ALBERT REYNOLDS

My Autobiography

with Jill Arlon

TRANSWORLD IRELAND

TRANSWORLD IRELAND
An imprint of The Random House Group Limited
20 Vauxhall Bridge Road, London SW1V 2SA
www.rbooks.co.uk

ALBERT REYNOLDS: MY AUTOBIOGRAPHY
A TRANSWORLD IRELAND BOOK: 9781848270473

First published in 2009 by Transworld Ireland
a division of Transworld Publishers
Transworld Ireland paperback edition published 2010

Addresses for Random House Group Ltd companies outside the UK
can be found at: www.randomhouse.co.uk
The Random House Group Ltd Reg. No. 954009

The Random House Group Limited supports The Forest Stewardship Council (FSC),
the leading international forest certification organisation. All our titles that are printed
on Greenpeace approved FSC certified paper carry the FSC logo. Our paper
procurement policy can be found at www.rbooks.co.uk/environment

Typeset in 11.5/13.5pt Granjon by
Falcon Oast Graphic Art Ltd.
Printed in the UK by CPI Cox & Wyman, Reading, RG1 8EX.

2 4 6 8 10 9 7 5 3 1

Mixed Sources
Product group from well-managed
forests and other controlled sources
www.fsc.org   Cert no. TT-COC-2139
© 1996 Forest Stewardship Council
FSC

To Kathleen

CONTENTS

ACKNOWLEDGEMENTS

I have been blessed with a warm and loving family, and I take this opportunity to thank them for their love, unwavering support, and for all the many happy memories we have shared through the years: my wife, Kathleen, who has been my anchor and my strength through everything; our seven children – Miriam, Philip, Emer, Leonie, Abbie, Cathy and Andrea; their spouses Niall, Anne, Kevin, Garret, Erika, Niall, Jamie, and all of our wonderful grandchildren. A special thank you to Andrea and Jamie for providing invaluable help in the writing of my memoir.

My thanks to Jill Arlon, for helping me to tell the story of my life so well. It has been a long and fascinating process and I am grateful to her for the attention to detail she has given to this book. Thank you to agent Deke Arlon for representing this project.

As I mentioned in the course of my story, although I never kept a diary I kept in touch with my friends. Some were there in my early years, some were there later and stood by me in government or worked with me during the difficult early days of the peace process. Many friends have generously given of their time to assist in the writing of this book and I extend my deepest gratitude and thanks to them all for being there when I needed them.

Special thanks must go to the following: Martin Mansergh, my adviser in government, who stood shoulder-to-shoulder with me in our determination to bring peace to our island; Sir John Major, former Prime Minister of Great Britain and my good friend who gave his all in the search for peace; President Bill Clinton, who was so supportive of our efforts; Senator Edward Kennedy and Vicki Kennedy; and Jean Kennedy Smith; Bill Flynn; my Press Secretary, Seán Duignan, who was always there for me; Taoiseach Brian Cowen; Archbishop Lord Eames; Father Alex Reid; the Revd Dr Ian Paisley; the late Revd Dr Roy Magee; Martin McGuinness, Deputy First Minister, Northern Ireland; Gerry Adams, President of Sinn Fein; Gusty Spence; Senator George Mitchell; Charlie McCreevy; Mark Killilea; David Andrews; Mickey Doherty; Derek Cobbe; Paddy Cole; Liam Collins; Father Brian D'Arcy; Dermot Gallagher; Noel Gallagher; Sir Roderic Lyne; Elizabeth McLaughlin; Tom Savage; and Sam Smyth.

Thanks also to Paul Allen and his assistants, Erin Mullally and Caroline O'Neill, for their enormous help; Yvonne Gilbert, who impeccably transcribed all the interviews, and Peter Woodward, who assisted so brilliantly with the recordings; Vanessa Burgess; Maire Grogan and Lisa Halpin; Anne Martin and Anne Stenson.

Finally, I would like to thank the team at Transworld Ireland for their invaluable advice and guidance: publisher, Eoin McHugh; copy-editor, Gillian Somerscales; Sean Magee; Brenda Kimber; and Lauren Hadden.

PROLOGUE

'Now you will know why I have been single-minded on many occasions in the pursuit of what I passionately believed in, often to my own detriment. In life, in business and politics, you cannot win them all. You win some, you lose some, but throughout my life in politics and business I have been delighted to be a risk-taker. If you are not a risk-taker you will not achieve anything. The easiest way in life is not to be a risk-taker. Yes, I was a risk-taker in politics and in business but I am quite happy that, having taken the risks – the successes far outweigh the failures.'

And so I ended the hardest speech of my life: my last speech as Taoiseach, my resignation speech in the Dáil.

I stepped down as Taoiseach, I stepped down as leader of Fianna Fáil, my party, the one I had served for the greater part of my life. It had been a short tenure but a rewarding one. I'd set out my goals and I'd achieved them, I'd taken risks and I'd come through them, I'd crossed the big hurdles and tripped on the small one.

In the course of that final speech I'd said, 'There'll be

another time when I will set the record straight.' John Bruton, leader of Fine Gael, the main opposition party, came back with the retort that 'a queue of publishers' would be waiting.

I looked up as I exited the Dáil that bleak November day. The boys and girls of the press corps, my sometime friends and foes, were looking down from the gallery, pens poised for the last story. I waved – 'I'm no use to you now,' I said, 'I never kept a diary.'

But – I did keep in touch with my friends! True, I hadn't kept a personal diary; yet as I left the Dáil that day I vividly recalled my first press conference on being elected leader, and my first speech, in which I set out the three main commitments at the forefront of my agenda, and the shock and incredulity on the upturned faces of the crowd as I promised to improve the economy and to tackle emigration – and told them that my greatest priority of all was to achieve peace in Northern Ireland.

I can still hear echoes of the cheers that followed, tempered with disbelief and puzzlement. People were asking, 'Where did that come from?' – not least my own family, and particularly my children. I suppose they had never really heard me talk about Northern Ireland. They had been born with the Troubles: always there, rumbling away up in the North, distressing but distant, with no solution. They knew I had links and friends and had done business in the North, but none of them suspected that I would be the one to really take it on. They expected me to tackle the economy but they certainly didn't know that for a long time I had been brewing over ways of resolving the problems in the North. It wasn't something I'd ever discussed, because I couldn't have done anything about it and the timing wasn't right; it wasn't until I was in a position to set those ideas in motion that I could express what I had in mind.

The celebrating had been long and hard that night and we ended up where we always ended up, in the kitchen, with Kathleen, my wife, dishing up sandwiches and cakes and endless pots of tea while the family, our seven children, gathered round the table, their excited voices rising in their efforts to be heard, vying with the good friends who had supported me in my campaign.

I remembered Kathleen and the children full of questions, and my good friend Pádraig Flynn, P. Flynn as we called him, warning the youngsters how they'd have to behave now I was Taoiseach and my words to them all: 'Don't get too comfortable now, I may not be there that long. The maximum I'll be there is six years.

'I have a plan, I know what I'm going to do and I'll get it done, but if I can't do it in that time, I may never get it done.'

Well, I wasn't there that long, far less than the six years, but my plan worked and I got it done – and, together with others prepared to risk it all, we brought peace to Northern Ireland and a growing economy to Ireland.

I had enough material for a book, oh yes, but back then I'd made myself a promise: I'd only write a book when time had proved that peace was permanent. Being a good Fianna Fáil man I'd like to have seen 'unity'. Maybe one day . . .

For now I'm content that what we started in the early nineties – the silencing of the guns, the end of the conflict, the lasting peace – still holds. Now I can write my book.

1

TO BEGIN AT THE BEGINNING

My story has a very ordinary beginning. I was a country boy, born on 3 November 1932 into a loving family living in a pretty little village on the banks of the Shannon. The green hills of County Roscommon in the West of Ireland rolled gently away from the river and the little rural community of Roosky, up to the border some thirty miles to the north.

Now it's a thriving tourist area, a centre for river cruising boats and fishing, grown out of all recognition; but back then there was nothing but a small village, set between Lough Bofin and Lough Forbes, dominated by Hanley's meat factory, the main employer in the area and the destination for the local farm animals. The main street, although surfaced, was more like a dirt track, ploughed up by the hooves of the herds that passed through on their way to market. Cars were a rarity: there were carts and the odd truck, and the rare bus, but mostly you either walked or travelled by bike. A picture of quaint rustic simplicity appears in the mind's eye, but it was also a time of great hardship and deprivation. Money and jobs were scarce, houses stood empty and cottages crumbled: sure signs of abandonment where people had been forced to move away, usually to emigrate, in their desperate search for employment.

My mother, Catherine Dillon, from Cloone in County Leitrim, was one of those young people who'd left Ireland. With little to no chance of employment in Ireland, she had emigrated to America to try to find work. She'd been home on a visit to see her sister, then married to a man from Roosky, when she met and married my father, known as John P., and they settled in a house opposite the old Court House on the main street in the village. They had four children, Joe, Jim, Teresa and myself, the youngest child, christened Albert Martin Reynolds.

I look at one of the few photographs I have of my parents back then. They are standing together smiling at the camera. She is a lovely woman with dark hair, blue eyes and high cheek-bones; my father stands next to her, a tall man, fair-haired, long face, strong nose. It's not hard to see who I take after!

My father was an enterprising man, a very hard-working man, in what were very difficult years. I suppose now he'd be called an entrepreneur. He worked all hours maintaining a number of small businesses. He was a carpenter, an under-taker and an auctioneer and, like most self-sufficient people then, he owned a small parcel of land which he farmed. He was also a coach-builder and owned a horse-drawn carriage, called a brake, which was used for carrying passengers. For years he operated a twice-a-week service only: on Saturdays the brake travelled between Roosky and Longford via Newtownforbes; Thursdays the destination was Mohill. The return fare was half a crown, and the carrying capacity was sixteen people. The service was regarded by many as the social outing of the week. Even today there are those who remember eagerly awaiting the clip-clop of the horses' hooves on the old tarred 'coach' road, as it was popularly called, announcing the brake was on its way. The old people at that time never referred to it as the Longford–Sligo road but harked back to the name that presumably originated at the time of the stage and mail coaches that travelled that route. When the brake arrived in Longford my father John P. and my brother Joe would arrange to stable the horses in the yard of the Midland Warehouse, then one of the most progressive business premises in town.

However, times were changing and coaches were being replaced with cars, so with great foresight and his usual flair for business, my father was inspired to convert his coach-building shed into a small ballroom, a dance hall on the banks of the Shannon where bands drawn from a thirty-mile radius were engaged to play for all the locals, who would arrive by whatever transport possible – horses, tractors, bicycles and Shank's pony – to dance to the bands.

I have distinct memories of these times because as youngsters we were always called upon to help sweep and polish the floor so that couples could glide across it more easily. We used buckets of a mixture based on paraffin; I can smell it still, it stayed on your hands for days and was powerful stuff. We were also expected to help out on the farm but I avoided that as much as possible: farming was not for me and I'd sneak off while no one was looking. For me the call of the river and being with my friends was irresistible. I can still feel the sun on my back on those endless summer days, lazing and swimming and playing down by the Shannon and hiding whenever one of my elder brothers came looking for me.

My family have always been at the centre of my life, my support and cornerstone. My profound belief in strong family values definitely comes from my mother. She was a purpose-ful, deeply religious woman, who believed in the value of prayer and a hard work ethic to get you through life, as did my father. They both had enormous energy, a trait I inherited.

My mother was also a great believer in education.

Like my brothers and sister I started off at the local national school in Roosky and I enjoyed it there. None of my siblings had gone on to secondary school, but for some reason my mother was convinced I had academic ability. She had heard that there was a young, very bright lady teacher getting great results at another national school some three or four miles out-side Roosky and she determined I should go there for the last two years of my junior education in the hope that I might get a free scholarship to secondary school.

I still see this teacher, Elizabeth McLaughlin, whenever I go over to Longford and though she's now in her nineties her brain is as sharp as ever. She was one of those wonderful, dedicated people who viewed their profession as a vocation. She never married but devoted herself to teaching. In 1942, aged twenty-six, she arrived in Carrigeen to take charge as sole teacher in the national school. She taught pupils through from infant level to sixth class and, as was common in Ireland in those days, she'd set work for one class while instructing another. Even so, she managed to nurture her brightest students and inspired them to win a number of coveted county council scholarships.

There were over forty pupils in the school and I became one of them. Unfortunately I joined the class too late to try for a full scholarship, so she encouraged me to try instead for a 'burse' to Summerhill College in Sligo.

Miss McLaughlin still remembers me as being very determined and willing to achieve everything she set me to do. Apparently I was also very good at Latin and Greek, which she encouraged me to keep up when I went on to Summerhill College.

I remember her as an inspiring teacher who made you want to learn. The school was a few miles away from home but I was always happy to cycle over there every day, even on Saturdays when I had extra tuition in Irish, which served me well for the future. She took this upon herself; I don't believe she was ever paid any extra to do it, although I do recall buying her a newspaper as a present on my way over to her house. She simply loved her work, loved her pupils and was determined to give them the best education possible in order to get all her students through their scholarship exams. It worked for me: I passed my exams, won a bursary and went off to boarding school in Sligo.

Summerhill College was primarily a training school for would-be priests and teachers. Most of my fellow students went on to study at colleges like Maynooth or Kiltegan. I wanted to become a teacher, maybe inspired by Miss McLaughlin!

Going to boarding school was a momentous change in my life. It was September 1946 and I was approaching my fourteenth birthday; I had never been away from home before, so leaving my family and Roosky was not easy, and it was with a great deal of trepidation that I said goodbye to my siblings. We were all very close and I watched as the little figures of my sister and two brothers disappeared into the distance, still waving, as the bus took me away to what felt like the ends of the earth.

I entered Summerhill a year after the Second World War ended. Ireland had remained neutral throughout that time – known as the Emergency – but we had suffered. Unemployment was rife, food was in very short supply and rationing was the order of the day. At school it was expected that wherever possible the family would help out. My mother was not well at the time. She'd had an accident a while back and now could only walk with the help of a stick, sometimes two, so she could not visit me herself. Occasionally she would send food parcels of home-baked cake and bread which arrived via the local bus, but for the most part we boarders had to fend for ourselves and we relied on the day boys for the supply of extra rations.

My first year at Summerhill was particularly tough. I missed my family and, to make things even more difficult, my arrival at the college coincided with one of the worst winters in Irish history. It seemed that for almost the whole winter roads were so snowbound that no buses or cars could get through, so there were no deliveries of food or parcels from home – and what was worse, the local bakery in Sligo, MacArthurs, was also on strike. Potatoes were about the only thing we had to eat. It was not a great introduction to boarding school life. Nevertheless I have happy memories of the friends I made there, of summers swimming in the school pool, and not so happy ones of the several beatings I received when caught in various misdemeanours.

It was there, too, I learned to play soccer – but secretly. The teaching staff, the priests, forbade the illicit English game, so a few of us bravely played on a field far from the watchful eyes of the staff peering from the college windows. I recently received a copy of a photograph of our team, the nine secret soccer players, sent to me by the boy who first introduced us to the game, a lively lad called Michael Devine from Ballygar, County Galway, now a monsignor in Miami.

It was during this period that I discovered an aptitude for business, which I suppose I must have inherited from my father. I've always had a sweet tooth and could usually find the money for the odd bar of chocolate, but then with a few shillings extra I found that if I bought several bars and a few more bags and sold them on to the other fellows for a small profit ... Somehow the school got to know of my little enterprise and appointed me to manage the tuck shop – which had not been a success for the simple reason that the priests who stocked it had no idea what the boys wanted, so they'd be left with stuff mouldering away in jars.

I set myself the task of reorganizing the shop, threw out all the old stuff and opened up once or twice a week. With a subsidy given to me by the school I'd go off to the local wholesaler, look for whatever bargains were being offered, carefully select only what I knew I could sell, and return with my bags of goodies which were eagerly awaited by the other boys. I was learning to follow the ultimate business principle of 'supply and demand' even then. All profits were ploughed back into the shop and as the takings increased, the staff used the money to help finance whatever was needed in the school, such as improvements to the sports facilities. It was my first taste of making money and I liked it; and what was more, I was good at it.

I was doing well in my studies, and although I was not the most skilled at sport I was good enough, and an enthusiastic member of various teams. I joined in most activities – football, swimming and so on – enjoying the camaraderie as much as the sport. As one of my fellow students, Seamus Creighton, wrote at that time in the *College Annual*:

'Albert Reynolds – one of the finest table-tennis players in the house ... a fine billiards and snooker player, has won many competitions ... his main hobby is dancing ... has danced to most of Ireland's leading bands, and Albert's decision on the merits of a band may always be regarded as final ... a most likeable personality ... our able tuck shop manager ... his ambition: to become a teacher.'

It was not to be. Coming up to final exam time, when we sat the all-important leaving certificate examination, I was playing football when in the course of a clumsy tackle I fell badly and awkwardly. My knee buckled under me at a strange and excruciating angle and I heard the ominous crack of breaking bones echoing around the field. By the time I got to Sligo hospital my knee was the size of a balloon. Somehow they attempted to manipulate it and set it in a cast – but the pain didn't go away. The surgery was obviously not a success, so it was back to hospital where they re-broke it and set it all over again. I was sent home with the warning that I must keep my leg up at all times and would be in plaster for at least another twelve weeks.

With my leg up, supported by a chair, I managed to do 60 per cent of my exams and luckily attained honours in Irish, English, Greek and Latin – but by the time I got to the geography and maths exams, my knee was throbbing again and I felt sick with pain. I'd answered two out of six questions on one paper and the first two in the other when I had to give up.

My knee had been set twice to no effect. The experts had failed. Not one to give up easily, in a final effort to resolve the problem my mother took me to a renowned bone-setter who lived some twenty miles away. Bone-setters were not doctors but folk practitioners, experienced in traditional old country ways of healing. What we would now call the alternative method, I suppose. Their main occupation was re-setting the broken bones of animals – especially horses – although they were known to re-set the odd human limb with great success. In fact the sister of the fellow who treated me specialized in animal welfare.

I suppose there was a touch of the old witch doctor about them – but certainly no magic, and no anaesthetic to dull the pain either. It took four men to hold me down while the bone-setter re-broke the joint and set it yet again. Fully conscious, or almost, I watched in alarm as he scooped soot from the chimney, mixed it with margarine, plastered it on the joint then bound my knee with this sort of poultice. Remarkably, it healed quickly and in no time at all it was better. I was eighteen at the time and it has never troubled me since. Sometimes there is a lot to say for these old remedies!

I could have gone back to school to re-sit my exams but somehow the prospect of teaching had lost its edge and the thought of more studying simply did not appeal. Besides, money was in short supply at home and I felt the urge to get out there into the big wide world and seek my fortune. I had enjoyed my little tuck shop venture into the business world; I wanted to taste it again. I wanted to make some money.

There was never any talk of politics within my family although, if asked, my parents would have admitted that at election time in Roscommon they voted for Fianna Fáil. I was made aware of politics through my friendship with the Hanleys. The boys had gone to the same boarding school as me, all six of them, although my particular friends were Seamus and Peter and there were also two sisters.

The Hanley family was the most successful in the village in those days. They gave me my first taste of association with wealth and business success, and I was very impressed. The father owned the meat factory in Roosky and employed most of the locals. They were also a big political family, well connected with the leaders of Fianna Fáil and very active supporters at election time. Through my friendship with the boys I was a regular visitor to the house, and so it was natural that I was frequently asked to help out with the political work too, and it was through them that I really began to understand the more recent history of Ireland.

I didn't really know that much about the Government of Ireland Act, although I was aware that it was that Act in 1920 that had led to the partition of the island of Ireland into two regions, Northern Ireland (the six counties) and Southern Ireland. As I was about to campaign for Fianna Fáil, the Hanleys felt it was important that I understood why I should support it.

I learned that de Valera, the then leader of Fianna Fáil and the Taoiseach, had in the past fought to free Ireland from the British, but what I had not realized at that time was that in the early 1920s, because of the political turmoil and the war of independence still going on in the South, only Northern Ireland was actually established under the Act; the South, after hard bargaining by Michael Collins, became a 'Dominion State' under the Anglo-Irish Treaty, concluded in December 1921 between the British and Irish governments. Under this new system of Irish self-government, Ireland could govern itself but would remain within the British Empire: thus the 'Irish Free State' was born. De Valera was one of those who refused to swear an oath of fidelity to the British monarch; in 1926, along with fellow politician Seán Lemass, who was to become my hero, he broke away from his colleagues and launched a new political party which they named the 'Soldiers of Destiny' – Fianna Fáil.

Such a swashbuckling pioneer of Republicanism appealed to me. I loved de Valera's spirited independence and I admired his willingness to lay down his life rather than offer allegiance to the British king. From then on the party's history won me over. I became a devoted follower and learned its aims by heart:

1   A united Ireland as a republic.
2   To restore the Irish language and develop Irish culture.
3   To develop a social system where there is an equal
     opportunity for all.
4   To have a fair system of land distribution in Ireland.
5   To make Ireland as self-sufficient as possible, with a
     proper balance between agriculture and other
     industries.

My family had never talked about the past, but I had grown
up during those difficult years of rationing and hardship
during the 'Emergency'. Although the Irish people had
generally accepted de Valera's policy of neutrality for Ireland
in the Second World War, it had inevitably led to a period of
great deprivation and the post-war economy was still plagued
with rising prices and growing unemployment.

I was aware of how hard it was for most people to make a
living. Wherever you lived you knew of people leaving the
country, emigrating for a better life. My own mother had been
one of them. Few, if any, escaped the effects of the economic
problems: often it wasn't a matter of money but of availability
– of food, of clothes, of everything. We were all affected.
There were wealthy families, like the Hanleys, who had a
more comfortable life, and I heard gossip among the locals and
the farmers who came down from the North that there was a
better, more modern way of life up there. On the other hand,
there were others who arrived with tales of hardship in the
North, especially for Nationalists, who felt cast aside and
abandoned by the British government.

There were families who had fled from the North and
settled locally in search of a better life, who told of the dreadful unemployment that existed, how they were shut out of
jobs, and out of the best schools and housing, and of how, no

matter how bright you were or how hard you tried, as a Catholic and a Nationalist you had little chance of getting a job in local government. Nationalists, they warned, were downtrodden and oppressed in the North, by the police and by the British authorities. They also told of the violence that frequently flared up between the Catholics and Protestants and of the 'no go' areas where you dared not tread. This talk of Catholics and Protestants living like opposing factions was quite alien to all of us young people in the South. We had grown up not exactly unaware of religious differences but certainly not anti anyone on religious grounds.

I knew people locally in the area where I grew up who were Protestants: admittedly they were in the minority in the South, and attended different schools and churches, but their choice of religion never led to discrimination as it appeared to do in the North. To a young man, naïve in such matters, these stories of discrimination against the Nationalists, and of neighbour fighting neighbour just because of religious differences, seemed so unfair and so unjust. They made a big impression on me.

But at election time in my boyhood years, listening to the Hanleys debating and arguing politics, and their explanations of all that had gone before, I little dreamed how thoroughly I was going to need to understand all this.

2

FORGING A FUTURE

It was 1951, I was coming up to nineteen and I was out of school with no idea of what I was going to do. All my aspirations of going on to university and becoming a secondary school teacher had been dashed by the accident to my leg, and although I was a devout Catholic I had no desire to become a priest or missionary like so many of my fellow students. My budding ambitions for the business life were there; but how to fulfil them was another matter.

It was a very difficult time in Ireland. The economy was in a dreadful state, there was very little employment and the majority of young people – people of all ages, in fact – were still being forced to emigrate to countries across the world: Britain, America, Australia, Canada. My brother Jim was one of them. Joe was running the family farm and business, which provided work for only one person and his family; so Jim left to start a new life, first in Canada, then in Australia. But I had no desire to leave Ireland – quite the opposite: I was determined that I would not be forced to leave and that, come what may, I would make my future in my own country.

One of the top jobs in Ireland at the time was banking. It was a much sought-after profession and difficult to enter, but my parents were determined that this was what I should do. At that time the only way into the world of banking was by applying to sit the banking examination, and applications were usually accepted only when accompanied by a letter of recommendation from someone already within the system. Luckily my parents were on good terms with our local bank manager and had managed to persuade him that I was a worthy candidate. So, armed with a recommendation from him, I set out for the capital, Dublin. The interview with the bank hierarchy was in the afternoon; the actual exam was set for the following day.

The interview went well enough and I sat the first of the exam papers the next morning. I hadn't found it difficult and thought I was doing OK, but when we broke for lunch I saw some of my fellow applicants walking around, chatting and joking with the interviewers and exam supervisors, and came to the conclusion that I was wasting my time. This was not for me. There's a saying, 'It's not what you know, it's who you know.' I didn't know any of them, so I left. To my mind the man who merits the job should get the job; what I was witnessing – or concluded I was witnessing – was a 'jobs for the boys' situation. Rightly or wrongly, I thought the decisions had already been made, and that I, as the boy up from the country, the outsider, didn't stand a fair chance. There and then I decided I'd make my mark elsewhere. So I did not go back for the second half of the exam; instead I bought the evening paper and started looking for a job.

The bank manager who had put my name forward as a suitable candidate wrote to my mother asking what had gone wrong, as I'd left having completed only half of the exam. However, he added, I had fared well in the first half and if I came back and did as well in the final part I would definitely be offered a job. My mother was devastated: it was hard enough to get people to recommend you at the time and there were very few jobs available. But I did not go back. I did not even look back: I'd moved on.

I'd already answered an advertisement in the paper and applied for an interview for a position as junior clerk with an engineering company. My first week's wages were £2 5s a week, and after paying my landlady I was left with 7s 6d.

A better offer was forthcoming. There was a chap staying at the same digs who, after listening to me complaining about having no money, said he could get me the cards to work as a carpenter. The unions were strong at that time and very strict in guarding their membership. I admitted to the fellow that I knew nothing about carpentry but he said it didn't matter as all I would be doing was putting polish on radios. So I became a cabinet polisher in the Pye factory in Dundrum for the handsome sum of £26 a week instead of £2 5s!

Unfortunately I got caught out by the union man, who found out I'd been sneaked in – so quickly I sneaked out.

The time had come for me to take a more serious view of my future. I applied for a job with the National Turf Development Board, Bord Na Móna. I passed the exams, was accepted and moved down to Kildare where I lived on campus, at Ballydermot.

The National Turf Development Board was a public company that produced electricity by burning turf. It had its origins in the national emergency created by fuel shortages during the Second World War, which had led to the establishment of turf production schemes to service Dublin and the east coast counties. Kildare was a prime candidate, having one of the biggest bogs in Ireland, the Bog of Allen. The scheme here had been based on the use of imported labour: fourteen residential camps had been erected, each with a holding capacity for over five hundred workers, and intensive recruiting had been undertaken, especially from the western counties, in order to build up a labour force of four thousand men. The National Turf Development Board was then faced with the immense task of providing twelve thousand meals a day, not easy at that time. Army advice was sought and discarded as, in the words of Todd Andrews, a leading figure in the early days of Fianna Fáil and managing director of the Board, 'the daily rations of a soldier were no more than a "daisy in a bull's mouth" to men doing eight hours of heavy bog work'.

The Kildare scheme at full production had yielded 600,000 tonnes before being closed down in 1947. However, the national turf industry had proved such a success that in 1946 it was officially recognized by the creation of Bord Na Móna. By 1952 the fuel emergency was over and production from the bogs was semi-automated; but although the labour force had been reduced, the camps were still functioning. I was twenty years old when, as a raw Bord Na Móna recruit, employed as a clerk, I joined the hectic humdrum world of Ballydermot camp life.

I received the princely sum of £3 13s for a five-and-a-half-day, 37-hour week. Most of this went on my rent for accommodation, but there was usually a little over for fun. I had always been a keen card player and certainly indulged in that, but I also cultivated what was to become a lifelong passion – horse racing! Despite such meagre earnings, with the odd money I sometimes won at poker I managed to save enough to cycle with a few friends from the camp to race meetings at the Curragh in Kildare.

One of the lads working with me in the office at

Ballydermot was a fellow by the name of John Corduff. His father was caretaker at the course and he used to get us in for free, which was great as it meant more money to bet on the horses! It was here I learned to keep my ears open to the racing gossip as we got to know the various riders and trainers and chatted about the chances of the different horses. Instinct and hearsay served me well and I'd often come away with double my week's wages. My love of horse racing and gambling was born.

I was still only a clerk among many others, but I wanted to be more than that. However, I realized that if I wanted to improve my circumstances and financial position, I would have to have better qualifications. I knew I had an aptitude for figures, so I decided to go for accountancy. Going back to school or college was not an option, so I signed up for a correspondence course and began studying at night.

Eighteen months later I passed my exams for a job with Córas Iompair Éireann. CIE operated the state transport service and was considered a secure place of employment. There was a popular belief at the time that those who had worked for Bord Na Móna always prospered – and oddly enough Todd Andrews, who became chairman of CIE in 1958, had followed the same route as me a few years earlier. Coincidentally, many years later in 1992, when I became Taoiseach, I, his former junior clerk in both companies, appointed his son, David Andrews, as my Minister for Foreign Affairs!

My experience working at the National Turf Development Board had also taught me a bit about turbary, which came in handy when I noticed that Bord Na Móna's custom of renting out turf-cutting rights to local families could be quite lucrative. I needed extra cash, so I decided to have a go myself. Turbary was quite an art and a plot could easily deteriorate if it was cut in a careless or imprudent manner: the turf roots could easily be damaged and the powers of reproduction destroyed, which would lead to the bog flooding with water. I rented a small plot myself and began cutting the peat and cultivating the turf every other weekend. Sales were good and my wages almost doubled.

By this time, my correspondence course with the Glasgow School of Accountancy had come to an end. I'd passed all my exams up to intermediate standard and decided that, with my new qualifications, it was time to move on again.

I was offered a promotion, a permanent post as a clerical officer (Grade 3) with CIE on the narrow-gauge railway in Dromod, County Leitrim, which was only two miles away from Roosky. Now I could not only live with my parents, I could even go home for lunch!

Weekends I'd play cards with the Hanleys. My time at Ballydermot had really improved my card skills and I considered myself a pretty useful player, particularly at poker – but the women in the Hanley family were something else, especially the mother: they were by far the best card players in the house. So much so, in fact, that sometimes they took me for every penny and I'd end up losing my whole week's wages, which was pretty drastic; but then, sometimes I'd win!

I was making my way, but for many people times were still desperate and emigration seemed the only way to find work. I was working in the ticket office in Dromod one day when a fellow came in whom I knew – we'd occasionally played cards at a neighbour's house. He wanted to buy a train ticket to Birmingham. Things were so bad, he admitted, there were no jobs to be found and there was nothing for him to do but emigrate.

The ticket was two pounds ten, which I deducted from the

three pounds he'd given me. As I handed him his change I asked him if that was all he had. 'It is,' he said. 'That's it.'

'Well, you won't go far on that. Give me back the ten shillings change and the ticket.'

Tickets were always dispensed from the bottom of a high pile. I took one from the very top, knowing that the missing ticket would not be discovered for some months, and gave it to him together with his three pounds.

Some twenty years later I was in Birmingham, giving a talk there to the Irish community, when this same guy sought me out. He was by this time married with six children and offered me back the three pounds. 'Don't give it a thought,' I told him; 'CIE is losing so much money, this three pounds will make no difference!'

My main occupation at Dromod was to organize the delivery sheets for lorries and the transport of goods by train. This meant I was working close to the border and often across it. I became very familiar with the people on and around the border, and saw that although it was quite defined and always watched, it was still reasonably free and open. Farmers from the North would come down to the Roscommon and Longford area to buy cattle, and I would organize trucks and transport back.

It was during this period that I got to know several leading figures in the North who would pay me in advance for looking after the transport of their livestock and frequently, because of the trouble in the border areas, they'd demand two drivers per truck instead of the usual one. We were pretty lax about rules in the South, but in the North they were very strict on the number of hours a driver could be at the wheel, and anyone caught transgressing could lose his licence. As one never knew where a vehicle might be stopped or roads be blocked, timing a journey accurately was almost an impossibility, so we provided two drivers just in case they over-ran the scheduled number of hours for one.

At Dromod, too, I met a man who was to become a future business partner, Matty Lyons, whose family owned Lyons meat factories in Dromod and Longford.

I also met up with some of the fellows involved in affairs that were not quite so legitimate. Smuggling cattle and pigs across the border was big business in those days, and many a night I would hear the sound of hooves clattering on the ground as they were herded down from the North under cover of darkness, on their way to be driven to Dublin and into the narrow streets of the Liberties, an ancient quarter of the city where they would miraculously disappear into the hundreds of small bacon- and meat-processing factories that provided the staple diet for most of Ireland.

At that time the North, under the British, was better serviced than the South, which was still struggling with the after-effects of the Emergency, so many a family that lived close by would depend on the quick sorties of their fleet-footed offspring across the border into the North in exchange for the odd thing that was in short supply down South – usually basics like flour and sugar.

In the fifties, CIE was in the process of a huge restructuring programme of its entire system, with old railroads being closed down as they sought new sources of energy to run their locomotives and rolling stock. The narrow-gauge railways which relied on the transport of coal were gradually being abandoned as CIE planned to move on to diesel as the new fuel, as well as experimenting with steam engines run by burning turf or oil. Dromod narrow-gauge was one of the lines being closed down, and so I was moved on to another narrow-gauge line at Ballinamore, Leitrim.

It was at this time that, sadly, my father passed away. I had loved and respected my father but had spent so much of my formative years away from home, first at boarding school and then away working in various jobs, that when he died I suddenly realized I didn't really know him as a person: he was just my Dad. But I knew I had inherited his energy, his will to achieve no matter what obstacles stand in your way, and his ability not to dwell on failure but to be positive and to accept that things change: there's nothing to be gained in looking back. The future lies ahead, and you have to move on.

I'd passed the first part of my accountancy final exams when I was transferred to the main-line railway in Sligo and the accountancy office in Ballymote. Here I used to do the accounting for all those receiving and sending goods by train, and it was here I met my wife.

One of my duties was to collect the money from various accounts in the town, including a very good customer in Ballymote, who took regular deliveries of drapery goods. His shop was called McGettrick's Outfitters. It was the last shop on O'Connell Street, and my final port of call. As was customary I'd spent time getting to know the staff who worked in the various offices attached to each of the premises, until finally I walked into the office of McGettrick's and saw this very attractive, very dark-haired young lady called Kathleen Coen, who was the one responsible for paying the accounts.

Kathleen's father had left the family farm and set off to seek his fortune in America. When the First World War was declared, despite his father's calls for him to return to Ireland, he joined the American forces and fought in Europe. Eventually he was demobbed in London and returned to Ireland, where he met his wife. Kathleen's mother was appointed as an assistant to the teaching staff of a local school where she remained until she married. They lived in the village of Culfadda and had three children, Kathleen, Paddy and Margie.

I had moved into lodgings in May Hunt's house on Wolfe Tone Street in Ballymote, along with a number of other young fellows who were working away from home. A crowd of us would go off to the local dances, and eventually I plucked up enough courage to ask Kathleen to partner me.

Dancing was the big thing in those days, and we'd all travel miles several times a week to different dance halls in different towns. We had wonderful visiting bands led by big names like Joe Loss and Victor Sylvester as well as some very good local bands. Not too many of us had cars then, but when someone did, we'd all share the price of the petrol and pile in. Sometimes there would be as many as ten in one car.

Things were going well with Kathleen and me, when suddenly I was transferred to Longford. I was worried that maybe we'd lose touch, but a little thing like distance was not going to stand in my way.

Sadly, during this period Kathleen's father, to whom she was particularly close, became very ill with multiple sclerosis, a wasting disease that was almost unrecognized in those days. Kathleen helped care for her father for a long time before eventually he died. In those days it was customary not to attend any functions or social events for a mourning period of twelve months after a parent's death, but I still travelled over to see her. Not until the twelve months was up could I ask her to marry me.

There was another reason it took so long. I just wasn't earning enough money to get married.

CIE was continuing to close down different lines and at Longford I was put in charge of reorganizing transport and delivery for the affected areas, not only for goods transport but for passenger travel as well.

It was here that I met two leading figures in the North who were regular visitors to our area and frequently travelled together: Harry West, Minister for Agriculture in the North, and Lord Brookeborough, who at that time was in his mid-sixties and Prime Minister of Northern Ireland. He was unusual in that he was one of the few Unionists to command respect across all strands of Unionist opinion, as was Harry West, and although he was known as a hard-line anti-Catholic, he always had time to stop and chat with me. He was a charming fellow, a real gentleman. Apart from politics, his great love was farming and the country pursuits of shooting and fishing. His estate, Colebrook Park, was in County Fermanagh but he was always in the South to attend the big cattle fairs and it was my job to organize the delivery of his newly acquired stock to the North.

With everything being cut back, the job with CIE was only taking me three or four hours a day to complete, and I was getting bored. I was not one to sit around doing nothing: I needed to find something else to fill in my time.

3

THE SHOWBAND YEARS

Religion has always been a very important part of my life and I've always enjoyed being involved with my local church; so it was inevitable that with time on my hands I would consult my local priest as to what I could do to help.

The church building was in need of repairs, he told me, and we urgently needed to raise funds to pay for its renovation. The main fundraiser for most parishes was the church carnival and dance. I'd always been a keen follower of music and had already danced to most of the big dance bands and knew them well – after all, dancing was one of my favourite hobbies. I suppose, too, the priest reckoned that as my father had owned the local ballroom and had booked many of the local bands, some of his expertise might have rubbed off on me: so there and then he asked me to take on the job of secretary of the Roosky Carnival Committee.

This was in 1955, by which time the days of the traditional Irish céilí bands were really over. During the war the American troops stationed in the North had introduced American music to the locals and that influence had spread across the island of Ireland: now every band wanted to play swing and copy the Glenn Miller Band. Dance bands were all the rage and Ireland had some very fine ones, like the popular Maurice Lynch Band from Castleblayney or The Regal.

Most dances in that era were held in small dance halls or community centres in the towns and villages, but in many of the rural areas large marquees were specially erected. In Roosky, although there was my family ballroom, its capacity was limited, so in order to raise money for the carnival it was essential we hired a marquee. It was my job to organize this and to book the bands. The most popular bands were in great demand around the country, and so to compete with other venues it was essential you got in first, which usually meant booking them months ahead, well in advance of the carnival date.

The Roosky Carnival dance was a great success from the start and the money poured in for the church fund – so much so that by the third year, the priest suddenly informed me that no more money was needed and therefore there was no need for a third carnival dance.

This threw me into a real dilemma. I'd already booked the band well ahead of time, and to cancel the commitment would have been not only difficult but expensive as the contracts were signed and binding. However, I had other ideas going round in my head. The priest's advice confirmed my decision.

'Why not do it yourself?' he suggested. 'Ask your brother and one or two others to help you raise the finances and pay for the hire of the marquee, and you can pay them back out of the night's takings.'

My brother Joe, although he was more concerned with his farming and undertaking businesses, agreed to support me and I set about promoting my first dance.

I was still doing my three hours a day for CIE, still

invoicing away, but this was far more exciting. I relished the cut and thrust of doing the deal, booking the bands and manning the box office. I enjoyed the company of the musicians and the excitement of the night, and with the priest's encouragement we had two more successful years.

In 1957 my brother Jim returned from Australia. He'd done well over there working in the construction business and was looking to set up a similar business back home. By this time the popularity of bands and dances was growing all over Ireland, and with the emergence of the showbands prospects for expanding the business were looking good. It seemed an ideal situation for us both, and we decided to go into business building and running our own ballrooms: after all, we'd been brought up in a family that had owned a small dance hall, and between us we had the experience, he in construction, I in management and promotion.

We decided to build a new ballroom in Roosky. With a little money of our own, including what Jim had brought back from Australia and a loan secured from our local branch of the Munster and Leinster Bank, we bought our first site, next to our old home. My brother was in charge of the building and I was responsible for the management, book-keeping and promotion.

Dance halls up until that time had been fairly primitive, mostly parochial halls, county halls rented from the local council or small local dance halls. It was hard on the musicians, who often trailed around the country playing in halls and marquees as many as six times a week; if we wanted to attract the best bands we had to offer better than that. My brother and I looked around the country, learning from others' mistakes. Many of the ballrooms were pretty basic and cheaply constructed: just four walls and a roof, with a separate room, often little bigger than a telephone kiosk, that served as a dressing room for the bands to change in. Some of the halls didn't even have electricity but relied on old-fashioned kerosene-filled tilly lamps. In Oram Hall, Castleblayney, for example, when the lights began to go dim, the caretaker, Paddy McGeough, would go around pumping up the lamps in case the lads got a bit amorous with the ladies!

The dust thrown up by some of those old wooden floors was so dreadful they used to throw paraffin on them to keep it down: the smell alone could knock you out. The other trick was to scrape candle wax over the surface, supposedly to ensure a smooth surface for the dancers. It was all very enlightening – but we had other ideas!

We called our first ballroom Cloudland. It had electricity, a polished floor, changing rooms and toilet facilities, and it held two thousand people. People thought we were mad to build such a big place in such a small village, but people would travel forty or fifty miles to the dances if you had the right band.

And the right band was a showband. Up until this time most of the bands were dance bands, led by men such as Mick Delahunty and Maurice Mulcahy: they dressed formally, wore black tie, sat down and read from sheet music set on music stands, and played for as much as four or five hours a night. The Clipper Carlton Band changed all that. They were a band from the North, from Strabane in County Tyrone. Some of the musicians had relatives in America who used to send them the most popular records of the day. Bored with playing for so long, the band decided to incorporate a different type of entertainment into the evening. In the middle of their session they'd take a break from playing, push back the chairs and the stands, and perform a little show. They'd even dress up in flashy clothes, mimic the comedy from the comedy records, act out sketches or parodies and impersonate American singers like Pat Boone or The Drifters.

They were unbelievably successful and the other bands simply had to follow their lead. Johnny Quigley's band from Derry was one of the first to convert to the new style. The first half, they'd sit and play the big band stuff; then away would go the music stands and chairs, the dress suits would be whipped off in the break and back would come the musicians all dressed in bright tangerine-coloured jackets ready to entertain for the rest of the night!

Showbands were a uniquely Irish phenomenon, part of a changing Ireland: the Seán Lemass era was bringing prosperity, and people had money in their pockets which they were willing to spend on dances. All the bands tried to outdo one another. There were The Indians dressed as Indians, and the Zulus – every style of gimmick. And there were the great bands: The Royals, born out of Waterford, led the way with their star attraction Brendan Bowyer; there were The Miami Showband, The Capitol from Dublin and The Dixies from Cork. There were also Dave Glover from Belfast, Gaye McIntyre from Derry, The Melody Aces and The Melotones, and many, many more.

The Royal Showband really paved the way. The name had been taken from that of their local theatre, the Royal Theatre, Waterford, but they had originally emerged as The Harry Boland Dance Band. The line-up then was Michael Coppinger (sax), Charlie Mathews (drums), Jim Conlon (guitar), Jerry Cullen (vocals) and Tom Dunphy (singer). They were greatly influenced by the style of The Clippers' brass section, and so they invited a young trombonist, Brendan Bowyer, to join them, as well as adding Eddie Sullivan on trumpet. They were an immediate hit, and became even bigger when Brendan Bowyer started to sing. His voice, his playing and his charismatic personality raised the band from a local attraction to a country-wide phenomenon. Their reputation attracted the attention of a businessman, T. J. Byrne from Carlow, who on seeing their potential took over as their manager and transformed their profile – and with it their earning power. Seeing their fan base rise into the thousands and the size of their box-office draw at the local dances, T. J. began to demand a percentage of the takings, with the biggest share in favour of The Royals. No serious ballroom owner could afford to turn him down. They played to vast audiences all over Ireland and the UK. At one gig in Liverpool an up-and-coming group called The Beatles supported them! (In fact, I had two bookings for The Beatles but couldn't get a venue big enough.)

The Royals were the exception. Most bands stayed in Ireland, but eventually they too were paid percentages of the box office. This was all cash, and they lived like rock stars. Back then in the late fifties and early sixties, the showbands travelled all over the island, north and south of the border, and attracted enormous crowds wherever they played – their music knew no religious boundaries. There were still tensions, of course, but for the most part bands moved freely across the border, playing to all communities. Sometimes they would work in a venue where the Irish national anthem, 'The Soldiers' Song', would have to be played; the next night it could be a Protestant venue where they would be called upon to play 'God Save the Queen'. Then there were venues where both communities came together, when both anthems were played. On those occasions, those who didn't want to be present for whichever anthem was being played left the room and returned when it was over, but this caused no friction and the bands, from both sides of the border, were accepted with open arms by both sides – until, of course, the tragedy of The Miami Showband in 1975.

The Miami Showband emerged on the scene in 1961, but it

was really only when their lead singer Dickie Rock joined the band that they enjoyed the huge success and string of smash hits that had them competing head-to-head for the number one spot on the showband scene with the legendary Royals. Dickie Rock had in fact left the band to go solo by that night in late July 1975 when, driving back to Dublin from a gig at the Castle Ballroom in County Down, they were flagged down on a lonely country road outside Newry by men in military dress. In those days it was quite usual for anyone travelling on the roads in Northern Ireland to be stopped at any time of the day or night by security forces manning makeshift checkpoints, and they presumed this was a normal security patrol. As usual, the band members were ordered out of the van – and then what turned out to be a group of UVF militants started to plant a bomb on the vehicle. The device suddenly detonated prematurely. In the ensuing chaos the remaining paramilitaries panicked and opened fire on the band members, killing Fran O'Toole, Brian McCoy and Tony Geraghty and seriously wounding Stephen Travers.

The killings shocked the entire country and overnight changed the showband scene for ever. From then on bands from the South avoided crossing the border to play gigs in the North. The tragedy struck at the core of the showband industry and in fact was the beginning of the end of that particularly Irish phenomenon.

Back in the fifties, however, the showbands took Ireland by storm, and it was against this background that we began to build our business. Cloudland was an immediate success; we drew crowds of thousands and began to look at ways of expanding.

At first the whole family joined in to help Jim and me get the venture off the ground. Brother Joe, after finishing his work on the farm or at the undertaker's, joined in wherever he was needed, while sister Teresa and my mother cooked and served hot meals for the visiting bands. There was never any alcohol sold in ballrooms at that time, only soft drinks and confectionery, but we made enough from that to pay the staff and we shared the door takings with the big bands. We began to look around for another site, and our next venture was Roseland in Moate. Young James Flanagan was one of our first employees: he stayed with us for years until the ballroom closed and lives in Moate to this day.

All this time I was still working for CIE, completing my work in just a few hours before I rushed off to do what I really wanted to do. I had a very tolerant boss at the time, but this was not to last. The next stationmaster took a very dim view of my activities. He called me in one day to tell me in no uncertain terms that either I worked for myself or I worked for CIE, and what was more, they were about to transfer me to Rosslare Harbour. There was no choice as far as I was concerned, and on 21 June 1961 I resigned from CIE.

Our reputation was growing and now, as well as going after bands to play in our venues, we started to find the top bands approaching us for dates, only too pleased to come and play in our modern ballrooms. My old friend Paddy Cole, then playing saxophone with the famous Capitol Showband, well remembers the misery of some of the venues they were forced to endure, especially those rural marquees on a wet night!

'At the start, modern ballrooms were few and far between. The rural areas still depended on the marquee.

'Often we'd arrive in a country town, the marquee would be up in the middle of a field, and come evening it would still be deserted with not a soul around, and then people would start to arrive on bikes, tractors, cars and farm carts, hundreds, thousands of them, and suddenly the place would be packed.

On wet nights it was dreadful as all the cars and carts would bog down in the mud. We carried a sound system and it was a wonder none of us were electrocuted.

'In those days we had huge speakers to carry the sound, not like the little combined speakers of today, and these massive speakers would have to be tied high up on the poles which held up the marquee.

'A good sign, when you were talking to the guys from other bands, was the number of poles. For example, they would say, "Did you play the marquee down in Castleblayney? That's a great one, it's a six-pole one whereas such and such is only a four-pole one!" By this you would indicate the number of people you could fit in, because needless to say six poles was a larger marquee.

'The facilities were dreadful, especially for ladies. And for the bands there was nowhere to change, only the van. You would have brand new, beautiful suits or in our case, pale blue jackets with white pants and white boots, and there we were trying to get through all this mud, trying to get on to the stage looking smart. So they'd set up planks across the field balanced on beer barrels, as a sort of bridge across the mud, which could be a bit rickety to say the least!

'It was all good fun and on good nights it was great, but it was good to see the end of them because it was nice to play in a ballroom with solid foundations.'

In 1961 my brother Jim and I bought the Longford Arms Hotel. Here we set up our base for the running of the ballroom business and established our new company, Reynolds Dancing Ltd. We were ready to build our empire.

Our pattern was set. We'd both research and plan the location, and then find the site. We always estimated that it would take about three to four months for my brother, who was responsible for construction, to complete the building, by which time it was my job to have publicity organized, staff hired and the bands booked ready for the opening of the new venue.

We'd always open with a big band such as The Royals. You could always depend on them to draw a huge crowd. The trick was to know who would be the best attraction for the area. The Melody Aces were a great draw in Roosky and the Midlands, whereas The Dixies were a hit down south. We went from strength to strength with a string of ballrooms: we established Fairyland in Roscommon, Dreamland in Athy, Lakeland in Mullingar, Jetland in Limerick, Barrowland in New Ross, Rockland in Borris-in-Ossary, Borderland in Clones and Moyland in Ballina. I think by the end we owned about fourteen ballrooms across the country and we rented even more.

As a promoter, I quickly learned that to attract the most successful bands to play in our ballrooms we had to offer more than our competitors. We had to treat the bands well. They would often travel long distances and play for very long hours – sometimes four or five hours a night. I knew our venues were well equipped but I also made sure that the boys were well fed with a good hot meal when they arrived, and that their dressing rooms were set out with refreshments, sandwiches and cold drinks to sustain them during the performance. It was little details like that that made the difference.

There was a young man called Sammy Smyth from Belfast who was managing bands at that time and who remembers our ballrooms. He's now a top political journalist, but he still recalls those hot meals:

'As a young man at that time I was managing bands who often would have to travel all day on a Sunday to get to a gig. They were usually in a draughty old van and in the middle of winter, in cold weather, when they arrived it was always part of the contract that a meal would be supplied. In many of the ballrooms, the really mean guys, promoters, would provide two wilting lettuce leaves, a tomato, two slices of very thin, shiny ham from a packet and bread and butter, but when they played for Albert, they would be directed to the local hotel where they'd get steak, chips, fried onion, tea and bread and butter, a proper evening meal.

'The other hazard faced by young bands was not getting paid. It happened often, but with Albert whether two people came to the dance or two thousand, you always got paid. He kept to his word, he was a man of his word and he had a sterling reputation in that.

'It was a cut-throat business, it was very competitive, it was also – culturally – how boy met girl. From the mid-1950s until some time into the late sixties that's what young people did, they went to a dance, they met, there was no talk of meeting in lounge bars and cabarets, people went to the dance ... that's how Irish people got to know each other ... where families were made. So, in a way, Albert Reynolds could be responsible for births and marriages ...'

I'm not so sure about that! But it was certainly time for me to start my own family life. Fortunately I had made enough money at that time to buy our first home in Longford. It was called Mount Carmel and was to remain our family home for years to come.

I had the car, I had the money and I had the girl – it was time for me to get married. It was June 1962 when Kathleen, my beautiful bride in white lace, walked down the aisle to join me in holy matrimony and we have never looked back. We spent our honeymoon in Majorca and returned to Roosky to live with my mother for a time while our house in Longford was being renovated.

I was working unbelievably hard, travelling all over the

country, North and South, organizing everything, promoting bands, collecting the box office. Often after a gig I'd chat with the band, close everything up and then have to drive all the way back home in the early hours of the morning. My saving grace was that although I smoked heavily, I didn't touch alcohol: tea was my drink.

One night after returning from honeymoon, I'd been up in Athy promoting a dance with Jim and a pal of ours from Moate, Pat Clavin. We'd had a hard time of it, running the bar as well as everything else for some big agricultural show night. Now, at that time there was only one night a year on which you were permitted to sell alcohol in the ballrooms and that was it, and so on that particular occasion we were returning home with bottles of unsold whiskey and spirits stacked in the boot of the car.

We were driving back on the road between Edgeworthstown and Longford when I must have nodded off and we collided with a lorry. The car ended up in a ditch and all the money from the night's takings, which had been in a bag in the back of the car, ended up scattered all over the road. Unfortunately, so were most of the bottles of whiskey, which shattered. The smell of alcohol was very strong on the night air, so when the Gardaí arrived they immediately thought we were all drunk and almost had us for drink-driving. Ironically, all three of us were teetotal! We were lucky, we all escaped with only slight injuries, but I still carry a small scar on my forehead to remind me.

As the ballroom empire grew, we appointed managers to oversee each venue, but we were still very much hands-on. You had to be; the showband business had grown into a lucrative industry and there was a lot of competition out there. Our main rival was Associated Ballrooms, set up by a group of independent promoters who tried to entice away the big players, but we were still favourite with most of the main attraction bands. The fact that we had such an extensive circuit meant we could fill their diaries by offering them four or five gigs a year, in some of the best ballrooms in the country with a capacity of thousands. Jetland alone, one of the biggest in the circuit, saw regular Saturday night crowds of anything between three and four thousand people, drawn from a catchment area with communities as far apart as Clare and Limerick, Tipperary and Kerry.

It was also an industry welcomed by the towns. Whenever there was a dance, all the local businesses benefited: the ladies' hairdressers, fashion shops, bars and restaurants, suppliers of soft drinks and refreshments, even the local petrol stations and bars – they all made money.

Bands would cross the border without a problem. Northern bands like The Clipper Carlton and Dave Glover would come South while The Miami Showband from Dublin or The Royals would play towns in the North, and the fans would follow. The showband players were like rock stars, and every band had its leader – Dickie Rock, Brendan Bowyer, Joe Dolan – and all were as popular in the North as the South. There had been a flurry of IRA activity in the late fifties and early sixties in what was known as the IRA border campaign. The most notable event was the New Year's Day raid in 1957 on an RUC barracks in Brookeborough, Fermanagh, when two young IRA volunteers were killed, Seán South from Limerick and Fergal O'Hanlon from Monaghan. The campaign activity was sporadic; lack of support finally rendered the campaign futile and in the early sixties things quietened down, but the story of Seán South passed into legend in an Irish lyric called 'Seán South from Garryowen'.

Future events overshadowed this period of IRA activity, but it was interesting to me in that this was the period when, after years of estrangement, Sinn Féin was finally adopted by the IRA as its ally in a bid to counter political isolation.

However, following the end of the border campaign there was this little window in the sixties when relations between North and South had never been better. Curiously, at that time more people would have travelled from Dublin to Belfast – for Belfast, with its British connection, had all the British high street shops and, for young fashion-conscious people, all the latest Carnaby Street fashions. Of course they were available in Dublin too, but to a more limited degree, whereas Belfast at that time was very progressive and prosperous. However, in following the bands people would also travel south, which led to the best relations ever within the two communities.

As further evidence of that improving relationship, in 1965 Seán Lemass, then Taoiseach of the Republic, went up to Belfast to meet with the Prime Minister in the North, Terence O'Neill, who then returned the courtesy with a visit to Dublin. Normalization did appear to be moving forward – but then in 1969 everything blew up with the start of the Troubles. Until then, those few years in the sixties were one of the most interesting periods in the short history of Northern Ireland and the Republic, and central to this was the shared love and following of the showbands. There wasn't much 'shared' history in Ireland, only trouble and conflict, and people did not want to dwell on that; but the same showbands were as popular in Belfast as they were in Bantry. It was an all-Ireland phenomenon and a uniquely Irish business.

I travelled to the North all the time because, apart from booking showbands for our own ballrooms, I had also started to bring in international artists to fill some of the major venues in the North.

I used to listen to Radio Luxembourg when I was driving

around, so I got to know the talent in the States and the UK: who was popular, who was on the way up, who was heading for the number one spot in the hit parade. Jazz was very popular in that period and I used to book acts like Acker Bilk and Kenny Ball six to nine months in advance for a fee of around £50 or £60 – sometimes even as much as £170 – and then sell them on to some of the big venues for a percentage of the night's take. Often come the night of the gig the act would be at number one, so I did well. In fact, I'd bought Mount Carmel from the risk I took in booking Kenny Ball! He was just becoming known when I got him; by the time he came to play the gig he had a number one with 'Midnight in Moscow' and I had booked him out for ten nights on the trot.

The Ulster Hall in Belfast was so packed out for Acker Bilk and Kenny Ball that we had to close the doors early. There must have been over two thousand people on those nights. Acker Bilk was happy as long as he got his ten pints of Guinness before he went on stage!

We were in a strong position to entice artists from overseas: we had big-capacity venues of our own stretched across the country and where we didn't have a site, we could offer a deal on other halls. It made it worthwhile for the bands to come to Ireland and tour. We attracted big names – Roy Orbison, Chubby Checker, Johnny Cash, Jim Reeves – and gave them full houses wherever they went, North and South.

Jim Reeves was a huge star from America and I counted myself lucky to get him. I even went out on a limb and paid the most money I had ever invested in an act. He was due to play two gigs on the same night, a common enough practice. His first venue was in Mullingar and the second, some time later that night, in Portlaoise. We had promoted the event well and paid a fortune in advertising, knowing that we could cover our expenses from the tickets, the merchandizing and the refreshments, especially as both houses were fully sold out.

The date was 3 June 1963 – and on that very day, Pope John XXIII passed away. Of course, the whole of Ireland closed down in mourning and every performance in every theatre, club, sports event and ballroom across the entire country was cancelled!

Jim Reeves was staying at the Gresham Hotel in Dublin when I called round to tell him that the night was off. He expressed his sorrow at the news and naturally I told him that under the circumstances, I would still honour our contract and he would be paid according to our deal. I was amazed when he thanked me but then added that that would not be necessary: he had no intention of taking the money! He understood why the date was cancelled and in respect for the death of the Pope, whom he had admired for his approach as a man of the people, he would forgo all payment. He was a rare human being as well as a great artist. It is little wonder that he was known as 'Gentleman Jim Reeves'.

Another rare human being is Father Brian D'Arcy. In the showband days the humour was something else and the friendships made then were so strong they have lasted to this day. Father Brian is one of those great friends, and has been there for all the important moments in the Reynolds family, including family weddings. He is a rarity and one of the most widely recognized characters in show business, regularly joining Terry Wogan on BBC radio. In the 1960s he entered the Passionist congregation, which seemed to mean saying goodbye to the world – but somehow Brian still found a way to be at every dance. He often jokes he held more confessions in the ballrooms than he did in church. Brian often reminds me that his career as a journalist might never have happened had I not recommended him to Jimmy Molloy of the *Dancing News*.

But the master of humour and the greatest trickster in show

business was Eddie Masterson. Eddie was legendary and would find a way to help every musician that approached him. He would often spend weekends at our house and I am sure it was he who taught my son Abbie how to back horses by studying the form.

There is a funny story about the first morning I became Minister for Posts and Telegraphs. The postman arrived at Mount Carmel with a big brown envelope. He had been coming to the house for years but on this occasion he looked a bit embarrassed. When I asked him was he all right he replied, 'I know you're my boss now but I'm going to have to ask you to pay for this package as there is no stamp on it.' I couldn't figure out who would not pay the fifty pence to send me a letter. I put the postman out of his misery, paid him for the stamp and congratulated him on doing a good job. Kathleen opened the letter and out fell a cigarette pack with a note scribbled on the back: 'Congratulations, this is the last one you will have to pay for. Eddie.'

Eddie's life was tragically cut short at the young age of forty-two. It was 1982 and I was on my way to a ministerial function when Father Brian called me to say he was with Eddie, who didn't have long to live. I rushed to his bedside and sat with him throughout the night until he passed away. To this day we all miss his larger-than-life character – but his stories are still told.

Most of the big promoters in the North were Protestants, and though this was irrelevant to me at the time, knowing them served me well in the future. Many of them were colourful characters – people like Sammy Barr, who owned the Flamingo Ballroom in Ballymena; he was always very proud of his hot dogs, the best in the world, he'd say, and his toilets. He'd always insist on showing you these. 'You could eat your dinner off the floor of my ladies' toilets,' he'd boast, 'they are so clean.'

He was also one of the first to introduce those kiosk-type machines to take passport photos. People would queue in their hundreds to get inside. He made a fortune from that alone.

Then there were the great managers and promoters like a good friend of mine, Jim Aitken.

I wasn't interested in politics then, but meeting and working with all those people gave me a good insight into how people thought and lived in the North.

On the night I had Acker Bilk playing in the Ulster Hall, Belfast – 1962 it was, just at the end of the IRA's border campaign – I put the bag of money from the night's box office in the boot of the car and set out for Longford. It was half-past two in the morning and I was halfway out of Belfast when I suddenly noticed I was running out of petrol. Jaysus, I thought – I'd filled the tank earlier in the evening but then left the car out on the street. Somebody had obviously drained the tank, stolen the petrol. What was I to do? Where could I go? It was the early hours of the morning, I was on my own with a boot full of cash and the IRA fellows were lively around and the other fellows were lively too! It was then I saw there was a fellow thumbing a lift. So I stopped. If I was going to run out of petrol, I thought, I was better having someone with me.

It turned out he wasn't saying very much to me, he just gave me his name and where he was going. I guess he knew where I was from by the way I spoke!

'Well,' I said by way of conversation, 'I hope we get to Portadown and I hope you know somebody there who'll get me petrol.'

'We'll see,' he said, 'I'll think about it.'

We got to Portadown, which I didn't think we would, and I asked him where we might go to get petrol. 'Drive down to the police station,' he said. Fair enough, I thought – besides which, I had no option.

The police station was surrounded by sandbags, the usual procedure to protect it from attack by the IRA. My passenger jumped out and said he'd be back. When he returned he explained that I was to follow a police car to a garage that he'd contacted and that was opening up specially to serve me! And thanks for the lift . . .

Years later, some time after my resignation as Taoiseach, I was up on the Garvaghy Road, still a sensitive area. The following day I was at a meeting in Belfast when a young woman, I believe she was a journalist, started questioning me. The conversation went something like this:

'You were up in Garvaghy Road yesterday,' she said. 'A friend of mine from Portadown saw you there, and I'm a Portadown lady.'

'And how does she know that?'

'She knows you to see, she saw you stopped at the lights. Are you denying you were there?'

'I'm not saying yes or no, do you think if I was in Garvaghy Road I'd be telling you?'

'Not at all. And it's not what I wanted to ask. What I really want is to ask you a question about my father. My father was a sergeant in the police in Portadown and he always says he saved your life.

'He says that you gave him a lift in sixty-two when you were stuck for petrol and he got a fellow out of bed who filled you up and set you back on your way to Longford.

'Now is that true or not? Because every time he tells that story we all call him a liar!'

'Well,' I said, 'never call your father a liar again!'

Like all good things, the showband bubble couldn't last for

ever and, in my view, was already showing signs that it was about to burst. The musicians earned so much money it often destroyed them. They were out on the road for weeks at a time, many of them drank too much, some did too much womanizing, broke up their marriages and lost respect for their audiences. Soon, instead of playing for four or five hours, they halved their playing time. 'Filler' bands were brought in by the promoters to entertain the audiences while they waited for the main attraction. Filler bands were usually new local bands – unknown, but often very good. People like Larry Cunningham from Granard, County Longford, started off as a filler for The Clippers. Joe Dolan and The Drifters, from Westmeath, were another filler band we booked.

Sometimes we'd even put up a small marquee alongside the ballroom to accommodate them while the star attraction set up their gear in the main hall. Joe Dolan and The Drifters, for example, played in the little marquee in Roosky beside Cloudland as the support for the British band the John Barry Seven. It was regarded as an important gig, a good career move, for young new bands to get dates with the Reynolds chain. It gave them status, built their audience and, if they had talent, it also guaranteed them future dates in all our key ballrooms in our circuit around the country.

The audiences, however, took a lot of persuading to support these filler bands. They were not ready to listen to something new, and as there was no alcohol served in the ballrooms, they'd drift away to the local pubs and bars. It was a catch-22 situation: the main band would hold off starting until the crowds came in, and the crowds would stay in the bars until the main band came on. Soon bars and pubs started to introduce their own entertainment to hold the audience captive. Hotels had a lot to offer, too: not only licensed premises but comfortable seating in a warm bar where you were served your drinks while you listened to the band. The death knell was tolling. It was time to move on.

For a while we diverted some attention into the new craze of bingo, holding bingo sessions as well as dances in various ballrooms. We started off in Roseland in Moate and were the first to offer a prize of a thousand pounds. I'd sell the tickets, call the numbers, and serve sweets and soft drinks at half-time. And it was about that time, the mid-sixties, that we also decided to diversify into property. Through the companies we set up, J. P. Reynolds Ltd and Lands Ltd, we did well buying and selling a number of properties in the Longford area.

We enjoyed great success throughout those ballroom days, so much so that the queues would stretch round the block. The queues were so long we aroused the interest of the tax inspector, who called me to a meeting in his office in Athlone. I answered all his questions, which showed that I owed no tax. Just as I was about to leave he suddenly said to me, 'Remember, Reynolds, I'll be watching you, and I'll get that tax even if you're on your deathbed.'

'If you leave it with me until then,' I said, 'we have a deal!'

But in 1966 my brother and I had a number of differences about the way the business should go. He wanted to stay with the ballroom business and expand it; I was convinced changes were coming and it was not worth more investment. I'd made up my mind that I wanted out, and so I resigned from the various companies I'd shared with Jim. He continued with the ballroom business for another six years or so but I believed that it had had its best days, that the venture was over – and I was ready to move on to something new.

Also my interest in politics had surfaced again. Over the years, we'd regularly hired out the ballrooms to politicians and organizations all over the country for various political fundraising events and I'd got to know many of the key figures in the different parties. Neil Blaney was one of those politicians who had become a very good friend. He was a prominent Fianna Fáil minister at the time and ran a very well-organized by-election team, and it was he who enticed me to become part of his task force. In 1966 I worked on the team to get John O'Leary elected for the first time in South Kerry; in 1967 it was the by-election in Limerick West that first got Gerry Collins elected; and in 1968 I canvassed in the by-election that saw Des O'Malley win his seat for the first time.

Neil was a hard taskmaster. He had us canvassers working every night until 2.30 a.m. and then insisted we were back on the job at 6.30 a.m. ready to canvass the train services and the early morning passengers. He was extremely methodical and efficient in his campaign planning: he apportioned districts to each of the canvassers, identified the Fianna Fáil and floating voters, and then carefully analysed the returns in each voting box to ascertain who had and had not got results. Each canvasser had to canvass every vote identified by Blaney, organize transport for it and get it out. If that was not done, Blaney would be devastating at the post mortems!

I learned everything I know about canvassing from Neil Blaney, and when the time came I practised his methods in my own election campaigns. Back then, I'd actually put my other business aside for the two weeks of the election, work like the devil and then, when it was over, I was gone. But the excitement of those days stayed with me, the adrenalin flowed and I found them exhilarating.

Over the past few years Kathleen and I had settled happily into our lovely new home, situated on a quiet country lane in Longford. I was on the road running the ballroom business for much of this time, frequently only returning home in the early hours of the morning. Kathleen loved the garden and gardening, but as I was really no help to her we had a gardener called Barnie Willis, who was with us for years. By this time we had three children, Miriam, Philip and Emer. Emer inherited the dark looks of her mother and was positively black when she was born. I remember Kathleen laughing when she related how one of the new mothers, coming into the nursery to find her baby, peered into every crib until she suddenly saw Emer and, startled, backed away quickly with the remark: 'That's definitely not mine anyway!'

Regrettably, I was not there for any of their births, and Kathleen had to rely on the goodwill of close neighbours to get her to the hospital on time. Luckily they were all good friends with young families of their own. Most people in the lane had large families at the time, and all were very supportive of one another. I'm afraid I was not a very 'hands-on' father when the children were very small, but I did make up for it as they got older.

Longford was our home. I liked the town and the people, and as I'd done very well in business over the years, I felt it was time to put something back into the community. So when Neil Blaney, who was Minister for Local Government at the time, started promoting the idea of encouraging local communities to build swimming pools in provincial towns, I, together with other local businessmen and friends – Dessie Hynes, engineer Larry Donegan, Matty Lyons and our local Fianna Fáil TD Frank Carter – decided to form the Longford Development Company, and to build the first heated indoor swimming pool in the country.

It was a very adventurous project at the time, employing various new technologies. We received a grant of 50 per cent from the Local Government Department. Longford County Council levied a penny in the pound on rates for its contribution, and to raise the money for the contribution by the Longford Development Company, in true Irish tradition we ran carnivals and dances. I used all my old connections to book the showbands, top-class acts who came as a favour, and with their appearances we pulled in huge crowds.

The cutting of the first sod was a ceremonial occasion. Neil Blaney came down, the bands played, the locals cheered and all seemed well set for the future opening date. However, as every day the construction company began to dig down and open up the vast pit needed to take the 82-foot by 25-foot pool, so every morning they returned to find that overnight the sides had collapsed and it had re-filled with sand.

It didn't take long to figure out that the site was completely unsuitable for building. The whole enterprise had to be moved to a different location.

The pool finally opened on time, to great publicity and a colourful fanfare. All the local dignitaries and politicians turned out, including Neil Blaney, who was to conduct the opening ceremony – and who was utterly baffled to find the pool in a completely different setting from where he had dug the first sod!

The project proved a great success and in the late sixties many other towns followed the Longford example.

4

DOING DEALS

I'd left the ballroom business, I had time on my hands and money in my pockets, and I needed a new challenge.

Show business was still fresh in my veins. However, it was not purely a love of music that had enticed me into the ballroom business or the passion for show business that drove me on: it was the excitement engendered by making the deal, seeing the potential of something, taking a risk and making it work. Of course, I had always enjoyed music and dancing, but equally I was interested in spotting the rise of up-and-coming young bands or artists, knowing exactly when to pitch for their services, where to place them for best effect, and how to sell them on when they were at their peak. Doing the deal was one thing, making it work was another. It was the rush of adrenalin that fired me to always aim higher, and when I had done all I could do within a certain situation, it was time to move on to the next challenge.

By the late sixties the era of the showbands was fading, the role of international artists and acts was on the rise, and licensed premises were essential. Cabaret clubs seemed to me to be the next stage in the entertainment industry. The pubs had introduced live music and been a big success; now people were looking for something different, more glamorous. I started looking for possible venues.

I found a property in Malahide, a pretty seaside resort on the east coast of Ireland some ten miles north of Dublin city centre. It had been run as a small hotel but had the potential to be developed into what was wanted, a luxury cabaret club. I called it The Showboat: it was very impressive, ahead of its time and large – at full capacity it could seat over a thousand people. For a while it met my ambitions. It was a new start and I enjoyed booking the acts, mainly foreign artists, and working behind the bar, or playing the role of master of ceremonies. Again it was hard work but pleasurable. But once it was successfully up and running, I leased it on: the seeds of my next venture had been sown.

It was Matty Lyons, my colleague in the Longford Development Company, who introduced me to my next acquisition.

He and his family had been in the meat business for years, and he had learned of a small bacon factory that was for sale and in need of major reinvestment. I knew nothing about the meat trade, but I had learned a great deal about business; so I went to look at it. It was situated in the Liberties, one of the oldest parts of inner-city Dublin, a run-down area of twisting small streets and crumbling houses. The factory was known as Patrick Kehoe's, formerly Kehoe of the Liberties, and had been established in 1742: it was the oldest bacon plant in Dublin. It was losing a fortune, but even so I estimated the property was worth as much as, if not more than, the asking price for the enterprise, so I bought my first factory and went into pigs.

The history of the Liberties goes back to medieval times and has often been turbulent and grim. Today it is a pleasant and bustling area, a haunt for antique hunters, but back then in the late sixties and seventies, before the boom of the Celtic Tiger years, it was a close neighbourhood that suffered a lot of deprivation.

I had a great relationship with the families of the district. I looked after them; I used to make sure that the local women, most of them natives of the Liberties, received whatever bits and pieces of meat we could spare from the factory – the odd off-cut, anything that could help them out – and in return they offered me security. The old buildings around the factory were divided into hundreds of little apartments, with windows overlooking the street and each other. There many of the women, particularly the older ones, would pass their days calling across to each other or simply gazing down on the streets below. I used to drive up from Longford every day and I could safely leave my car outside, even with the doors unlocked and my coat or briefcase on the back seat, knowing it would never be touched. It was the same with the factory: no one dared ever break into the premises under the watchful eyes of those women.

They were there for me on another occasion as well. There came a time when we nearly had to close the factory because of industrial problems and a strike by the Irish Farmers' Association. For a while our local supplies of animals were cut off, so I had to look elsewhere. There was a fellow I knew in the North who had a plentiful supply, so I arranged for him to send his pigs down to Dublin. Unfortunately, the IFA got to hear about this and started picketing the factory. They knew we closed at six o'clock, so around this time in the evening they'd call it a day and all go home. It was then the women came into their own. Over the weeks they'd got to know the fellows driving the pigs down from the North. 'You leave us a set of keys, Mr Reynolds,' they said, 'and we'll do the rest.'

I didn't ask any questions, but come the morning the pens would be full of pigs.

It seemed the women had negotiated with the fellows from the North to deliver the pigs at night to an appointed place at the end of the Coombe which borders the Liberties; there they'd collect the herd and drive them through the narrow streets by torchlight into the factory. Next morning when the pickets arrived at eight o'clock, it was too late: there were the holding pens filled with pigs. Weeks after the strike was over, the pickets were still bemused as to how they'd got there.

I had put the day-to-day running of the factory in the hands of two men well known for their expertise in the business, leaving me free to concentrate on the export side of things and on raising productivity. Within a year we had turned the business around from a loss to a profit, employing a steady rota of staff, and it continued as such until, under a government scheme aiming to rationalize the industry, I surrendered my bacon export licence. However, just before the factory closed down, it was severely damaged by fire. The Liberties were old and many of the buildings presented a constant fire hazard.

Some time later, in 1973, I rented out the property on a trial basis to the Coyle brothers, who were keen to start up the bacon business again for the home market. I deducted the money it cost them to repair the fire damage to the building from their rent and they went on to build a very successful business that is still operating today.

My energy levels were high. I'd turned the bacon factory around, now I needed something else. Someone, somewhere, had suggested the notion of exporting Irish salmon.

I'd done it with bacon, why not fish? In one season I bought up the entire catch from Donegal. Marketing it was another matter. Suddenly I was the outsider and all the fishing cartels ganged up against me: even the famous Billingsgate fish market in London refused my salmon. I kept my nerve and my fish, frozen, until the end of the year when I sold it on, smoked, for the Christmas season.

The live lobster and crayfish I'd bought at the same time were not so easy to dispose of. I had markets all ready and waiting in France and Spain, but a sudden air strike put the whole operation in jeopardy. Not to be beaten, I bought a plane, a second-hand de Havilland executive jet that I had converted. I also hired a pilot, a colourful character from the Caribbean called Captain Charles. He too had been involved in some way in the meat industry and had various contacts across the world. Unfortunately we could not get enough supplies to meet the demand and, burdened with the costs of running the jet, the enterprise failed.

For some unknown reason the plane had a cocktail cabinet on board which somehow ended up in the garage at Mount Carmel. It served for years as a source of great amusement for the children and their friends.

Luckily this had not been the only venture to occupy my time. I now owned a share in the Odeon cinema in Longford, had invested in a hire-purchase company involved in financing the buying of cars and machinery, and, more importantly, I was germinating the kernel of an idea that would become my biggest business success.

I was also in the first stages of being drawn further into local politics. Throughout the years of owning the bacon factory, the tedium of driving every day from Longford to Dublin had been lightened by the company of a very good friend of mine,

Joe Sheridan. Joe was a man who had been a strong member of Fine Gael in my constituency. He had expected to be elected as TD and his name had been put forward over the course of three elections in the fifties, every one unsuccessful. In the end he left Fine Gael and went Independent. For many years thereafter he had been elected as Independent Deputy for Longford–Westmeath and had been a strong supporter of the Lemass government of 1965–9 at a time when Fianna Fáil did not have an overall majority and relied on a few Independents for their support.

He had often worked out of the Longford Arms in the days of the ballroom business, so we went back a long way. It was those long drives with Joe that started to make me think politics could be another career. Joe was a genuinely decent man who'd made an art of getting things done for people. Although he was not a great speaker – I don't believe he ever spoke in the Dáil – he was a man of action. I remember there were two gay men living in Longford, and this was way back, when it was not even acceptable to admit to being gay. But when one guy died, Joe got the other fellow a widow's pension!

I decided to get more actively involved in local politics and was elected as a constituency representative from Longford–Westmeath to the Fianna Fáil National Executive. A grand title for a lowly job, but at least I was in a position to help bring a better quality of life to the people of Longford.

All this time, too, my family had been growing. Another daughter, Leonie arrived; then Albert junior, known as Abbie, entered the world in 1969; and he was followed by two more daughters, Cathy and Andrea. I was very conscious that I wanted to ensure a better future for my children than the last few generations of young people had been forced to endure. They wouldn't have to face unemployment, emigration and instability – not if I had anything to do with it!

Meanwhile I bought a newspaper, the *Longford News*. It was a small-time paper with a small circulation, but I could see the potential for developing it into something to rival the other local papers. From my days with the showbands I also knew the value of advertising, and I foresaw that this would become an important part of the future: as towns and commerce modernized and developed, the world of publicity would grow too.

Longford in the early 1970s was a poor town even by Irish standards and there was not much going on. However, it was unusual in that for a relatively small community it had two newspapers, the *Longford Leader*, founded in 1897, and the *Longford News*, founded in 1936. The *News* had been the brainchild of its owner, Vincent Gill. He was a legendary figure in the world of journalism in that he not only owned the paper but wrote his own copy. In an era when local newspapers confined themselves mainly to factual reporting of local events, births, marriages and deaths, Vincent regaled his readership with colourful articles and columns reflecting his own bizarre, off-beat view of life.

However, he was getting on in years and was convinced he was going to die before long. His mother's name had been Reynolds, so he decided that if he was going to have to sell his beloved newspaper, it would have to be to someone in his family or to someone named Reynolds. In no way was it to fall into the hands of his lifelong rival the *Longford Leader* – on this point he was adamant. The paper had been established some forty-odd years and although Vincent's methods of publishing were somewhat 'individual', the paper had a following, it had potential – so I bought it.

I hired a young freelance sports reporter, Eugene McGee, to act as editor, that is until I recruited Derek Cobbe, the former

director and editor of the *Longford Leader*. Derek Cobbe
became my first editor. He'd known Vincent well and
frequently regaled me with stories about this ultimate
eccentric.

Derek Cobbe:

'Vincent had spent the early years of his working life in the
army and the Gardaí. He'd been based in County Kerry but
left when he was told he had to evict people from their homes
and confiscate their cattle: he would walk around with stones
in his pocket which he'd throw at the cattle to make them run
off, so that he wouldn't be able to confiscate them. He
returned to Longford to set up a local paper which he
intended to publish and write himself. He started off by calling it the *Canal Herald*, and the strapline was "A journal for
God's men and little fishes". He later changed it to the
Longford News.'

Vincent was vehemently anti-establishment and anti-
Church, and at a time when Ireland was very anti-communist
he would cover a full page with photographs of some marshal
in the Soviet Union. On days when he had no news, he'd fill
the front page with a large block of black ink headline,
'Caught in the Pub after Hours'. Then he'd take great delight
in listing genuine names of people who lived in and around
Longford. On another occasion, the paper carried the big
headline ... TOWN IMPROVEMENTS: underneath, the
copy carried all the names of those who had emigrated! When
he had nothing to report he made up the news stories. He was
totally anarchic and more than outrageous in some of the
items he devised, especially in pulling in advertising.

Derek Cobbe had been working for the rival paper, the
Longford Leader, until he joined me as first editor on
the *News*, but he was very familiar with some of Gill's
schemes, and delighted in telling me about them.

Derek Cobbe again:

'Vincent was a great man for paying his bills if he had the money, which he rarely did because he never sent out any invoices for advertising, for example, so he obviously didn't get paid. So every now and then he'd put a notice in the paper that he needed money and that anyone who owed him should pay him. At other times he would be more devious. He would print in one of the issues a notice in which he would warn the courting couple "seen on the canal line the previous week" that if they did not take out a subscription to the paper, they would be shamed and their names would be published in the paper the following week. Often seven or eight subscriptions would suddenly fill the coffers.'

I knew nothing about the newspaper business, although I'd learned a great deal about promotion and the power of the press in my showbusiness ventures; this was another challenge, a risk, and I relished taking it on. However, I had neither the time nor the experience to run the paper myself, so I brought in people who did. While Vincent stayed on to write his column for as long as he wished, Cobbe became joint managing director with me; plus, he was given a small shareholding in the paper, which would rise with performance results. As the circulation was only two thousand, we had a long way to go.

The first thing was to move to new premises. The smell of cats and dogs in Vincent's place was overpowering. However, moving was not so easy. The extension building in Harbour Row had been constructed around the machinery, so now we had to knock it down to get the machinery out. We finally set up shop in Breadon's old bakery on Dublin Street in Longford.

At about the same time Cobbe persuaded journalist Liam Collins, now a senior journalist with the *Sunday Independent*, to join the team as a journalist and set him to do his first job. Liam Collins remembers it well:

'I was clearing out Vincent Gill's things in Harbour Row – drawers full of unopened letters, scandalous pictures and bundles of back issues of his beloved *Longford News* and stacks of the *New Yorker* magazine to which he contributed the odd witty line – when I first met Albert Reynolds. Tanned, wearing a well-cut suit and stepping out of his deep blue Daimler car, he was the epitome of the successful businessman. The new owner of the *News* said "Hello" and exchanged a bit of banter. Then he left us to get on with the job in hand.'

I have always believed that if you choose the right people for the right job then you should let them get on with it. There was never too much money about in those days and I wasn't around that much. I left it to the fellows and just went in to sign the cheques. I was there if they needed me, I'd listen and advise if they asked, but I also knew how to delegate and expected them to play their part. Even so, I was hands-on at the beginning. In those early days with the paper everything had to be cut by hand, and that first Saturday trying to get the paper out even Kathleen came down in the middle of the night to help cut the paper – and both of us were up early the next morning trying to distribute it before the shops opened.

It was a big leap for the paper to become more professional. The linotype machine from Harbour Row was in good working order, but we also needed a new printing machine and this I bought from the Guinness plant. We set it up in the bakery, next to the old ovens. There were odd holes in the roof where the birds still flew in to pick up the grains of flour that somehow clung to the rafters.

As things improved and the circulation rose, we decided to buy a second printing machine for the *News*. I'd heard of one for sale in the North and Liam Collins came with me to look at it. It was the first time he'd ever been in the North, which was not unusual. The border was only thirty-five miles away but few people at that time went across it: the North was another country. The new machine was being sold in Enniskillen by the local paper, the *Impartial Observer*. It was a Protestant paper, and this really surprised Liam: he had no idea that each town in the North generally had a Protestant and a Catholic paper.

I still had lots of contacts in the North and had run into someone, somewhere, who had told me this machine was for sale. I had never been interested in the political or religious aspects of business dealing: it was just a question of 'Let's get this sorted – now! Let's find a solution.' However, Liam's bemusement at the situation where one town would have two newspapers, one for each religious community, suddenly brought home to me the madness of current attitudes and the distraction this presented to progress and things moving on.

My interest in politics was growing, albeit at local level, and although I had originally been attracted to buying the paper as a simple business venture, I began to realize the possibilities it presented in furthering my political ambitions.

Under Derek Cobbe's editorial direction the *Longford News* continued to expand. For the most part it still published factual accounts of court cases, local events or announcements: there were no articles as such. However, we were starting to do well and one of the main reasons was that we started reporting news of local people who had moved to Birmingham.

I had a lot of friends who had left the area in the search for jobs – school friends, local Longford people and so on – and many of them had moved to live in Birmingham. As a local politician, I had started going over to speak at meetings of the Birmingham Irish Association; these events were then reported in the *News*, along with items of interest from various individuals, and the paper's circulation really benefited from this. I have maintained a strong link with the Longford Irish in Birmingham ever since.

Derek Cobbe also had a great idea for an addition to the paper's sports pages. I was still as passionate about horse racing as I had been ever since that first introduction to The Curragh during my days in the camp at Ballydermot working for the National Turf Development Agency. Whatever or wherever the race, I'd be there whenever the opportunity arose and I was available, be it Cheltenham, Aintree, Ascot, Galway or Listowel – and if I couldn't be there, I'd watch it on television. My younger son, Abbie, had inherited the same passion. As far back as I can remember, when he was just a little fellow, he'd be out walking the course with me, Roscommon at weekends, Galway for holidays (the family holiday always coincided with that particular festival!). Kathleen would join me on most occasions but her interest was more in the social side of racing, whereas Abbie intuitively started studying form. For my part I still relied more on word of mouth and tips; Abbie, however, was good! I'd always put money on his choice for him, and more often than not he'd win.

So impressed was Derek Cobbe with Abbie's ability that he actually gave him his own column in the *Longford News*. It was simply called 'Abbie Tips 3' and that's exactly what it was: a list of three of Abbie's hot tips, be it for the local event or the Grand National. What nobody who followed it realized was that Abbie was only seven years old at the time! Derek Cobbe paid him £3.50 a week and this helped finance his betting. Until school intervened Abbie would often walk the course with me on race days. He was fortunate that when he went on to the Cistercian College in Roscrea his Irish teacher just happened to be Brendan O'Rourke, the TV race commentator on TG4: Abbie had found a soulmate! Although he now lives in America, Abbie still goes with me to the various festival meetings whenever he's over and it can be arranged.

Racing is an integral part of Irish culture and I met many of my 'soulmates' through racing, beginning great friendships that lasted throughout our lives. There was one particular group, Peter Reynolds (no relation), Gerry Reynolds (no relation), Davie Sheeran, Tommy Noel-Donlon and myself, and every year we would take the same house for a week in September for the Listowel festival in Kerry. Sadly, Peter and Davie are no longer with us, but the rest of us still go. I believe I've only ever missed one year – and that was when I was Taoiseach and I had a few other things on my mind.

It's not just the excitement of the race I enjoy, it's the camaraderie in the racing community and the people you meet. There was a horse called Rag Trade, part-owned by a colleague of mine who supplied raw materials for C&D Petfoods, a subsequent business venture, and part-owned by a guy called Pierre Raymond Bessone, a personality hairdresser, known as 'Raymond' or Mr Teezy Weezy, a flamboyant character, notable for his colourful suits. In 1976 Rag Trade was quoted at 14–1 in the Grand National at Aintree, ridden by Irish jockey John Burke and trained by Fred Rimell. Worth a bet – but he was up against Red Rum, a wonderful horse who had already won the race twice.

It was a great race – and the greatest moment of all was when Rag Trade came in first, beating Red Rum, ridden by Tommy Stack, into second place! It was an extraordinary win – everyone was over the moon, and I was invited down to the winner's enclosure where Raymond insisted I led in the winner. It was a thrilling moment and I have the photograph of it still in my study.

Under Derek Cobbe's editorial guidance the *Longford News* continued to prosper, and its circulation grew all through the seventies. However, my life was becoming increasingly taken up with other preoccupations, with different ventures claiming my interest, and as the paper was now well established, I decided the time had come to sell.

It had all started when I was running the bacon factory in Dublin. There was a lot of waste in the butchering of pigs to produce bacon – bones, offal and blood – and all of it, by law, had to be removed every evening from the premises, otherwise it would have created a health hazard and the authorities would have closed me down. So at the end of every day we paid for it to be removed.

One day I was watching the guys collecting the waste, and in the course of chatting and handing over the money, I asked them what they were doing with it all. They explained that it went to a plant to be frozen and was then exported to England where it was made into pet food, not just to be sold in the UK but also to be re-imported for sale in Ireland.

And there was I paying for them to take it away.

It didn't take long for the idea of doing it myself to take root. Suddenly I could see a big potential market in pet food. Of course I knew nothing about it, so I started investigating and looking around for someone who did.

Matty Lyons turned out to be the man. Just by coincidence he too had been toying with the same notion. His family were also in the meat business in Longford and Leitrim, and he too had noticed a sudden rise in pet-food sales. People were no longer willing to give their cats and dogs the odd scraps from the table but were now buying tinned food specially produced for pets. The market was looking good: in Britain alone pet-food sales topped £240 million per annum. So we decided to go for it together. We wanted to build our plant in Longford town but that was not possible, so we started looking in the surrounding area and found a field on the outskirts of Edgeworthstown, six miles up the road. With financial help from the Industrial Development Agency, the ICC and various bank loans, we began to build. Unfortunately the early 1970s was a time of industrial upheaval in Ireland. Particularly damaging was the infamous 1970 cement strike; there was also a bank strike. Both of these actions affected us and delayed the opening of the plant. With the help of two additional shareholders, we finally opened the factory in 1971 and began operations with a staff of five. Matty Lyons was appointed managing director as he was the more experienced in the meat business.

C&D Pet Foods Ltd was launched with a big reception in Dublin at the Cats' and Dogs' Home on Grand Canal Quay. We chose this venue because we wanted to draw attention to the work of the Dublin Society for the Prevention of Cruelty to Animals, and we also wished to press home the point that our product was made only from animals killed in the most humane way possible. Many high-profile personalities supported us in this aim and came to the event, which received excellent publicity. We were on our way.

Inevitably, success did not come easily. There were many teething problems and difficulties, and customers were hard to win over. We needed them to try our product but we faced a lot of resistance, from British buyers in particular. Sales were not what we had hoped for and canning and promotion were costly, so that by 1972, just one and a half years after our grand opening, the auditors were advising liquidation on the grounds of insolvency.

I was determined not to close down. However, Matty Lyons

was losing faith; we owed so much money that he wanted us to get out, and at the end of a very heated argument he threw me the keys and said, 'Do what you like!'

Matty was still managing director and the major shareholder, with 51 per cent as against my 29 per cent; but, although we had nothing in writing, he walked out leaving me to make whatever decisions I chose. So I took over the responsibility for the debt, bought out two other shareholders who each had 10 per cent, and went back to talk to the IDA and the ICC and persuaded them to support us with further financial grants as they had at the beginning of our project.

We employed a marketing expert and with his help we began to develop sales in Britain and Italy. Sales gradually started to rise from 70,000 cases a year to 200,000 cases. Unfortunately, at this point Matty Lyons returned and started trying to change the whole operation. Again he and I had a difference of opinion. He wanted to go in one direction, I wanted to go in another. I did not believe that what he wanted would be an effective way to run the company but Matty, being the majority shareholder, had the final say; and, as was his right, he decided to take it to the High Court and to let them decide on C&D's future. Against all the odds, as the minority shareholder, I won the case.

This was a visionary decision on the part of the High Court judge, Judge Kenny, and set a precedent. He ruled that while the throwing of the keys by Matty Lyons did not amount to a formal or legal arrangement, I had nevertheless accepted the responsibility of employing the staff and of servicing the debt, and it was only when Lyons saw the business starting to build up again that he came back and wanted to resume control. However, it was my commitment to the banks that had kept the business operating, and he judged that, as I had taken responsibility for other people's lives, and had acted in the best interests of everybody, I should continue to be the one to run the business.

Initially Matty was allowed to keep his majority share-holding on the basis that I ran the business. Ultimately, it was ruled by the judge that Matty had not complied with that order and the judge compelled him to sell his 51 per cent to me at a price to be decided by the court.

The big target for C&D was Sainsbury's. To be contracted to supply Sainsbury's 'own label' pet foods would be a real coup. It would not only be a substantial order of some magnitude itself, but would also attract other potential buyers.

Suddenly the call came. However, as well as demanding that the product itself was of the highest quality, Sainsbury's also required the most meticulous standards of operation from their suppliers, and before any contract could be initiated the factory had to be inspected by both their pet-food buyer and their technical adviser. The factory passed the inspection and the buyer was impressed with the quality of the product. We made a deal.

It was a hard bargain, and profit margins were extremely tight. I've always believed that if your profit margin is too low, then you can double it by doubling your output. So I put on a second shift. Then came our lucky break when Britain, hit by industrial unrest in the power industries, was put on a three-day week. As a result, Sainsbury's found that some of their biggest suppliers could not fulfil their orders – and we were very glad to help them out. We never looked back.

Although my career in local politics (which had been develop-ing at the same time as C&D) was taking more of my time and energy in the mid-seventies, I was still working very hard at developing the pet-food business. We had increased our output, and our profits were gradually climbing. Most of the meat was supplied locally, but canning materials were sourced from across the border and I was travelling back and forth between North and South. For sales and distribution in the North I appointed a close friend of Ian Paisley's. At that time things were difficult following the civil rights marches and Bloody Sunday: the Troubles in the North were serious and I was often stopped at checkpoints en route; sometimes the border was simply closed. Nevertheless, despite everything we were gradually increasing sales.

Sainsbury's were hard taskmasters who rigorously monitored their suppliers' product and plant, and to keep up with their draconian hygiene requirements we were constantly having to reinvest in machinery and plant. It got to the point where they accounted for 60 per cent of C&D sales and owing to lack of capacity some of our other customers were losing out. Soon further strains were put on the company when Sainsbury's too demanded an increase in supplies – and if we could not provide it, they would look for another supplier. We were confident our product was the best, we were still working double shifts and to full capacity, yet owing to increased competition our profit margins were decreasing. In that position, with inflation high and no prospect of increasing production, we had few options: we could either stay as we were, sell, or expand the plant.

We decided to expand. The prospect was daunting; the cost of constructing a new plant was estimated at about IR£4.5 million. Where were we going to find the money?

At this time Ireland was in the depths of depression, but the country had become a member of the EEC and we found that we met the conditions to apply for what was known as a 'FEOGA' grant – from the European Agricultural Guidance and Guarantee Fund. We supplemented this grant with various other loans and grants, and the building began.

This was in late 1981, by which time I was an opposition

TD shadowing a minister. Perhaps inevitably I came under fire, accused of using my position to get the EEC grant. This was not so. It was not Fianna Fáil but a Fine Gael–Labour coalition government which sanctioned the FEOGA scheme. Had we not taken this route then we would have had to seek help from the IDA and the Irish taxpayer would have borne the brunt of a loan. As it was, we won the first grant of its kind from the EEC, and it opened the way for other Irish businesses to benefit.

I had hoped to be on the spot to supervise the construction of the new plant, but circumstances dictated otherwise. In 1982 another election saw Fianna Fáil back in power and I was appointed Minister for Industry and Energy. My political career had now taken over my life, and instead of being there to oversee the C&D building project I was off selling Kinsale gas to the British: although I watched the struggles and successes of C&D with great interest, from this point it had to be from afar.

Over the years the reputation and fortunes of the company grew; different personnel drove the company forward and eventually, in 1990, I was very proud to see my son Philip take over the business and become managing director and later chairman. Today, C&D's produce is found on supermarket shelves not only in Ireland but right across Europe.

I always knew it was a good idea!

5

BUSINESS ON A BIGGER SCALE

As my involvement in politics deepened, I was becoming more aware of the background to the situation in Northern Ireland. No one could ignore what was happening in the North.

When the civil rights marches erupted into violence in 1969, we were all thrown into a state of shock. There had been a window of peace in the preceding years; now old wounds were bleeding again and anger against partition raged. People from the North fled south out of fear, to seek refuge, while they looked to the government in Dublin to send help.

The IRA declared a return to its military campaign and the British sent in troops. In this worsening situation and in the face of the IRA declaration, government policy was clear, and the Taoiseach at that time, Jack Lynch, held fast to that policy, as had his predecessor, Seán Lemass. I knew from my own contacts in the North that they were relying on the South to intervene and were bitterly disappointed when the statement was issued making it clear that any IRA military action would not be tolerated; that only the lawful government of Ireland, freely elected by the people, had the authority to speak and act on behalf of the Irish people, and that the government would not tolerate any attempt to usurp the power legitimately conferred upon it by the people.

In September, as violence escalated and the calls for intervention became louder, Jack Lynch emphasized again that the government had no intention of using force to end partition. Unity by consent was the only way forward, he argued. We had to create conditions of mutual respect and tolerance if ever we hoped to break down partition and see Nationalists and Unionists live together in harmony, and that was going to take a long time.

A friend of mine from the North, a Republican, Noel Gallagher, was a teenager in Derry at that time and he paints a bleak picture of what it was like growing up on the Bogside:

'As a young man, a fourteen-year-old, I joined Éire Nua, basically the IRA youth movement. You must understand there was nothing to do. Then came the summer riots in 1968–9 and we were all involved. I can't describe to you how desolate and desperate we were. We really were at a stage where we couldn't take any more and if you are at that stage of desolation, nothing matters to you. So the summer riots come and they're gone and in sixty-nine the British sent down the soldiers and they were greeted fantastically well, my own people took them out biscuits and tea – but that didn't last long. They came in as a great hope but if the Unionists had given us housing and a few jobs we wouldn't have needed any soldiers.'

The government refused to respond, but there were others in Fianna Fáil who wanted action. Among them were my old mentor and staunch Republican Neil Blaney and an ambitious young Minister for Finance, married to Lemass's daughter,

Charles Haughey. They succeeded in pushing through cabinet a decision to provide emergency assistance and relief for the victims of violence in the North. Two sub-committees were established, one consisting of Blaney and Haughey and the other of two ministers from border constituencies, Pádraig Faulkner and Joe Brennan. Blaney and Haughey had their own ideas about how funds for aid to victims should be dispensed. A government fund of £100,000 was set up, and Haughey was given sole authority over the money.

In October 1969 a meeting of the Northern Citizen Defence Committees was held in Bailieborough, County Cavan, with an Irish army intelligence officer, Captain James Kelly, in attendance. The meeting was told that £50,000 would be made available from the fund to buy weapons for the defence of Nationalist areas against the Loyalists. Haughey even met with the IRA Chief of Staff, Cathal Goulding. When Minister for Justice Michael O'Morain later reported this meeting to cabinet, Haughey dismissed it as a chance encounter.

It was alleged that Neil Blaney conspired with Captain Kelly to import arms from Europe, with funding provided by Haughey. It was further alleged that Haughey even tried to arrange customs clearance.

Revelations about the 'plot' were passed to Jack Lynch who, pressed into action by the leader of the opposition Liam Cosgrave, confronted Blaney and Haughey. When they refused to resign, he had no option but to sack them.

On 28 May 1970 Haughey and Blaney went on trial in Dublin, together with Captain James Kelly and two others. And I was there. At that time I was still running the bacon factory in the Liberties; my office was not far from the courts and I was keen to see the outcome. I had met Haughey very briefly when he'd visited Longford but Neil Blaney was a long-time friend. I was also becoming more and more intrigued by politics and the situation in the North had had a big impact on me – not least because I was deeply concerned at what was happening to many of my business colleagues and friends in the North.

The two other defendants, along with Haughey and James Kelly, who were called to stand trial for treason, were a Belfast Republican leader, John Kelly, and a Belgian businessman and former socialist, Albert Luykx, who had allegedly used his contacts to purchase the weapons.

On 2 July Neil Blaney was cleared of all charges and was not tried. The main trial collapsed a week later after allegations of bias: the judge refused to continue and the trial was abandoned.

At the second trial, held in October, there was a direct contradiction of evidence regarding the sanctioning of the imports between Haughey and the prosecutorial witness Jim Gibbons, who was Minister for Defence at the time of the imports. Haughey admitted arranging customs clearance for the shipment but claimed he did not know it consisted of weapons.

That trial too finally collapsed and the four defendants, Charles Haughey, Captain James Kelly, John Kelly and Albert Luykx, were cleared on 23 October. The evidence showed that, despite the suspicions of some, the government was not funding the IRA.

The cut and thrust of politics intrigued me. It was another business on a bigger scale, and it was during this period I decided that, when the time was right, national politics would be my next big challenge.

My local political life began to edge forward. I had not only served as the Longford delegate to the Fianna Fáil National Executive from 1971 to 1974, but in 1973 I had also been appointed Director of Elections for Fianna Fáil in Longford. For me a key achievement was when I was selected as president of Longford Chamber of Commerce in 1972. This really opened up my chances to help with the urgently needed development of Longford. Communications at the time were very poor, so my first project to bring the town into the modern world was the development of an airport at Abbeyshrule. We set up Longford Aviation Airfield Development Ltd and at our first meeting to discuss the proposed airfield, in January 1977, we raised share money totalling £40,000 from members of the public.

In 1974 the local Fianna Fáil organization, and the long-time sitting TD, Frank Carter, approached me and asked me if I would stand for the local county council, and also if I would start preparing myself to arrange my business in such a way that it would allow me to do politics as well. I was very happy to agree.

I had always been very impressed by Seán Lemass. He was my inspiration and my political hero.

De Valera and Lemass founded Fianna Fáil together, but though de Valera had caught my youthful imagination, he was always buried in history; Lemass was about the future. I liked the way he tried to change the nature of the country, to move it on from the old ways. He was forward-thinking, he wanted to develop Ireland to produce jobs and business, and he had the ability to inspire people to reach out for what they could do.

When I was growing up, a full education was limited to the privileged few and too many people were going abroad for lack of opportunity at home. Lemass tried to change all that. He also tried to forge new links between the Republic and the North, and never gave up on seeing the unity of Ireland restored. He was entrepreneurial and pragmatic – 'the architect of modern Ireland' – and I believed in all that.

Lemass was the inspiration for all my speeches to the people during my election campaign of 1974. What he had wanted for Ireland, I wanted for Longford. Longford had been too complacent, I told them: for too long we had sat back, content with what we had. We had watched industry and business opportunities pass us by and go to other towns like Wicklow, Clare, Limerick and Mayo. Now we had to fight back: our future depended on the creation of new jobs, the development of the county and our ability to attract new industry. Remember, I told them, in the words of Lemass, 'a rising tide lifts all boats!'

When the votes were counted, I topped the poll. As the *Longford Leader* reported: 'The popularity of Albert was evident when crowds who had gathered at the Temperance Hall for hours beforehand cheered loudly when they heard the results.'

Longford was my home and I was proud of it. Six of our seven children had been born there; all seven were growing up there and had started their education in the local schools. Kathleen and I were happy there. Our house, Mount Carmel, had been extended to accommodate our expanding family and we had bought extra land on which to build a tennis court and a swimming pool. My business career had brought us success and financial security, but politics had got into my blood and I found it exciting. I also believed my business background and experience would serve me well in politics and I wanted to put it to good use to achieve something positive, not just for Longford but for my country; I wanted to be part of ensuring a better future for Ireland. The urge to move to national politics was growing stronger.

* * *

I was still smoking and every day my pockets bulged with a growing 'file' of notes as everywhere I went people stopped me on the streets with different ideas or requests which I noted on my cigarette packets. It's still a habit today: no cigarettes now, but the bundles of bits of paper still fill my suit pockets. It's my 'filing system'.

As Liam Collins commented:

'The sixties didn't really get to Ireland until the seventies, communications were so much slower. Albert Reynolds was a new breed of businessman, a show-business entrepreneur, involved in politics but at the lower end . . . even so you could see then there was something special, he was already a political animal.

'When you went to county council meetings he would stand out. Most members were of the old style, looking for the odd favour for a local farmer or tarring for a road; Albert Reynolds had vision, he wanted to do something for local enterprise, to help get jobs. There was very little industry in the area so employment was limited. People were just about "getting by", houses, roads were in a dreadful state and cars were just about held together for years.

'Albert wanted to go to the IDA, to build factories and services for employment. He was committed to bringing prosperity to the town, he had already built the C&D plant, he owned the *Longford News* and a finance company, as well as other businesses. He was far more than your ordinary run-of-the-mill politician – he had vision and creativity.'

I was approaching middle age, in fact I was forty-five years old, when I eventually decided to take the big step from local to national politics. I'd been considering it for some time and, with Kathleen's support, I had made up my mind that if the opportunity presented itself, I'd go for it.

Then came the general election of 1977. The current coalition government of Fine Gael and Labour had run its course and there was every chance that, in a general election under the leadership of Jack Lynch, Fianna Fáil could win back a second seat in Longford–Westmeath. This it had failed to do in the previous election of 1973, when of the four seats available in the constituency, Fine Gael had won two and Independent Joe Sheridan one, while Frank Carter had held the fourth for Fianna Fáil.

Although at that time I was a novice, my name was put forward for nomination as the Fianna Fáil candidate for Longford, to be voted on at the convention in Mullingar in the run-up to the general election, which was to take place on 16 June.

Frank Carter had been the uncontested sitting TD for a number of years, as had his father before him. He was a good friend of mine, and we had worked closely together for a long time in local politics. Now, getting on in years, Frank had decided that it was time for him to stand down. He then changed his mind – which, as Derek Cobbe pointed out, didn't do anyone any favours, 'because whatever chance there was of a clear-cut campaign was gone with all his messing around. I think he'd been listening to people talking, persuading him he should still stand. He was the last of the old-school politicians whereas Albert Reynolds was of the new generation of bullish fiery young people.'

It isn't easy for anyone to reconcile himself with the passing of time, the ending of a career and the sudden realization that the 'active' years are over: so, although Frank had made up his mind to retire, I think when his loyal friends persuaded him to stand again, he was suddenly filled with hope that his career could continue.

The *Longford Leader*, although a rival in the newspaper world, came out in support of my nomination:

'The needs and prospects for youth is much more than a cliché with Albert Reynolds – it is a firm commitment backed up by action. Already, in his capacity as Chairman of the ambitious Mall Development project, he is engaged in the development of a Town's Park for Longford with special facilities for all sports in the Community ...

'One might well ask why a man with proven industrial and commercial ability would want to involve himself with politics and seek the nomination as a candidate for the Longford–Westmeath Constituency – the answer is simple – as a committed member of Fianna Fáil, he is convinced that the progress of this country is dependent on the return to Government of the Fianna Fáil party, and the people best suited to represent the Party must have the energies and ambitions to face the present day problems of Government. Albert Reynolds possesses all of these, and is seeking nomination as Fianna Fáil candidate at next Sunday's convention.'

There were almost three hundred Fianna Fáil members gathered in the County Hall in Mullingar that Sunday to vote on who should represent the party. At the time I put my name forward for nomination, Frank was not in the running; now he was my competitor, which was not what I would have chosen. However, I had entered the arena and I did not want to lose. It was a tense night: so many people had admired and respected Frank and he had been a very good TD for Longford, but there were also those who could see it was time for him to make way for new blood and a new Fianna Fáil candidate.

There was a dramatic build-up to the count but when it came, I was selected by 209 votes to Frank Carter's 77; the third candidate, Councillor McCarthy, had a disappointing 12.

Frank took it badly. It was a crushing defeat for a man who had served his constituency well, and hard for him to accept that it was time for things to move on. Nor was he the only one to go: the sitting TD in Roscommon was also ousted that night. Jack Lynch was preparing a new team for the election and I was delighted to be part of it.

The *Longford Leader* again:

'A delighted Albert Reynolds brought life to the three hundred plus attendance with a rousing and rallying speech ... He said there had been no winners or losers at the Convention. The Fianna Fáil party had come to pick their team and on June 16th they will know whether to rejoice or not ... We will get back the Republican spirit and the Republican principles and we will get the fire back in the Irish bellies. The country has suffered badly in the hands of the Coalition and once again the people will look to Fianna Fáil to put them on the road to prosperity ... Mr Reynolds concluded by congratulating all the candidates and by paying a special tribute to Mr Carter for his 30 years service to the party.'

The general election was but a month away. I intended to secure every possible vote for the party and called for an immediate start to my campaign. In my view publicity was everything, so I decided to make my official signing-on as the Fianna Fáil candidate a memorable event. My ploy worked, as witness the report in the *Leitrim Observer*:

'Albert "Get things Done" Reynolds lived up to his name when signing at the Courthouse as a candidate, he wasn't content to hand in a £100 deposit, so he commissioned Bob "Of a thousand smiles" Cumbers to do a hunt around the town's banks for a £100 note – one was found at the Ulster Bank after a lot of searching and handed over to Leo Brannigan (County Registrar) – who could believe it was hard to find a £100 note in Longford!'

I had a good group of friends and supporters around me led by Mickey Doherty, a local county councillor, Noel Hanlon, Ned Reilly and Derek Cobbe, all of whom had helped with my nomination election and now set up the organization of my campaign for the big election day of 16 June. For me all those campaigns with Neil Blaney, the master canvasser, those crack-of-dawn mornings and those late, late nights on the road, were about to pay off.

My years in show business had taught me many things, but above all that in the world of promotion advertising was king, and the design appeal of the poster was of prime importance. I decided to go for colour.

It's hard to believe now, but at that time colour printing in elections was usually confined to posters of the Taoiseach or party leaders. I was familiar with it because of my business: I'd been using it from the days of show-business posters to the advertising and labelling of cans and jars of pet food, and printing technology had come a long way.

There was no actual law to say you couldn't use colour, it just wasn't done. The most you'd ever get was yellow paper with a picture in black and white with maybe a bit of red type at the top. I went for full colour. Then we needed a slogan. My campaign lads worked long and hard. Joe Sheridan had led the way with, 'Vote for Joe the man you know.' We decided on, 'To get things done, Vote Reynolds 1.'

A great photograph was vital. We were working against the clock and unfortunately on the very day of the picture shoot I got a cold sore on my lip. Here Kathleen came into her own. She was always a great dresser, so she was the one who chose the right outfit for me, a grey suit, a white shirt and the right tie, picked from a long succession, plus a dab of makeup on the lip.

Fianna Fáil had decided that whenever three candidates

were standing in one constituency, no one individual could do publicity alone and that any poster had to feature all three. To get round this, one of my great friends, Larry Cunningham, a well-known singer and musician from Granard in County Longford, had come up with the idea of sponsoring me personally. This way I was not promoting myself; Larry was issuing the poster in support of his chosen candidate – Albert Reynolds.

The biggest advantage I had from my years in show business was that I had learned to meet and be comfortable with all sorts of people on their own level from bishop up to bishop down, as well as with the man on the street. All the other politicians were always formally known by their surnames; I was the only one to be known by my Christian name. Even today people rarely address me as Mr Reynolds; it was, and is, always, Albert.

I had geared my campaign to confront the issues that were of most importance to the people of Longford and the needs of the young voter. Young people had been ignored or forgotten by most politicians, but unemployment among school leavers was a serious problem that had to be addressed. I had seven children myself, and I wanted to ensure that when they grew up they would be able to earn a living in Longford or at least in Ireland. This meant more industrial development in the area, more job creation and a better standard of living. The farmers around Longford, too, were still suffering the effects from the recession of 1974–5.

I had been working sixteen to eighteen hours a day canvassing the country areas around Longford, but the town campaign could not begin in earnest until the formal visit to the town by Jack Lynch, the leader of Fianna Fáil.

I was living on little sleep and the night before Jack Lynch arrived I'd had hardly any at all, but I certainly was wide awake at one remark he made when he took me to one side and said, 'Don't give any commitments in this business.'

I said, 'I gave them and I intend to keep them and if I don't, I won't be back the next time.'

'Well,' he said, 'I've never heard any other man say that in my lifetime.'

As election day drew near the campaigning intensified. People were disillusioned with the coalition – their repressive policies, high inflation and the anti-Republican feeling exemplified by the ministers Conor Cruise O'Brien and Paddy Cooney – and across the country the political pundits were predicting a swing towards Fianna Fáil.

It was one of the most exciting elections ever. All over Ireland people came out to vote. In Longford and Westmeath 81.5 per cent of the voters used their constitutional right and in doing so helped to oust the coalition government. Fianna Fáil won by an outstanding margin, returned with an unprecedented twenty-seat majority in the Dáil. I was elected TD for Longford and Seán Keegan TD for Westmeath. As the *Observer* reported at the time:

'Last Thursday was an historic result in Longford. Jack was back with a vengeance throughout the country, and Longford– Westmeath contributed to his victory by returning two Fianna Fáil TDs for the first time since the late P. Lenihan held the second seat along with Frank Carter.'

The celebrating that Friday night following the count went on into the early hours of the morning, with bonfires blazing and crowds gathering to greet Seán and myself as we toured the constituency to praise and thank our supporters. Finally, at the unearthly hour of 3.00 a.m., Seán and I were chaired on to a platform in Longford and, along with our Fianna Fáil colleague Seán Fallon, spoke to the enormous crowd still gathered in attendance. Afterwards a cavalcade of cars drove back to Mullingar and on to Rochfortbridge, Tyrrellspass and Kilbeggan, where crowds cheered our progress.

The partying went on for days. Kathleen and I threw a party at the house to which everybody came, a party to remember.

My new career in politics was about to begin – as well as new friendships that would last for the rest of my life.

That election saw a raft of young Fianna Fáil members enter the government for the very first time, among them a young man who was to become my very good friend, Charlie McCreevy:

'Even Jack Lynch didn't know half of us but we were to dominate Fianna Fáil for the next thirty or more years. People like Albert, Bertie Ahern, Seán Doherty, Pádraig Flynn and Máire Geoghegan-Quinn. A gang of us came in together to the Dáil that time and found a common bond and friendships grew. Albert was quite well known, he was the big, successful businessman from Longford and I'd met him before, but knew him only slightly from our shared love of horse racing. Nobody had heard of the rest of us, bar a few from our own areas.

'We came in on this avalanche . . . It was totally unexpected, we didn't do opinion polls at the time, so it was a complete surprise to the political élite that this monstrous swing occurred, the media hadn't predicted it, yet all these votes came pouring in.'

I made my maiden speech in the Dáil on 30 November 1977. I don't believe I was nervous but the adrenalin was definitely pumping as I looked around at the encircling benches and the expectant faces of the opposition and the other Fianna Fáil deputies.

It was the debate I had been waiting for on the Industrial Development Bill. This was my territory, my forte, and I was passionate in my belief that there was a better way forward for Ireland. I was determined to see improved opportunities for my own home town of Longford; I was ambitious for its economic future and especially that of the young people in my area.

In my speech I called upon my years of experience in business and as an employer to address all that I believed in and hoped for in the future of Ireland. I put particular emphasis on the role of the IDA with which I had become very familiar in my own dealings: I urged it to become less conservative and more adventurous, and I called upon members of the house to back it to the hilt in their endeavours to develop existing industries and attract new ones.

I talked about the need to help our home industries to prepare for a competitive world market, in particular what I believed to be a scandalous position whereby Ireland, whose main asset was agriculture, had had an import bill of around £200 million the previous year; and about how we needed to widen our horizons to encourage Irish entrepreneurs to seize opportunities which were there for the taking.

My life had been business and I was only too aware of how much we had to draw on our own resources, our wealth of natural assets. I said:

'A nation consists of people and natural resources and therein lies the key for future job creation and future prosperity . . .

'History has made us a dependent race and we always look to someone else to solve our problems. Down the country they look to Dublin and to this House to solve the unemployment problem and of late people are starting to look to Brussels to solve our problems. Nobody will solve our problems for us; we must find the solution ourselves. The world does not owe us a living. We now have greater opportunities than ever before . . . I know of people with skills and enterprise that would undertake new projects if they had venture capital. Although the Irish banks are making large profits, they are not providing venture capital. It is time for the banks to play a part in our development. American banks back the man and the idea and our banks back assets and securities. If they continue to behave in that fashion, private enterprise will fail . . . I put it to the Irish banks that they should face their responsibilities and adopt the American system.'

These were the things I believed in passionately, and I wanted to inject this hope for the future of our country into families and young people who were facing a bleak prospect unless things changed.

'We have the resources and can solve our problems if we have the will to do so. We have a growing and educated population on which many mothers and fathers have spent well-earned money, but what are they educating them for? Some months ago I spoke to 90 vocational students. When I asked them what they intended to do when they left school, 85 per cent of them said they wanted office jobs. We all know the market for office jobs is poor. The blame for the emphasis on office jobs must lie with the educational system and the stigma that is attached to the technical school . . . To the mothers and fathers of Ireland I say the future is in industry, not office jobs. I started work during the recession as a pen-pusher and I was prepared to take whatever was available at the time. There is nothing more frustrating for young people than sitting around doing nothing . . . If we do not solve the problems for these young people who are now educated and who are not prepared to emigrate . . . and that I admire them for – we will be seen to have failed. The system will be seen to have failed and they will rebel against society. Revolutions do not grow, they just happen.'

Enterprise and markets create jobs. That was the message I wanted to give, and I was determined to help make it a national commitment and to start in Longford.

As Derek Cobbe recalls:

'When Albert became TD there was a sense of pride but also a great expectation that everything was going to happen, that things were going to change within a week. People here thought we were going to get a new factory and that every government department would invest within the week! They had great faith in Albert. What impressed me most was that he never changed; he was as accessible as he was when he was a councillor.'

I had always tried to be accessible to the people of Longford – sometimes to the detriment of family life. At this time when the government was in session I was living for most of the week in Dublin, but weekends I always went home. Saturdays I would hold my 'clinic' for my constituents. Kathleen, as supportive as ever, despite having seven children to care for, would always arrive with flasks of tea and sandwiches to sustain my hard-working secretary, Pauline, and myself throughout the day. Back home the doorbell would never stop ringing, even on Sundays which was the only day set aside for the family. Sunday mornings after mass we would return home to see several cars parked outside Mount Carmel, with constituents lined up to see me. I have to say the family gave me every support and there was never any sense of resentment. It was what I did. So many would arrive, even during Sunday lunch, that we set up a little reception area by the side of the front door where people could sit and wait until we'd finished eating.

Sunday afternoons, however, were reserved for my children

and we'd regularly take drives into the countryside, often stopping for ice-creams.

Then it was Monday and back to Dublin.

Jack Lynch, the Taoiseach, was a gentleman. In his youth he'd been regarded as one of the greatest dual players of Gaelic games. He had specialized in both hurling and Gaelic football, and in his fourteen-year sporting career he had won five all-Ireland titles.

He was also a follower of Lemass and, like his predecessor, he believed fervently that the future of Ireland lay in improving its economy through industrial development. As Taoiseach in January 1973 he had successfully negotiated Irish entry into the European Economic Community. In 1977 he came back into power on a policy platform that set out a range of new economic measures; but they were hard to implement in these difficult times, and setbacks were not long in coming. A new Department for Economic Planning and Development was set up and certainly unemployment fell, but at the same time the national debt increased and there were protest marches by PAYE workers. His authority was also undermined when, in a vote on contraception, his Minister for Agriculture, Jim Gibbons, ignored the parliamentary whip and refused to vote with the government. The Minister for Health, Charles Haughey, had introduced what he called 'an Irish solution to an Irish problem', in which contraceptives would be sold by prescription to married couples only. Gibbons was a very conservative Catholic and simply did not turn up for the vote. Lynch was expected to discipline him for this, and when he didn't he was perceived to be losing his grip on discipline within his party.

There quickly followed a series of events which further undermined his leadership, notably a five-month postal strike and a second oil crisis which led to long queues at petrol stations. Then in August 1979 came the tragic assassination of Earl Mountbatten and members of his family in County Sligo, and a very poor showing in European Parliament elections at which Fianna Fáil was seen to be losing favour with the electorate.

By this time Jack Lynch had already determined to resign at the end of the year, allowing himself time to complete his tenure as President of the EEC. He knew the popularity of his party was fading and that the mood within the party was moving towards a change of leadership. Two men in particular were known to be in the race for the top job, George Colley and Charles Haughey. Lynch was on a flight to America when he received the devastating news that Fianna Fáil had lost two by-elections in his own native Cork. The time had come to go, and sooner rather than later.

As Charlie McCreevy recalls:

'What we had in common – Albert, Seán Doherty, all of us – was that although Jack Lynch was the man who had got us in with this monstrous majority, we didn't really want him to remain leader of the party . . .

'We believed more in the business kind of approach, the Republican kind of thing, we would have preferred Charlie Haughey's Nationalist–Republican stance to that of Jack Lynch.'

I was an admirer and a supporter of Charlie Haughey. I'd got to know him when he'd visited Longford at the election and also when, as Minister for Health, he had come down to announce the good news that a new twenty-bed acute medical unit was to be installed at the Nursing Home in Edgeworthstown, and he'd lunched at Mount Carmel with Kathleen and me. Kathleen is an excellent cook and the cheesecake she served that day had been relished by all – none more than Charlie Haughey, who had phoned the next day for the recipe. From then on it was known as 'Charlie's cheesecake'!

Jack Lynch had been a good leader, but I believed the time had come to move on and that Charlie Haughey would be the right man to lead us into the eighties.

It was December 1979, and Kathleen and I were actually about to board a plane at Dublin airport when the call came from Ray MacSharry that Jack had resigned. We cancelled our holiday plans and returned immediately to lend our support to Haughey's campaign.

George Colley had been the one to persuade Lynch to announce his retirement earlier than planned. By so doing he had hoped to pre-empt the Haughey campaign. He had a loyal band of supporters too, although I know it shocked him when Ray MacSharry, who had been his junior at Finance, came out against him. There were a number of us working hard on Haughey's behalf, among them Pádraig Flynn and Charlie McCreevy. Together with others, those two and myself, the three non-drinkers, consumed gallons of tea as we phoned and persuaded and plotted over the next few days on Haughey's behalf. It paid off: Charlie Haughey won by forty-four votes to Colley's thirty-eight. He displaced Lynch and became the new leader of Fianna Fáil.

6

GETTING THROUGH

I was not expecting the call. It had not come all day Monday or Monday evening, when Government Buildings was alive with gossip as to who had been appointed and to what cabinet position. So it was a complete surprise when at 8.00 a.m. on Tuesday, 11 December, Catherine Butler, Haughey's private secretary, informed me that the new Taoiseach-elect had been trying to contact me all weekend and that on my arrival at Leinster House he wanted me to go directly to his office.

Charlie was waiting and greeted me with the words: 'I've a right bastard of a job for you – Posts and Telegraphs. Do you want it?'

I hadn't been expecting anything, let alone a cabinet post – after all, I was a fairly new boy in politics, only two years on the back benches – so I was delighted to be given, as I thought, a position in a junior ministry and accepted. It wasn't until someone explained the situation that it dawned on me that it was a full cabinet post.

I rang Kathleen immediately but the line, never good at the best of times, was constantly engaged. In the end I got electricians to go round to the house to check it, and finally I got through.

The appointment was to be announced that day, so I immediately dispatched my good friend Noel Hanlon with a list of my measurements and instructions to buy me a new suit, shirt and tie. He also managed to contact Kathleen and they immediately set about rounding up the entire family (some were away in boarding schools) so that everyone was present to hear the announcement of my first ministerial role. My daughter Andrea was particularly excited, as she well remembers:

'I was seven years old and the youngest when all this took place but I remember being at a friend's house when the call came to go home immediately as we were all going up to Dublin, to the Dáil, where it was being announced that Dad was to be Minister for Posts and Telegraphs. I was aware it was a big deal but at that time Posts and Telegraphs was always shortened to P&T and all I knew was that there were vans going round with P&T painted on the sides, delivering letters, so I was very proud to inform my friends that my father not only had a new state car, a black Mercedes, but that in his new job, he was now "Head Postman".'

Up to this point I'd been splitting my time between our family home in Longford, a series of hotel rooms and a small flat in Dublin. Kathleen was in charge of my domestic life as she was of our growing family: now she decided I needed a more permanent base, one that our eldest daughter Miriam could also share. She was planning to go to university in Dublin and Kathleen decided it would be a good idea if we looked after each other: so Kathleen and I purchased a Dublin apartment in Hazeldene, Ballsbridge.

Miriam thought it was wonderful:

'When Dad first became a TD he stayed in a hotel in

Dublin. In those days he never drank, smoking was his thing, but he'd be there holding up the bar with everybody else and he was always the last one to bed. There were journalists then who were with him who never realized he didn't drink until years later.

'My mother thought that kind of life, hanging around bars, wasn't great and as I was off to university, it made sense to get a foothold in Dublin which we could share and which would give Dad at least some semblance of family life. So Hazeldene became my base too. There was this strange scenario where everyone else was in digs and I was in this magnificent apartment with my bike outside, leading a completely surreal life with Dad coming and going.

'I'd be in lectures at nine in the morning then up until three or four at night making tea for Dad and his political friends. I was never bothered about having four or five hours' sleep, I loved the excitement of it and Dad loved talking politics.'

As the Minister for Posts and Telegraphs (P&T) – and Transport, once the portfolios were amalgamated shortly after I was appointed – I was responsible for a workforce of about 52,000 across the departments: all the people in CIE, P&T and the national broadcaster RTE.

The recent postal strike had been long and bitter, and although it was now finished it had been badly handled: the staff were disillusioned and the postal system was in total disarray. Despite the strike, little had changed or improved. The unions were very strong at that time and industrial relations were not at all good. The system was antiquated and disorganized, with mail, even that posted locally, sometimes taking weeks to be delivered. No money had been spent on its infrastructure for years. So I decided to make Posts and Telegraphs a priority.

A week after my appointment Charlie Haughey assigned

Mark Killilea as minister of state for P&T, a man who was to become a lifelong friend. It was the second week in December, and Mark had not even been into the department when we set off to attend our first GPO Christmas party. We were so new to the game that in fact when we arrived at the venue, an old hotel somewhere in Dublin, we were refused entry, and it was only after a lot of persuasion and Mark pointing out that I was indeed Albert Reynolds, their new minister, that we were finally allowed into the celebrations by a young man by the name of Harry Cooke.

It was Mark's responsibility to find a private secretary for me to help in the running of the department. He tells a lovely story of how he asked the retiring secretary, a real gentleman by the name of Mr Regan, if he could pick out four or five likely young candidates for him to interview for the post. The first one into the room was the very same young man who had behaved in such a diplomatic manner at the party, Harry Cooke. There was no competition: Mark sent the other applicants home.

Harry proved to be a brilliant young man who worked every hour demanded without question. He ended up as secretary of An Post, the state organization for the Post Office, which employed 37,000 people at the time.

It was near to Christmas and, as an employer myself, I had always made a special point of visiting staff at that time of year, particularly those in plants or areas where people were working on night shifts. I decided it was time to pay a call on the GPO.

It was a cold evening, I remember, with a stiff wind blowing when we arrived later that night at the sorting office in Sherriff Street. It was a miserable place, as dark and depressing as a dungeon. I was told that there was a change of shift around midnight, so I hung about chatting to the workers, watching some go and others arrive. As I went around, I was aware that the temperature inside was almost as cold as that outside and that there was a freezing cold draught blowing in from somewhere. That somewhere, I discovered, was a large window edged with shards of broken glass through which the wind was howling. With people being forced to work throughout the night and day in these freezing conditions, I was not at all surprised there had been industrial problems.

I called one of the supervisors over and was told the window had been broken for some time.

'Then get it fixed,' I said. 'Send someone out first thing in the morning and get a new pane of glass put in.'

'We can't do that, Minister,' I was told. 'We're not allowed to touch it.'

'So whose job is it to touch it?'

'The Office of Public Works, we've asked them so many times but they just don't come. They tell us they'll only do it in their own good time.'

They were obviously a different department from the Post Office, and as everything was strictly regulated and bound by government and union rules, I could understand their problem.

'Right,' I said, 'if that's the case, don't be expecting people to work with that draught blowing in all the time. I tell you what you do: when the shops open, send somebody out to the local glazier and get them to order a pane of glass to fit that window, then get them to fix it. Meanwhile I'll look into the system and if necessary I'll pay the bill myself.'

The supervisor was shocked. 'But I've no authority to do that, Minister, and we'll be in terrible trouble when the Public Works people come, they'll take their men out on strike and they'll bring ours out in sympathy.'

'You're telling me they may not come for a couple of

months and it's been almost three months like that as it is, so it's time you fixed it. You do it, and if you want to stop a strike happening, when you know the Public Works fellows are coming, break the pane of glass again before they get here and leave them to put in a new one – they'll never know the difference!'

The end of the seventies had been a turbulent era of serious industrial dispute in Ireland, in almost every sector: so much so that 1,460,000 working days were lost in 1979 alone. The bitterness and misery in the aftermath of the recent Post Office strike were still very keenly in evidence. It had been the longest stoppage in its history, lasting some twenty-odd weeks, and had caused great distress to the employees and their families. I knew it was going to be a hard struggle to get over such a desperate dispute, but until Mark and I turned up at the union's annual conference in Castlebar, I had no idea just how deep feelings ran. We were sitting at our table when suddenly we were surrounded by knife-wielding extremists, and for the first time ever our two security guys had to put their hands on their guns to calm the aggravated and highly distraught situation.

It was essential for me to rebuild confidence between the workforce and the government. Because there had been no investment in the industry and no real development in any of the government departments within my new ministry, there was no progress and no encouragement to work: so spirits were low among civil servants and employees alike, and the union leaders were totally discouraged. The country had no communications to speak of, so business and commerce were losing out both at home and internationally, and our road and rail systems were poor. The only enterprise that was working professionally was RTE.

The Post Office had become a joke. It was unreliable in every way and its leaders had become apathetic. It was understandable. The lack of investment had removed any incentive either to encourage their work force or to improve efficiency. I was not surprised they were resentful of criticism levelled at the standard of service provided. In many ways it was not their fault.

I decided to find out for myself just how bad the system was by posting letters to myself from wherever I happened to be as I went around the country. I needed proof before I could start to demand the changes I wanted to make to the infrastructure of our postal service.

As a businessman, my philosophy had always been to keep close to the people who do the work: that way you would hear of any problems before they became major crises. It was a principle I adopted throughout my career and it served me well.

I was in my office one day at the GPO in O'Connell Street when I received a call to return immediately for some business at the Dáil. My car was unavailable for some reason but there were a couple of P&T vans parked just outside, and in one of them I could see the driver. I went over and knocked on the window and said that as I was in a hurry to get to the Dáil, would he mind giving me a lift. He looked a bit taken aback and pointed out that as it was a P&T van it had no front passenger seat. I told him I didn't care and that I'd sit on a couple of sacks if I had to, which I did. I don't think a minister had ever been in his van before or even chatted to him, man to man, but chat we did.

We talked about how antiquated the whole system was. For a start, I complained about how time-wasting it was for me that, as Minister of P&T and Transport, I spent half my day traipsing between the two separate offices, my Transport headquarters in Kildare Street and P&T in O'Connell Street, a journey of some half an hour or more if the traffic was bad. He moaned about the state of the main sorting office in Sherriff Street, the conditions under which they were forced to work, and how such an outdated system could only lead to inefficiency in the service which was not their fault.

It was on this occasion that I learned just how fed up the workforce was at being ridiculed every time they mentioned that they worked for P&T; they had lost all credibility with the general public and needed someone or something to restore their pride in their work and themselves. I understood their attitude; I had heard the same complaint from the bus drivers, who suffered unbelievable abuse from a public frustrated with choked roads and chaotic traffic conditions and old buses long past their sell-by date.

The Irish telephone system was even worse, primitive beyond belief. I know: I was trying to run an international business under conditions where little or nothing had been done to improve the system since it was first installed. There was no automated service available for most of the country, so if you wished to make a call it had to be through the local operator. Telephones themselves were in short supply and great demand. In all my years working in commerce I had suffered the trials of trying to run a business without a proper and reliable means of communication with the outside world. Our private lives, our business calls, our export and import affairs were conducted via the local operator in Edgeworthstown, and we, along with everybody else, were dependent on her availability, that is, on her being free to put you through or accept your call. Anyone could listen in, so nothing ever remained private. All the locals knew your business dealings as well as those of the rest of the town, and so much business was lost, especially internationally, because no one could get through to you. I can remember vividly the frustration we experienced when we were trying to put our deal together with Sainsbury's and we would be forced to queue up for hours while someone on the other side of Longford was gossiping with a relative in Roscommon.

At that time there was a drive to export all manufactured goods from Ireland, and that included nearly all the actual telephone equipment: only a very small proportion was retained for the home market. Consequently telephones were prized and rare. Doctors, lawyers and the elderly received preferential treatment, but for the rest it was everyone for themselves, and stealing and bribery were rife. Often thousands of pounds would change hands just for a single telephone. There were even instances where the P&T, when called out to repair a breakdown, would maintain that the phone was not only out of order but beyond repair, and then sell it on to someone else, often for as much as two thousand pounds, although if they were caught they were sacked.

It was a totally ludicrous situation. Here we were, with a ready market of thousands of people around the country all demanding a product and more than willing to pay for it, and yet we were unable to supply it. It was a businessman's dream – a textbook case of supply and demand. But it wasn't just the equipment we needed: the whole communications system needed a complete revamp. I decided that if Ireland was to develop its economy to play a role on the international stage we had to develop the most modern system possible in line with all the new technology that was being introduced in other areas of the world.

Ireland had not joined the EEC until 1973 so our relationship with Europe was in its infancy. However, because of my own business dealings in Europe I was well aware of the various grants available to enterprise, and had indeed made use of them and various long-term loans at subsidized interest rates for C&D. I knew that this was the way forward for development in Ireland. The Irish government had no funds; the EEC did.

I arranged a meeting with the P&T union leaders. There were still minor wildcat strikes called from one week to the next, particularly at Sherriff Street, the main sorting office for the whole country, where Mick Sheridan, the union liaison man, was constantly battling for better conditions. So Mark Killilea and I, together with Seán O'Kelly, the deputy secretary of the department, Regan and Sheridan held a meeting to help resolve the situation; we found the best way to do this was to take the union people down to the local pub, buy them a few pints and let them talk through their needs.

There had been no investment for so many years that they never knew from one year to the next what they would have to spend; consequently, any future planning was always haphazard. I set out to address the system by implementing a five-year programme, and I gave them my word that I would get them money if they told me what was required.

Then came my first cabinet meeting as a minister. It was a big day for me, and I wanted it to be a big day for my portfolio. I wasn't so much nervous as wound up and ready. I was about to propose something revolutionary for Ireland, and I knew there would be scepticism and resistance. Many of the old guard establishment were not ready or willing to embrace change under any circumstances, especially when it involved something they didn't understand – like new technology. I also knew I was the new boy on the block, and a country fellow from the Midlands, a fact many of the élitist politicians were ready to knock. It was not going to be easy to get what I wanted, but I was determined to win. When I went into that cabinet meeting I had done my homework: I knew the figure I needed, and I told the rest of them in no uncertain terms that if we didn't invest in modern communications and technology the country would lose out, and that if we didn't have a modern phone system we would have no business, and without business there would be no jobs. I had a five-year plan, I told them, to turn the Posts and Telegraphs system around, and I needed IR£1.1 billion to do it. There was a stunned silence of disbelief, I remember. Finally, someone said: 'You'll never spend it!'

'Ah, yes, I will,' I answered.

'But what if you don't?' they said.

'Then the money comes back into Finance.'

Let me say this, I warned them, if I don't get this and we ignore what is going on around us, this new surge forward in communications and technology, then not only will we be plunged into more bitter industrial disputes but Ireland will lose out as the world moves on and our economy will sink deeper and deeper into debt.

It took a while, but finally the Department of Finance agreed.

The first thing we did was to buy sites on which we could build a series of new exchanges across the country. As soon as the unions saw we meant business, their confidence in us grew, the industrial disputes stopped and they became enthusiastic about the future. We had only one problem and that was with a fellow down in Cork, an engineer who was proving very obstinate and resistant to change; however, over a very nice lunch at the Gresham, Mark and I soon resolved that. 'There's plenty of green grass up here in Dublin,' I said. 'We'll promote him to a "little grass job" upstairs in O'Connell Street [the GPO].' And that solved that!

Next we turned to the problem of new telephone

installations and telecommunications. As Killilea remarked, 'Bad pigeons were better than the postal service we had and our telecommunications.'

We promised the boys a bonus: the more lines they could install, the more they'd get paid. We had to start with places where the new exchanges were up and running, and as each one was completed so the lines were installed. That year we had set ourselves the target of 60,000; we put in 62,400! It was an incredible achievement.

As each exchange system was completed we attracted buyers for our new lines by offering special deals to people in the local areas. Three years later the whole country was wired for service.

It is hard to believe now, but in the 1970s there was a two-year waiting list for phones. By the time the Pope came to visit in 1979 I had reached many of the targets I had set and phones were becoming readily available. There was a joke doing the rounds that getting telephones to Ireland was one of the great miracles the Pope performed on his visit!

I didn't know anything about modern telecommunications at that time, but I did know that AT&T, the big tele-communications company in America, were making major developments and that I needed to talk to them. I planned to attend a convention in New York, and decided to set off a bit earlier and combine it with a family holiday in Hyannis Port. While we were there we were invited to the home of Senator Edward Kennedy, where we were warmly welcomed by his family. His mother was being cared for by a young Irish nurse from Ballymahon, County Longford, and there was a young girl working there too who happened to be from our own home town of Longford, so we were really well looked after.

It was the first time I had met Senator Kennedy. He was a very good-looking fellow, athletically built and totally charming, and we became firm friends immediately. I knew well that the senator and his family always had the interests of Ireland at heart; he was very approachable and always willing to help in any way that he could. I also realized that if he introduced me to AT&T, I would get a better reception and more help than if I tried to introduce myself.

We met up again at the convention and I explained the gravity of our lack of expertise in telecommunications in a country that depended so heavily on exports. Immediately he organized a lunch with the AT&T board of directors, some of whom were also of Irish origin, and I spent several hours being instructed on the advances being made by the company and talking things through with the technicians. It was a great insight into the advanced world of digital communications and technology. The Americans were developing new systems all the time. They had vast resources for their research and their new methods were advancing rapidly, although at that stage they were still focusing on electronic rather than digital systems. We had nothing and no money to start with; we didn't have even a basic knowledge about the new technology. I knew that if we were to progress we would have to look to other countries in order to set up a new ultra-modern system for ourselves.

New technologies in telecommunications were being explored everywhere. France was already well ahead of the Americans in the development of video-text; however, though it operated well within the Paris area, over greater distances it lacked the capacity and needed far more powerful technology. Japan was experimenting with another method of video-text, but this as yet remained untested. The Swedes appeared to be closer to developing a successful digital system than anyone, through their electronics company Ericsson.

I made my choice and ended up contracting 40 per cent of

our telecommunications venture to France and 40 per cent to Sweden: that left me with 20 per cent competition to play between the two.

I was accompanied on one of our visits to France by both Mark Killilea and Seán O'Kelly, together with an expert in high technology from the department. Because of the importance of the French expertise, we went to Paris to look and to buy. The price was high and, always one to enjoy making a good deal, I managed to beat them down, though not quite far enough for my liking. So, to sweeten the deal and as a gesture of goodwill, they also threw in for free a little something called 'mobility'. I had no idea what this was and turned to our expert. He hadn't heard of it either; however, I accepted the 'gift' with good grace. Just as well, as the gift turned out to be the installation of an up-to-the-minute exchange for mobile phones! The highest technology in the modern world and we got it for nothing; now that's a good deal.

It was several years before AT&T finally decided that digital was the way forward; by then Ireland was in the lead, with the most advanced digital telecommunications system in Europe, and everyone was coming to see it.

Meanwhile, I had money to raise. The EEC was my first port of call; I followed success here by getting financial aid from the French government in the form of a ten-year loan at a very low interest rate, to help set up the new equipment. My own government was well behind me now and agreed to bring in a new man to head up this exciting new telecommunications project: a high-profile businessman, Michael Smurfit.

This innovative strategy was introduced at that time in order to help improve the efficiency of our emerging industries. The thrust of the strategy was to seek out the most accomplished entrepreneurs in the country, and to use their experience and expertise to help oversee the progress and development of different enterprises. Michael Smurfit was an extremely successful and imaginative businessman, and although our new telecommunications project had a long way to go to approach the size of the hugely successful commercial ventures he commanded, he took it on and with it the arduous task of sorting out the 150 years of legislation governing communications in Ireland. I spent my time putting in place all the necessary investment needed, so that whenever the preparation was finalized the new system could be installed.

It was a very proud moment for me and the fulfilment of an ambition when in 1981 we opened a new IR£1 million Telecom Éireann engineering headquarters in Longford.

While I was Minister for Posts and Telegraphs and Transport I had my first brush with Ian Paisley, the leader of the Democratic Unionist Party in Northern Ireland and a man well known for his extremely strong views. This was over the transmission of RTE into the North.

It started with a conversation I'd had with the then head of the Roman Catholic Church in Ireland, Cardinal Tomás Ó Fiaich. He was from Armagh, and had a great knowledge and understanding of the problems in Northern Ireland on both sides. We met at a function organized by Aer Lingus, and in the course of conversation he suggested that the best thing I could do to improve communications and understanding between the two parts of Ireland, North and South, was to extend the broadcasting capacity of RTE, our national network, so that it could be seen by people as far north as northern Donegal, across to Derry and west of the river Bann. He was right; I knew from my own experience doing business in the North that there was a lot of superstition about the South, many people believing that everyone in the Republic was in the IRA and went around with a revolver in their hip pocket.

'Let the people in the North see for themselves what everyday normal living is like in the South,' the cardinal continued. 'It would be good to break down the barriers between ordinary people, it would lead to a better understanding of one another. There's a bitter divide that doesn't have to be there but if they could watch your programmes they'd be able to judge for themselves and get a better balance to make up their own minds about what it is like down here and a lot of the fear between us would disappear.'

I presented the idea to the chairman of RTE, Mr Moriarty, and he immediately asked his technicians whether they could do this. They worked out that if a powerful booster station was erected on the highest point of the Cooley Mountains on the eastern side of the country RTE could transmit right up beyond the north of Belfast, and with another positioned just outside Letterkenny we would be able to cover the six counties. However, I was informed, international broadcasting rights did not allow it.

'What about the BBC?' I said, 'and Ulster Television? They both recently put up boosters at Enniskillen and Strabane so they can beam their transmissions down to the South. I didn't see them asking permission, and I didn't complain. Go ahead and build your boosters and I'll find a way of financing them.'

The first man to complain in the House of Commons, when questions were asked about the sudden transmissions into Northern Ireland from the Republic, was the Reverend Ian Paisley. I made no immediate response, but when the call came from the Taoiseach for me to explain my actions, I had my answer: 'When they come asking for our contract for permission to transmit to the North, tell them we want to see those of UTV and the BBC permitting them to transmit to the South!'

We heard nothing more about it. I knew it was the right thing to do. My business experience in the North had taught me that.

My main distributor for C&D pet food in the North was a strong right-wing Unionist man, and he and I got on well. He also advised me well, and the advice he gave me said a lot about the suspicion that existed at that time. 'Don't send the product up on CIE,' he said. 'It's your national truck people and everyone will know where the pet food comes from. And don't put on the label "Manufactured in the Republic of Ireland". Just put "Made in Ireland".'

Years later I was telling this story to Gusty Spence, the former Loyalist paramilitary leader. He told me that he had been the one who had originally suggested the idea of booster stations to Cardinal Ó Fiaich when the cardinal visited him in jail.

Gusty Spence:

'I said to him, let the ordinary people in Northern Ireland see they're no different from us, let them see programmes like Gay Byrne and that the RTE news is not in any way vitriolic towards Britain or Northern Ireland. You're living a few miles down the road and people don't know each other. Let them get acquainted – and there's only one way to let them get acquainted, and that is to show them your life. Let people see Albert for example, he's a down-to-earth man, he's saying positive things and wants to do positive things, let's accommodate that in some shape or form.'

There were suspicion and misunderstandings on both sides of the border; indeed, even in my own town of Longford there were those who had fled from the Troubles in the North and who still faced suspicion and persecution from certain quarters. In fact, there were a number of people in the Republic who were members of Sinn Féin, and one of the reasons why the previous coalition government had fallen was the strong anti-Republican feeling among some of the government members – none more so than a previous Minister for Posts and Telegraphs, Conor Cruise O'Brien.

I was in Longford one day when I met up with a local fellow, Mickey Nevin, who had worked for many years for P&T. He had sought me out, he said, because he had a problem and he wanted to know if there was anything I could do about it. He explained that he had worked for the Post Office all his life, as did many younger members of his family, but because of the law which forbade anyone affiliated with Sinn Féin from being employed on a permanent basis, he and his family faced a future with no pension. They were all followers of Sinn Féin, he argued, but in a free society it was unjust and unfair that they should be penalized for their beliefs.

I agreed. I was also shocked. I was completely unaware of this order that had been ratified by Minister O'Brien and the previous government. I promised him I'd look into it and set out to change it immediately as long as they were people cleared by the Garda Síochána. I also pledged never to reveal any names of those without clearance. Further, I instructed that the names of every man and woman cleared by the Gardaí but affected by this order be immediately removed from the records. The individuals concerned would have their rights restored. These actions earned me the trust of many for fairness and honesty, which was to be of immense value when I became involved in the peace process some years later.

Despite my ministerial duties, I was frequently in Longford – after all, my family was still living there, and it was not only my home but also my constituency. In my election campaign I had promised to do all I could to address the problems besetting the town and to bring development to the area. Andrea, my youngest daughter, was well aware of the situation at that time when Longford had so little to offer young people:

'We had nothing in Longford, we didn't even have a leisure park – then Dad took over and there was huge input in the community. Suddenly people had phones, potholes were filled in, roads improved and a new sewage system was installed, which was very important for the local people. He was really popular with the grass roots but as a family we only really saw him at weekends. He would be asked all over the country and would travel wherever and show up anywhere, any time, for anyone who needed him, whether it was to put in an appearance at a fundraising event or to offer advice. I've known him leave at three o'clock in the morning to attend a meeting in a far part of the country. My mother would accompany him to most social occasions, until she became too ill to do so, and then one of us girls would accompany him.

'I remember once driving past the clinic he ran in Longford. It had a huge sign over it that read "Albert's Clinic" and there was a long queue outside stretching the whole way up the street. I gasped that there were so many people. I remember him laughing and saying, "That's right, Andrea, let the people form a queue, so that others passing will think just how successful you must be that so many are waiting to see you!"

'His old show-business tactics never left him.'

Derek Cobbe, who was out fighting my corner at every election, remembers:

'Albert had great support. You see, he never forgot the people who elected him in the first place. He was still coming up and down to Longford for funerals for the man in the street. To the people of Longford, Albert was the miracle worker. There was a joke in Longford, " 'Tis an awful bad day today, yes it is – I'll have to get a letter from Albert and get that changed!"

'Albert could do anything, and a letter from Albert was as good as anything and could change everything. Nobody asked, Albert who? They'd say, "Ah, the next thing you'll be doing is giving me a letter from Albert!" It was a common expression. Whatever Albert said he was going to do, he did it and nobody was surprised.'

I had always prided myself on having good relations with the people who worked for me, but industrial relations in the country generally were still not good and it was part of my portfolio at P&T and Transport to improve them. We had to get management to realize that the viability and stability of their companies were their responsibility, not that of government. We were still suffering high inflation and it was hard to make the general public understand that wage restraint had to be enforced. Employers had to learn to relate to their workforce and to communicate that it was not a question of 'them and us' but a matter of all pulling together to root out inefficiency, if we were to build a future together in Ireland.

I tried to set up a factory in Shannon to manufacture new buses but immediately there was trouble from the unions in Dublin, who did not want the plant moved to Clare. I was used to dealing with the unions, but I had to be blunt: if I was paying I wanted the job done. Government funds were limited, but there were other deals to be made; it was a matter of finding them and setting them up.

I pushed forward the issue of electric trains to take some of the traffic off the roads, partly financed by low-interest loans from the French. It was the first suburban railway in Ireland and ran overground across Dublin. Known as the DART, which stands for the Dublin Area Rapid Transit, it was finally opened in December 1984.

To alleviate congestion and to get things moving I also introduced bus lanes, giving buses priority on the roads. Yet even to begin to introduce something as simple as that meant getting agreement from at least five different government departments. There was a lot of jealousy among them as each sought to defend its own interests. The only way round it was for me to get authority that none of them could challenge. So I went to the government and got an agreement that gave me the right to put in bus lanes, and that stated my decision was final and could not be over-ruled. Even so, there was a fight between two departments, each of which insisted that it alone had the right to paint the white lines marking the bus lanes. It became so absurd that in the end I had to say: If you can't solve the problem yourselves give me the paint and the brushes and I'll do it myself.

The founding of Knock airport is legendary. It had started as the dream of the late Monsignor James Horan, at a time when money and employment were scarce and emigration was at its height, nowhere more so than in the West of Ireland. Monsignor Horan had come up with the idea that an international airport built to service that part of the country would help alleviate the impoverishment of the community, not only by providing employment locally but also by helping to introduce tourism into an area which had a great deal to offer in the way of natural beauty. His idea was ridiculed – the cost of such a project was prohibitive – but Charles Haughey could see the potential and so could I. However, there were many who were vehemently opposed to it and prophesied that it would be a white elephant. Monsignor Horan, despairing about the poverty he witnessed in the West, persevered against all adversity until eventually, with Haughey's support, I asked my junior minister in Transport, Pádraig Flynn, to take over the project and to announce to the press that the airport had been 'approved in principle' and that it was just its size that remained in question. The idea thus suggested, that it might be just a 'grass strip', was an attempt to allay the fears of the opposition as to the potential cost, but in reality we fully intended to finance and develop an airport capable of landing jets. Finally, in 1986, Knock airport was completed, and over the following years it became a huge success story, as well as providing the region with one of its finest pieces of infrastructure.

It was during the Knock airport saga that I became involved in a bizarre hijacking. By 1981 Monsignor Horan and the people of Knock had fought the battle and won, and as Minister for Transport I had the honour of turning the first sod. It was a very happy occasion; Kathleen was with me and we were about to go in for lunch when I was suddenly pulled away from the ceremony and before I knew it – and before I had even had a chance to warn my wife – I was being whisked away by helicopter to a small airfield in Castlebar. My briefing by phone from Charlie Haughey was brusque and to the point. An Aer Lingus flight en route between London and Dublin had been hijacked; the pilot had been forced to fly to Le Touquet in France and had landed at Côte d'Opale airport, where the plane was being held by the hijacker, with the full complement of passengers still on board.

'And what am I supposed to do about it?' I asked the Taoiseach.

'You're Minister of Transport. Your decision.'

Thanks, Charlie!

My immediate reaction was to get on to the man at the top in France – but there was no point in calling the French

President, I was informed; the local authorities and the Mayor were the only ones legally able to deal with this situation, and then only under my instruction once I got there.

I was rushed out to a little plane which was ready to fly me to Dublin, where an Aer Lingus plane was waiting to take me to France.

There were rumours coming through that the hijacker was some madman who wanted to be flown to Iran. I arrived in Le Touquet and was immediately taken to the control tower and put through by radio to the hijacker. I started talking – told him who I was and that I'd flown in from Ireland and could he explain what this was about and what we could do to resolve it.

He explained he was an ex-Trappist monk and his only demand was that the Pope release the 'Third Secret of Fatima'! Fair enough.

'So, if I get the Pope to release it, how will I get that in-formation to you? How will you know?'

'I want the story published in the *Sunday Independent*.'

By this time it was about half-past midnight and the printers were about to put out the first edition when I got through to the editor, Michael Hand, now sadly deceased, who happened to be a pal of mine, and gave him the story. He acted instantly, stopped the press and printed up a special front-page edition reporting that the Pope had handed over the 'Third Secret of Fatima'! He had it flown out to me immediately.

Meanwhile I told the air crew to play along with the hijacker and to distract him from looking out of the windows, while I kept the guy talking. By this time the fellow was getting tired and, without him knowing, under cover of dark-ness, French security forces had crept across the open ground and were waiting out of sight under the belly of the aircraft ready to seize their chance. Aware this was happening, the co-pilot quickly asked to be allowed through to the lavatory which happened to be at the back of the plane. Here, out of sight of the hijacker, and while the pilot kept him occupied as they had agreed, he quickly opened the back safety door.

It was some hours before the special edition arrived. As soon as it did, I instructed the hijacker to open the door at the front of the plane so that someone from the French authorities could show him the evidence as reported in the paper. As the Frenchman walked slowly up the steps he deliberately distracted the waiting hijacker by waving the *Sunday Independent*. This was all it took for the waiting security guys to enter from the back of the plane and to quickly overwhelm the lunatic hijacker, who was totally absorbed reading the front-page story of his demands and the Pope's release of the 'Third Secret of Fatima'.

The French then suggested that I should take the hijacker back to Dublin with me, so that he could be sentenced and jailed under Irish law. It was now the very early hours of the morning, my sense of humour had deserted me and I told them, not too politely, to keep him. 'Do what you like with him,' I said, 'he's your terrorist, not mine!'

Later that morning – but still early – we landed back in Ireland, where I received a phone call from a grateful Taoiseach who offered his congratulations for a job well done. News of the hijack had quickly spread, and crowds had gathered to greet the returning passengers and crew. I was amused to find myself hailed as the returning hero and did a number of interviews as I stepped onto the runway. I remember one question:

'Minister, what is "The Third Secret of Fatima"?'

'How would I know?' I said. 'It's a secret.'

There is a sequel to this story. Some years later, as Taoiseach, I was on a state visit to Australia. Kathleen and I were alloted the best suite in a very luxurious hotel in Perth, with top security to guard us. One morning I found a note pushed under our door. It was a charming letter from some man, informing us that it was now his job to show people around the old historic prison in Perth and asking would we care to join him for a tour? We didn't take up the kind invitation, and it was only later it became clear that it was from your man the Trappist monk, the lunatic hijacker! I showed the letter to the police in Perth. How, I asked them, with all the security in place, how could the fellow get in and put that under my door?

7

TROUBLED TIMES

Despite all the promises made by Fianna Fáil in the 1977 election, the national debt was still seriously damaging the country. To get the economy moving, more money had been spent, with the results that taxes had risen, unemployment was still severe and people were beginning to have doubts about Charlie Haughey's style of leadership. Within the cabinet itself certain personal relations with the Taoiseach were strained, most notably those between Haughey and George Colley, his former rival for the leadership, and Colley's close confidant Des O'Malley.

Victory at a by-election in Donegal South West gave Haughey a boost and, in the hope of gaining an overall majority in his first election as leader of Fianna Fáil, a general election was planned for the spring of 1981. However, the tragic fire on St Valentine's night at the Stardust ballroom in his own constituency, in which so many young people died, caused him to postpone the election.

It was the most appalling tragedy and the whole island, and most of the world, mourned the loss of so many young lives. It is still not clear how the fire started and even now, in 2009, investigators have not ruled out the possibility of arson.

On that fatal night in the early hours of 14 February 1981, the club was still packed with over 840 revellers when fire was suddenly noticed inside the building. It was later suggested that it had started when a cigarette burn ignited the exposed foam beneath a slashed seat cover, and that paper decorations intended for the impending St Valentine's night celebrations had quickly caught alight, causing the building rapidly to turn into an inferno.

Those attending the disco, and others at a trade union function in another part of the building, were hampered in their frantic efforts to escape when they discovered the main fire exits padlocked and chained; other fire exits had chains draped about the push bars, and even the toilet windows were blocked with iron bars. Forty-eight people died that night and 214 were injured as a result of that fire. The country was shell-shocked at the enormity of the tragedy.

That year of 1981 brought further dark news from the North of the fate of the H-Block hunger strikers, and with the death of Bobby Sands, the Fianna Fáil Árd Fheis was also postponed.

The hunger strikes had begun some years earlier, when, repudiating the official British criminal classification of 'terrorist' imposed on them, IRA prisoners in the Maze Prison, Belfast, had demanded a change in their status to that of political prisoner. When this was refused, around three hundred of them began a 'dirty protest' that had lasted some three years and was followed by a short-lived hunger strike. However, on 1 March 1981 a second, and more major, hunger strike was begun by IRA prisoner Bobby Sands which was to prove to be no short-term measure and was to bring about not only his own death but a distinctive change in the future of the

Republican movement. It was a seminal moment in the history of the island of Ireland. As Martin Mansergh, starting out as an adviser to Charlie Haughey, recalls:

'It had a national and international impact different from anything else that had occurred during a 25-year conflict. It put the spotlight on human rights and dignity in a particular situation, in a way that no armed action was capable of doing ... The hunger strikes were a turning point in the Northern conflict as well as a catalyst for the greater politicization of the Republican movement. They struck a chord that the conflict itself had not done.'

Margaret Thatcher's hard-line policy on prisoners, her insistence that Sands was a 'common criminal' with whom there would be no negotiation, exacerbated a worsening situation and put an enormous strain on Anglo-Irish relations. News of Bobby Sands' death on 5 May 1981 led to riots across Northern Ireland, and when a second hunger striker, Francis Hughes, died on 12 May, over two thousand people descended on the British Embassy in Dublin. By the end of the campaign in October 1981, ten Republican prisoners were dead.

The Twenty-first Dáil was dissolved at the end of May 1981 and an election was called for 11 June. For me it was back to Longford and the election campaign, the first of three in the next eighteen months. My campaign, masterminded again by Derek Cobbe and Mickey Doherty, was under way immediately: the team they had assembled was already out canvassing and drumming up support locally, and our message was good. In my constituency manufacturing employment had risen by almost 33 per cent, we had the new Telecom Éireann engineering headquarters established, and our development results in the area, achieved under the IDA Small Industries Programme, were double the national average.

Earlier in the year, on 5 March, the death of the MP for Fermanagh and South Tyrone, Frank Maguire, presented the Republican movement with the opportunity of proving the huge public support for the hunger strikers' campaign by nominating Bobby Sands as a candidate for the vacant Westminster seat. Many leading figures in Sinn Féin were reluctant to do this, however, as it meant going against all their vows of abstentionism in relation to electoral participation. There was also the added complication that he might lose the by-election and they would face humiliation. They decided to take the risk, and on 9 April Bobby Sands was elected to a seat in parliament, beating his Unionist opponent by a thousand votes. This monumental victory won the Republican move-ment worldwide support and an inflow of cash not enjoyed since the 1970s. Encouraged, they decided to put forward more candidates for the general election to be held on 11 June in the Republic, in certain hand-picked areas.

Hunger striker Martin Hurson was put up as the local candidate for Longford. This led to a terrible fear locally around that time that there would be a bomb or an explosion of some kind in the town. It never happened, but no one would have been surprised; we were all expecting it. There were protests, but they were all verbal, not violent.

It was common practice in the run-up to an election for a minister to be given the right to speak first when he happened to meet a rival contestant on the campaign trail; however, out of courtesy to the family, I preferred to give the Sinn Féin candidate priority. Martin Hurson's parents and relations were down from the North and represented him in his campaign, which they ran from Longford. There was always great respect between us and people recognized it. I believe that is why, although we feared something might happen, a riot or an explosion, it never did.

The election was overshadowed by the tragic deaths of two more of the hunger strikers, Patsy O'Hara and Raymond McCreesh, which had occurred earlier on 21 May.

The result overall was close. I was re-elected to my seat in Longford with a comfortable majority, as was the second Fianna Fáil candidate, Seán Keegan. Significantly, in a show of strong support for Sinn Féin, Martin Hurson polled well over half a quota. He died not long after, as did so many more protestors before the strike was over.

All in all, nine protesting prisoners fought the general election. Just as Bobby Sands won Fermanagh and South Tyrone, and the Westminster seat, Kieran Doherty and Paddy Agnew were elected to the Dublin parliament. Kieran Doherty, a native of Andersonstown in West Belfast, who won in Cavan and Monaghan with 15 per cent of the first-preference vote, died on 22 August.

The significance of these two victories in the South was that the results for Fianna Fáil did not live up to expectations and we ended up with our poorest showing for twenty years. Although we returned seventy-eight TDs, in the end a government was formed by a minority Fine Gael-Labour coalition which relied on the support of a few Independents.

I was now in opposition; it was time to return to C&D and the new plant we were planning.

Not for long. Within seven months the coalition led by Garret FitzGerald had fallen. The economic climate and the ever-increasing national debt had forced ministers to go against all they had promised in their electoral manifesto, and instead of cutting taxes they had increased them. The final straw was the budgetary proposals to impose VAT on clothes and children's shoes and to abolish certain food subsidies. The Independents on whom they depended refused to support the budget and the government fell.

The lead-up to the government's collapse had consequences for Fianna Fáil. When Charlie Haughey, in opposition, attacked the coalition's approach to tackling the national debt by accusing it of being deflationary and monetarist, he earned the anger of one of his erstwhile supporters, the Kildare TD and close colleague of mine, Charlie McCreevy, who spoke out in an article in the *Sunday Tribune*, voicing his disillusionment with his leader's views on the economy. Because of this McCreevy lost the Fianna Fáil whip and became Independent for a time; but he was not the only one who was becoming wary of Charlie Haughey and his leadership.

When the general election was called for February 1982 McCreevy was automatically nominated as Fianna Fáil candidate for Kildare, which meant he did not have to reapply for the party whip; however, his show of dissent had high-lighted the damaged profile of the party leader and the difficulties we faced in persuading the public and certain members of the party of Haughey's appeal and of our confidence in him as a future Taoiseach.

I had always found Haughey a very fair leader. As a minister, if you did your job well, he did not interfere but only encouraged. True, he always wanted the job done yesterday and was a stickler for time – but he lived by the same rules himself. He was also strict and though he was always ready to praise good work, any raw recruit caught not performing would be eaten alive!

When the votes were counted on the night of Friday, 19 February 1982, it was obvious that no party was going to win outright. Charlie McCreevy came through with a very high poll, proving how much support his action had engendered, and I too topped the poll in Longford, where Fianna Fáil had won three seats out of four. However, when the overall result was announced, though Fianna Fáil's eighty-one seats put it three seats ahead of the combined Fine Gael–Labour total, it was still three seats short of an overall majority. This was a disappointment and meant we had to look to the Independents and smaller parties to decide who would form a government. It also led to the first of what were to be several challenges to Haughey's leadership.

The challenge was led by Jim Gibbons, an anti-Haughey member, who on the night of the count inflamed the situation by saying in a television interview that the leadership issue would be discussed at the meeting of the parliamentary party before the House reassembled. To pre-empt the challenge Haughey brought forward the meeting, which meant any opponents would have little time to prepare. Des O'Malley was the chosen candidate, supported by Martin O'Donoghue and Seamus Brennan; others of us believed we had to defend the existing leader. There was a lot of speculation in the media, but it was really no contest: the timing was not right and in the end the challenge collapsed.

Charlie Haughey did a deal with the three Workers Party deputies and the Dublin Central Independent TD, Tony Gregory, and we were back in government.

I was appointed Minister for Industry and Energy. Another past pupil of Summerhill College, Ray MacSharry, was made Minister for Finance. Together, we were responsible for a new initiative to develop employment and to improve industrial relations. That same evening we were called in by the Taoiseach to our first cabinet meeting. The outgoing government, he told us, had not only fallen on the rejection of their proposal to impose VAT on the sale of children's shoes, but because that proposal had been defeated they had failed to raise the necessary income needed to fulfil their budget and had left us with an outstanding deficit of IR£6 million. It was up to each minister, instructed the Taoiseach, to go through the finances of his or her individual department and find areas where money could be saved in order to make up the shortfall. There could be no more increases in tax; so, as ministers, we were under pressure to find funds, somehow, somewhere 'in the system'.

The following day I set my department the task of going through all the files and papers, checking every figure to see if we could work out a way in which we could contribute towards the shortfall. We worked at it on through the night until, around four in the morning, we came upon a document that showed that the outgoing government had estimated a certain income from the sale of gas for the last quarter of the year but had failed to verify it before they included it as the final figure in the budget. They had neglected to check the final sales figures and had taken the estimate as the actual figure. Now, for some reason, during that last quarter there had been a surge in the consumption of gas, and the actual income raised was in excess of the estimate – by a long way: by some IR£13 million, in fact. In other words, the previous government had not needed to fall!

The next morning we all gathered with the results of our searches, and I waited as each head of department offered what he or she could to make up the deficit. I was sitting next to the Minister for Finance, my pal Ray MacSharry, and finally it came to my turn.

'How much short are you now, Ray?' I said, and he told me, whatever the figure was. 'Well,' I said, 'you can keep all that and on top, there's a full IR£6 million extra from me – but the balance of the money I found, the IR£7 million, I'm keeping for expenditure within my own department.'

Everyone was delighted that the money was found, including the new Taoiseach.

Nuclear power was the big option in government energy policy at that time. I had done my research on this. The Lynch government had already made plans to develop nuclear energy and had even chosen a site down in Wexford. I wasn't at all convinced that nuclear was the way forward: it was expensive and to my mind presented a health risk. So, on my first day as Minister for Industry and Energy I overturned that decision.

There were other factors to be taken into consideration, too. Natural gas had been found off the coast of Cork and as yet it had not been exploited. This was going to be my first priority. And it wasn't going to be easy.

There must have been over four hundred objections from landowners whose property would be crossed by the proposed gas pipe that was planned to run from Cork to Dublin. We had to consider all of them: some would involve a little persuasion, most would involve compensation, many ended up as court cases, often going on to courts of appeal. It was my decision to decide on a course of action for each case, so I took on the task of going through them all personally.

State contracts were regarded at that time as a bit of a 'gravy train' because there was always a way to add on extras, demand more money for more time, extend the budget, and so on. I was determined to keep this project on time and within budget, and I warned the contractor that he should give me a realistic budget that we could both agree and live with: I would expect him to abide by our agreement, I told him, otherwise there was no deal. I also brought in an expert from outside, an engineer from a large construction company who understood the job, and I instructed him to supervise the whole lot and to report to me directly. Ignore the department, I said to him, ignore everybody but me, and don't change anything on the contract, no matter who asks you, without first discussing it with me.

There were a few cases left outstanding when we finally started the work. It was 1 April, April Fool's Day. I'm not superstitious; however, I told the project manager, 'If you want to start on 31 March, it's up to you!'

It wasn't easy. Getting our gas lines across private land was always going to be difficult. There were all sorts of hold-ups as people tried to hold us to ransom with last-minute requests for more compensation or a sudden newly lodged complaint. Caught up in all the added complications, I could see why the previous government had abandoned the idea. However, I took them all on, although a little lateral thinking was needed at times.

We were almost there, the project was nearly complete, and there was one last parcel of land we needed to cross. It was on a property on the Dublin–Kildare border. Much of the land we'd acquired had been quite cheap, but this was not: this was a prime area and the landowners, a father and two sons, were determined to stop me any way they could. I would take out a court order for them to appear and they'd go sick. This happened a number of times, with excuse following on excuse. Finally I decided the only way was to requisition the land. Under the law, this still allowed them time to appeal, and every time a hearing was called their lawyer found an excuse to postpone it. We were now being seriously held up; it was time for action.

The contractors were called and asked, 'Can you get your men down there and just get the job done?'

When the landowners next went into court they were told there was nothing they could do; they were too late.

There were plenty more incidents in the course of this

enterprise, and one in particular was a good example of people looking on the state as fair game.

I was chatting with some of the boys on site who told me that they had been approached by a farmer in Tipperary who had offered them a deal, a tip of a few hundred pounds if they would divert a bit of a pipeline from the main line and connect it to his property, so that he'd have his own free private supply of gas and no one, especially the state, would be any the wiser.

Apparently, they agreed that they would finish the contracted work in the area, and then start on his connection. A number of weeks later the gas supply to the farm ran out and, so the story went, the farmer dug around, expecting to find a fault on the line. He followed the pipe from his house – to find that, instead of leading to the main line, it finished at a small gas tank which the men had buried in the ground, with a connection to his house. He had been well and truly duped; there was nothing he could do and by then the men were well away.

When the project was finished, inevitably there was a court case with the contractors suing for more money for extra work; but as there had been no extension of contracts their claim had no legal basis and the contract and budget we had originally agreed were upheld. The gas pipeline had been laid, and the project was completed on time and on budget.

Notwithstanding my track record in overcoming obstacles, some things were totally beyond my control. The Falklands War had started in 1982 and the government's decision to remain neutral meant that all my efforts to encourage British investment into Ireland often went for nought. There were hard choices to make, and where state companies within my area of responsibility were not making a profit, I was forced to close them. Ardmore Film Studios was one such company;

Clondalkin Paper Mills was another. Such action was necessary but not popular, and for all Ray MacSharry's promises of a 'boom and bloom' economy and my efforts to get industry going, the economy, in the short term, was still showing little sign of improvement.

There were other factors, too, that were reflecting badly on us as a party. One, although innocent enough in its origin, led in August 1982 to the resignation of the Attorney General, Paddy Connolly, who had unwittingly allowed a murderer, Malcolm MacArthur, to stay in his apartment. MacArthur was a friend of Connolly's girlfriend; she persuaded the Attorney General that the man was going through a bad time, and in a kind and innocent gesture he allowed him to stay.

On 1 October 1982 Charlie McCreevy put down a motion of no confidence in the second challenge that year to the party leadership. Des O'Malley, who had been away on holiday, flew back to support the motion and both he, as Minister for Trade, Commerce and Tourism, and Martin O'Donoghue, the Minister for Education, decided to resign from the cabinet and back McCreevy. I was sorry to go against Charlie but again I felt compelled to support the Taoiseach. This time, though, the dissidents were more determined. They fought their campaign on the lowering of political standards, the mismanagement of the economy, and the party's failure to win a majority in two successive elections. They called for a secret vote. Haughey insisted on an open roll-call vote so that the dissidents could be identified, and called for discipline within the party.

The vote taken at the Parliamentary Party meeting was orderly; the conduct following it was not. The meeting went on most of the day and late into the night, with McCreevy calling for a return to party decency and Haughey defending his position, insisting that his new manifesto 'The Way Forward' had not yet been put into operation and given the chance to prove itself.

When the vote was finally called, Charlie Haughey carried the vote by fifty-eight to twenty-two. Outside Leinster House crowds of Haughey supporters, many of whom had been drinking all day, surged forward, and as Charlie McCreevy tried to make his way through to his car he was pushed and abused both verbally and physically. Jim Gibbons, too, was attacked and hit to the ground. It was a shaming sight, a disgrace, and served only to further discredit Fianna Fáil.

Looking back, it seems such an extreme reaction to a party contest; but, as Charlie McCreevy reflects:

'What I did in 1982, my outspokenness, was totally unheard of at the time. It's far easier now for fellows but what I did then was unheard of in the Fianna Fáil party. We were a closely knit group and that's how it had been for the previous sixty years. Consequently the Fianna Fáil supporters, the organization's members, were aghast and appalled at what I had done because that was not in the tradition of the party. It was still the old system of all for one and one for all, we kept things to ourselves. I was this independent fellow and I'd taken on the leadership, which was unheard of. Consequently, for very genuine reasons, whole lots of well-meaning people would gladly have taken me out and strung me up to the nearest lamp-post.

'Even my own mother, had she been alive, would have come out against me because she was brought up in the tradition of Fianna Fáil and you just did not do that.'

Following the assault on him that night, Jim Gibbons suffered a severe heart attack and was hospitalized. The death of Billy Loughnane, a deputy from Clare, diminished our numbers even more; and when the vote was taken on 'The Way Forward', which proposed substantial cuts in public spending, the key Independent Tony Gregory and the Workers Party deputies withdrew their support and we faced our third election in eighteen months.

Another election, another campaign. It was called for 24 November 1982. We all knew it was an election too far and that the general public would hold Fianna Fáil to blame – and they were right. Too many shotgun elections and changes of government prevented the country from moving forward. There was little heart for it, especially as there were few differences in policy between the main parties on the dominating issue of the day – the economic crisis. The Haughey factor, and his style of leadership, served only to blight our campaign. In the end, although I once more topped the poll in Longford and was elected on the first count, Fianna Fáil was decisively beaten, down six seats in just eighteen months. Garret FitzGerald became Taoiseach in coalition with Labour, Dick Spring became Tánaiste, and I returned to the opposition benches as spokesman on Industry.

Defeat at the polls was followed by a further blow to the party reputation when the incoming Minister for Justice, Michael Noonan, revealed that his predecessor, Seán Doherty, had authorized the tapping of the phones of two leading political correspondents, Geraldine Kennedy and Bruce Arnold. He also disclosed that during the time when both Ray MacSharry and Martin O'Donoghue were ministers, MacSharry had ordered bugging equipment from the Gardaí to record conversations he was having with O'Donoghue. This had happened at the time of the vote of confidence in the party leadership.

It all reflected very badly on Charles Haughey and his leadership of the party, in and out of government. Of course, he was quick to deny any knowledge of such affairs, claiming that neither he nor his government were involved. However, in a front-page article in the *Sunday Press*, Geraldine Kennedy reported that the previous July, Haughey had asked the publisher of the *Sunday Tribune*, where she then worked, for details of her sources.

Within days, MacSharry and O'Donoghue had resigned from the Fianna Fáil front bench and an internal party inquiry was under way. Haughey was exonerated, but the press had a field day with rumours of his resignation, and before long another onslaught on his leadership was put in motion, this time by Dublin South Central Deputy Ben Briscoe, demanding his resignation. Others challenged for the leadership but once more when the votes were counted Charlie Haughey had survived. For myself, although yet again I gave him all my support, my faith was being eroded bit by bit.

Over the next few years in opposition, as spokesperson on Industry and Commerce I fought hard to do what I could to further economic progress and industrial relations, but there were other things happening too which interested me more and more, although at the time there was nothing I could do about them. I was critical of the lack of economic decisions, and of the coalition for focusing more on studying problems than on solving them – 'the paralysis of analysis'.

Charlie Haughey and Margaret Thatcher were two strong-minded individuals with strictly opposing views on Northern Ireland, and while Charlie, with his strong Republican ties, was in power there was no hope of a political breakthrough. Garret FitzGerald, on the other hand, nervous at the rising strength of the Sinn Féin movement, which was threatening to rival that of the Northern Nationalist SDLP, was eager to improve Anglo-Irish relations. He stressed the need for a 'constitutional crusade', and the need to make the Republic more accommodating to the Unionist tradition in the North. The idea of a new Irish Forum was born as a means of working together, not just through the British and Dublin governments, but involving all the constitutional parties, North and South, in round-table discussions to find a political accommodation. The Unionists refused to take part, as did the Alliance Party, and the forum became dominated by constitutional Nationalism – the very thing it had tried to avoid.

The setting up of the New Ireland Forum in May 1984 caused further controversy within Fianna Fáil when Haughey dictated that, in respect of Forum discussions, party members must follow the party line. The core value of Fianna Fáil was the unity of Ireland, and as far as Haughey was concerned that principle was not for negotiation. Des O'Malley accused him of stifling debate, and the ensuing dispute led to the whip being withdrawn from him.

The following year, early 1985, the Fine Gael–Labour coalition introduced a Bill to liberalize the sale of contraceptives. Fianna Fáil opposed it; O'Malley, however, considered it a matter of conscience and wanted to support it, although when it came to the actual vote he abstained. Summoned to a Fianna Fáil party meeting, he was charged with 'conduct unbecoming' and on a roll-call vote was expelled from the party.

Increasing violence in the North was inevitably damaging the economy both sides of the border. FitzGerald sought to convince the British government of the need for a joint political response, but the intransigent Mrs Thatcher insisted instead on an even greater concentration of security in the North, with more troops and more border controls. Following the IRA bombing of the Grand Hotel in Brighton at the 1984 Conservative party conference, in which five people were killed and Thatcher herself escaped only narrowly, FitzGerald again appealed for cooperation on the idea of joint

Dublin–London authority. The Prime Minister responded with her famous 'out, out, out' speech.

Relations between London and Dublin remained strained, but all was not lost and in November 1985 the Anglo-Irish Agreement emerged. It gave Dublin the right to be heard in relation to Nationalist concerns in the North, and it re-affirmed the long-standing British position in place since 1920–1: that if the majority of the population in the North voted clearly for a united Ireland, then legislation to give effect to that wish would be granted in Westminster. To Nationalists this was seen as a Unionist veto; but the principle of consent had been agreed by the two governments as a policy commitment. It also drew strong opposition from the Unionists, who were appalled that the Dublin government had been granted an advisory role in the running of Northern Ireland.

The Dáil ratified the agreement by eighty votes to seventy-five, but Charles Haughey and Fianna Fáil voted against the agreement. Personally, I regretted Fianna Fáil's position. The situation in the North was at stalemate: compromise and political accommodation on all sides had to be the way forward if the violence was to stop. In my opinion the agreement wasn't the complete answer, but it was a step forward. Unfortunately, far from helping to ease tensions, it served only to alienate both sides: the Unionists because they saw Dublin having influence in the North, and the Nationalists because it confirmed the partition of Ireland by the Government of Ireland Act. Two of those who went against the Fianna Fáil position were Des O'Malley, now an Independent, and Mary Harney, both of whom went through the government lobby when the vote came. Mary Harney was consequently expelled from the party and for a short while she sat on the Independent benches. In reaction to what she and many other people saw as Fianna Fáil's negative and destructive attitude to the Anglo-Irish Agreement, she joined with Des O'Malley to found the Progressive Democrat Party. Feelings were running high and people surged to join the new party. Americans in particular were loud in their protests at Fianna Fáil's actions against the agreement; they simply could not understand it.

On 20 January 1987 the coalition fell when Labour went against Fine Gael over a proposed budget. Another general election was called. This time we could leave nothing to chance.

In my own constituency, the retirement of Fine Gael's sitting TD, Gerry L'Estrange, created an opportunity for Fianna Fáil to try for three out of the four seats. Alongside myself as the candidate for Longford and Mary O'Rourke in Athlone, barrister Henry Abbot from Mullingar was added to the party ticket.

My loyal friend Councillor Mickey Doherty was again the Director of Elections. 'If we are going for three out of four seats, and we are,' he advised, 'then the North Westmeath people will have to vote for the North Westmeath candidate [Abbot], the South Westmeath people for the South Westmeath candidate [O'Rourke] and the Longford people must vote entirely for the Longford candidate [myself]. We will only fail if someone messes up!'

This time there was not only my old team of Derek Cobbe and Larry Cunningham to join in the fight: the whole family came home to Longford to help with my campaign.

My son Philip directed operations from the house:

'We had a plan that every single house in Longford would be canvassed and it was. There were seven of us – Mum just didn't like canvassing, so she would do the hospitals or a nursing home or she might go to the convent, but that would be as much as she would do. As there were seven of us, it was my view that there was no reason why between us we couldn't knock on every door on every house in the county. The only way of doing that was to put up a map. Every area has its own electoral register, and every one of them is numbered, so I gave each of them an area to cover and when they had contacted every name on the electoral register, they brought back the results to me and I shaded in the area covered; that way nothing was missed. Admittedly I used to get a bit of stick from the others but I did a lot of canvassing myself, and I loved it, I have to say. Maybe more than some of them did. All through Dad's campaigns one of the strengths was the intensity of the canvass, and all I was trying to do was follow on with that in the latter years, and the more of us there were as we got older, the easier it was for us to do.'

Neil Blaney's campaign methods still worked well, although things had become a little more colourful, as Andrea recalls:

'In those days people used to write songs for politicians and in the verses would be listed all the things they had achieved over the last twelve months, things they'd done for the community. These would be broadcast through loudspeakers from vans as they drove through the towns, or from the backs of lorries covered with posters promoting the candidates. It seems bizarre now, but communications were still limited then. Dad had had a huge input into developing Longford, so there was always evidence of what he had done and he was incredibly popular with the grass roots.

'Even so, we were all called upon to speak on his behalf. One of my earliest memories of when I was about twelve was going out with the local activists to different churches and waiting for the people to come out of mass on Sundays. They'd give me a little box to stand on, hand me a loudspeaker, and instruct me as to what to say. Things like, "You see that community hall over there," or that road, etc.,

Left: One of the few photographs I have of my parents, Catherine and John P. Reynolds.

Above: Schooldays at Summerhill College, Sligo. Here I am, slap bang in the centre of this happy group.

Right: At home with friends and family in Roosky. *With me, from the left*: Jack Bohan and my brother Joe; Charlie Reynolds (my brother-in-law) and my sister Teresa; *seated*: my mother Catherine.

Left: A very happy day for me and Kathleen, June 1962.

Below: The early days of our marriage, with Kathleen and our good friends Jack and Eileen Moriarty.

Below: At a Fianna Fáil annual dinner dance at the Prince of Wales Hotel in Athlone, with (*from left*) Mary O'Rourke, Jack Lynch, Frank Carter and Mairín Lynch.

Left: When Charlie came to visit Longford. *Back row, from the left*: Jim Coyne, Seán Doherty, Noel Hanlon, Paddy Farrell. *With me, front row, from left*: Charles Haughey, Noel McGeeney, Tony Egan.

Below: I could always rely on family support. At an election count in Longford. *Left to right*: Emer, Abbie, Andrea, Kathleen, Cathy, Miriam, Philip and Leonie.

Left: Des O'Malley, Minister for Industry and Commerce, and I, Minister for Finance, deliberating at an OECD Council meeting in Paris, 30 May 1990.

Right: The Three Taoisigh: Charlie Haughey and his two immediate successors, me and Bertie Ahern.

Below: At Ashford Castle in March 1990 John Major, Chancellor of the Exchequer, and I, Minister for Finance, got to know each other. On the right is Theo Waigel, German Federal Minister for Finance.

Above: Delivering the budget as Minister for Finance, 31 January 1990.

Below: 'Welcome home, Taoiseach.' The celebratory homecoming, February 1992. On the steps of the courthouse in Longford with (*left to right*) Ned Reilly, Padraig Flynn, Donie Cassidy and Mickey Doherty.

Above: Receiving the Seal of Office as Taoiseach from President Mary Robinson for the second time in a year! 12 January 1993.

Left: Getting my message across. Making an impassioned address at the Fianna Fáil Ard Fheis.

Above: Fianna Fáil and Progressive Democrats Coalition Cabinet, February 1992.

Below: Fianna Fáil and Labour Coalition Cabinet, January 1993.

Top: At an EU summit meeting, shortly after the successful June 1992 referendum on the Treaty on European Union (Maastricht Treaty).

Centre: A formal reception for EU leaders attending the Edinburgh Summit in December 1992, hosted by HM Queen Elizabeth on board the Royal Yacht *Britannia*.

Right: A little more than merely 'a working visit'. Meeting Federal Chancellor Helmut Kohl in Bonn, 12 November 1992, for mutually beneficial discussions in advance of the European Council meeting in Edinburgh, December 1992.

"well, it wouldn't be there – if it wasn't for Albert Reynolds!"'

I had trained the home team well from the beginning, as Philip recalls:

'From a very early age we were all involved. Once the election was called any of us who could talk were put on the road, either canvassing or doing after-mass meetings, so Miriam and I were sent to them all. We were given a rota and the whole county would have to be covered in the period, which was three or four weeks at that time. We were sent out with drivers and local party activists most Sundays. The schedule of mass meetings would appear in the paper, so Dad would perhaps cover South Longford, where there might be four or five churches. First mass would be at nine o'clock and last mass would be at twelve noon or twelve-thirty, so physically you just couldn't get to any more than three or four. Dad would do three or four in South Longford, Miriam might do three or four in North Longford, I might do three or four in West Longford and that's the way it went on.'

There was a little rural church in my constituency right on the border between Longford and Westmeath in the village of Tang, and many of my supporters from Longford went to mass there, as did many constituents from South Westmeath, from where Mary O'Rourke drew much of her support. It had actually been assigned to O'Rourke, but as my voters were there too, I reckoned both candidates had the right to speak there – after all, we were all out for every vote we could get. On this particular occasion both O'Rourke and I turned up at the same time, me with my team of supporters, she with hers. Unfortunate, but it happened! Sparks flew for a few minutes, earning the incident fame as 'the battle of Tang', but the battle was short-lived and we both took it in turns to speak, remembering that we were both on the same side.

At the final count, I topped the poll in Longford, O'Rourke

won Athlone and Abbot took Mullingar. Fianna Fáil had returned two ministers and a TD – and we had won three out of the four seats!

This was the first election contested by the newly formed Progressive Democrat Party, led by Des O'Malley, and their performance was quite impressive in that they gained fourteen seats. Overall, Fianna Fáil came in with eighty-one seats, still three short of an out-and-out majority. This was the fourth time that Haughey had failed to win an overall majority, but he was still in the strongest position to form a government.

When it came to his nomination as Taoiseach he was supported by Neil Blaney and Tony Gregory and elected on the casting vote of the Ceann Comhairle, the Independent TD Seán Treacy from Tipperary.

It was time to form the new cabinet. I was keen to continue my work with Industry, but this time when Charlie Haughey called me into his office, he began talking about Forestry and Developing Tourism – a worthy ministry, I admit, but not what I wanted or expected. 'Who's got Industry and Commerce?' I asked.

'Ray Burke,' said Haughey.

'In that case I won't be working!' And I left the room. Ten minutes later the phone rang. It was Haughey again, asking me to stay on. 'Not for Forestry,' I replied. 'I've got better things to do with my time. I've a new factory being built.'

Next thing Haughey's secretary came in to see me asking me to reconsider, but I was adamant. 'It's Industry and Commerce or I'm leaving!'

I returned to the Department of Industry and Commerce and Ray MacSharry resumed his position as Minister for Finance.

There was little doubt that the country faced a huge economic crisis. The national debt had doubled to some IR£25 billion, which meant one pound in every four raised went on servicing the interest on it, which amounted to one-third of all tax revenue. There were rumours that the slump was so severe that the International Monetary Fund, the IMF, would have to step in and impose tough conditions – even that it was about to seize control of the Irish economy.

There were also predictions that once Haughey and his government were in power they would resort to their old ways and embark on unrestrained spending once again. In fact we did the opposite: instead of increases in public spending, swingeing cuts were introduced, earning Ray MacSharry the nickname of 'Mac the Knife'. Cutbacks elsewhere brought forth a crop of nicknames for ministers – Minister for Health Dr Rory O'Hanlon was dubbed 'Dr Death', for example – but people realized that the state of the economy was so bad that there was nothing for it but to accept the new draconian conditions if the country was to have any chance of recovery.

All this, and everything else, was overshadowed by the Enniskillen bombing on Remembrance Day 1987. Television pictures around the world conveyed the horror of the tragedy, in which eleven people were killed and more than sixty were injured when the bomb explosion demolished a wall and rubble and masonry crashed down. No one would ever forget the words of the bereaved Gordon Wilson, when he described being trapped in the debris holding his daughter's hand and her words, 'Daddy, I love you very much.' And the silence that followed. It was the dignity and magnitude of his forgiveness, when he said, 'She was a great wee lassie. She was a pet, and she's dead. But I bear no ill will. I bear no grudge.' No one who heard those words will ever forget them, and years later when I became Taoiseach I nominated that extraordinary human being to become a member of the Seánad.

* * *

As Minister for Industry and Commerce, my path was clear: I had to bring in more investment. One of my main concerns was to get American money coming back in. Many Irish Americans were high-fliers, but because of the situation in the North and the dire state of our economy, they were reluctant to risk their finances in Ireland. I flew to America to encourage them to rethink, to assure them that we had the manpower and the raw materials to rebuild our industry: all we needed was faith and investment. Padraic White, the chief executive of the IDA, frequently travelled with me, and was there when we attended a lunch for four hundred top financiers in New York. I had prepared a speech but in the event, when I stood up and saw all those potential investors in front of me, I put it aside and went for broke! It paid off. Nor was it the only success of that four-day trip: as a result of that visit several big American companies invested in Ireland, including Chase Manhattan in Dublin and Metropolitan Life in Galway. I also created a very powerful group of Irish American business leaders in the US – a forum which focused on inward investment to Ireland.

As a party we had set out our strategy for industrial job creation in what was called the Programme for National Recovery, in which we had identified areas for improvement and the goals we were aiming to achieve. We knew we had to make best use of our natural resources, encourage new advanced skills, and increase share in selected areas and markets. It was my job to see that we expanded and diversified our industrial base, thus creating the right environment for investment: for example, we introduced the development of software as a new industry, encouraging companies such as Intel to set up in Ireland. This became a huge winner for the Irish economy.

To get the economy moving, I firmly believed we had to start at the base and build upwards, just as you do when building a house: 'foundations first', I told the Dáil.

I was working hard, maybe too hard, and at one point was rushed to hospital. The symptoms and tests revealed I had diabetes. A few days of rest and soon I was back on the job.

All the tough decisions and cutbacks were beginning to prove effective, and in small ways the economy was at last improving. However, on the personal front I had to swallow a bitter pill when I became embroiled in a strike in my own constituency, at the ambulance factory set up by my close friend Noel Hanlon. The factory had been established in Longford as far back as 1966, when Hanlon, who ran a garage, had been approached by Longford County Council and asked if he knew anyone who could do conversion work on ambulances. He decided to do it himself and began to assemble ambulances on a small scale. The enterprise became a phenomenal success; however, at this stage, owing to cutbacks both at home and in Britain, his market had diminished and he was forced to reduce his workforce. This action led to a bitter dispute which I seriously believe was orchestrated by a certain militant faction. It was my home town and I knew the union branch secretary to be a decent man, but there were others who acted irresponsibly. After months of in-fighting a peace plan was drawn up, but it was rejected by the workers and the plant was closed down. It was a severe blow for Longford.

In 1988 Ray MacSharry, who saw his future with the EC, was appointed Ireland's European Commissioner in succession to Peter Sutherland and I was promoted to the most important cabinet position of Minister for Finance.

There was still a long way to go despite the upturn in our economy and fiscal rectitude was still the order of the day.

However, recent results showed that the total number of jobs in the economy had increased appreciably for the first time since 1980: unemployment was falling and the prospects for economic growth were looking good.

The programme I had initiated as Minister for Posts and Telegraphs, modernizing our telecommunications systems and pushing us to the forefront of world leaders in high-technology education and software production, had paid off; as a result foreign investment had poured into the country, and now that investment was set to turn in the best performance in a decade. Overall I was optimistic that growth in domestic output was likely to accelerate, and indeed it did. The more competitive we could make our economy, the quicker and better the results for employment would be. I needed to get money out of people's pockets and into the economy – but that meant I also had to put money in!

My first budget was well received and proved to be effective. Two budgetary factors underpinned the strategy: first, and most directly, tax cuts and income transfers released a net IR£178 million into the hands of consumers; second, and more importantly, by keeping a fairly tight rein on public finances I gave people confidence that the economy was set to improve further and that employment was secure. It was that feeling of optimism that I anticipated would encourage a domestic consumer spending boom. I believed that, by significantly increasing investment in buildings, machinery and plant, we could accelerate the rate of economic expansion which in turn would further stimulate domestic demand and inward investment.

Financing government borrowing was still a huge drain on our economy, and only by getting our economy moving could we service the interest on the mountain of debt that burdened us every year. And the way to get things moving had to be

through the tax system: tax relief for manufacturing companies, cutting corporation tax, making our country highly
competitive with low tax rates for foreign investors and, at the
other end of the scale, lower personal taxes and special income
tax assistance for the more impoverished sector of the population. I introduced wider tax bands and eased the personal
income tax burden. I cut the standard income tax rate by 3 per
cent (from 35 per cent to 32 per cent) and the top rate by 2
per cent, the first reductions in income tax for twenty years.
Overall I was pleased with the reaction to my first budget, but
I also realized it was just one small piece in the overall
financial puzzle and a hard task lay ahead.

During my time in Industry and Commerce, I had seen the
positive effect that driving down costs had had on reviving
the economy. It was not a popular policy with some of the
powerful lobby groups in the country, but it was a necessary
measure. Now I took on the oil companies by introducing a
maximum prices order, moved to prevent price fixing in the
drinks industry, leaving the market to be sorted out through
competition, and banned 'hello' money and below-cost selling
in supermarkets – anything to ensure a fair deal for the
consumer.

Slowly things were turning round – so I was concerned to
hear that Haughey was again facing scandal. More and more
questions were being asked about his lavish lifestyle, and there
were insinuations that he was abusing his position as Taoiseach
to enrich himself. He was accused of receiving valuable gifts
from a Saudi prince, both for himself and for his wife, allegedly
in contravention of the Cabinet Procedure Instructions. There
was another political storm but, in the face of Haughey's failure
– or refusal – to give any excuse or explanation, once again it
died down.

Haughey's high-handed style of leadership and the various

scandals surrounding him were making him more and more difficult to defend. I was also acutely aware of just how badly this was reflecting on the party.

A close circle of friends would frequently turn up at Mount Carmel or the apartment at Hazeldene and we'd gather as always in the kitchen – Pádraig Flynn, Mickey Doherty, Charlie McCreevy, Noel Hanlon. As always, the chat was all politics, and now it kept coming back to the spiralling number of scandals involving the Taoiseach and, inevitably, the party. Kathleen would make dinner, or there would be tea and cake and scones, and the young ones would be there too, not just hanging on every word but quick with their opinions. We called it the kitchen cabinet as we resolved the country's problems round the table. Andrea still remembers the excitement of being involved in politics:

'Cathy, Emer, Leonie, Abbie and I were usually there, sometimes Philip would pop in or Miriam if she and Niall [Miriam's husband] were over from Edinburgh, but there was always a houseful and the conversation would be politics, nothing else. What we loved doing best was pretending – if Dad was Taoiseach who would be in cabinet and who would he sack?

'We always knew that at some point Dad would go for it, that one day he would be Taoiseach. It was very exciting when it eventually came to fruition.

'There was one person we girls definitely put into our cabinet and that was Charlie McCreevy – and to this day he says he wouldn't have got the job except for us!'

Charlie McCreevy was a constant visitor to the house:

'The thing about the Reynolds family was, you seriously couldn't have been to a nicer or happier home. I spent oodles of time out there when they lived at Hazeldene, so I got to know the kids well. It was very special and we all became great friends. Kathleen in particular; Kathleen was Albert's prop and the relationship he has with her is very, very unique, even in Irish marital terms.'

Gradually the country was pulling through the economic crisis: the level of government borrowing was down, foreign investment was growing, Fine Gael were supporting our budgetary policy and public spending was coming under control. Then Haughey, returning from a trip to Japan, called us in to announce that if we were defeated on a pending motion concerning compensation of IR£400,000 a year to haemophiliacs who had been infected with HIV through defective blood products administered by the state, he would consider it appropriate grounds for calling an election. We had been defeated at private members' time on a number of minor issues but there had been no question of any of them leading to an election, and certainly there seemed to me no reason why this motion, important though it was, should force us into yet another election at such a vulnerable time, just as confidence in our economy was building. I urged Haughey to reconsider.

On 29 April 1989, Labour put the motion to the vote and the government was defeated. I was firmly opposed to an election, but as cabinet discussions continued it was obvious that other members were convinced that the time had come to go to the country again in the hope of gaining an outright majority. I pleaded in vain. Haughey was one of the few Fianna Fáil Taoisigh up to then never to have had an overall majority – in fact it had eluded him four times – and for some reason he was convinced the timing was now right. Pádraig Flynn and Ray Burke supported him, influenced by a strong showing for Fianna Fáil in the opinion polls prior to the elections for the European Parliament. Holding a general election on the same day, 15 June, they argued, would give the party the opportunity to gain an overall majority. There was further reason for optimism in the collapse of support for the PDs; but there were strong stirrings of discontent in the electorate over health cuts imposed by our government, and these were either ignored or underestimated. The public was always very anxious and angry about health cuts. Even individuals not directly affected by the cuts knew of neighbours or family who were, and they felt outraged on their account. They also feared for themselves in the future.

So we were back on the campaign trail again. This time the opposition had more time to prepare, but once again I headed the poll with first preference votes in Longford, as did Mary O'Rourke in South Westmeath, but the party lost the third seat when Henry Abbot was defeated. Across the country it was one of the lowest turnouts ever, proving that the people had no heart for an election at this time. Fianna Fáil, far from winning an overall majority, was in a weaker position than ever, having dropped from eighty-one to seventy-seven seats. The forcing of an election had proved a big political mistake and the possibility of forming even another minority government looked slim. Things grew even worse when, for the first time in the state's history, the nominee for Taoiseach, Charles Haughey, failed to take a majority vote in the Dáil. Constitutionally this meant Haughey was obliged to resign, which, obstinately, for a short period he refused to do. He eventually tendered his resignation to President Hillery but continued as Taoiseach, albeit in an acting capacity.

The PDs had taken only six seats, down from their previous fourteen, but those six seats could give us a majority, as was clearly pointed out to Haughey when we met at Fianna Fáil Headquarters. We had no option but to go for it.

Haughey had already held private, exploratory talks with other parties but no agreements had come out of them. The

PDs' response when asked to support a minority Fianna Fáil administration was firm: the price of PD backing was coalition.

I was totally opposed to a coalition; others saw it as the only way of staying in government. Haughey, in a private meeting with O'Malley, conceded.

Bertie Ahern and I were appointed to negotiate on behalf of Fianna Fáil, Bobby Molloy and Pat Cox for the PDs. There is no doubt that, unbeknown to us, Haughey was taking decisions without any reference to us at all, and that the negotiations we were conducting were being undermined in secret meetings between himself and O'Malley. Negotiations had ground to a halt over the number of PD cabinet seats. They insisted on two, we offered one; both Ahern and I went on radio to assert that the PD allocation would be one and one alone, only to learn that on the very same day Haughey had conceded two in his meeting with O'Malley without inform-ing us.

At this stage, I was becoming more and more disillusioned with Haughey's overbearing presidential style. I was not the only one. Several other members of cabinet, all former strong supporters of his leadership – Flynn and Geoghegan-Quinn in particular – were totally opposed to a coalition and angered that we had been forced into another unnecessary election.

For once Charlie McCreevy and I did not agree, as he recalls:

'That was the only time that Albert and I ever fell out. He was very aggrieved about that and about my role in it. Fianna Fáil always wanted a clear majority and Haughey in all the elections he'd run had never got an overall majority himself, not like Lynch or de Valera or Lemass. A coalition was unthinkable at the time: Fianna Fáil had never done this, and people from the cabinet like Albert and Pádraig Flynn were totally opposed to it. I wasn't in government at the time but I had mended my differences with Charlie Haughey, so I did help to convince both sides – why not go into coalition?

'So Haughey appointed Albert and Bertie to negotiate for Fianna Fáil and O'Malley appointed Molloy and Pat Cox for the PDs, and they were discussing policy and everything else about the arrangement when Albert cottoned on.'

I realized something was going on between McCreevy and Charlie Haughey when Bertie and I returned unexpectedly from our negotiations at the Berkeley Court Hotel to Government Buildings and I saw McCreevy coming out of Haughey's office. He was so startled to see us that I immediately suspected another game was being played out in our absence. I was incensed. I remember calling after him, 'This is a waste of time!' But I also recognized it would be a game that could cost Haughey the leadership in the end. It was the moment I lost all faith and made up my mind – enough of Charlie Haughey!

Fianna Fáil suffered a further blow in the 1990 presidential elections when Brian Lenihan, the Tánaiste, our nominated candidate, and favourite to win, lost to Mary Robinson. But what soured the episode for me was not so much the result itself as the conduct of the campaign and Haughey's treatment of Brian when things did not go according to plan.

Brian was a bright man and a popular figure, a much-loved politician and a worthy candidate for the position of President. At first he was considered unbeatable until Dick Spring put forward Senator Mary Robinson as the Labour choice and Fine Gael nominated Austin Currie as their candidate.

Brian was actually a very intellectual man, but he liked to mask this side of his personality by playing the comedian, and during the run-up to the presidential campaign he appeared on a *Late Late Show* TV special devoted to him in which friends and colleagues projected an image of him as a 'cute hoor', a popular saying which denotes someone who would pull any stunt and offer the electorate any promises without any intention of fulfilling them. Consequently his popular profile became tainted with overtones of untrustworthiness.

Unfortunately this perception of him was heightened in the second half of the campaign when an event from his past resurfaced. In January 1982 Brian was alleged to be involved, on behalf of Haughey, in an attempt to pressurize the sitting President, Patrick Hillery, a close friend of Lenihan's, into refusing the then Taoiseach Garret FitzGerald a parliamentary dissolution. At that time the minority coalition of Fine Gael–Labour had gone over its budget, and calls for dissolution of the Dáil were strong and furious; but for Lenihan to have tried to involve the President, who is traditionally above politics, contravened all the conventions.

In the intervening years, Lenihan had never denied being one of those who had made those controversial phone calls that night to Áras an Uachtaráin, despite several articles in the press naming him with Sylvester Barrett and Charlie Haughey. Now, suddenly, he refuted all knowledge of such a call. However, a few months previously he had been interviewed by a young research student, Jim Duffy, and in an 'on the record' interview he had revealed his participation in the event. The *Irish Times* was aware of this interview and, following Lenihan's denial, confirmed the story. In the furore of denials and accusations that followed, a copy of the recorded tape of Lenihan actually admitting he had made the phone call to the President at Áras an Uachtaráin was brought in as evidence.

Brian changed his story again, claimed extenuating circumstances and sudden 'mature recollection'; but the damage was done. His credibility had been fatally undermined. The opposition put down a vote of no confidence in the government and O'Malley gave Haughey no option: Lenihan must resign as Tánaiste or the PDs would force an election. Haughey, although insisting he would put no pressure on Brian Lenihan, his friend of thirty years, drew up a letter of resignation for him to sign. It was a grave demand and Brian, who had a lot of support within the party, refused to comply. In the end Haughey sacked his old friend Lenihan from the cabinet.

I had just returned from the US and was called to Haughey's office. He asked me to support the sacking, which I refused to do. At that point I quite expected to be sacked myself for taking this position.

This episode was to have severe consequences for Haughey in the future. His lack of support for his friend, and his readiness to bend to the wishes of the opposition, signalled his overriding ambition and a willingness to do anything in his power to hold on to his leadership. This served only to damage his reputation.

Brian had been a loyal and active member of the party, and for a while, despite the dismissal, his campaign for the presidency seemed to be going well; but more bad publicity damaged his chances when an ill-judged remark from Pádraig Flynn in support of Brian insulted Mary Robinson, one of the other contenders.

In the end, although Brian topped the poll, it was not enough to win, and Mary Robinson became President. Unfortunately this result reflected badly on Fianna Fáil. Brian was the first, and to this day the only, Fianna Fáil candidate to lose the Irish presidential election, and there were more and more mutterings that the time had come for a change of leadership.

* * *

Meanwhile I had been reappointed Minister for Finance. The economy was improving, but we still had a national debt of some IR£25 billion that meant a heavy tax burden on the public to service the interest payments. I was determined to widen and lower the tax bands again at the first opportunity. Having done that, it was up to me to make things work, to reduce public expenditure and to get the civil service working more efficiently. Business ventures were expanding, our indigenous industries of fishing, forestry and tourism were growing, and I was feeling optimistic about our future. We were about to take on the presidency of the European Community and I felt sure the 1990s would bring a new era of opportunity for Ireland.

It had been well recognized internationally and at home that my Department of Finance had done a good job in negotiating loans and in achieving a well-balanced debt portfolio, but the enormity of the national debt continued to be a huge problem. Although we had been successful in reducing the rate of increase over recent years and the debt had fallen as a percentage of GNP, interest payments alone on the IR£25 billion owed came to over IR£2.1 billion annually, which meant that each one of the 1.1 million people employed in the country was paying almost IR£2,000 per head each year out of his or her own pocket! Somehow this had to be brought down.

At that time management of the debt had become so complex and sophisticated that it became apparent we had to introduce an independent office which, with flexible management structures and suitably qualified personnel, could fully exploit the potential for savings. To this end I announced in my 1990 budget speech the introduction of a Bill to provide for the establishment of a new office to be called the National Treasury Management Agency. It was an idea put to me by Michael Somers, an investment manager working within my own department, who had proposed it to the former Minister of Finance, but it had not been taken up at the time. I thought it was a brilliant concept and it certainly proved effective.

The new agency would act on my behalf and under my control. Although my responsibility to the Dáil remained unchanged and the powers of the Minister for Finance were undiminished, the Bill enabled the government to delegate statutory borrowing and debt management functions to the agency.

At the most basic level, we could have continued servicing these huge debt costs by attempting to limit or stop the rise in our debt and indeed further reducing borrowing, but I knew that shrewd management of that debt could also yield savings and actually improve our budgetary position. The National Treasury Management Agency, or 'Auntie Mae', as it is still affectionately called in Ireland today, basically took the national debt out of the hands of government and gave the running of it to a group of professionals. They then borrowed money on behalf of the government and, with their specialist knowledge, invested it for them; they also had the power to negotiate the interest rate. It was so successful that it led to savings of more than IR£1 billion to the Irish taxpayer over five years – and continues today as one of the key agencies with the cash and the know-how to help Ireland out of the current recession.

It was during this period that I met Noel Gallagher, who was in the South on a mission to see Haughey. He was a dedicated Republican and, like so many young men in the North, he had grown up knowing only deprivation, discrimination and conflict and was desperate to see an end to the Troubles.

I was introduced to him in the Dáil restaurant by a colleague from the Senate, Willy Farrell, and I noticed he seemed fraught and anxious. He started talking about the problems in the North and said that he had a document which he had taken to Charles Haughey that conveyed some of his ideas for a way forward to get peace in the North. He was very upset at the time because apparently his document had not been well received and Haughey had told him there was nothing that he could do about it. I sat down with him and chatted about the situation and found that he was not only very knowledgeable but also well connected with some of the leading figures in the IRA. He was from Derry and good friends with Martin McGuinness – in fact, he was best man at Martin's wedding. Their wives, too, were and still are very good friends, who had grown up as neighbours.

Noel was a very decent fellow, passionate about his country and about finding a better life for his children. As we chatted we realized we both smoked the same cigarettes – and smoked a lot of them – we both drank a lot of tea and we both didn't take any alcohol. We talked about the people I knew in the North and about the border and smuggling – especially about pigs being smuggled over the border, because he knew an Orangeman who used to drive his pigs down to me in the Liberties in Dublin when I'd had my bacon factory there. But the consuming topic of conversation was politics, and we talked and talked and talked about the North, the North, the North.

Noel was and is well versed in what goes on there and whenever, over the following years, he came down to Dublin he would call in to see me for a cup of tea. I valued his friendship and his opinion, and throughout my time as Taoiseach he was often a well-informed and helpful link in introducing me to many people in the North, on both sides, who would become very active in working with me to make the peace process a success.

* * *

One of the great pleasures of that era was my first meeting with John Major. He was Chancellor of the Exchequer at the time and we met at one of the EC's regular finance meetings. We hit it off immediately, little realizing at the time how much our friendship would be tested in the years to come. He was at once easy and charming and new to the job. He admitted as much as he sat down next to me at one of the luncheons. 'And you,' he said, 'I believe you are one of the seniors here. Would you mind filling me in?'

'Well,' I answered, 'that's easy. Yes, it's very easy to fill you in here.'

'How's that?' he asked.

'Well, there are twelve countries represented here, and the best way for me to explain,' I said, 'is in racing terms. Any time there's a horse here running, it's usually up at 11 to 1, and the best I can do for you is to make it 10 to 2.'

He laughed and said it was the best and quickest introduction he had ever had. 'Can I rely on that?' he asked.

I said if I agreed with him I would, and if I didn't I wouldn't, and added that if something was important to him – and different issues would be – then I didn't mind going against a ten every now and then. The others might have a different view from me in many areas, but we agreed that if he and I could support each other in any way we would. Over the years that followed we were very fair with each other, although for me back home in Ireland at that time supporting Britain politically was not the done thing, and neither was supporting Britain against Europe – Britain was not the favoured nation at the time. Nevertheless, I'd made my own judgement about John Major and every time we met we got to trust each other more.

I learned that John Major, although a member of Margaret

Thatcher's government and consequently expected to follow her policies, was very much his own man. Thatcher was a powerful figure who expected her team to be loyal to her in a big way, and I've nothing against that, but I do know that Major was not afraid to go against her in voicing his own opinions. We became, and still are, good friends.

Meanwhile, back home Haughey was beset by even more scandals when controversies arose over malpractice in the Goodman meat plants. Larry Goodman was a good friend of Charlie's, and there were suggestions that he was involved in the granting of favoured export credit insurance. The PDs immediately reacted with condemnations and accusations and so, in an effort to avoid a possible revolt by his PD coalition partners, Haughey was forced to set up an investigatory tribunal into the whole of the Irish beef industry.

There then followed a series of resignations by chairmen of semi-state companies. One of them was Michael Smurfit, one of the country's most prominent businessmen, who had been appointed by Jack Lynch as chairman of Telecom Éireann some years earlier. He became embroiled in controversy when it was discovered that he had a share in the company which had sold the site of the new proposed headquarters in Ballsbridge to Telecom. Haughey exacerbated this crisis when in a radio interview, without consulting any of his colleagues or advisers, he suggested that Smurfit should step aside from the situation.

It was during this same interview that Haughey suddenly announced his intention to lead his party into the next election. This provoked even more dismay within the party and yet more questioning of his leadership. These voices grew even louder when another scandal erupted. This time it concerned public money that had been given to University College

Dublin to buy land belonging to Carysfort College – land that, it appeared, had been acquired a short time before by a close friend of the Taoiseach. Righteous anger raged even more when it was revealed that the purchase and sale of the land within a period of just six months had made the Taoiseach's friend a personal profit of IR£1.6 million.

Haughey was rapidly losing his grip on power and there was a definite feeling of restlessness in the party. Open pressure was finally put on him when four backbench deputies, M. J. Nolan, Noel Dempsey, Seán Power and Liam Fitzgerald, issued a statement expressing their disquiet over the handling of recent events. A parliamentary party meeting followed at which Power and Dempsey told Haughey he should go. Still he held on, narrowly defeating a motion of no confidence.

Charlie McCreevy, as outspoken as ever in his criticism of Haughey, was quick to challenge the disintegrating leadership of the party. In October 1991, in an article in the *Irish Times*, he expressed his concern about the future of Fianna Fáil:

'No more than a decade ago, the accolade of the greatest political organisation in the democratic free world was commonly ascribed to the party by friend and foe alike. Now not even the diehard of the diehard Fianna Fáiler believes such a description to be accurate. The proud boast that Fianna Fáil was not a political party but a national movement is no longer sustainable. Changing leaders will not solve the problems of Fianna Fáil. The party needs direction – any direction.'

I was continuing to lose faith in Haughey's ability to lead the party, and I had already been persuaded by a number of party members that the time had come for me to put myself forward as a candidate for the leadership. I had been asked in Cork back on 10 November 1990 if I would be a contender for the leadership in the future, and I had replied that, when the occasion arose, my hat would be in the ring. News of this had already alienated me from the Taoiseach. The tension, bordering on animosity, between us was clear when we shared the same stage at an EC summit in Rome. When asked a question about British financial policy, Haughey deliberately and maliciously responded:

'We all know that Chancellors of the Exchequer and Ministers of Finance are neurotic and exotic creatures whose political judgement is not always best.'

Things between us went from bad to worse when the government rushed into the Programme for Economic and Social Progress. This was a new agreement between the government and the social partners, who comprised union representatives and business leaders. It provided for public pay costs to rise by 10 per cent over three years. I totally disagreed with this – it was against everything I had been fighting for – and I adamantly argued against the deal, but Haughey went ahead anyway.

From then on, the gloves were off. My discontent with Haughey had been simmering for some time, and although originally I had been one of his most loyal supporters, and would always remain grateful that he had given me the opportunity of becoming a senior minister in his first cabinet, the relationship we had once shared had definitely cooled. Over the years I had not liked seeing Haughey become more and more dictatorial, and I resented the series of shotgun elections that had caused instability within the party as well as the country.

Towards the end of 1991 the relationship between the two of us had become quite acrimonious. On 6 November Seán Power, without my prior knowledge or approval, tabled another motion for the parliamentary party requesting the deputies to 'discontinue forthwith the leadership of Charles J. Haughey'. Though I believed the move was premature, I had no choice but to support it. I did not believe the motion would succeed, but I did not want to be labelled a hypocrite.

I had been out of town when I received the news of the motion being tabled. I returned to Dublin and told my close colleagues of my decision. Some tried to dissuade me, but I knew that in the interests of my own credibility there was no alternative, even though I fully realized that, having supported the motion, I would inevitably be sacked from my cabinet post.

My daughter Cathy remembers well the tensions of that difficult time:

'It was all coming to a head and there was a lot of speculation that a rebellion against Charlie Haughey was imminent. Charlie McCreevy had spoken out saying there was going to be a revolt in the party and the obvious person to lead it would be Dad.

'It was the night of the annual Fianna Fáil dinner: Mum was showering, getting ready for the event, and taking an unusually long time. Finally she called me in and told me she'd found a strange lump under her arm. Peter Staunton [the family doctor] was sent for immediately and was there within fifteen minutes. Peter didn't want to alarm us but he advised that Mum should go into hospital for tests first thing in the morning. We were all in shock, and she was scared, but she insisted that although by this time they were running late for the dinner, they had to go. They arrived late and as the speeches were about to start, as was customary, the doors were closed and my parents had to wait outside until an opportune moment arrived for them to go in. The media, of course, had a field day: every paper carried the story of how Albert and Kathleen had been deliberately locked out of the dinner.'

The whole family was frantic with worry over Kathleen as we waited anxiously for the results of the biopsy. Our worst fears were realized: it was a malignant tumour and the diagnosis was breast cancer.

The news was devastating, hard to take in, and no matter how many doctors or friends assured us of the high success rate in combating breast cancer, the fear never left us. Kathleen as always remained strong and insisted that nothing must change and life must go on. She was determined she would beat it and she prayed to her special saint, St Rita.

Suddenly the future was uncertain, but Kathleen's support for me and the family never wavered. She was adamant that everything had to go on as usual and I must not back off from what I believed was right. I had little heart now for the fight that lay ahead – it all seemed so insignificant in the face of Kathleen's diagnosis – but she insisted that I must summon up my courage and go for it.

I had no option but to stand up and be counted. I issued the following statement:

'For some time now there has been considerable political instability which has led to an erosion of confidence in our democratic institutions. This uncertainty must not be allowed to continue. The well-being of our country requires strong and decisive leadership of government and of the Fianna Fáil party. I am not satisfied that such a leadership now exists. In the circumstances I will be supporting the motion tabled for the party next Saturday.'

As I had anticipated, my support for the motion of no confidence led Haughey to demand my resignation from the cabinet; and when I refused he sacked me, along with my supporters Flynn, Geoghegan-Quinn, Brendan Smith and Noel Treacy.

The announcement to the Dáil of the termination of my

appointment led to uproar. Proinsias de Rossa forcefully argued that it was unprecedented for a Taoiseach to sack within twelve months both his Minister for Finance and his Tánaiste, while Jim Mitchell demanded to know, following the motion to be debated, what other ministerial resignations would add to the disarray of the government.

I knew the timing for my move was not right and that we did not have the numbers we needed. I knew too that, when the time came to vote, many TDs who had encouraged me to make a move would be too fearful of ending up on the losing side and would remain supporting Haughey.

The meeting to debate the motion, on 9 November, went on long into the early hours of the morning. Pádraig Flynn made an impassioned speech, as did McCreevy and others, all expressing their great belief in the ideals of Fianna Fáil and their fears at what it had become under Haughey's leadership.

Haughey remained present throughout the entire procedure. In his closing speech he said he would not be there for ever and wished only to see through upcoming important European Community business. As I had anticipated, he defeated the motion of no confidence, by fifty-five to twenty-two. TDs who had sworn their allegiance to the motion so recently, and had denounced Haughey so vehemently, at the last minute rose up to sing his praises. There were many others who told me it would not be too long before another occasion arose and that when it did they would be there to support me.

I had stood up along with the others for what we believed had to be the only way forward if the reputation of the party was to survive. We had lost the motion but not the fight, and we knew that Haughey's control was crumbling.

That night Charlie McCreevy, Pádraig Flynn and the usual gang all came back to the apartment. There was a great feeling of anger, not just because I'd been sacked there and then but also because my state car had been confiscated immediately and I had had to get a lift home.

The family were stalwart as ever in gathering round Kathleen and me during that black time. And there were always times to make you smile, as Miriam recalls:

'Knowing Dad was to be sacked we'd all gathered, in the way that we do whenever there's a crisis or a good time, so we piled into Dublin and decided we'd put on a brave face and go for lunch. We all believed Dad had done the right thing and we were proud of him even though we were gutted for him too, so we all went for lunch in Jury's Hotel. We were sitting there when the late Ronnie Drew, lead singer of The Dubliners, passed us by on his way to his table and Dad looked up and said, "Ah Ronnie, have you e'er a job?" and Ronnie said, "You could try singing, I got away with it!"'

And Cathy tells this one:

'Friends were great. They knew things were bad but they kept your spirits up and made you laugh. I remember the day after Dad was fired as Minister of Finance – they handed me the jobs pages and offered me my bus fare home!'

There are some times in your life you don't want to remember, desperate days of worry and empty days when the one you love is not there. This was where my children took over for a while. As Emer recalls:

'Then Mum went into hospital and had the operation for breast cancer and I remember us all saying, if Dad was still in a ministerial role instead of just a TD, he wouldn't be able to be with her. She was always there for him and incredibly strong, now this was her time to be cared for.'

It was the worst time, the darkest time. But then the chemo worked, the lymph nodes were removed and the diagnosis that Kathleen would be fine, though hard to believe at the time, proved to be right.

The world of politics moved on, and although I was out of power I was still in touch with what was happening. In place of Flynn and myself, Haughey, instead of promoting two junior ministers to the two senior vacant positions, had taken the unusual step of appointing two backbench TDs, Noel Davern to Education and Jim McDaid to Defence. This provoked yet another government crisis when it was revealed by the Workers Party that McDaid had been photographed a year earlier by the side of a leading IRA man, James Pius Clarke, one of his constituents, and other anti-extradition campaigners, outside the Supreme Court after a request for Clarke's extradition had been defeated. McDaid made it clear that it may have been insensitive but he nevertheless supported the government's policy on extradition. However, following O'Malley's demand for a meeting with the government McDaid decided, in order to defuse the situation, that he had no choice but to resign. Again the result was upset and anger among the party members, for McDaid had actually done nothing wrong: but Haughey, instead of supporting his man, once again had simply caved in to the PDs' intervention.

Then came the *Nighthawks* revelation.

Ray Burke, Minister for Justice, had just published a Bill dealing with legislation to govern phone-tapping. It was by now ten years since one of his predecessors in that post, Seán Doherty, had taken responsibility for the phone-tapping of two journalists, Geraldine Kennedy and Bruce Arnold, and had been forced to resign. Doherty had spent the intervening years in the political backwaters, but by this time he was Cathaoirleach to the Seánad, and in order to avoid the embarrassing duty of presenting the new Bill to the Seánad he asked Ray Burke to either withdraw it or defer its publication. Burke refused. This obviously put Doherty in a predicament, which angered him. In any case it seems that Doherty had decided it was time to come back into mainstream politics and time for the truth to come out. The opportunity came in an interview for RTE's *Nighthawks* programme, when he was asked about his version of the phone-tapping affair. He replied that as Minister for Justice he'd had a job to do which was to stop matters leaking from cabinet. He added, somewhat significantly, that 'people' knew what he was doing. He expanded on this some time later, calling a press conference at which he gave a clear statement: 'I am confirming tonight that the Taoiseach, Mr Haughey, was fully aware in 1982 that two journalists' phones were being tapped and that he at no stage expressed a reservation about this action.' He went even further and claimed that he had given transcripts of the taped conversations to Haughey himself.

Haughey, of course, denied all knowledge of this and made some spurious claim that it was all part of some plot thought up by my supporters. He convinced no one. For the PDs it was the opportunity they had been waiting for: they called an emergency meeting and declared their withdrawal of support from the Haughey government. Charlie's position was now untenable, and a week later, at a Fianna Fáil party meeting, he announced his decision to step down from the leadership. The Haughey era was over.

The timing could have been better, but, with the blessing of Kathleen and my family, my name went forward as a contender for the leadership along with those of Mary O'Rourke and Dr Michael Woods.

As David Andrews, former Fianna Fáil TD and my good friend and supporter, recalls in his autobiography:

'Albert Reynolds was the leading contender and there was a

very strong flow of support from the main body of the party for him. Having resigned his portfolio his hand was strengthened even further. It was John Wilson and I who were the first, I believe, to suggest at the time that the "dream team" to lead the party would be Reynolds as leader and Bertie Ahern as his deputy, the implication being that the latter would succeed to the leadership with Reynolds' retirement in the normal course of events.

'I was very pro-Albert. It wasn't that I had anything against Bertie. I felt his time had not yet come. I also felt that he was more closely associated with Haughey than Albert had been. My belief was that Albert's time had come and he deserved his chance.'

Bertie, too, was happy to wait. I had already given him my word that my stay would be a limited one, at the most six years, and that when he was ready I would support him as the one to take over as leader.

My loyal band of campaigners worked long hours drumming up votes from the party deputies, and the other contenders too fought vigorously and well.

The vote was held on 6 February 1992. My family and friends from Longford were out in force and filled the visitors' bar. When the vote was called – Reynolds sixty-one, Woods ten, O'Rourke six – there was a roar of cheering from the crowd. Under cover of the celebrations I escaped home to tell Kathleen the good news.

Then I went back to Jury's Hotel and my first press conference as leader of Fianna Fáil.

8

BAPTISM OF FIRE

On the evening of Albert's press conference, which lasted from 5.30 to 6.30 p.m., the Angelus bells, broadcast by RTE at 6.00 p.m. every evening to call all good Catholics to prayer, were silent for the first and only time in their history as the nation listened to Albert's speech.

Derek Cobbe

In my first press conference as leader, on 6 February 1992, I expressed the objectives I hoped to achieve in my tenure as Taoiseach, however long or short that term might be. The first and of prime importance was peace in Northern Ireland; the second, to develop the economy; the third, to reduce unemployment and emigration.

People were surprised, shocked even; they had expected me to talk about the economy, but not of my concern for Northern Ireland. True, apart from the position I had taken over the Anglo-Irish Agreement in 1985, I had never commented on the problems of Northern Ireland – but that was normal procedure: in government it was always understood and accepted that only the Taoiseach spoke on Northern Ireland affairs. However, through my life in business I had gained a very good grounding in attitudes in the North, I had friends and colleagues there across the religious spectrum, and I understood their thinking and concerns. In my time in government, as Minister for Posts and Telegraphs and Transport, I had attempted in whatever way I could to build relations between North and South. I had introduced the RTE booster stations, established air routes between Dublin and Derry, and greatly improved our communications system.

This was what I tried to put across in my speech to the press and to the people on that first night: the background to my way of thinking, the influences and initiatives that had made me put peace in Northern Ireland at the top of my agenda.

Since 1969, I explained, all the outside world was seeing of Ireland was bombs and bullets. It didn't matter that it was in the North: as far as the world was concerned it was Ireland, the island as a whole. Yet here were we trying to develop an economy where tourism and inward investment were important. Who was going to holiday in a place where there was trouble, where atrocities were being committed every day of the week? Who was going to invest in a country that hadn't a solid political position? That's why I wanted peace in Ireland, I said. Whatever it took, that's where I was going. If I get that, I added, whenever I get it, it will inject investment into the country, investment will create jobs, emigration numbers will fall, and so will unemployment.

We had a wonderful university system, I told them, and alongside that we had developed another, technological, education system, one that put us at the forefront of the fast-developing world of technology, an asset that would make us even more attractive for investment. All we needed now was peace on our island and a solid political foundation.

People thought I was mad – so many had tried before – but I believed it was imperative to make it work.

The world of business looking for investment had a choice: continental Europe or Ireland. We had one great advantage over the other countries – we spoke English. We were also the first stopping point for American overseas development, but the trouble in the North was a big minus factor. Asking American high-fliers to come over here and invest their money when you have all that trouble just up the road is not a good sales pitch.

That was where I was coming from – a financial, invest-ment and technological viewpoint – and I knew that there were many in the North who understood that way of thinking and that they too wanted peace, and I'd made up my mind I was not going to fail.

Kathleen was weak, recovering from her operation and undergoing chemotherapy, but as always she selflessly en-couraged me in all I hoped to achieve as Taoiseach. However, I was very aware of her condition and I wanted her close to me and cared for, so she moved from Longford to be with me in the apartment in Dublin.

It was time to get on with the job. One of the final duties of an outgoing Taoiseach is to brief his successor in the political scene, so Charlie Haughey fulfilled his task. His briefing was exactly that: brief, efficient and to the point. He was ever the professional. On the subject of Northern Ireland, all he had to say was: 'Ask Mansergh.'

Martin Mansergh had been a highly valued and loyal adviser to Haughey throughout his leadership, and indeed had fought valiantly on his behalf during the recent leadership battle. He was a well-known figure in Leinster House and we had chatted socially on many occasions. He had been a power-ful influence behind the scenes in Fianna Fáil and was generally acknowledged for his fine intellect and commitment to the Republican ideals of the party, particularly on policy concerning Northern Ireland. I learned that he had already, at Haughey's request, had two covert meetings with members of Sinn Féin in 1988, although this was denied at the time. I knew that if we were to make progress towards peace he was a good choice for my team. I asked him to join me as an adviser and he agreed. It was not a hard decision for Mansergh – even though he had served with Charlie for a long time, his loyalty to Fianna Fáil was paramount and his dedication in bringing peace to Northern Ireland unshakeable. As Seán Duignan, who joined me as government press secretary, remarked, 'The Taoiseach clearly regarded Mansergh as a most valuable adviser. I soon noticed that, although they might not see eye to eye on issues such as the economy or whatever, they seemed to think almost as one on Northern Ireland.'

Other changes in government were to follow. I wanted new people. I had nothing personal against some of those I asked to leave – they had served their country and done their jobs – and I knew that it was unusual to change so many personnel, but most of them had been friends of Haughey for many years, even before my time, and their loyalty lay with him.

There had been bad blood between Haughey and me at the end, and I knew that I was unlikely to get 100 per cent commitment from his old followers. Also, with some of them – not all of them, of course – I felt their day was done: I was a man with things to do and I wanted people in government who would do things with me. It was time to inject new blood into the party, to bring in people who would restore faith in the party, people who were ready to fight the challenges that lay ahead and ready to initiate the changes necessary to move Ireland forward in the modern world.

There were also people who were just too valuable to lose.

People like Dermot Nally, secretary to the government for twenty years, an astute and highly respected government official, a dignified man who had served under the last three Taoisigh, Haughey, FitzGerald and Lynch, guiding them through a number of crises. He was almost at retirement age, but his experience was vital and after some persuasion he agreed to stay on. Then there was Bart Cronin, who had handled press for me in Industry and Commerce and then Finance, and knew me well – sometimes too well. I appointed him head of the Government Information Office. And there was Tom Savage, my communications adviser, a trusted colleague who had served me well and who brought on board Seán Duignan, a former RTE political correspondent, as government press secretary.

Bertie Ahern remained as Minister for Finance, but I also chose some new ministers, among them men who had been strongly critical of Haughey, such as Charlie McCreevy, David Andrews and Seamus Brennan. I also promoted promising younger TDs like Brian Cowen and Noel Dempsey.

I'd met Cowen's father, Ber Cowen, when I first entered the Dáil in 1977. He was the Fianna Fáil TD for Laois–Offaly and like me his passion was politics. In fact he'd stayed with me at my apartment in Ballsbridge, and we'd been up all hours talking politics, the night before he so unexpectedly died. I'd left before my dear friend early the next morning and it wasn't until the evening that I heard he had collapsed while attending a convention in Tullamore. I rushed straight to St Vincent's Hospital and it was there I first met his three sons, who were clinging on to the hope that he would survive and were distraught when he died so suddenly. He was just a week short of his fifty-second birthday. Brian was twenty-four and had just qualified as a solicitor, but his father's death changed everything: he contested Ber's seat and entered politics.

Because of his father, I'd kept an eye on him and we became family friends.

Brian had inherited his father's political awareness, and he impressed me. I had observed him for a number of years since canvassing with him in his by-election in 1984. I thought he was very talented and showed a great deal of potential. He was still young when I brought him into my first cabinet, in his early thirties, and by rights should have first served in a junior ministerial role: but I played my hunch, decided to give him an early chance and appointed him Minister for Labour. I was not disappointed and neither was anybody else. He is now Taoiseach and leader of Fianna Fáil.

Obviously, I also brought close party allies into my new government, among them Pádraig Flynn, Máire Geoghegan-Quinn and Michael Smith.

I spent some days considering whom I wanted by my side and whom I would have to ask to leave. It was not easy, but it was necessary, even though I knew there would be resentment from many of the old guard. What I was about to do was unprecedented. I knew it would cause uproar and I also knew that it would make enemies. The changes I was about to make were drastic and went against all the traditions of Fianna Fáil, which was used to people holding on to their ministerial positions and remaining in power for a very long time. I wanted to bring a new public face to the operation, a new team who would best suit the objectives I had in mind for my new administration. True, I might lose continuity and there would be political fallout; but I was prepared to risk that to have the right people around me.

Before I left Government Buildings to go to Áras an Uachtaráin I gave my secretary, Donagh Morgan, a long list of names of senior and junior ministers I wished to see on my return. Many on the list were well-known figures. Donagh reminded me there would only be half an hour before I was due to lead my cabinet into the Dáil, and presumed I wanted to see them all together. I told him I would see them individually.

It was all over in fifteen minutes. I called them in one by one and I said, 'You won't be appointed, thank you.' And they went out, most of them too shocked even to question me. It was all so fast I could have done with a revolving door!

Only two queried my decision, Mary O'Rourke and Dermot Ahern, who asked me: Why? Why was I doing it to them? I told them quite simply: 'Nothing personal, you just backed the wrong horse!'

The press and the media had a field day – they nicknamed me the 'Longford Slasher' after our famous football team, 'The Longford Slashers'. Fair enough!

It was Seán Duignan's first day as my personal press man, a hard initiation, as he wrote in his diary:

'You'll never see the likes of that ever, in British or Irish or even European politics. That morning, I remember it was my first day at work, imagine the shock. Albert Reynolds had succeeded Charles Haughey. Now Haughey was legendary as being ruthless and tough, people quaked even being in his company, but Charlie was a pussycat in that he never fired anybody. Albert Reynolds comes in and the whole place was in shock.'

He also warned: 'The other thing I would add to that, if you're going to do something like that you have got to be sure that when they're down, they stay down and they don't crawl off into the long grass, and that may have been the only problem for Albert, that they kind of existed out there and naturally gravitated over to Bertie's [Ahern's] wing of the house. Albert had fired them, so they moved over to Bertie's side and to that extent they were waiting.'

In fact, even at my first Árd Fheis, Bertie's people were gathered in a pub in Ballsbridge, already canvassing my removal.

It was all just beginning.

The evening before I led my new government into the Dáil, Des O'Malley, the leader of our coalition partners the PDs, came to see me at the Berkeley Court Hotel to discuss their position in the new government. I had informed him of the cabinet changes and we had agreed he would hold on to his two members of government as before, when he suddenly raised the question of the Harry Whelehan situation and asked if I was aware that Harry, in his capacity as Attorney General, was involved in a case with the High Court? It was the first I'd heard of it. Certainly in his briefing to me Charlie Haughey hadn't mentioned it, although it is hard to believe he wasn't party to such information; neither had the Attorney General himself, but then he had no need to inform me because until I was officially appointed Taoiseach it was not the usual practice that I should be included in such government confidences.

It was to prove a baptism of fire.

Abortion was the all-time dividing issue in Irish politics. Abortion in Ireland was already illegal; however, in the early 1980s, following a limited liberalization of the laws on contraception, and the introduction of a relaxed federal law in the United States, there was concern that such laxity could be introduced into the Irish constitution. This led to a heated debate in Ireland and a call from the pro-life lobby for a constitutional guarantee on the right to life of the unborn child.

Neither Haughey nor FitzGerald was happy about a

constitutional referendum, but the matter blew up in pre-general-election time and both bowed to lobbying pressure by conceding that an amendment to the constitution would be sought.

The draft amendment was published, reading: 'The State acknowledges the right to life of the unborn and, with due regard to the equal rights of the mother, guarantees in its laws to respect and, as far as practicable, by its laws to defend and vindicate that right.'

There were many who argued against this wording, but as no alternative was found it went to a referendum and was passed by the people. It was incorporated into the constitution in 1983, as Article 40.3.3.

My first day at Government Buildings in Merrion Street, the storm over the 'X Case' broke and I was briefed. It was my first cabinet meeting and this was not the way I had wanted to start, but as Charlie McCreevy recalls:

'That first real cabinet meeting I remember Albert saying, "Before we go on to any other business, the Attorney General has something to tell us." And Harry Whelehan, the Attorney General, explained the history of the 'X girl', as she was called:

'I remember clearly turning to Michael Smith, a close friend of mine, and saying, "Jesus, Mick, I know this is going to haunt us." The ramifications of the "X Case" on abortion followed us throughout Albert's government and on into one of Bertie's [Ahern's] governments. That whole period with Albert, it was there in the background.'

My heart sank as I listened to the Attorney General that first day.

A fourteen-year-old girl, raped by a family acquaintance, had become pregnant. Her distraught parents, having reported the crime to the Gardaí, left Ireland for England where abortion was legal. On their arrival, the responsible parents called the Gardaí investigating the case against the father of the unborn child, to enquire whether or not the foetal remains should be saved as evidence for investigative purposes.

The Gardaí immediately informed the Attorney General, Harry Whelehan, who, following the letter of the law, sought a High Court injunction forbidding the abortion and ordered the immediate return of the family. They complied.

Now, it was well known that hundreds of Irish women made their way to England for abortions every year, but Harry was the Attorney General and he had a constitutional role to follow. The political fallout that followed had us all reeling.

The family appealed to the Supreme Court, pleading that the girl was threatening to commit suicide and quoting the equal right to life of the mother.

The Supreme Court overturned the injunction by a majority of four to one. The majority opinion held that a woman had a right to an abortion under Article 40.3.3 if there was a 'real and substantial risk' to her life. This did not apply if it was a risk to her health, only if it was a risk to her life, and that included the possibility of suicide. In fact the girl in the X Case suffered a miscarriage shortly after this judgment, but we were left sinking in a political quagmire.

The referendum on the Maastricht Treaty was looming and it was vital that the result was a resounding 'Yes'. However, the previous Haughey-led government had fought hard for the inclusion of a specific anti-abortion protocol for Ireland to make it 100 per cent certain that abortion could never be introduced into the state, either now or under any future EU law, thus ensuring that nothing could affect the application of Article 40.3.3.

However, Article 40.3.3 had now more or less been

overturned by the Supreme Court judgment. Now it was possible under certain defined circumstances to have an abortion, even though the rights to travel and information were still restricted.

The laws on abortion were complicated, but the urgency of the impending 'X Case' meant I had to study and grasp their complexities practically overnight. I was determined that I was not going to fall at the first fence. The question of abortion has always raised passions to fever pitch in Ireland, a Catholic country, and it always will. Now the government was caught right in the middle of a serious moral dilemma and in my new position as Taoiseach, inasmuch as I could, I had to become an authority on the subject.

A new addendum was written, ordaining that the protocol could not limit travel between EC member states or the obtaining of information lawfully available in member states. It was submitted to the EC Council of Ministers, who said 'No!' to this convoluted and overcomplicated proposition.

All hell broke loose. People, media, the Church all joined in. I was besieged by opinions of every passionate persuasion, from bishops to pop stars – and not just from the people of Ireland: half the world was only too eager to get in on the act. We were accused of taking Ireland 'back to the dark ages'. An editorial in the *Irish Times* on Tuesday, 18 February 1992, entitled 'Descent into Cruelty', asked:

'What has been done to this Irish Republic? What kind of State has it become that in 1992, its full panoply of authority, its police, its law officers, its courts are mobilised to condemn a 14-year-old girl to the ordeal of pregnancy and child birth after rape at the hands of a "depraved and evil man"? With what are we now to compare ourselves? Ceauşescu's Romania? The Ayatollah's Iran? Algeria? There are similarities.'

Passions were raised and criticism poured down on the government even from Catholics within our own party. The pressure from the bishops was immense – they were vociferous in their disapproval – but it wasn't just the establishment hierarchy who joined in: there were liberals and women journalists all on the pro-liberal wing, the pro-choice as well as the pro-life, traditional Catholics – even some of my own deputies joined in the tirade against me and what I was doing. I took them all on.

To compensate for the refusal to accept our amendment, Brussels came up with what it called a Solemn Declaration. In fact it gave the same assurances on travel and information restrictions as our addendum but it was written in a slightly different way and it satisfied their needs.

I proposed that the referendum vote on this change to our constitution be taken after the Maastricht referendum vote. It was a risk, but a calculated risk. I wanted the vote on Maastricht to be clear and understood, to stand on its own merits, unencumbered by any argument about abortion. That was for another day. It was imperative for our future that Ireland ratified the vote with a 'Yes'.

Our coalition partners, the PDs, disagreed. As far as I was concerned, they had effectively offered no support throughout the crisis and I expected none now. Des O'Malley was adamant that the referendums should be taken in the opposite order. The government agreed otherwise, by majority. It was telling at that time that Mary Harney, one of the founding members of the PDs, remarked that the abortion row would not bring down the government. However, I suspected it would not be long before the PDs tried again.

There was opposition from certain members of my own party, but it was limited. Senator Des Hanafin, chairman of the pro-life campaign, was most vocal and marshalled many conservative-thinking party members against concessions on abortion under any circumstances; but when, as Fianna Fáil party whip, he voted against the Maastricht referendum Bill in the upper house, a parliamentary party motion to have the party whip removed from him was overwhelmingly carried. And the bishops went a step too far when on 14 April at the Catholic Bishops' Conference they declared that they had noted with alarm that the right to life of the unborn child 'does not appear to be on the Government's agenda at the present time'.

Such irresponsible, inflammatory rhetoric could not be ignored. After all the heartache and the personal moral dilemma I had wrestled with over the past few weeks as a devoted and practising Catholic, especially as I was also the father of five daughters, I was totally incensed at their uninformed insensitivity and expressed my outrage in no uncertain terms. They immediately retracted with defensive responses and excuses. It seemed that several of them had not been present when the statement was drafted and they agreed that it had been an exaggerated response.

It took the sensational affair of the Bishop of Galway, Dr Eamonn Casey, to really turn them around. Dr Casey was forced to resign after admitting that he had enjoyed a lengthy relationship with an American divorcee, Annie Murphy, fathered a son with her and used more than IR£70,000 of Galway diocesan funds to support them both. A week after this exposé the bishops issued a statement which modified their position and which we welcomed as 'recognition of the practical difficulties and complexities of the situation'. In other words, they now accepted that ratification of Maastricht did not equate with the introduction of abortion in Ireland.

I may have had very strong personal views on abortion but I did not get involved in any moral judgement where the bishop was concerned, although the whole of Ireland was shocked at the downfall of such a prominent and outspoken figure in the Church hierarchy. Dr Casey was popular and respected as a progressive church leader, and his resignation was seen as pivotal in the decline of the considerable influence of the Catholic Church over society and politics in Ireland. However, for me religion is a personal thing and I leave others to follow their faith as they decide. I cared only that the bishop was a devout man and that following the scandal he had become a missionary in Ecuador. He was also a champion of various charities and was exemplary in his work with the homeless in London and in helping Irish emigrants in Britain. Years later the people of Ireland forgave him and in 2006 he returned to live in Galway.

We were caught in a maelstrom of conflicting views. The PDs were still insisting on alternative dates for the referendum and Maastricht, plus they produced alternative wording to the addendum, but it went nowhere. Then, on 2 June, when the Danes voted by 50 per cent to 49 per cent to reject the Maastricht Treaty, the pressure grew even greater for me to postpone the 18 June vote. Even Jacques Delors, the Commission President, called in panic. The anti-Maastricht campaigners saw it as vindication of all their arguments, but I was convinced we could not afford to reject this opportunity of being part of the bigger European picture and I believed the majority of the Irish people were with me and would agree.

Then came 18 June and the vote confirmed it: 69 per cent 'Yes', 31 per cent 'No'.

The pro-lifers exulted that the way was now clear for the next referendum on travel and information relating to abortion, and that they fully expected the result to humiliate the government. At about this time a Kilkenny rapist walked free after being given a good character reference during his arraignment. The nineteen-year-old girl he had attacked, far from hiding behind her right to anonymity, had come out to publicize her outrage and anger that such an aggressor should go free while she, the victim, still suffered from his despicable savagery. Women across Ireland rose as one to express their horror and disbelief at the judgment and took to the streets in their thousands in support of the girl and to proclaim that they would no longer cower in silent disgrace in the face of rape.

It had been a difficult initiation into my life as Taoiseach, and things had not been that easy at home either. Kathleen had moved back to Hazeldene where some members of the family were living and was slowly recovering from cancer, but the effects of the chemo were debilitating. Thankfully the family rallied round and Miriam came home from Edinburgh to help. In fact the girls, those who lived at home, took it in turns to accompany me to the various formal occasions that were part of my agenda as Taoiseach, even though sometimes it broke into their social life.

But as Kathleen grew stronger she accompanied me to certain social events, even though she was still in chemo and having to wear a wig. On one particular night we were all dressed up to go to a State Dinner. As usual, she had cooked dinner for the family before leaving and then, despite being dressed in her finery, insisted on checking on the meal in the oven. When she popped her head up the wig was completely singed. She simply handed me the scissors and told me to cut off the burnt bit! Then we swept off to the ball. She was amazing!

It was a long-standing policy of Fianna Fáil that we would never go into coalition. I had personally fought against it following the result of the 1989 election, when Haughey had agreed to share government with the PDs, and I had not endeared myself to them when on another occasion I had referred to the coalition as 'a temporary little arrangement'. There was also a shared antipathy on a personal level between Des O'Malley and me that went back some years, to around the time Jack Lynch had announced his retirement and Des O'Malley was one of those planning to declare for the leadership. It was the Sunday before the Fianna Fáil party meeting. O'Malley had arranged to meet with me at the house of a mutual friend where he asked if he could rely on my support. I was off to London that day and was not even sure if I would be back for the party meeting, but I was completely honest with him and told him that I would not be supporting him but that I wished him the best of luck. Of course he was annoyed; I could have said, as did so many others, that I would consider it, but I preferred to be direct. I could not support him because I did not believe he had the right personality to bring people with him and I didn't think that would be good for the party. For me he was the wrong man for the job.

As a member of Fianna Fáil, O'Malley had challenged Haughey for the leadership on a number of occasions and he had strongly criticized many of his decisions – so much so that eventually the whip was removed from him and he left Fianna Fáil to form and lead a new party, the Progressive Democrats.

In 1989 the PDs, inflated with ambition by their success at the polls, had been determined to get their pound of flesh from the deal over coalition and had forced Haughey, bound by his efforts to maintain his hold on power, to give in time and again to their demands. He had sacked his Tánaiste, Brian Lenihan, dropped his nominee for Minister of Defence, Jim McDaid, and in the end had been ousted himself as leader. My head was going to be next.

I knew when we went into partnership it was going to be

difficult. I told O'Malley plainly that it was clear he had no respect for me because I had refused to vote for him, but that was the way it was. I sensed from the very beginning that our relationship was already too soured for the coalition to survive for long. I guessed it would be a very rocky road and it was. I knew too that they would never support me in what I had in mind: my ambition to see peace in the North, and to that end to encourage Sinn Féin to a ceasefire.

It seemed to me the PDs were determined to bring down the coalition – Mary Harney had implied as much during the abortion debacle. Anti-Fianna Fáil feeling was demonstrated at every opportunity. They were just waiting for the right excuse.

As a partnership government we were still struggling to get the economy moving forward. The 'national recovery pro-gramme' that had been in place since 1987 was doing fine, but we were not getting enough economic growth; we were getting some but not enough! The country was starting to recover, our new telecommunications system had made a big difference, our infrastructure was improving and foreign investment was beginning to have an effect, yet despite all this unemployment remained high.

I insisted that schemes, activation programmes, were set up to get people back working. I was adamant we had to drive our high unemployment figures down. Looking back, it seems every debate, every meeting was governed by the need to get new ideas and approaches in play that could hack back those figures and change the balance, to get economic growth up and unemployment down.

The reason this problem was so hard to solve was that although competitiveness was slowly coming back into the economy, it was still taking time for that activity to generate a situation where people felt confident enough to actually expand their businesses. For the most part they were still hanging on, locked in survival mode, afraid to plunge into the necessary adjustments needed to make real progress.

As Brian Cowen, now Taoiseach, then Minister for Labour, reflects: 'On economic terms the government was OK and policy positions were coherent. It was the dynamics of the government that changed the most with tribunals and differences of opinion.'

The Beef Tribunal, which was to bedevil me throughout my years as Taoiseach, gave the PDs the opportunity they were looking for to bring down the government.

The tribunal had been instigated by the PDs, against fierce Fianna Fáil opposition, as a means of bringing down Haughey. In the Dáil, Des O'Malley, backed by his PD Deputy Pat O'Malley, had repeatedly charged Fianna Fáil with displaying favouritism in their allocation of export credit insurance to the Goodman beef empire. It was further alleged that Haughey had abused his position as Taoiseach, in that Larry Goodman was his close friend. However, as Haughey pointed out in a speech in the Dáil on 24 May 1991, when he announced that a tribunal would be established to examine the many and serious allegations made in the house and on a recent television programme in regard to the beef processing industry, the beef export credit insurance debacle in fact went back many years to 1982, when a coalition led by Fine Gael was in power:

'During the debate in this house on 15th May 1991, Deputy Spring said that he had been told by a number of sources that Mr Goodman had been guaranteed immunity from civil prosecution as part of his settlement with the banks, and from criminal prosecution. I want to state categorically that no such immunity can be given or was given by any member of the Government or by the Government collectively as part of his settlement with the banks or in any other connection . . .

'For a number of years now one of the most persistent and venomous political campaigns ever has been waged in an attempt to discredit the Government over the affairs of the Goodman companies. The whole basis of this attack is by innuendo and association, to create the impression that Mr Goodman and his companies enjoyed some unique and ill-defined protective relationship with the Fianna Fáil Government of 1987–89, a kind of relationship that they did not have with the previous Fine Gael–Labour Coalition Government. Nothing could be further from the truth as the records clearly show.

'One of the very first decisions of the Fine Gael–Labour Coalition Government on coming into office in late December 1982 was to grant export credit insurance for the first time in respect of beef exports to Iraq to Mr Goodman's company, Anglo-Irish Meats Limited. Concerns were expressed at the time about the unacceptable financial risk in the middle of the Iran–Iraq war, but these were overruled. Incidentally, this was done on the basis of a proposal put to the Government by the Minister for Trade, Commerce and Tourism, the late Deputy Frank Cluskey, former leader of the Labour Party. It will be noted that the decision was made in favour of one particular meat exporting company, Mr Larry Goodman's AIBP.

'And it was actually only six months later in June that a general scheme was put in place for export credit insurance in respect of trade to Iraq. I wish to make it clear that I am not criticising the Government of that time for doing what they did in acting for the benefit of a single company belonging to Mr Goodman. It is the sort of difficult decision that a Government in the best interests of the economy may have to take from time to time. What I wish to do however is point up the double standards being employed by the people who have been making the allegations now for some time . . .

'The views of the last Fine Gael–Labour Government are clearly set out by the then Minister for Industry, Trade, Commerce and Tourism, Deputy John Bruton, in a letter to the Minister for Finance of 27th May 1985 proposing a further increase in export credit insurance to Iraq. I quote:

' "My disposition is to do what we can to help exports to Iraq. There is no doubt but that Iraq will be a very good market in due course – assuming they win the war and that the war does not go on indefinitely and that they sooner or later manage to complete the oil pipeline outlets. They will certainly remember the countries which have stood by them and this has been a factor which has influenced many countries to offer them financial, military and other support in such large amounts. I believe we have developed a particular relationship with Iraq and that they have been consciously putting business our way. I believe also that this accounts for their excellent repayment record."

'The House will also recall that the Fine Gael Minister for Agriculture, Deputy Austin Deasy accompanied Mr Goodman to Iran in February 1984 to help secure an IR£80 million beef contract. The following year Deputy Deasy as Minister for Agriculture . . . was flown out to Egypt specially at Mr Goodman's invitation to set the political wheels in motion with the Egyptians.

'. . . We have heard a lot of misleading talk about the cancellation of export credit insurance by the Fine Gael–Labour Government in June '86 with the implication that somewhere they had lost faith in the Goodman group. This was not in fact the case. What we have not heard about is that there was first a decision by that Fine Gael–Labour Government to double export credit insurance to Iraq in February '86. Coincidentally or not, the then Taoiseach,

Deputy Garret FitzGerald had a luncheon meeting with Mr Goodman shortly afterwards on 17 February, at which export credit insurance was identified as one of the subjects of discussion.

'...The record clearly shows that, contrary to all the false propaganda, when Fianna Fáil came into office in '87 we did not bring Larry Goodman in from the cold and place him and his companies in some new specially favoured position as has been so often suggested. He was already inside in a very favoured position and had been since 1982. For the entire period of the 1982–87 Fine Gael–Labour Government, Mr Goodman had a close personal working relationship with individual members of that Government and especially the head of that Government, Dr FitzGerald, the Taoiseach. Again I am not prepared to attach any blame or odium to the Fine Gael–Labour Government for that situation. I accept that they desired, just as we did, to promote the Irish beef industry for the benefit of the nation, and to help farmers and those working in the meat business. But they should not now try to distort the record and attribute blame to a Fianna Fáil Government for a policy they themselves had resolutely implemented.'

Despite such unequivocal exposition and evidence there is no doubt the scandal tainted Haughey, but he left office before the tribunal had time to really get under way. O'Malley, however, had already made it clear that he had no intention of shirking a Beef Tribunal hearing, be it with Haughey or anyone else. And the anyone else would be me!

True, I was Minister for Industry and Commerce at the time and my department had handled insurance for exports. Beef was an important source of revenue for Ireland and it was our responsibility to protect those who were exporting it, especially when it was going to countries like Iran and Iraq, both very volatile at the time but nevertheless important markets for the industry. Among the biggest exporters at that time were Goodman International and Hibernia Meats, so they were justifiably covered by the beef export credit scheme, but as far as I was concerned they were no more favoured than anyone else.

What incensed me was O'Malley's unproven assertion that these two companies had received special benefit above all others – and his even more inflammatory claim that in some cases the operation of the beef export credit scheme represented a fraud on the taxpayer.

The problem was, as Brian Cowen now says of that time:

'The tribunal started to dominate the politics of the place. It was affecting all that was going on in parliament. It was simply a very major distraction in some respects from getting on with the job. Nowadays, unfortunately, we still have a few tribunals, but at least they are not dominating the work of government; then they did. It was a big political story and people were allowed to generate ideas and theories about what was happening, and how this or that came about. It became something that eroded the trust and confidence that is necessary for a coherent government to continue.'

It was a complex case that few people could understand. The press didn't seem to try: they cast me as the bad guy and went in en masse in a feeding frenzy, which poor Seán Duignan, as my personal press secretary, had to combat. 'Diggy' recalls this time in his book *One Spin on the Merry-Go-Round*:

'My main headache . . . was an inability to sufficiently grasp the more arcane aspects of the sorry saga. This contrasted with Reynolds' own capacity for fathoming the essence of any report, analysis or submission pertaining to the case. As Bart [Cronin] put it: "He can go on for ages about what might appear some abstruse points of detail, but they are all part of a jigsaw, and he knows every piece" . . . However, Albert was to be dogged by his own tribunal description of his attitude to decision making . . . "I operate a department on the basis of no long files, no long reports; put it on a single sheet and, if I need more information, I know where to get it . . . the one-sheet approach has got me through life very successfully in business and in politics."

'It was a perfectly tenable modus operandi. "I know where to get it" was the important caveat, but that was skilfully deleted to portray him as a virtual semi-literate whose limit-ations dictated that he should not be taxed with more than could be kept to a single page.

'In fact the "one sheet" man had a disquieting ability to absorb and retain reams of detail – we used to joke that it had something to do with a brain undamaged by alcohol – and I was present when economists and financial experts discovered that trying to faze him with jargon or technicalities almost always backfired.'

More recently, in an interview, talking on this very point, Diggy said:

'Albert could quote you the whole of the Downing Street Declaration off the top of his head, clause, sub-clause, the whole shebang. He would go into something and completely absorb it. The abortion thing, which was astonishingly complex, he had a total grasp of what it was.

'In fact it used to drive me nuts with the amount of detail he could regurgitate about anything that interested him or that he had to apply himself to as Taoiseach. Amazing that he could absorb it all. The Beef Tribunal . . . half the time I didn't know what he was talking about. I couldn't understand a word of it . . . it was so complicated but he had a grasp of every detail of that. It was quite extraordinary.

'But . . . over the "one sheet" . . . the press said "No, he's just stupid" . . . I accept that's legitimate politics, that's what politics is; you throw whatever you can at the guy.'

Brian Cowen remembers how I liked to run things:

'Albert's was a strong business type of approach to the politics and his own background as a businessman was very evident in how he conducted his politics – very good networker, very good at the detail when necessary – very persistent, very focused, impatient to get things done, not one for long analysis: What's the problem? What are the options? What are we going to do about it?

'So, very much a straightforward, businesslike approach, that's how he ran the cabinet. He expected people to be on top of their brief, to know what they are talking about, to do their job and to come forward with ideas. He liked people to come forward with new ideas. He was very open, for example, to the whole question of alternative energy; he was very interested, he could see the potential in all of these things and was anxious to see initiatives piloted and people trying – not afraid to take risks. He . . . calculated what was the road to go in any particular area of policy and then he expected people to get on with it and not to be disheartened or to walk away from something because you met a difficulty. He expects you to get over the difficulty.'

I have always upheld my honesty and integrity as inviolable and I will defend them with my utmost being. Before I was called to the tribunal myself, the daily process was reported back to me.

In his first day in the witness box, without actually naming me personally, O'Malley apparently tried to defuse his accusation by stating that 'the manner in which cover was given didn't constitute fraud, but was unusual'. The following day Ray Burke, my successor in Industry and Commerce, was called. Burke, O'Malley alleged, had been 'seriously in error' in telling the Dáil in 1989 that there were no defaults in payments by the Iraqis to Irish exporters. Burke felt free to hit back with the response that O'Malley's attitude was questionable. I had a similar opinion.

O'Malley then turned his guns full on me. He declared that decisions I had taken on export credit insurance had been 'grossly unwise, reckless and foolish'. He had not actually used the word 'dishonest' but as far as I was concerned the ghost of it was there pointing a finger as clearly as if he had. I suspected it was his way of licking old wounds. It was a display of antagonism that one did not expect from a coalition partner.

The whole issue became even more heated when Ray Burke was further questioned on discussions at government level on 8 June 1988 during which it was decided to raise the ceiling on cover for trade with Iraq under the export credit insurance scheme. In particular, the chairman of the tribunal, Mr Justice Hamilton, wanted to know if this provision was exclusive to Goodman International and Hibernia Meats. His enquiry was immediately questioned by Henry Hickey, senior counsel for the state, who cited Article 28.4.2 of the constitution, which stipulates that the government must take collective responsibility for its decisions. The issue involved cabinet confidentiality. Mr Justice Hamilton maintained it was a necessary line of enquiry, while Harry Whelehan, in his capacity as as Attorney General, insisted equally adamantly that there was no question of revealing cabinet discussions and demanded a High Court decision.

The High Court judgment was delivered by Mr Justice O'Hanlon: Whelehan's application to halt the line of enquiry was rejected. Whelehan promptly applied to the Supreme Court on behalf of the government. Meanwhile I was reviled by the PDs and the press, who claimed that I had deliberately spiked the wheels of justice by inciting Harry to frustrate the tribunal in order to protect myself! Harry Whelehan, whose iron integrity and adherence to the letter of the law had brought the 'X Case' to court, was now, bizarrely, being accused of suddenly bending to my whim!

The Supreme Court, to the great irritation and incredulity of PDs and press alike, ruled by a majority that there was an absolute constitutional duty of secrecy in relation to cabinet discussions. For reasons I will never understand, I was vilified by the press as the villain again!

The *Irish Times* then quoted five unnamed Fianna Fáil ministers as disagreeing with my account of decisions taken at that particular meeting. When Ray McSharry demanded that their names were published, no more was heard, but pressure was mounting. The press, which had once been so supportive, had turned on me with open hostility and Fianna Fáil's relationship with the PDs was fast deteriorating.

That deterioration was exacerbated when O'Malley, in a blatant departure from established protocol, appointed Mary Harney – a minister of state, and a junior minister at that – to represent the PDs at important talks between North and South. It was known that only members of cabinet were to be present at the meeting and, as no cabinet member from the PDs made themselves available, the talks went ahead without them. It wasn't just that Harney was a junior minister: the talks were sensitive, we needed a team we could rely on, and Harney was not only inexperienced but had publicly attacked the government on its Northern policy. Whatever was happening in government, I would tolerate nothing that might in any way hinder the delicate first stages of the peace process, and infighting was not a risk I was willing to take.

Then it was my turn to be called to the tribunal. It might have been expedient to say things differently, but when the time came for my response to O'Malley's statement under oath, the word 'dishonest' said it all.

O'Malley had asserted that a claim by Goodman International against the state was for IR£172 million. But, as I told the tribunal: 'When he [O'Malley] said that to the Tribunal, he knew that the figures were wrong. He knew that the Iraqis had been paying right up to August 1990. He gave no credit for that, but he knew the figures. He puffed up Goodman's claim for what I regard as cheap political gain. He was reckless, irresponsible and dishonest to do that here in the Tribunal.'

The fact was that the Iraqis had paid over IR£53 million of Goodman's losses on contract to Iraq and the potential liability therefore stood at IR£119 million. O'Malley's own department had been notified of that fact, as had he. I pointed out the actual extent of the liability to the tribunal. The IR£172 million claimed by O'Malley was only a potential liability, not an actual liability. Furthermore, the total liabilities under the export credit insurance scheme had at that time amounted to no more than IR£6 million.

The arguing was bitter and divisive. I was pressed by O'Malley's senior counsel to withdraw the charge of 'perjury' against O'Malley. I insisted that I had accused him of 'dishonesty', not 'perjury'. After the wrangling that ensued over nuances and wordplay, over terms used in the course of the tribunal, from O'Malley's accusation that I had made 'untrue statements' to my calling his statements 'dishonest' and counsel turning that around into accusations of 'perjury', my patience was running thin. In my book you are honest or dishonest, and whether I was well advised to use it or not, I believed 'dishonest' was the word that applied, and I used it.

The PDs, in a spurious show of moral indignation, demanded an abject withdrawal of the 'dishonesty' allegation, and informed the media that O'Malley was only remaining as a minister in order to ensure that files were not tampered with, or civil servants intimidated in relation to the Beef Tribunal! The PDs knew as well as I did that the files could not be changed, nor were they – nor was the matter ever raised after the election that was now looming.

It was the end of the Twenty-sixth Dáil, we were facing a general election in November 1992, and I knew it was going to be tough, really tough.

The press, the media and the people laid the blame for another election directly at my feet and consequently my personal rating plunged a massive 20 per cent, which was hard, as the accusations levelled at me were simply not true.

Liam Collins, now a reporter with the *Sunday Independent*, recalls:

'Albert was always very good with the media. He didn't favour any one journalist but he got to know a lot of them. Then when he came into office, as often happens, the media became not just anti, but they began to look for answers they weren't always getting and they thought he should be more forthcoming. Definitely a lot of them wanted to bring him down and there were certain columnists who were particularly vitriolic about Albert.

'He must have found that difficult because suddenly things had turned.

'I had the impression when he came to lunch at the *Independent* that he must have been wondering why they were so anti what he was trying to do, not necessarily with the peace process, but with the economy. Things were not good but they were getting better – but people expected more.

'He had a bad relationship in coalition with Des O'Malley ... There was a lot of snobbery too, about him being from the Midlands, not like Haughey who was a bit of a maverick but had the Lemass connection, nor from a political dynasty like Lenihan or O'Rourke. And they misused sayings like "one-sheet man" ... It was a big insult when someone called him a "blow-in", an Irish term which means someone is not from the county. A "blow-in" could live in a place for thirty years but if you were not born there ... There was that kind of attitude in the Dáil and Leinster House, that he had come in and taken over. Bertie Ahern was a Haughey man and so was Ray Burke, both powerful men. Albert and Brian Cowen were known as the "Country and Western wing", but it was used in a pejorative way.'

It looked as though we were dead in the water. My own campaign had been a difficult one. I was unutterably tired and worried over the effect this damaging and hateful press campaign was having on Kathleen's health. She was still very frail following her chemotherapy treatment for cancer. I was anxious too for the safety of the children, who went out canvassing on my behalf every day and who insisted they would not give up despite the pressure of ill-will.

In the eyes of the press I could do no right. If I stumbled in an interview I was condemned as 'foolish', 'inarticulate' and even 'out of control'; if I asserted anything vigorously, I was castigated as 'abusive', 'arrogant', 'argumentative' and 'pushy'. My personal rating tumbled as John Bruton's 'rainbow' rose.

Fianna Fáil was in a spin. We knew our numbers were going to drop considerably, but we still clung to hope. I was advised from every side, some insisting on 'no coalition what-ever', others suggesting 'maybe a post-election alliance with Labour' or 'let's take our time and regroup in opposition'. I listened to them all.

Polling day dawned and with it came another international monetary crisis. Spain and Portugal had devalued, and analysts threatened the same fate for Ireland and for the punt.

The only upside to that was that such a crisis would demand a stable government, not the divided opinions of a rainbow coalition.

The election was difficult in that it was caught up in what Brian Cowen describes as a 'cauldron of controversy that was swimming around in the ether everywhere'. He reflects: 'I thought we fought a good campaign. Where we lost out was it polarized opinion. We lost out on transfers in a whole range of constituencies – if you watch for the last sequence of ten to fifteen constituencies, I think we lost every one of them. There might have been one out of fifteen. Now we'd be hoping for six or seven of those to come our way near the end, unfortunately that didn't happen. And, like everything I suppose, when a sudden election is called, the question of organization and preparation wasn't what it would have been if you were planning for an election in two or three years' time. Then you'd have all your ducks in a row and all your candidates' selection made. So decisions had to be made very quickly in a matter of days.'

The national result was a disaster for Fianna Fáil. We lost nine seats, Fine Gael lost ten; the PDs got an extra four, while Labour gained a massive eighteen seats, which brought them up to thirty-three in the Dáil. It was a real achievement for Dick Spring, the 'Spring Tide'.

The election was over; it was time for musical chairs. Dick Spring, elated at his result, suggested a 'rotating' Taoiseach! In other words, he and John Bruton would take turns at the top. Fine Gael had definitely rejected any thought of an alliance with Fianna Fáil, while the PDs were waiting to jump into bed with anybody; O'Malley even suggested he might consider going back into government with me! 'I don't rule out working with anyone,' he said in an interview, 'if the people and the party concerned work reasonably in a spirit of cabinet government.' However, he added in ominous warning: 'It would hardly be a propitious circumstance if the allegation of "dishonest" evidence stood.'

The final judgment of the Beef Tribunal had been postponed until after the election; we'd have to wait and see what it came up with. There were also mutterings that – maybe? – Fianna Fáil and Labour? But then, only two weeks previously Dick Spring had stood up in the Dáil and, in a devastating attack on Fianna Fáil, had said: 'We will not support any government with this track record.' So maybe not!

It was time for me to bide my time. I had good reason.

In the aftermath of the election, Martin Mansergh had confided to me that he had been looking at the electoral figures and as an intellectual exercise was studying Labour's party manifesto and looking at ways of squaring the circle should the occasion arise. I gave him carte blanche to continue, just in case of an approach. Martin's own values lean more to the left, so I suspect he enjoyed the challenge of researching Labour's policy and coming up with a complementary Fianna Fáil response that they would find too attractive to resist.

Finally Labour, already allied with the Democratic Left, decided the play for partners was over: it was time to make a choice. Obviously the two of them together would never make a government, but they had decided that a joint front would strengthen Labour's hand going into negotiations with Fine Gael, because that was all they were thinking about at the time. They had a document prepared which more or less set out their platform for government and they presented it to the other parties for their responses. They obviously doubted the chances of sharing any common ground with Fianna Fáil, but at the last minute decided to approach us too.

What they didn't know was that Martin Mansergh, as he readily admits, was prepared:

'Remember, I would have had both the Labour Party and the Democratic Left documents before the election and I suppose I could work out roughly what their paper was going to be, but I had the paper virtually ready when someone leaked to me a copy of their agreement several hours before it was sent to us officially. You see they were going through the motions of sending it out to the other parties, but I got an advance copy some five or six hours beforehand and I was able to adapt our paper. I had it fairly well anyway, let's say I had it 95 per cent there, but the extra 5 per cent I was then able to manipulate and adjust, and the result is, when it finally came to us formally, we were able to send it back by return.'

It was 10 December and I was about to leave for a crucial EU summit in Edinburgh when I received a copy of the Labour–Democratic Left policy document together with a request for a meeting. They knew I was away for a period of days and obviously calculated that I would not be in a position to reply until my return. They must have been amazed when our response was delivered within an hour or so of their document being dispatched. Not only that, but it was a twenty-page response brilliantly constructed by Martin that wove together the two party policies in perfect harmony:

'One of the most crucial things it said was that this would be a quite different, partnership government – in other words, we would be treating them as equals rather than a small minority party. That was the key to it.

'Then we also took on board something that never happened and that they didn't push when they came into government but had been suggested when they were in opposition, and that was the "Third Banking Force", where there would be a state-controlled bank in addition to the Bank of Ireland and AIB. Anyway, we made it clear that we would have no deep ideological objection to this and they were very pleased with that because it was their idea played back to them. Now, it never came to anything, and that's fine, but it was important to them at the time!

'It also stopped them in their tracks because they had been about to open negotiations with Fine Gael. Fine Gael did badly in the election, they had lost quite a lot of seats, but they were behaving as if they had won and Spring was settling a few scores back from the 1980s when they had been very much in opposite camps and had been rivals and enemies. Basically Spring told Bruton where to get off, and that left things a little bit in limbo. But when our paper came across, they suddenly realized they had a real choice instead of only one option.'

Irresistible!

Now, if I could pull off a coup in Edinburgh . . . I flew off with a smile on my face.

Although Fianna Fáil was out of government I was still acting as Taoiseach, but whether I remained Taoiseach or not, I was determined to come away from the EU summit in Edinburgh with the best possible deal for Ireland.

This was a particularly important summit for Ireland as it was to focus on establishing the amounts of the Structural Funds and Cohesion Fund to be allocated to the EU member states over the course of the next five to seven years.

Realistically everyone expected we would receive EU funding of about four and a half to five billion pounds. IR£6 billion was a hoped-for possibility; I maintained I would get more. The media had dismissed any chance of this happening. As far as they were concerned I would be gone in a matter of days, and they made it clear that they thought my presence in Edinburgh would do little to increase the likelihood of a good deal for Ireland. The *Irish Times*, even as I left for Scotland, claimed I had 'hung' myself in aspiring to the IR£6 billion. The opposition jeered that I would be lucky to make even IR£4.5 billion. Even the punters were betting I was on a loser.

However, only a short time previously John Major had asked if Helmut Kohl could meet with me in Ireland. It was during the election period at a time when I knew I wasn't going to win, so I was happy to get away and said that I would certainly meet with him, but in Germany.

Helmut Kohl was a big man in every way – he could be overpowering just by his physical presence – but he was also a good man, and he and I got on well. He had a problem, he informed me, and he needed it solved. British troops stationed in Germany were being attacked, he said; British soldiers were being shot by the IRA on German soil. Was there anything I could do to help the situation? Kohl and Major were obviously very concerned and embarrassed that so far they had not been able to stop these attacks; I think that during their discussions John Major had inferred that as I was in the process of trying to negotiate peace in Northern Ireland, and as I seemed to have connections in the North, maybe there was a chance I could get a message through to the right people.

There was a big allocation of funds coming up at the December meeting of the EU in Edinburgh, Kohl explained, 'and I will give you whatever help you need if you can give us any help with this'.

Kohl was a very influential figure within the EU; I knew that his decisions could sway other members, and that once Kohl had agreed a figure they would go along with it too. John Major was chairman of the meeting that year, and as he had the same interest in seeing an end to the attacks, I knew he too would be a powerful ally. I agreed to do my best. I admitted that there was only one man who could put a stop to the attacks; if I could get a message through to him, I said, explaining that in return for a halt to the campaign in Germany I could do a deal for Ireland that would bring in funding of x billion pounds, then he and his colleagues, as Republicans, would understand the economic benefits of such a deal and, being in favour of all things Irish, might possibly agree to cooperate.

The message was fed through the appropriate channels. In concluding I asked whether, if I did a deal for Ireland at those negotiations in Edinburgh, they would stand behind me, not publicly but privately, in confidence as men of our word. I knew I could trust them on this. The reply came back: 'Agreed'. They left me to do the best deal I could.

John Major recalls the episode.

'I was chairman of the meeting and we were re-designating the budget and there were lots of changes. There weren't only changes to Ireland. And it wasn't only for that reason, there were other reasons why we thought it was viable and Albert made a good case. But Helmut was an emotional man, he was concerned. He was always hugely interested in what Albert and I were trying to do for Ireland and his influence in those meetings was always good, but there was a case for a better deal for Ireland. I was attracted to a better deal for Ireland on its merits and for wider reasons and Helmut was supportive.

'I don't know what Helmut said to Albert but from the surrounding information I have, I would say that story is probably correct . . .

'Albert was battling for more money for Ireland and he was fortunate that he had two advocates, in Helmut who at the time was the single most influential figure in the EU, and in me who was chairing the meeting. It was a fortunate concatenation of events.'

The talks took place at Holyrood Palace. Bertie Ahern,

David Andrews and Tom Kitt accompanied me, as did other knowledgeable stalwarts such as Dermot Nally and Pádraig O hUiginn. It was a time for hard consulting and negotiating, lightened by a very enjoyable reception given by Her Majesty Queen Elizabeth aboard the royal yacht *Britannia*. She was accompanied by Prince Philip, Princess Margaret, Princess Anne and the Prince and Princess of Wales, who had just announced that they were to separate. They were all there not just for the summit, but to attend the wedding of Princess Anne, set for the following day.

The next day we too had cause to celebrate. After a gruelling round of negotiating, I got it: I came out of the conference hall with not IR£6 but IR£8 billion pounds! Seán Duignan was there to meet me, and I said to him:

'Eight billion, Diggy, eight billion – now watch me put a government together!'

The Irish media had gleefully been awaiting my humiliation – so much so that they had no idea how to react to the news that Ireland had been granted the huge sum of IR£8 billion. I think if I had only come away with IR£3 billion they would have cheered, but the fact that I had succeeded in getting IR£8 billion left them with egg on their faces.

We got the deal we wanted – and in Germany the bombing stopped.

The meeting with Dick Spring was set for the day of our return from Edinburgh. It was a Sunday afternoon when we gathered in the penthouse suite of the Berkeley Court Hotel in Dublin. Our success at the EU summit had certainly turned things around. Far from being anti-Fianna Fáil, Labour was now eager to talk. The press, too, had swung around to the opinion that a coalition of these two parties, with our complementary policies, could be interesting. Even Fergus Finlay, the Labour leader's adviser, admitted in his autobiography that the opinion of the press was an important critical sounding board for them, as for all political parties, and an important indicator of public opinion. The political correspondents were obviously very intrigued by this novel initiative and were eager to see where it would lead. In fact, it was made quite clear to Labour at the time that if they turned down our policy-compatible offer out of hand, there would be a lot of explaining to do.

Dick and I began negotiating our positions that Sunday afternoon. There were many difficulties ahead, but I believed we could form a government based on equal responsibility, a partnership of two strong parties rather than one weak and one strong, as had been the case in our partnership with the PDs, where the weaker party was forever vying to overcome the other in an effort to reach a position of strength. I also believed he would be a more understanding partner in the search for peace in Northern Ireland. O'Malley had never believed in the possibility of peace, and I had deliberately avoided involving him in what was going on. Spring, although reasonably sceptical, was definitely intrigued and I felt I could trust him to go along with my ambitions.

Diggy was outside waiting in another room with his opposite number, Fergus Finlay, who apparently asked if I could deliver. Diggy answered firmly that with eight billion on hand there would be no problem. However, Finlay then told Diggy they could not take Flynn. I had other plans already for Pádraig Flynn, who had expressed an interest in taking on the European Commissioner's job. So, again that presented no problem, but it was intriguing.

Given all the speeches he'd made adamantly declaring his antipathy to Fianna Fáil, I knew it was going to be a difficult decision for Dick Spring and his party and I guessed it would be some time before they reached an agreement.

After all the taunts and jibes my family and I had suffered during the election campaign, and the accusations and denigrations that had been flung at me by my fellow politicians, I enjoyed returning to the Dáil a few days later, on 16 December 1992, to report on the successful outcome of the Edinburgh summit, and I felt quite justified in my statement:

'During the course of the referendum campaign earlier this year on the Maastricht Treaty, I said that our objective was to obtain about IR£6 billion over the five years to 1997, as implied by the original Commission proposals. Many people accused me of raising unreal expectations. From the Maastricht referendum campaign right through to the recent election the issue was used to denigrate my credibility.

'Deputy Bruton on 6 May last in this House accused me of making wild promises and of presenting the IR£6 billion as a bribe from the European fairy godmother. Deputy de Rossa on 23 October, claimed the IR£6 billion was always an exaggeration and spoke of a "sorry saga of dishonesty, particularly during the referendum campaign, and plain wrong-headed negotiating tactics and objectives". Much of this was echoed in the media. For instance, in the current December issue of *Fortnight* magazine, one of our senior commentators writes of "the infamous IR£6 billion" receding into the mists. My strategy and my negotiating tactics have been vindicated.

'The agreement now reached ensures – and I say this with complete confidence – that Ireland will obtain in excess of IR£8 billion over seven years. This will comprise up to IR£1 billion from the new Cohesion Fund and more than IR£7 billion from the Structural Funds. A great deal will depend on how well we use this massive supplement to our national resources; but it is beyond question that our country is offered an immense opportunity to raise investment and growth, improve our infrastructure and economic efficiency, and tackle the jobs crisis, further narrowing the gap between living standards here and the Community average.'

However, rarely do things run smoothly and there was further disturbing intrigue when word came back from Brussels that the Irish claim of IR£8 billion was not valid. Pádraig O hUiginn immediately contacted the Secretary-General of the Commission, David Williamson, who confirmed that the rumours were just that – rumours, without any basis in truth – and that the IR£8 billion was definitely assured. Despite such promises, on more than one later occasion Jacques Delors attempted to renege on the deal, but without success.

As Des O'Malley continued in his anxiety to thwart any possibility of a Fianna Fáil–Labour partnership, Dick Spring faced further sneering from the Fine Gael leader John Bruton. Following Spring's return as a witness in the Beef Tribunal, he refused to reveal his sources of evidence. On previously taking the stand he had torn into Fianna Fáil and my name had been frequently abused; now it was not even murmured. To be clear, none of the allegations Spring had made in the first place had concerned my part in the procedure, but I took this new restraint as a further sign of his good intent.

Finally, on 12 January 1993, our new partnership was signed under the terms of an agreement concluded by our negotiators, called 'Programme for a Partnership Government 1993–1997'. It gave the government the biggest majority in the history of the state – forty-two seats. Labour, with Dick Spring as Tánaiste and Minister for Foreign Affairs, now had six cabinet seats; Fianna Fáil had dropped from thirteen to nine.

Máire Geoghegan-Quinn had already come to me requesting that, in the event that we won, she could have first call on the position of European Commissioner in Brussels, but I'd already offered that to Pádraig Flynn. I didn't tell her that at the time, but promised that she would definitely be in the new government. As it was, I remained as Taoiseach; Bertie Ahern was back in Finance; Máire Geoghegan-Quinn was appointed Minister for Justice; David Andrews got Defence and Marine; Charlie McCreevy, Tourism and Trade; Michael Woods, Social Welfare; Joe Walsh, Agriculture; Michael Smith, Environment; and Brian Cowen, Transport, Energy and Communications. Loyal colleague Pádraig Flynn was appointed to Europe.

I was very happy with the new arrangement and I was confident that the two parties could work well together. Both seemed to have accepted the new partnership with enthusiasm and a belief that the combined policies could really work. True, the economy was still in a poor state; but the IR£8 billion, albeit over a period of seven years, would be of huge benefit in our efforts to develop Ireland's future. The Beef Tribunal was still there in the background, but I knew I had no reason to fear the outcome.

It was time to concentrate my attention on Northern Ireland.

9

LOOKING NORTH

The 'X Case', difficult as it had been to have such a bomb-shell land on my desk on my very first day as Taoiseach, did not detract from my determination to put Northern Ireland at the top of my agenda.

In one of my first press conferences as Taoiseach I elaborated on this when I said that one of my priorities was to build a new relationship with Great Britain and that I intended the 1920 Government of Ireland Act to be on the agenda. Sometime later, via a certain conduit, I was informed that on hearing this Martin McGuinness had said that if it was on the agenda, he would come to the table. That gave me hope that there was a chance things could move forward.

Martin McGuinness:

'Sinn Féin's view all along was that the Government of Ireland Act had to be part of negotiations. We emphasized our own view, which coincided with Albert's view, that the Government of Ireland Act should certainly come under the microscope and be dealt with effectively.'

My great good fortune was that in December 1990 John

Major had succeeded Margaret Thatcher as British Prime Minister. Just two weeks after I had been sworn in as Taoiseach, John invited me to Downing Street.

John Major:

'I had no background in Northern Ireland when I became Prime Minister, but I had observed it at a distance and it seemed to me to be no more tolerable killing people in Northern Ireland than it would have been had they been killing one another in London, and if that had been the case it would have been the first item on the British government's agenda. Albert agreed with that. We hadn't, I don't think, discussed it when we were finance ministers but we did when we met as prime ministers in the upstairs study in Downing Street. We both agreed then that it would be improper not to put it at the head of our interests and we should try and see what we could do.'

It was an informal meeting. I remember Dermot Nally, secretary to the government, and his counterpart preparing to take notes, and John suggesting that both gentlemen put away their pens and notebooks as the talk he proposed was to be frank and open and off the record. It was important, he said, that we expressed our views freely and without prejudice.

Northern Ireland dominated our conversation. We were both of one mind in a determination to do everything in our power not to condemn another generation to a life of violence and sectarian killing. Whereas Thatcher and Haughey had distrusted and disliked each other, John and I shared trust and understanding. Efforts to build bridges between our two governments had stalled during the years of our predecessors, and apart from the Anglo-Irish Agreement of 1985 the Troubles in Northern Ireland had been sidelined into stalemate; consequently there had been little to no effort made to push towards a peaceful solution.

John Major:

'When I met Charlie Haughey I was horrified that there was no regular system for the British and Irish prime ministers to meet. They met occasionally and usually in disagreement. My thinking was, we are both members of the European Union, we've both got an interest in Northern Ireland, we ought to routinely, regularly meet. What I'd agreed with Charlie Haughey was that we would agree to meet routinely for summits twice a year where there may or may not be an agreed agenda but we would be there to talk about what was happening. We hadn't got much beyond that but we did agree that.'

John and I were of the same opinion that from then on Northern Ireland would be on the front burner of our agendas. Having been finance ministers, we both understood the economic benefits that peace would bring to our two countries. We knew that the violence was driving away the vital investment we all needed. The British government, John explained, had been making steady progress throughout the 1980s to address the problems that had led to the Troubles. It had introduced legislation on fair employment for all religious groups in an attempt to dispel the severe grievance of discrimination suffered by the Nationalists. Public services had been improved, as well as education and housing, but this was not enough to encourage the investment needed to build the economy. The bombings and the violence were losing us all business, with the result that unemployment was rising and so was emigration. It was not only a vicious circle that had to be stopped, it was also a humanitarian crisis in that many people were living in fear and suffering atrocities.

I believed that the time was right for change. Everything I knew from my contacts indicated that the IRA was considering a different approach. Gerry Adams of Sinn Féin had started talks with John Hume, leader of the Nationalist SDLP in the North, and I knew, from Martin McGuinness's response to my press conference, that Sinn Féin and the IRA leadership were behind him, ready to seek a political way forward under the right circumstances. And the right circumstances, I told John Major, would exist if the Government of Ireland Act was on the table and open to discussion.

John was intrigued. At that time, although he knew of the Act, he was not entirely aware of its significance to the current situation.

John Major:

'No, I wasn't that well informed, that's perfectly true ... Was I aware of all the intricacies of the "green" language and the "orange" language and the Government of Ireland Act? No, I wasn't. I was reading myself into it all. I probably knew more than Albert realized, but no, I didn't know remotely as much as I came to know ...'

I left it to Dermot Nally to explain how it was that the Government of Ireland Act of 1920 was at the root of our current problems.

The partition of Ireland into North and South set out in the 1920 Act and recognized in the Anglo-Irish Treaty of the following year had always been a compromise: it contributed to civil war in the South and sporadic violence leading to civil war in the North even after the passage of some fifty years. Back when Michael Collins had agreed to partition in the treaty of 1921, many thought it no more than a temporary solution, although de Valera refused to accept it even on those terms. However, nothing was ever done to change the treaty and it had therefore remained in operation more through apathy and usage than desire or indeed intention. In the end the Southern Nationalists and the Northern Unionists were content with the outcome of the treaty; it was the Northern Nationalists who had always suffered.

The 1920 Act had guaranteed four safeguards for the Nationalist community in the North, all of which over the years had been dropped or ignored: proportional representation to protect the minority; the Council of Ireland, intended to keep Ireland in economic and administrative terms as a single unity; the guarantee of religious non-discrimination; and the Boundary Commission, which would have allowed certain areas, where Nationalists were in the majority, to join the South. All failed to deliver. Finally the Nationalists, frustrated by years of discrimination and feeling betrayed by the Free State policy towards the North, had rebelled and the result was the current bitter conflict.

Both governments had a responsibility to end the conflict, I argued, and if we could demonstrate to Sinn Féin and the IRA that we were prepared to either alter or repeal that Act, I felt they would embrace a political rather than a violent future. Besides which, since the atrocity of the Enniskillen Remembrance Day massacre, which had shocked not only Ireland but also the outside world, the IRA's tactics were seen as more and more futile and they were fast losing credibility, even with their American supporters.

Sinn Féin had seen two hunger strikers from the H-Blocks elected to the Dáil in 1981, but their attempts at winning seats in the 1987 election in the South had failed as the continuing violence eroded what remained of public tolerance and conflicted with any hope of a political strategy.

John understood all this, but was still doubtful that the solution lay in tackling the Government of Ireland Act.

'I knew the importance of the Government of Ireland Act and I knew that from the point of view of the Unionists and everybody else, we had to deal with the important Articles –

Article 3 in particular of the Irish Constitution; I knew we had to deal with those, of course I did, but so much of that was more to do with reassuring the component parts of the peace process than an intrinsic piece of substance. That was always the reality. So much of the time you were dancing round – well, call them prejudices, call them convictions – you were dancing round them in order to persuade people that progress should be made.

'The fundamental of this was simple – people had to stop killing one another and you needed to draw the Republican armed forces into the political system and at the end of the day forget everything else. That is the core of what you had to get. I talk of the Republicans but it is equally true of the Loyalist paramilitaries.'

John and I agreed, whatever our differences, that we would have a better chance if we were seen to be working towards an agreement that would go some way to righting the wrongs of the 1920s.

Driving back to the airport after that first informal meeting with John Major, Dermot Nally commented that he had been a long time listening to debates on Northern Ireland and that he had been at every meeting with every prime minister since 1972. He said, 'If it's ever going to be settled, you're the two boys to settle it!' The changes we were proposing would happen in time anyway, he prophesied: demographic figures would redress the balance of Catholic and Protestant population and eventually give us the results we were demanding now; but if the British and Irish governments could work together in the way we were planning, that future could be the present. I remember that he finished by saying to me, 'Your gut feeling is so right, and John Major too seems genuine in his desire to bring peace, and if there's a price to be paid he seems prepared to pay it. I won't be at all surprised if you two fellows succeed.'

* * *

When I took over as Taoiseach, I had invited Martin Mansergh to join my team. Mansergh's philosophy was rooted in history. He constantly looked back to go forward, drawing strength and wisdom from the likes of Parnell and de Valera and Lemass. He was of Anglo-Irish descent, a Protestant Republican and a dedicated 'Soldier of Destiny' within Fianna Fáil.

In character we were complete opposites – he was the total intellectual, I the entire pragmatist – but in that we complemented each other, and on the subject of Northern Ireland we were in harmony.

His approach was based on the strategies of Parnell, who in the late nineteenth century had drawn on the strengths of the Irish American faction and harnessed all the elements of nationalism in one common cause, a self-governing united Ireland. The grouping had eventually split, but it did mark a step forward. This had been the strategy Mansergh had proposed to Haughey as a way of leading the militant Republicans of the North out of a situation of violence into a new role as a political force that could engage with the democratic process, not only to achieve a withdrawal of British troops but more importantly to achieve a state of self-determination.

Haughey had always prided himself on his Republican connections – he was after all a Derry man – but his involvement in the 'arms trial' of 1970 had forced him to withdraw into the wilderness for a few years, and once back at the top he would not do anything to endanger his position: he was therefore reluctant to be seen in any way negotiating or talking with the Northern Republicans. For that reason he was not greatly trusted. Maggie Thatcher had not trusted him either. The hunger strikes had left a bitter aftermath, and following the setting up of the Anglo-Irish Agreement relations between the two governments were at an all-time low: whatever contacts there had been between governments and spokespersons for the paramilitaries stopped, for fear of giving the latter the impression that they were winning.

There had been a certain line of communication between the British government and the Republicans in the North over the years but that had broken down too. As Martin McGuinness, a member of the Sinn Féin Árd Chomhairle, the party's governing body, wrote in 'Setting the Record Straight', the Sinn Féin document of 2 December 1993:

'The line of communication goes back over two decades. I had no dealing with it before the Hunger Strikes although I was aware of its existence. The line of communication was dormant from the breakdown of the '74–75 truce until the Hunger Strikes. The two Hunger Strikes were a period of frenzied contact between us and them. The contact between us and the British Government at this time is not disputed. Incidentally we were assured during this period that Margaret Thatcher had authorised the line of communication with us and with the political prisoners in the H Blocks and Armagh Prisons. The British Government representative was appointed by London not Stormont.

'After the Hunger Strikes the line of communication was dormant until mid 1990. Even though the line of communication was dormant the contact remained in touch with the British Government representative and occasionally with me.'

However, although Haughey had been reluctant to make advances to the North, the North had come to him in the person of a Redemptorist priest, Father Alex Reid – a man whom I was to get to know well.

Father Reid had moved to live in Belfast in 1961:

'I was sent to Clonard [Monastery] in 1961. There were no Troubles then but there was tension. I remember the time when you went over the border, even the Unionists used to say it, when you crossed the border into the North, there was an atmosphere, because you knew there was division there . . .

'Then in 1968–69 we had the civil rights movement and the Unionist parliament in Stormont tried to ban it, I think they banned every civil rights march and every time they tried to march, the police were there telling them it was illegal. I remember Gerry Fitt, who was leader of the Nationalists at the time, with blood streaming down his face, trying to lead them . . . Derry was very Nationalist, 60 per cent at least were Nationalist. They had a big march planned, 30 January 1972, and Derry being Nationalist they knew they would get a big following – and for whatever reason the British paratroopers were policing it and they opened fire on the parade and killed thirteen. As a result, the young people, the young IRA people (Gerry Adams used to say to me the dangerous people in the IRA are the nineteen- and twenty-year-olds) got together and said, look, we have tried in '68 and '69, and they have batoned us off the streets, they've shot us off the streets, there's no point in trying to do this peacefully . . . so the IRA campaign started, they couldn't deal with all the applications to join them.

'. . . Clonard Monastery bordered the Nationalist Falls Road area and the Loyalist Shankill and there would be riots out there. There were two IRAs – there was the Official IRA and the Provisional IRA, always feuding . . . there would be ten people killed in a day if they started fighting and they were neighbours shooting neighbours. I came to know their leaders in Belfast. You could deal with them, you could trust them. There were occasions when they were fighting and a member of the Official IRA would come to me and say, "So and so lives in that area in a Provo street, is he safe to go home or will they go in and shoot him?" And I'd go to the Provos and say, "So and so wants to go home, is he safe?" And they'd say, "Yes, we won't touch him." You could rely on them. They gave their word and their word was their bond.'

As he told me later, it was during this period, witnessing the escalating violence, the two IRAs' rivalry and feuding, their campaign against the Loyalists and the Loyalists killing the Nationalists, and the violence directed at the security forces, that Father Reid decided to try to get involved. He already had access to the IRA leaders; he now felt an obligation to see what he could do to stop the whole IRA campaign in terms, primarily, of saving British soldiers and RUC men – Northern Ireland policemen. There was one night in particular he recalled:

'I was at a funeral of a man who had been shot by the Loyalists. I was saying the rosary and I don't know now if it was his wife or his mother, but she was keening – that crying that goes on and on, it was heartrending and I remember saying to myself there's something wrong here, people should not have to be going through that suffering, that agony, something has to be done.'

Father Reid belonged to the Redemptorist Order, which, like the Franciscans, is spread all over the world, and his superiors were Redemptorists; had he been a diocesan priest, subject to the bishops, he would probably not have been allowed to get involved. As it was, he was given 100 per cent support with complete freedom to act as an official minister of the order in a peace ministering role. It meant he was acting under authority, not as some maverick priest.

Father Reid remembered another significant event which for him was a turning point:

'There was one day a UDR man, a part-time soldier who was captured by the IRA. I was advised of it by an IRA leader in Belfast who was against them picking up part-time people and shooting them. He came to me and said he had the authority to get the man released and would I go with him. We arrived too late.

'The next day I sent for Gerry Adams. I knew Gerry from internment . . . I used to go in and out of the prison saying mass for the prisoners in Long Kesh, so, as a result of this UDA man being shot, I sent a message for Gerry, and I said to him, "There's another person dead. Can nothing be done?" And he said a very interesting thing, he said the Church was the only organization that could do anything . . . Now Gerry knew more about what the Church should be doing than the Church!

'He was the political leader of Sinn Féin, . . . I knew he was a peace man. He told me he could do nothing unless he was able to communicate with the SDLP, the main Nationalist party in the North, led by John Hume, and the Irish government. Then he'd be able to go to the IRA leaders and say, "Look, you see what happens when you take the political route. Here am I talking to the head of the SDLP and the Irish government. This is what happens when you stop, if you stop. We can really get into politics here!"

'He said that the Church had to set it up, it had the lines of communication, it had the status, it had the credibility, what it would have to do was to set up the lines of communication between the different parties. First of all between the Nationalist parties, because in those days nobody would talk to Sinn Féin, they just condemned them, they were outlaws.

'I remember saying to myself, this is the last chance: we'd tried all kinds of things over the last few years and nothing had worked. This is the last throw of the dice . . . I went up into the Dublin Mountains to write this letter to John Hume, and I put in everything that described the opportunity we had to get the IRA to stop . . . if only he and the other Nationalist parties would talk to Sinn Féin . . . I put everything in it, fourteen long typed pages, about Gerry Adams being a great politician, committed to peace, and I sent it to John Hume, in May '86. The next thing was, John Hume got the letter and phoned me immediately ... He didn't know me then but he came down to Clonard and said, "I'll co-operate with you."

'I got my Superior in [and] we both said, "John, we think we can move the whole thing forward if you're prepared to talk to Sinn Féin." And he agreed to meet with Gerry Adams.'

Father Reid also sent his fourteen-page letter to Charlie Haughey, who at that time was leader of the opposition, which made it difficult if not impossible for him to get involved.

Gerry Adams recalls the instrumental role played by Father Reid in those early days:

'Father Reid was a friend of mine. Father Reid I first met when I was in prison. He had played a very important role in trying to resolve some inter-Republican faction fighting that was going on at the time and he and I were debating those issues and he, as part of his ministry, believed that the Catholic Church had a role to play, that it shouldn't just be one of condemnation, that the gospel message in his view was actually about producing justice and dialogue and that had to be given primacy. He started to talk to Charlie Haughey, initially as leader of the opposition, and then as Taoiseach, putting it to him that he should meet with me which he refused to do.'

The letter had been sent to Haughey in November 1986, but even when he was back as Taoiseach in 1987 he was unwilling to involve the government while the IRA campaign continued. Father Reid had explained to Haughey that he wanted him to meet face to face with Adams as he was convinced that Adams believed the time was right to persuade the Northern Republican paramilitaries to enter the political arena. Haughey refused to meet either of them, although at a subsequent meeting he introduced the priest to his adviser, Martin

Mansergh. It was not until 1988 that Haughey finally agreed to contact with Sinn Féin, and then not at sanctioned government level, but at a secret meeting of party to party representatives only. The Fianna Fáil representatives were Mansergh, Dermot Ahern and Richie Healy; Adams, Mitchel McLaughlin and Pat Doherty represented Sinn Féin. It was a high-risk endeavour and Haughey warned that should news of it leak out, those participating would be disowned. As Mansergh said: 'The government per se was not involved but the party of the government was.'

The meeting took place on a Monday morning in a wood-panelled room at the Redemptorist monastery in Dundalk. It was the first ever face-to-face meeting of Fianna Fáil and Sinn Féin, and after introductions by Father Reid, it lasted for two hours. According to Mansergh: 'There was no raising of the voice and certainly no harshness, no bullying and no heckling. People were trying to get a dialogue off the ground.'

In briefings with me later, Martin Mansergh reported that it was a preliminary setting out of positions. The Sinn Féin delegates expressed their opinion on the status quo in the North, where the Nationalists felt disturbingly alienated from Dublin, and they insisted that they felt that an alternative political strategy had to be found if the violence was to stop. They also pointed out the ineffectiveness of the Anglo-Irish Agreement, which they viewed as not worth the candle, as the cost of the provocation of Unionists was not commensurate with any substantial gain.

The Fianna Fáil representatives, on behalf of the Nationalists in the South, expressed their abhorrence of violence. They stressed that they regarded it as the single most potent divisive factor in weakening Irish Nationalism. As well as dividing opinion within all Nationalist communities, whether in the North, the Republic or Irish America, violence only served to prevent the combining of forces for electoral or other purposes.

There was one other secret meeting, but little progress was made. Haughey was reluctant to authorize any government contact or dialogue with Sinn Féin and, as Gerry Adams wrote in his autobiography *Hope and History*:

'The effort to develop an alternative was painfully slow. The Sagart [priest – Father Reid] and his colleagues continued to do their best, but we were met with rejection – either of the outright variety or a less forthright but nonetheless negative, long-fingering kind that was debilitating and corrosive.'

In 1987 Father Reid had drawn up a paper outlining 'A Proposal for a Democratic Overall Political and Diplomatic Strategy for Justice, Peace and Reconciliation'. It was a remarkable document, approved by Cardinal Ó Fiaich, the head of the Catholic Church in Ireland: it accepted the Republican position of self-determination by the majority of the people of Ireland as a whole; it affirmed that self-determination meant consent, but that this could only be realized by the twofold consent of the people of the Nationalist tradition and the people of the Unionist tradition, and this in turn could only be achieved through dialogue and agreement. In other words, he was proposing a peace convention.

At the same time John Hume and Gerry Adams, who were trying to put together a proposal for a joint declaration for the two governments, incorporated some of these ideas into their document. Hume delivered this to Haughey, who passed it on to Martin Mansergh. Seán O hUiginn and Dermot Nally also deliberated over the document and modified it. However, according to Gerry Adams:

'It was a rehash of the contemporary position of both the British and the Irish governments. It was totally unacceptable to us.

'It was useless. The Irish government was giving us a position which it thought the British government would accept. It should have been putting together a position required for peace in Ireland, standing up for all the people of our island, mobilizing Irish diplomatic and political resources in so doing.'

This was the position, then, when I took over as Taoiseach in February 1992.

Father Alex Reid:

'When Albert came in as Taoiseach after Charlie in 1992, I remember everybody saying to me, "Look, you're going to have to be patient because this is the way politics goes – you start a process and it all changes – it's like a stream flowing along until it runs into a whole lot of boulders . . . You're going to have to be very patient because this could take another five years. This man here really hasn't shown any interest in the Northern Ireland situation, he's just a politician."'

That was the general consensus, of course, but I'd known business people in the North, Roman Catholic and Protestants of all political parties, and when something significant happened we'd inevitably talk about it, which was why I had experience of the different nuances of language on both sides and I understood where they were coming from. They weren't all involved in the violence, nor were they politically extreme: most were ordinary decent people who could not understand why the problems couldn't be worked out, why we all couldn't live together in peace.

I think they spoke freely to me because I had no 'history' to answer or account for. The 'arms trials' had tainted Haughey and the Unionists were always suspicious of his intentions. I had no such 'baggage' to contend with.

As Seán Duignan, who was working closely with me at that time, recounts:

'Remember Haughey had allegedly Republican sympathies – and he was seen to be that way, so he had that kind of "baggage". Martin Mansergh was interested by this, he used to say to me, "Albert doesn't come with any hang-ups about Republicanism or this or that, he simply says – there's a problem there, let's deal with it."

'He didn't have this aura of being a "snaking regarder", as we call them. It's an Irish expression, meaning "sneaking regard". During the Troubles people who could be classed as vaguely sympathetic to the "Shinners" [Sinn Féin] or the IRA would be accused of being "snaking regarders". Albert had no such problem and this gave him the ability to talk to them long before anybody thought they could be talked to – just because he didn't have any baggage.'

I knew my history, I understood the reasons for the current Troubles, I understood the strategies of Parnell, for example, but sometimes you have to learn from history and then move on. Sometimes you have to put history aside to get a result.

I was very clear in my mind as to what I thought might work and I was prepared to go the distance with it. I knew we could only make progress if we developed a relationship with all the elements – the Republican and Nationalist parties of Sinn Féin, IRA and the SDLP, the Unionist parties (UUP and DUP), and the Loyalist paramilitary groups, the UDA, the UVF and their army council, the Combined Loyalist Military Command: everyone had to be brought to the table and into dialogue. It was the only way.

We couldn't be seen to favour only the Nationalists: nothing would work unless we treated the Unionists with the same consideration. In business terms, a good deal is when everyone feels they have benefited. That was what we had to do – bring everyone to the table and send them away believing they had secured a good deal for their side, that they'd won.

One of the first calls I made was to a friend of mine from the showband days, Sammy Barr, who I understood was very influential within the Democratic Unionist Party and a personal friend of its leader, Dr Ian Paisley. Dr Paisley at that time was doing everything he could to win members away from the Ulster Unionists into his own party. He was very extreme in his views and determined to build the DUP into the biggest majority party in the North.

I had known Sammy since the early sixties. He was the owner of the Flamingo Ballroom in Ballymena and I had supplied him with world-class acts like Acker Bilk and Kenny Ball. He was a good friend, he told it straight and I knew he was a man of his word.

I put it to him that there was something I wanted him to do for me, and that I also knew he was the man to do it. I explained that I had a new job in Dublin and that I wanted him to find out if Paisley would be interested in talking to me or not.

He took some persuading. He wanted to know how I knew about his association with Paisley. I said that didn't matter, but that if he could get to Paisley and ask him to answer 'Yes' or 'No', it could be helpful to all of us in the future. He finally agreed and promised to get back to me by the end of the week.

He was as good as his word. 'The answer's in two parts,' he said. 'One – don't be wasting your time. Two – not until he is number one!'

'Ah,' I said, 'so he doesn't have control of enough of them yet?'

'I think you're reading it right,' he answered.

From then on I knew to leave the DUP alone and to concentrate on the others.

About this time Father Alex Reid came to see me. I had to

warn him that as Taoiseach I could not be seen to be talking directly with members of Sinn Féin or the IRA, but I said that if they had any messages for me, he was to bring them and I would answer them directly. I wanted word to get through that I was receptive and open to whatever they had to say.

Father Reid:

'That was typical of Albert, he was very direct and very businesslike. Gerry Adams was delighted.

'Albert was prepared to take risks. There's a little place behind the Taoiseach's office and he invited me there for lunch and he said, "I know what I'm doing is risky from the point of view of the government, the fact that I'm talking to you or that you're seen coming to this office is risky because people will know I'm talking to the Republicans and that could cause this government to fall." He was in coalition with the PDs at the time. But, he said, "I don't care, I'll risk it, there's life outside politics, so if the government goes or my office goes, no matter, I'd lose it all, I'm only interested in saving lives."

'He was prepared to lose his job as Taoiseach if he could save a life. That was important.'

The report back from Father Reid was positive: Gerry Adams was ready to respect the confidentiality of our secret communication, with Father Reid acting as conduit, even though, as Taoiseach, I was prevented from meeting Adams directly.

Gerry Adams:

'My very clear view was that we weren't going anywhere with Charlie Haughey and I don't want to say anything derogatory, but that was a fact and his Republicanism was overstated, he continuously raised the rhetoric of his position. Albert was much more understated. Our position was to work with whoever happened to be Taoiseach; I think we were lucky with Albert. I think he brought a lot of just commonsense to the position. In fairness it was one that he had inherited, it had reached a certain point, but he came at it in a straightforward, "OK, let's see if something can be done here" . . . He encouraged Father Reid.

'Charlie Haughey had set up a meeting, a deniable meeting, led by Dermot Ahern and Martin Mansergh . . . We accepted it. We did the meetings in good faith but we also thought that he should have met us – or if he had not met us, it should not have been put into a sort of "party sideline".

'It is my strong position . . . that for a Taoiseach to try to make peace is not something the electorate would have disapproved of, and in fact, if it was an honest attempt, the electorate would have strongly approved it . . . So I thought that there would have been no political downside for a Fianna Fáil-led government to engage in such a process and Charlie Haughey was much too cautious . . .

'I think Albert went with his instinct and I think that while his was a much more understated Republicanism, when I did meet him I was surprised, pleasantly surprised, at his grasp of these issues and even that he knew Republican people that I knew around Longford and around Roscommon and that he had lots of his own contacts about the North and that was good. I know it's a cliché but he brought a "can do" approach.'

Father Reid gave me hope. Gerry Adams must have been in his forties at the time and he'd lived with the Troubles all his life. As a father myself, I knew he would not want his children to inherit more years of violence. It seemed to me that the timing was right for the violence to stop. Father Reid endorsed this when he told me of a conversation they had had between them:

'It was a lovely summer's day and we were sitting on our hunkers outside the Sinn Féin office up in Andersonstown and Gerry said, "If you want to get a strategy for peace, for democratic peace, then we have to have the backing of the main Nationalist parties and that would be the SDLP, Fianna Fáil, Fine Gael and the Irish Labour Party and Sinn Féin."

'He always spoke about settling the conflict in the North in a "democratic" way, which meant by implication we had to respect the Unionists. We had to consider everybody's rights, he said, and that he was prepared to do. But the dynamic had to come from the Irish government itself, uniting with the SDLP and Sinn Féin to find a settlement; only then would the IRA stop because they would see that as a credible, political way to peace.'

I completely agreed with that, but getting all those people around a table to talk had so far proved impossible. Still, straight talking and straight dealing was what it was about, and I was good at that. Martin Mansergh had already had two meetings with Sinn Féin, and although the last one had been in 1988, I determined to sanction further contacts on my behalf.

Martin McGuinness:

'Prior to Albert coming on the scene there were, I think, maybe two meetings between representatives of Sinn Féin and representatives of Fianna Fáil, but at no stage did anybody within the leadership of Sinn Féin meet with Charles Haughey, which was always viewed as a particular disappointment, given that Charles Haughey had portrayed himself as being from the North and effectively ingrained in Republicanism. So I think that it came as a surprise to many people on the island that during his time as Taoiseach there was no effort made by himself personally to talk with the leadership of Sinn Féin. And of course, when Albert became Taoiseach, given his past knowledge of the North, and experience, he was an unknown quantity as far as people like myself and Gerry Adams and others were concerned. But it quickly became clear to us, particularly through my conversations with Martin Mansergh, that we were dealing with a Taoiseach who understood the importance of dialogue for the purposes of trying to resolve a conflict which was effectively the position that the North of Ireland had been in for some time – I suppose since 1968/69 right through to the beginning of the nineties.

'I think Albert, in terms of the position of all the governments that existed since Ireland was partitioned, was certainly in my opinion the first Taoiseach to make a real effort to engage the four sectors of the community of all political tendencies in the North with a view to trying to contribute to the finding of a political solution and the end of conflict.'

Obviously the government was aware of my official agenda on Northern Ireland, but I could not divulge to O'Malley or anyone else in government anything of my covert plans. Government policy still endorsed non-communication with those who sought to rule by the gun, or those associated with them. It was too dangerous. O'Malley was already looking for ways to bring down our coalition, and any hint of my being in contact with Sinn Féin or the IRA, or indeed the Loyalists, would have been just the excuse he was looking for. It would not have been acceptable to most members of the government. I simply could not afford to let it be known until I was sure I could get the IRA paramilitaries to agree to a ceasefire – and a permanent one at that.

That was my aim: to get the violence to stop. Until I had that cessation in place there was little prospect of the government supporting me, or even staying with me. I had to take the risks. Martin Mansergh was the only one I could trust, and he too was prepared to risk his career for the sake of peace. He owned a farm in Tipperary. His attitude was – he could always go back to farming!

I knew enough about the Republican movement to know that a leak would make them break off all communications. This had to be a tightly kept secret between Martin and me. That way, if there was a leak it could only be one or the other of us. We both realized the dangers should word get out and the damage it would incur. It was vital we got, and kept, the confidence of the Republican movement.

Charlie Haughey's 'caution', as Gerry Adams calls it, together with his stand-off with Margaret Thatcher, meant little had been achieved over the past few years. Now, with John Major as my opposite number in Britain – a man, like me, ready to put everything on the front burner in his efforts to resolve the conflict in Northern Ireland – I believed we had the right combination to find a formula for peace. I was conscious, too, that a feeling was gathering that now was the time to make a move. People were ready and eager to embrace peace, and although I was aware that many individuals, like John Hume and Gerry Adams, were valiantly working behind the scenes, ultimately the conflict could only be resolved by the two governments agreeing on a joint statement that would satisfy all parts of the community on the island of Ireland. Our officials could continue working towards that end with all the constitutional parties – but first the violence had to stop.

I was confident that Sinn Féin was ready to talk and deal. Gerry Adams and Martin McGuinness, judging by the information I had received via my contacts in the North, were receptive and waiting for me to act, and Father Reid had conveyed my message to them that I was willing to negotiate. I knew there would be a minefield of words to test us before we found something that both Nationalists and Unionists would accept, but for now I concentrated on getting Sinn Féin on side.

I called in Martin Mansergh and together we reappraised the situation. The division of our island under the Government of Ireland Act had torn apart the constitutional Nationalists and the Republicans: now we had to find common political ground to draw them together. All wanted the same goal – Irish unity – but the journey there was beset with problems, not least the aspirations of the Unionists. The heart of the problem lay in the principle of self-determination and consent, the trouble being that Irish Nationalism endorsed it in a way that did not cater to the wishes of the Unionists and the British government, who under the Anglo-Irish Agreement of 1985 stipulated that Irish unity could come about only with the consent of the majority in the North. For the Nationalists, on the other hand, the principle of consent required British acceptance of the principle of concurrent self-determination, in other words consent of an island-wide majority, North and South.

It was an impasse, but we had to get things moving. Martin Mansergh and I, using the twofold principle of self-determination and consent as the pillar of our negotiation, drafted and revised a document which we saw as a starting point that Martin could present to Sinn Féin through Father Reid.

Father Reid delivered the Sinn Féin response when he met with Martin Mansergh in Dublin. They had accepted three-quarters of it, but had reworded it. There were also certain objections that we set about overcoming. Our policy was to never say 'take it or leave it'. I insisted we always tried to meet their concerns – but we also never forgot that whatever we came up with had to be within the boundaries of what was acceptable to the Irish government.

Martin started work on the draft again. Over the following months, observations were exchanged in writing with

Sinn Féin, and once again Father Reid acted as intermediary.

Negotiations were slow. The initial draft went to the outer limits of what was acceptable. Even when difficulties of communication were partially overcome – and in the circumstances they were difficult enough among Republicans themselves – the whole initiative was understandably treated with extreme caution on both sides. I knew and appreciated that unless we had a document that would also encompass the aspirations of the Unionists and satisfy the British government, it would be doomed to failure.

At that time there were grave doubts that peace or even a ceasefire was possible. No one believed the IRA could be stopped, neither the Loyalists nor the Nationalists. The British army had tried and failed and things seemed to be spinning further and further out of control.

For my part I decided to go the political route and let it be known that all sides had to make a contribution. I was encouraged that Adams accepted that any form of settlement had to include not just the Nationalists but the Unionists too. Paisley had already given me his answer, so I put the DUP to one side for the time being and set about drawing in the other Unionists. I had to find a way to talk to Jim Molyneaux, leader of the biggest Unionist party in the North, the Ulster Unionist Party.

Archbishop Robin Eames, the Anglican Primate of All Ireland, was a close associate of John Major and a good friend and respected adviser to Jim Molyneaux. If anyone could break through the cordon of fear and suspicion surrounding Northern Protestant politicians, he could. Archbishop Eames was often in Dublin, and Kathleen and I got to know him very well. Indeed, he was often seen in Government Buildings, which would have been impossible for Molyneaux. In those days, a Unionist politician seen coming to Dublin would have been viewed with the utmost suspicion by their party constituents. There was always that fear that they were about to sell out and 'surrender' to the South and a united Ireland.

Since the signing of the Anglo-Irish Agreement, Unionists were equally suspicious of Westminster. The agreement had institutionalized the right of the Irish government to be heard in relation to the concerns of the Nationalist community in the North. It had also reaffirmed the British position that had been adopted in 1920–1, restating that if a majority of the citizens in Northern Ireland voted clearly for a united Ireland then legislation to give effect to that wish would be passed at Westminster. For the Republicans, this amounted to a Unionist veto. It also set up an intergovernmental conference, based at Maryfield in County Down, jointly chaired by the British Northern Ireland Secretary and the Irish Minister for Foreign Affairs, and serviced by British and Irish civil servants. As far as the Unionists were concerned, the agreement was the first step to a sell-out and a thorn in their side, and they refused to take part in any conferences or talks under its auspices.

In 1990 two Unionists, the brothers Chris and Michael McGimpsey, argued in the Supreme Court that Article 1 of the agreement contradicted Articles 2 and 3 of the Irish constitution. Their case was rejected because it was noted that Articles 2 and 3 were a claim of 'legal right': they were not merely 'aspirational' but a 'constitutional imperative' intended to achieve Irish unity.

However, as it was, the agreement was an international accord that was binding on the governments of Dublin and London. It could not be ignored; but if, with the agreement of John Major, we could delay the frequency of the meetings at Maryfield and, by leaving long gaps between them, create a de facto suspension, then that would encourage the Unionists to believe I meant business.

I invited the archbishop to see me in Dublin as a representative voice of Unionism.

Archbishop Lord Eames:

'Along came Albert. I met him, I don't know how many times, but from the outset Albert struck me as somebody who wanted to do business and above all else he realized what I was trying to tell people, that unless something is taken a grip of in this, we're going to go hell bent into civil war. And we started to talk: he asked questions about what was the real fear of the Protestants in Northern Ireland, why it was so hard to get a dialogue with the political leaders in Northern Ireland . . .

'[Albert] had been Minister for Finance when John Major had been the Chancellor of the Exchequer, so that there was an understanding there, they knew each other. And I knew John Major. John Major was someone that I always felt if he was Prime Minister, he would have a better hold on the situation than Margaret Thatcher. Margaret didn't read the scene, I'm afraid.

'Along into No. 10 came my friend John Major, and Albert in Dublin, and it seemed to me this was the ideal set-up to get something going. So the friendship and the confidence with John Major built up equally with my confidence in the Taoiseach and we began to analyse the situation beyond the rhetoric of politics and everything else.'

I met Robin Eames on a number of occasions, both socially and in business. Kathleen, always a very good judge of character, had a high respect for him, and she and his wife, Christine, enjoyed each other's company.

Robin had a clear understanding of the Northern Protestant position, and gradually he helped me to a better understanding too, not in a party political sense, but in comprehending their aspirations. His was the authentic voice of moderate

Protestantism that helped me to understand their fears that changes could be made to the status of Northern Ireland without their being consulted or their consent sought. They were already incensed that there had been no prior consultation with them over the content of the Anglo-Irish Agreement, and they felt betrayed that the Irish government had been granted a defined influence over Northern affairs, signalling a shift in British attitude, and in their view a step closer to a united Ireland.

Robin assured me that unless Dublin recognized the problem of the principle of consent, as set out in the Anglo-Irish Agreement, in relation to the Northern Protestant demographic, there was no hope of any settlement. It was the beginning of many discussions between myself and the Primate and between the Primate and John Major, and in the search for peace we were of one accord.

My discussions with Archbishop Eames were not just a means for me to get to know the views of the Unionists: I also wanted them to understand me. I wanted word to go back that I was intent on drawing them to the negotiating table as well as the Republicans, that I intended to break through the old suspicions, and I hoped that the Primate would reassure them of my intentions.

Archbishop Lord Eames:

'I wouldn't say I went so far as to reasssure them completely. I certainly said: "Take this man seriously," and I said to them that this man is listening to you, he's not going to do the "broadcast edicts" of Haughey, as they used to call it. I think there was a grudging understanding that Reynolds was a man that ultimately they could do a deal with, but all Southern politicians were painted in the same light by most of the Unionists because they felt that ultimately the Republic would grab back the consent principle again. They had this whole idea that the real aim of the Dublin government was to take the North into the Republic.

'That was part of the Fianna Fáil history and that was part of their policy ... I think that any Southern politician in those days started from a negative point of view. They had to win confidence if they were going to do dealings with the North. Of course not all of them felt they had to deal with the North, they would deal with Britain, after all Britain was the sovereign power ... Albert's secret was that he never had the airs and graces of Haughey, he was a man on the run, hands-on, come and see me – I'll talk to you, and that got through to the Ulsterman.

'... He was a self-made man. He knew Tyrone and he knew Fermanagh. You have to put it in the context of a man who was hands-on and who was prepared, at times, even to surprise me with the risks he was prepared to take ... I would say something like, "But Albert, you can't agree with that without consulting someone," and he would say, "I agree, and if I agree, it's done."'

John Hume came to see me not long after I had become Taoiseach. He told me that he had had talks with Martin Mansergh about a draft proposal for the British government that paved the way for a declaration by the two governments, but he needed to get it directly to John Major. I knew it was politically impossible for the British Prime Minister to be seen to be dealing directly with the leader of the Nationalist SDLP, and I said I would take it up with Major.

When I approached the subject with Major, he explained that he was in a very precarious position himself. An election was looming, his party was vulnerable and dependent on the Unionists' vital vote, and not only would the opposition jump on him at any hint of dealings with Irish Nationalists in the North, but so would some of his own strong right-wing ministers.

'Anything I do and anything I agree', Major confirmed, 'has to be between the two governments.' And he asked me to make that clear to John Hume.

Besides, I knew the document could not run. Put together by Gerry Adams and Hume, it was written from the Nationalist point of view. It was far too 'green'.

Archaic language was the problem, the expression of ideologies buried in history. Martin Mansergh had been following more or less parallel exchanges with Gerry Adams and Father Reid, and I left him to run with it. He was possibly the only man to truly understand the historical prejudices, the words and nuances that blocked our way to a settlement. I left him to pursue more exchanges, lines of thinking, to find new ways of putting on paper the conditions that could appease both sides and bring them together, in a blend of 'green' with 'orange'.

Progress went at snail's pace and documents were passed to and fro over weeks. With painstaking care phrases, words, the placing of a comma, a full stop, would be analysed so that they exactly and meticulously expressed the philosophy, policy and aspirations of Sinn Féin. At the same time they needed to take into account the concerns of the Unionists, the demands and rigours of the British and Irish constitutions, and the innumerable agendas and agreements at the root of the Troubles. Everything was challenged, amended, suspended in a hundred different ways as progress alternately inched forward and stalled towards the end of my first year as Taoiseach.

Gerry Adams:

'Well, the process of engagement actually became more complicated as it matured, because at the same time as we were in contact with the Irish government and with the SDLP, we were also in contact with the British government and then separately from that again we were doing our best to engage and outreach with people of the Unionist background in our own right – which was just as diligently.

'If someone wrote to me who was obviously a Unionist, or even a Protestant person, we tried to do a meeting, and Father Reid's work in Clonard had also matured to the point where they founded a ministry in Clonard. Clonard was just right on the peace line and is in the area which had been very badly affected by the first outbreak of violence and the first attacks in 1969 on the streets. One street in particular close to Clonard, Bombay Street, was entirely destroyed, so Clonard had for a long time been involved informally with dialogue with our neighbours on the Shankill Road [a Protestant area] and this under Father Reid and the tutelage of Father Gerry Reynolds took another step forward and again they would have invited Sinn Féin at different points into those discussions . . .

'As a party we established a small group to do Unionist out-reach. Tom Hartley, who's now the Mayor of Belfast City, and Jim Gibney would be the two best-known people involved in that, and that work continues today. We met people involved in the community sector in civic Unionism, in the Protestant churches, and as that process continued with people represent-ing business Unionism, and some people involved in chambers of commerce, or people who were, I think, very sensibly look-ing increasingly towards Dublin, looking for an all-Ireland economic approach as opposed to what we had previously. In fairness to them, the reason they were coming to meet us was because they wanted peace and while there was this maybe wider vision, because of their business experience, their desire to meet us was human. They wanted things sorted out and against this, you know Sinn Féin was increasing our electoral support and we were increasingly articulating a peace strategy, so I just presume that was of interest to people and people were being curious.'

I understood why Northern Unionists in business and commerce were starting to look to Dublin. It wasn't for a united Ireland but for a plan of economic cooperation. They could see the benefits that we were beginning to enjoy from our privileged position within the EU. Of course Britain was part of that too, but Northern Ireland was suffering in that some of its social and economic demands were not really being met in the way that was needed. They didn't have the tax advantages of the South to help encourage investment, and whereas agriculture represents only 3.5 per cent of the entire economy in Britain, in Ireland it counts for 55–60 per cent. In these circumstances the pursuit of support for agriculture would always be a higher priority for the Irish than for their British counterparts.

The business world of Ulster also recognized the advantages that peace would bring to the economy, from attracting business investment back into the country to encouraging tourism and trade. They needed peace and they were not afraid to negotiate for it.

Intergovernmental relations were improving. I had appointed a ministerial team of David Andrews, Pádraig Flynn, John Wilson and either Des O'Malley or Bobby Molloy pursued ongoing discussions with the Northern Ireland Secretary Sir Patrick Mayhew, his junior minister Jeremy Hanley and whichever of the Northern parties would come to the table; Seamus Mallon, deputy leader of the SDLP, would be there, and Jim Molyneaux, leader of the UUP, or his party security spokesman, Ken Maginnis, would sometimes come; but as for Paisley, leader of the second biggest Unionist party, the DUP, and his party officials, though they would occasion- ally put in an appearance, they were more likely to walk out than participate in dialogue, either socially or politically.

These talks lasted for six months and though many words were spoken and ideas exchanged, little was achieved.

John Major and I continued to inform each other of what progress was being made, but we met only twice during that period. It was a difficult time for both of us. He went through an election, war broke out in Bosnia, and Britain pulled out of the Exchange Rate Mechanism, while I was trying to get through my own problems with the PDs, the abortion debacle and the Beef Tribunal. Apart from that, there was little encouragement from within our own governments, and our hopes and aspirations for peace were regarded with a great deal of scepticism and pessimism. When we did meet it was always to confirm our determination to find a way to prevent another generation being condemned to a life of violence.

John Major:

'We knew there would be difficulties. The difficulties on my side were fairly apparent. Firstly, there were the political difficulties. There were a lot of people prepared to say if you entered into any form of peace process that you were doing so from weakness and you were bowing to terrorism in trying to reach an agreement. There was always a market for this argument on this side of the water.

'There was also the problem that for a long time the stance had broadly been: "We'll only talk to the IRA when they come out with their hands up and say they were wrong." I parody that slightly, but you know what I mean.

'That seemed to me to be boxing in the IRA and also boxing in those people within the IRA who might have thought the armed struggle had failed and it was time to go in a different direction. You needed to liberate a route for those people to begin to express themselves and take risks themselves for peace. It also seemed to me that if you maintained the traditional stance it was a very easy political stance to make and it is seen to be very strong. Unfortunately, it has a defect, and the defect is that people go on killing for a long time ahead because nothing moves.

'So that was broadly how we saw it.

'The political problems I had were the perceptions . . . The Ulster Unionists in particular had been very close to the Tories for a very long time – even though they were no longer a part of the Tory party as they had been thirty years earlier. But the affections and cross-currents between the Ulster Unionists in particular and a large part, but not all, of the Conservative Party were very real, so the slightest stirring on behalf of the Ulster Unionists was going to cause domestic political problems. And that was true not just in the political party but in many parts of the media as well, though not all. So there were genuine political problems. I think it is true to say that there never was a moment when there was enthusiastic majority support in the cabinet. They did not oppose what we were doing in most cases but they were lukewarm – some did, though not publicly, but they were lukewarm. There were some who were very much in favour of what we were doing, Peter Brooke, Paddy Mayhew, people like that, strong supporters, but they were a minority.

'It wasn't that people didn't want peace, it was because, as one very big beast in the cabinet put it to me, "I think that there is a very real risk that you will be taken for a ride and that it will have a very heavy political cost with no gain. I do not believe you can make progress on this."

'That was from a very significant cabinet member who was prepared for us to try but thought it would be fruitless and we would end up with egg on our faces.

'So that is a very broad summary of the problems and of

course they manifested themselves at almost every aspect of progress.

'Whenever anything happened people peered at it suspiciously to see whether we had done some underhand deal or surrendered some important principle, and there were usually people prepared to say that we had, even when we hadn't. So that was the constant problem.

'There were moments – was it the leak of the framework document that caused so much trouble? I think it might have been, which had been leaked maliciously in order to do damage to the process, so we had little firestorms, sometimes quite big firestorms at regular intervals, so that was broadly the risks that we were taking.

'On Albert's side I think he took risks too. Albert was plainly much closer to the Republicans than I was ever going to be, but even so there was always the fear in their minds that the British government would betray Albert, would upset Albert, would take Albert for a ride. There were always those problems that he had to face. I think I knew that Albert wouldn't deal unfairly with me, and I think Albert knew that I wouldn't deal unfairly with him. But the people surrounding us at a distance were not necessarily prepared to accept that, so I think Albert took risks as well.'

I had continued to try to draw in the Northern politicians. I invited Jim Molyneaux to come to Dublin. I explained that John Major and I had decided on a de facto 'suspension' of Anglo-Irish Agreement meetings for a period of six months, in order that Unionists could come to Dublin and we could meet without the shadow of the agreement hanging over us. He accepted.

In the course of our talks I explained that we needed to negotiate a new agreement, one in which Unionists' aspirations would be recognized and included. I said I understood their current feelings of exclusion, but it was important that they participated in the search for a new formula for peace. I wanted their input and we could only progress if they joined in with talks. Molyneaux was sympathetic to what we were trying to achieve, but Unionist suspicions were hard to allay and progress was slow. The Unionists requested that the six-month suspension be extended, but that was not possible. I suspect they thought that by extending it unconditionally they could claim that the agreement was nullified, and I could not allow that. However, despite their protests and their refusal from then on to return to Dublin, they were aware that we were prepared to accommodate them as best we could. In fact, before it was official that these talks were breaking down, the Unionists complained to John Major that after the six months they still did not have a position paper. Major called and asked us to have one more meeting to give them the opportunity to put a position paper on the table, which we did. In everything I was trying to talk, to draw people in without creating problems or making a big deal of simple requests. My door had to be open for everybody.

The talks with Martin Mansergh were progressing, but too slowly. Trying to find ways of drawing the parties together from totally opposite sides to join in an agreement on the middle ground was a challenge to even the most astute minds.

Gerry Adams:

'We came at it from the point of view that you had to decide what you wanted, and then find a means of describing it. The negotiation of course was to move your opponents to that desired position while realizing also that you may have to move your own position. We had a sense that others moved to try and find words that were acceptable, as opposed to necessarily fulfilling the requirement.

'I remember being very influenced just flicking the channels one time late at night, and there was a BBC2 programme that had a number of very senior British civil servants talking about Cyprus. One of them was head of the British civil service at that time, and he said that their job, and the task of the drafters, is to find words which are capable of being interpreted two or three different ways, even including totally opposite meanings. That to me was an insight. This is a guy who had been very frank and had also expressed regret that in the case he was referring to, that was the way they had approached it. He thought, had they brought greater clarity to the draft that they would have made more progress.'

In September of that year I received a personal letter from Gerry Adams.

He wrote expressing his opinion that there was a danger of misunderstandings, that engaging with the Irish government in separate talks between the Sagart (priest) on one side and John Hume on the other was making the creation of a joint declaration even more problematic. He stressed that the June 1992 document they had presented had been well received by the IRA but was now being argued over in this indirect process of negotiation. Only face-to-face contact could help solve it.

I had sworn I would not meet with any IRA representative until we had a permanent ceasefire, and yet the only way to get peace was to talk. It meant a complete change of policy, and it was a decision only I could take. In his letter to me Adams had said that he understood the dangers should any rumour of this get out. He promised and assured me that although it was a political risk for us all, the Republicans would not breach confidentiality. I believed him. I knew it to be true. I knew too that I could not take anyone in government into my confidence over this. O'Malley for sure would have walked immediately.

The Stormont official talks had stalled. My focus had to be on moving things forward, so whatever the risk, I was determined to take it. I knew that if things went wrong, if word got out, then I'd have to resign. I couldn't impose such a major risk on anyone else; I had to keep it to myself and, of course, Martin Mansergh. It was essential it remained secret: there could be no records, it had to be kept close between ourselves if it was to have any chance of success.

I asked Martin if he was prepared to take on such an assignment, and told him he should give it serious consideration before he said yes. I promised him that if anyone found out, I would take full responsibility. He said he thought it was an extremely courageous decision on my part and he agreed to do it.

Although I knew my career as a politician would be over if word of this got out, I didn't for one moment fear that Adams or Sinn Féin would sell me down the river and I'd no intention of selling them down the river either. They were highly confidential people and I had complete trust in that.

Yet again Father Reid organized the meetings. Again they took place at the Redemptorist Monastery in Dundalk, only this time Martin McGuinness was involved as well as Aidan McAteer, a close and trusted friend of Gerry Adams who had joined his personal staff in 1985.

According to Mansergh:

'Meetings were generally held up on the first floor in a seminarists' common room, and very often a meal would be brought up from the kitchen. Martin McGuinness was always accompanied by another person from Sinn Féin, normally Aidan McAteer, but occasionally others like Tom Hartley.

'Discussions ranged widely with what may be described as

analysis of the political situation in the first part of the meeting, followed by detailed discussion of points in the draft document.'

As always, the various strands of talks continued exclusive of one another. Certainly I knew John Hume was not party to these meetings and had no knowledge of our discussions with Sinn Féin, although he continued his separate negotiations with Adams. I did at one point discreetly mention to John Major that I was involved in a new approach that I thought had the potential to lead to peace, but I did not divulge exactly what.

October 1992 was a crucial time. Talks were progressing well when, suddenly, the coalition with the PDs broke down. For a while everything had to stop. The talks were interrupted and we were thrust into the next election and a new coalition with Dick Spring and the Labour Party.

10

TIGER IN THE SHADOWS

It was 1993 and I had high hopes for our new partnership. Dick Spring was Tánaiste but he had also taken over as Minister for Foreign Affairs, with responsibility for the North and Anglo-Irish relations. I was optimistic that with him by my side we could move forward much more easily than with Des O'Malley. Even though he was not as positive about success as I would have liked, he nevertheless was willing to be convinced.

I briefed him on the work in progress to produce a draft declaration drawing together the three strands of Irish Nationalism, as represented by Sinn Féin, the SDLP and the Irish government, and on the uphill battle being fought to resolve the opposing views on the principles of consent and self-determination which, in my view, were central to any agreement. Although I did not reveal too much of the secret negotiations I had sanctioned between Mansergh and McGuinness, Spring appointed his Labour Party adviser Fergus Finlay to join the official government team working on the draft declaration.

The killings and the violence were continuing in the North, but while they were a constant threat to our hopes for a resolution they also served to urge us on. Dick Spring allowed our ongoing discussions, be they secret or official, a chance to show results. He also understood the imperative for discretion where the secret talks were concerned. We were both aware that should the opposition PDs, or John Bruton's Fine Gael, get the merest whiff of covert contacts, we would be buried under universal criticism.

I left Dick to pursue political negotiations with the Unionists. In my early talks with John Major I had said that consideration would be given to changing Articles 2 and 3 of the constitution if the British government would repeal or amend the Government of Ireland Act. It was these articles that were frustrating any change in the Unionist position. We needed to be more accommodating: Dick clearly understood this and made it his responsibility to reach out to the Unionists in an attempt to break the logjam that was so far stalling the talks with Mayhew.

The Labour Party, despite misgivings on the part of many of its ministers, had joined with Fianna Fáil determined to run an efficient, responsible government. The 'Programme for a Partnership Government' had introduced a system whereby each minister had a programme manager to ensure that the coalition programme was achieved. The Labour managers were recruited from party activists and advisers; we employed civil servants. As Charlie McCreevy, the new Minister for Tourism and Trade, noted:

'It was the most efficient government of which I have been a member. Most efficient. Albert was a great chairman. The Labour Party's idea of having "programme managers" allowed a lot of business to be done outside the cabinet room and so cabinet meetings were very clean and sanitized and business was conducted very efficiently.'

Brian Cowen was now Minister for Communications and he too, like so many of the new administration, was pleased to be back in government:

'I was pleased that first of all Albert was getting another opportunity to serve as Taoiseach, because I think it was obvious that he had many important projects on hand and it would be a great pity if his own personal drive was not applied to them, because he was unorthodox. It was the fact that he wasn't orthodox, I think, that was probably the difference between him and the others. He wasn't orthodox in the way he went about solving problems, and was prepared to go in many different directions to get to the end point, and he was a big risk-taker that way. So it seemed we needed someone like him if this project regarding the North was to go anywhere. We needed him at the helm, there was no doubt about that, because many others would have stepped back from it, for fear of what public exposure of what he was doing at the time would entail in terms of how people would react to it.

'I was also glad from an economic view that Fianna Fáil was remaining at the helm as well as working with a regenerated Labour Party. The Fianna Fáil philosophy would be, in many respects, left of centre in terms of our support basis and we are a very widely representative party of all social and economic classes, more so than any other party in every income group you want to look at. So there was no ideological problem once we got the programme right. There was no reason why we wouldn't be prepared to enter into a partnership government, and that's what we did.'

I truly believed it was a government that could run and run: all I had to do was captain the ship. We hit rocks immediately. On 16 September the previous year, on 'Black Wednesday',

John Major had been forced to devalue the pound and to suspend British membership of the European Exchange Rate Mechanism; now it was our turn to face the same financial crisis. It was the first great test of the partnership. Bertie Ahern, as Finance Minister, fought hard to win EU support in general and German support in particular. It was a fine balance: we could either hold on for a recovery of the pound sterling or hope for a reduction in German interest rates. We were not in a position to support an Irish pound trading at as much as 110p sterling; we could only hope that the Germans would throw us a lifeline. This time they did not. We had no alternative but to devalue by 10 per cent.

Unemployment continued to rise to the worst level in the history of the state. The Labour Party had stood by us over devaluation; now we both had to stand by our first budget. Economically we were plunged into gloom with a new 1 per cent levy on income tax. Unusually, the public seemed to be holding Labour to blame.

Labour's fall in popularity was further exacerbated when it was revealed that most of the numerous new job appointments under Labour, from programme managers through to secretarial staff and ministerial drivers, had been given not only to Labour activists but also to family and friends. Such nepotism was well broadcast across the media, and public admiration quickly turned to assault, which seriously shook the Labour hierarchy. The highly publicized 'new standards and fresh start' were rapidly turning sour.

The Celtic Tiger was there in the distance but as yet it had not come out of the shadows, and we were beset with problems, many of them born out of the two parties manœuvring for public favour.

Brian Cowen sums up some of those problems:

'I think what happened was that during the course of that

campaign certain promises were made, as are made by all parties during a campaign, so everything would be all right if the Labour Party came in and certain things would happen and certain things wouldn't happen.

'I came into that second administration and as Minister of Communications I was in charge of the whole semi-state sector. There were also a lot of new Labour deputies, particularly in the Dublin area, who, I suppose, felt they were going to be in a position to dictate policy; obviously they would have a contribution to make, or an input, but the programme for government that we set out was such that all state companies or any other company had to have a viable plan for going forward and the taxpayer wasn't in a position to support companies that hadn't a viable plan. At the end of the day that would be throwing good money after bad. There was also the EU dimension in terms of competition policy, state aid policy, so you could only inject capital into a company under certain conditions, part of which was the ability to show that if you made an investment you had a plan that would in fact solve the problems that were causing you to look at rationalization in the first place.'

The Aer Lingus crisis was under way and Brian Cowen was doing a great job in trying to sort out the financial problems besetting the airline, as well as TEAM Aer Lingus, the aircraft maintenance wing of the organization, which had recently separated from the main company but had virtually run out of money: it was losing over IR£1 million a month at the time and was only paying its wages and bills with support from the national airline.

To help rectify the situation Cowen had brought in Bernie Cahill, who had led the sugar group Greencore as executive chairman. They came up with the Cahill Plan, involving weekly meetings to discuss progress. Cowen had many astute thoughts on how to develop the company, including examining ideas put forward by TEAM Aer Lingus workers themselves, who together held a majority of the company shares. He was a firm believer that this gave them the right to play a substantial role in how the company could make itself commercially viable.

However, the implementation of some of Brian's ideas sometimes caused friction between him and his Labour counterpart, Ruairi Quinn. As Brian explains, there were sometimes inter-party tensions:

'I was liaising with Bernie Cahill and others in Aer Lingus regarding the plan that was being devised, but by the same token, I was having to report, obviously, to cabinet as to what progress we were making. Government then decided that the Cahill Plan offered the best prospects for Aer Lingus to go forward as a strong company and that was accepted at cabinet.

'I then had the unusual request to go to a Labour Party meeting to address them and to explain what was in it and that's exactly what I did. Some of them then started to question me about what bits they liked and what they didn't. I simply reminded them that this was government policy and I was there to explain what that policy was, and that if they wanted to have an internal discussion about whether it was acceptable or not, that was a matter for the Labour Party, it was not a matter for me, so I withdrew from the meeting at that point.

'There was no hostility as such, there was a lot of animated discussion about things, but we got through that problem. A few of the deputies eventually couldn't support the government and there was a private member's motion and some of them voted against it. Obviously the Labour Party leader had to discipline them by taking away the whip from them for a while. So that was sort of the political fallout over that.

'In fairness, my first appointment under Albert was as his Minister of Labour, so I had a good rapport and a knowledge of the trade union movement and the employer organizations; the social partnership model that we still have was a great way of getting a common analysis of what the nature of the problem was and how government would deal with issues, particularly in the semi-state sector.'

Greencore, the Irish beet sugar company, was a case in point. Fianna Fáil had put forward a suggestion that we should sell the government's 30 per cent share in the company to a big US multinational food consortium instead of offering it to an Irish company. It was a deal worth about IR£60–70 million. The Labour Party were not in favour of the US deal – but instead of discussing it in the Dáil Chamber as normal, they leaked the story to the press that I was trying to ram the deal through against their wishes! They had been very upset by all the recent attacks on them in the media and I believe they were trying to make it look as though they were standing up to Fianna Fáil.

The previous year, in order to encourage American investment into the country, I had initiated a new venture that I'd discussed with Dermot Gallagher, Irish ambassador in Washington.

Dermot Gallagher:

'It was the establishment of what is now called the Ireland–America Economic Advisory Board. It was set up in the summer of 1992, and the first meeting was held at the Waldorf Astoria in New York that September. The IAEAB, which still continues, brought together a group of fifteen to eighteen Irish American businesspeople who were invited to be members of a special board set up by the Taoiseach. He would then meet them twice a year in the US and brief them on economic developments in Ireland and in return get their thinking on global economic developments. It was also a way of developing relationships with each of them. They were all chairs or directors of major businesses and corporations, so you could not only meet them as a group but also individually. It gave you access to some of the top boards in the US, people like Dan Tully, chair of Merrill Lynch, Jack Welsh of General Electric, Don Keough of Coca-Cola, Chuck Feeney the billionaire and Tony O'Reilly. They were key people and rising out of that Dan Tully brought Merrill Lynch to Dublin. It was going to Switzerland but it came to Dublin instead . . .

'I always felt that we needed to tap into that top business network more effectively than we had, but Albert moved and brought them in. And into another strategy. Every time he met them he always briefed them on the peace process. Bill Flynn [chairman of Mutual of America] was a member of that group as well, and he had a very close relationship with Bill. So he was briefing them and linking them into the peace process.

'Albert's business background meant there was an instinctive ease of dialogue and communication between them.'

Building up employment in the country and curbing the tide of emigrants was high on my agenda from the start. The American connection was of prime importance in this. Just as an example, Kieran McGowan came to me one day; he was head of the Industrial Development Agency, whose mandate was to attract investment into Ireland. He took me to one side and asked me if I would make time for a businessman from the States who could only see me that afternoon. That same businessman brought Intel to Ireland, against fierce competition from Scotland and Israel and others. We started with two thousand jobs and ended up employing over five thousand.

Thc advantage we had was the tax – our attractive corporation tax rate of 12.5 per cent. However, if America itself were to introduce punitive taxation on overseas investment, then those companies who had come to us would be gone. With one-fifth of our total manufacturing workforce now dependent on US investment, this was a situation we monitored carefully,

There was a moment of high anxiety that summer when Washington suddenly passed a measure to limit tax concessions to US firms based abroad which could have had serious long-term consequences for the Irish economy. It was at this point that our close relationship with the US was called into play. Dermot Gallagher immediately contacted the chair of the congressional committee and got him to agree to an amendment, as he recalls:

'I then went and had a very difficult session with the chair of the Senate Committee, Daniel Patrick Moynihan. Albert then rang him and Moynihan said, "I'll agree if the White House agrees."

'I had to get to Clinton. Ethel Kennedy, Bobby Kennedy's wife, was organizing an annual dinner. I phoned and said, "Ethel, I need to be at that dinner and, more importantly, I need to be seated beside Clinton." She sat me beside him and he agreed and I went back to Moynihan and it made the front page of the *Irish Times*.

'The story suggested there could have been one or two elements that could have been damaging but in fact there were none. We got 100 per cent of what we wanted ... In fact a number of American companies coming to Ireland had put the final decision on hold to see whcther this would go through. Albert in fact phoned Moynihan and the President to thank them.'

It was evidence of the close relationship we shared with

Irish America and the White House that Dermot Gallagher could lobby so effectively, and more importantly could get the ear of the President. It was also a time of shared cooperation and great relief for Dick Spring and me.

At other times cooperation was harder to achieve. Finances and how to make the most of our assets were a constant source of disagreement. Labour was in uproar over the sale of 25 per cent of Telecom Éireann, the state communications service, to the giant Cable and Wireless for £1 billion. I saw it as a great deal; they threatened to leave government if the deal went through.

Fianna Fáil succeeded in securing an 'amnesty tax'. This allowed wealthy individuals to bring their assets back into Ireland on penalty of a fixed 15 per cent levy on disclosed untaxed funds. The press denounced it as a 'cheat's charter', a 'fiddler's freebie', but it brought in a significant level of much-needed revenue.

Dick Spring was again very upset at the public and media reaction.

I was determined not to join in with this tit-for-tat policy of vying for position that seemed to be evolving. I had Northern Ireland at the forefront of my attention and I did not want any-thing in government to distract me from that, so when the Labour minister of state Emmet Stagg was exposed in the press for being involved in a sex scandal, I sent out a message to Fianna Fáil members not to join in the controversy. I knew Labour would be embarrassed enough. Calls were made for Stagg to resign, but he refused to do so, which led to very strained relations between him and Spring.

I was in Cyprus on holiday when I received a fax from Dick Spring warning me that Labour could not countenance the new 'amnesty tax' as it served only to benefit the super-rich and that he was meeting with Bertie Ahern to go through the forthcoming budget. Yet again Labour threatened that if I didn't agree with their decision it could lead to a general election – in other words, back off or else!

This time I sent a firm message to our coalition partners, warning them: no leaks to the press, no spin in the media. I did not want to see headlines about how Labour's principles had won over my policies!

By the time I returned things had calmed down. However, I heard rumours that Bertie Ahern, far from backing me, had not only offered his support to Spring but agreed to drop the current discussions on the 'amnesty tax' or to postpone it until the autumn. This was not on as far as I was concerned: the tax concession would bring in finance that we needed for developing our infrastructure; it would also bring business investment back into the country and everybody would gain.

When it finally came up at a meeting I spoke in favour of it and so did Bertie Ahern, even though Labour had claimed Bertie had promised to support them. However, though the measure went through, it was another sign that our so called 'partnership' was faltering.

Under the Irish Nationality and Citizenship Act, passed in 1956, the Minister for Justice may grant a passport to a foreigner if he or she has what are termed 'Irish connections'. The exact qualifications for such 'connections' are not defined – and as Michael O'Morain, a Fianna Fáil deputy at the time of the original debate, said, 'an Arab who drinks Irish whiskey' could claim 'Irish connections'.

This particular scheme had been revived some years before I took office as a means of attracting foreign investment into Ireland through the Business Migration Scheme. Such schemes already existed in many other countries, Australia and Canada being two. For Ireland it meant that a foreign national who made a substantial business investment – over IR£500,000 – into a job creation scheme would be granted naturalization and rights of residence in the Republic. From the investors' point of view this had the added bonus of allowing them free access to the whole European Community and all that that meant.

The scheme had been running successfully for several years, and a number of accountants and lawyers were involved in brokering such deals between investors and Irish companies.

Labour were about to publish their Ethics Bill when a story broke in the press that C&D had been involved in such a deal two years earlier and had received a IR£1 million investment loan from the Masris, a mother and son who were attracted to the scheme, thus creating approximately fifty jobs straight away, and many more later.

'Passports for Sale' ran the headlines, and a row erupted in which I was vilified as having misused my position as Taoiseach to attract the Masri investment into my family company. True, I was a shareholder in the company; but as soon as I became a minister I had resigned from my position as chairman and my son Philip had taken over. At that point he was managing director, with complete authority over the running of the company, and such day-to-day business decisions were entirely under his mandate – and indeed there was no reason why he should not have taken advantage of a legitimate business scheme open to every other business. In fact, I knew nothing about the Masri family or their involvement with C&D. (As it happens, they recouped the value of the investment within five years of making it.)

The press, the opposition and, of course, the Labour Party, had a field day. Questions were tabled as to my role in the affair, while PD Deputy Michael McDowell, a senior counsel, drafted a private member's Bill to revoke the Masris' citizenship unless they made a declaration of loyalty to the state in an open court before 31 July.

The excitement was deflated when Minister for Justice Máire Geoghegan-Quinn announced in the Dáil on 31 May 1994 that the Masri family had already undergone such a procedure, and that all legal requirements had been complied with. She further declared that they had also invested IR£1,500,000 in a forestry project, creating around fifty jobs, and had indicated that a further investment of IR£1,500,000 would be available for another venture.

She then asked the deputy if he was aware of the length of time that the scheme had been in existence, and continued:

'If the representative of any party which has been in Government in that period is tempted to stand up and challenge what I have just said, I would strongly advise him or her, right now, to remain seated and have a word instead with his or her party colleagues. I would also strongly advise that they ask their colleagues whether any of them ever sought to extend the scheme so as to allow for the grant of naturalisation applications on the basis of investments not necessarily falling into the direct job creation category – for example, for investments in golf clubs. If they are told the truth about this they will also be told that the Government, on the recommendation of a Fianna Fáil Justice Minister, opposed the golf club move and that it failed. Deputy McDowell will not require cross-party consultations to get the facts, if indeed facts are of any interest to him.'

I told Dick Spring that he was welcome to inspect the Department of Justice files on the Masri deal and was somewhat taken aback when he said he'd already done so! For once I was speechless. Nevertheless, having perused all the papers he was forced to admit that everything had been conducted in an 'ethical and above board, arm's-length way'.

McDowell then turned on Spring, pronouncing him 'morally brain dead'. Attacked from all sides, Spring promised new legislation to toughen up the rules and to place the passport scheme on a statutory basis. When McDowell confronted me with the 'promise', I said no such 'promise' had been made as yet and that when the government had decided on legislation it would be brought before the Dáil.

The European elections and two key by-elections were but a week away. Dick Spring seemed to grow more and more enraged as the question of legislation was deferred. He seemed to believe he had to prove his party's superiority over Fianna Fáil, and in a TV broadcast said that henceforth Labour would become more assertive.

It was a great pity that all this political manœuvring was distracting from what was essentially a successful administration. Towards the end of 1993 and throughout 1994, despite our initial problems, our economy was beginning to move forward and grow stronger. Europe's role in this recovery was an important one and the deal I had negotiated for Ireland was starting to take effect as the IR£8 billion began to feed into our economy. In fact, the country actually ended up with IR£8.8 billion, which was all accounted for at the end of the payment period in 1999.

Brian Cowen assesses the situation at that time:

'It was a strong deal for Ireland. Albert obviously was a strong negotiator and had the ability to represent the country well and get the best possible deal.

'He was a networker, and was able to call in various favours from different colleagues in Europe. Basically, we just wanted a bit of fair play for those on the periphery of Europe. We were talking about the establishment of a single market. Jacques Delors had brought forward the idea of Structural and

Cohesion Funds that would enable those on the periphery to compete in what would otherwise be a difficult and competitive market. We were on the extremity of the Union and this was going to be a very important strategic outcome for us and we had to have the wherewithal and the resources to make sure that as the impact of the single market started to evolve, we had the means to compete.

'So all of that money went into very important areas like infrastructure, and into significant social funds that helped us to reskill and retrain our people. We did a lot of good work with that allocation.'

The advanced telecommunications system I had introduced some years earlier now came into its own as the EU's High Level Group on the Information Society, led by the German Commissioner Martin Bangemann, published the Bangemann Report, introducing a very strong framework for the liberalization of telecommunications in Europe. This was of huge benefit to us as by definition telecommunications and technologies overcome the disadvantage of being on the periphery and we were well set up to enter the market in software, for example, at a highly competitive level.

We were starting to become a very enticing location for investors. A large part of our industrial policy was geared towards attracting foreign direct investment and our Industrial Development Agency, which had become very professionally organized, was at this point doing well successfully marketing the country not just as English-speaking but also as an integrated member of the European Union with a consumer market that was becoming bigger and more sophisticated every year.

The Celtic Tiger was beginning to roar. I was very aware that the North would be watching and that, as our economy grew, so they would want to be a part of it.

Since the division of the island of Ireland many people in the North, of all persuasions, felt that the Republic had nothing to offer, that an economy based on subsistence-level agriculture could not compare with the benefits offered by Great Britain in the post-war years, with its social welfare system and, for the most part, thriving industrial economy. Now suddenly all that was changing: we were becoming a stable and flourishing economy.

I had always believed that if we could create a strong enough economy in the South, to equate with that offered by Britain, we would have the basis for bringing peace to Northern Ireland. If Nationalists in the North, who were still excluded from economic and political power there, saw our economy progressively growing and modernizing, they would be encouraged to increase their own demands to be part of the expanding economic, social and political infrastructure of Ireland; and the Unionists – the more progressive-thinking Unionists, that is – would also see the advantages of trading with a newly developing market right on their borders, with all the possibilities that offered – more jobs, more investment and more trade. As a member of Fianna Fáil I held the unity of the country to be a noble objective and I was determined to see it realized.

However, at the start of my second administration in January 1993, our peace efforts in Northern Ireland were moving very slowly indeed, particularly the intergovernmental talks and our own secret negotiations with Sinn Féin. Dick Spring had seemed a positive force as a coalition partner and I certainly felt that as Tánaiste and Minister of Foreign Affairs, his input would assist in getting things moving with the constitutional parties. But to get things moving towards a permanent ceasefire with Sinn Féin and the paramilitaries, we had to start thinking outside the box.

11

ST PATRICK'S DAY AT THE WHITE HOUSE

I'd always believed that to get a lasting peace in the North we needed to draw Irish America into the equation.

Since the mid-nineteenth century, in the wake of mass emigration, the Irish in America had sought to use the US as a launch pad to stimulate political change in Ireland. In 1858 the Fenian Society in America was founded by John O'Mahony, Michael Doheny and James Stephens, in a ceremony in front of Tammany Hall, New York. All three men were members of the Irish Republican Brotherhood, and the objective of their new society was to rally Irish America to the cause of Irish independence from Britain. Although they had not succeeded in their planned military attacks against the British in Canada, they had helped to finance the Fenians back home in Ireland.

Now we needed to turn to Irish America again.

Edward Kennedy was already a strong supporter of all things Irish and his influence was a vital ingredient in the fight against violence. As far back as 1977 Senator Kennedy,

267

together with John Hume, had worked to set up a group of high-powered Irish Americans that became known as 'The Four Horsemen', whose aim was to help break down the traditional reluctance of certain other Irish American Democrats to condemn Republican violence and to encourage instead constitutional Nationalism as a viable altern-ative. The four members were Senator Kennedy himself; the Speaker of the House of Representatives, Thomas 'Tip' O'Neill; Senator Daniel Patrick Moynihan; and the Governor of New York, Hugh Carey. In fact, it was Tip O'Neill who began the now traditional White House lunch on St Patrick's Day when a token bowl of shamrock is presented to the President on behalf of the Irish Government.

On St Patrick's Day 1992, in my first year as Taoiseach, my Foreign Minister David Andrews had lunched with President George Bush and the First Lady, Barbara Bush, along with other Irish politicians and dignitaries. However, as he reported back to me and noted in his autobiography, *The Kingstown Republican*:

'On St Patrick's Day, I made the usual shamrock delivery trip to The White House and met President George Bush Sr and his Secretary of State James Baker. One thing I recall about James Baker was his keenness to talk to me about rugby, for which he had a great enthusiasm. At this time President Bush was dealing with some financial scandals in Congress and was somewhat preoccupied. However, he was very courteous and his wife Barbara was a charming lady who regaled us with stories of her grandchildren. We sat and chatted with them in the Oval Office for a short time. The talk was mainly and predictably about American–Irish relations. We then went out to the famous Rose Garden for the standard photo opportunity – me presenting the President with a bowl of shamrock. There was a large gathering of the press corps waiting for us. I'm afraid they had little interest in St Patrick's Day or shamrocks and were more concerned with the financial scandals bedevilling Congress.'

Bush's predecessor Ronald Reagan had drawn very much on the blue-collar Irish vote, and was always interested in all things Irish. He had backed Maggie Thatcher over the Anglo-Irish Agreement and had supported it through an annual US contribution of $20 million to an international fund for Ireland. Bush, too, in his campaign for the presidency had advocated family values and the same hard line on communism that had attracted the normally Democrat-leaning Irish vote to his party, but he demonstrated only polite acknowledgement and non-interference when there were problems to be sorted.

However, news had reached us in Ireland of the rapid rise of a young lawyer from Little Rock who had been appointed Governor of his home state of Arkansas. He'd particularly caught our attention because, as a champion of civil rights causes, urged on by a young civil rights activist from North Belfast, Rita Mullen, he'd signed a decree on St Patrick's Day 1978 declaring it to be 'Human Rights for Ireland Day' throughout Arkansas.

I'd followed the career of this young man, Bill Clinton, who was of Irish descent, as had several wealthy and influential Irish Americans. He was charming, charismatic and ambitious, and seemed destined to go right to the top. When he decided to run, his presidential campaign was led by his former Georgetown University room-mate, Chris Hyland. He had been made deputy national political director with the job of bringing those blue-collar Irish Americans back to the Democratic fold as supporters of Bill Clinton.

Hyland brought on board Niall O'Dowd, New York publisher of the *Irish Voice*, which dominated the Irish

American media market in the United States. O'Dowd, as it happened, had been urging his friend Brendan Scannell, a diplomat in the Irish Embassy in Washington, to find a way to join the Clinton campaign, convinced that the Democrat candidate was the only one who would be willing to help in the developing search for peace in Northern Ireland.

The three had met and proposed setting up a committee to rally Irish America to the cause, under the name 'Irish Americans for Clinton'. Bruce Morrison was suggested as chairman. Morrison was a Connecticut lawyer who had been responsible for writing recent legislation for Congress, under which entry visas were granted to many Irish emigrants to the US; they were known as 'Morrison visas'. He had been successfully helped in this by a huge lobby at grassroots level, and had the support of important legislators like Senator Edward Kennedy. Boston's mayor, Raymond Flynn, signed on as co-chairman.

Bill Clinton had attracted the attention of such high-fliers when, during the New York primary election for the Democratic nomination, he had appeared at a forum on Irish issues. The presidential hopeful stunned his audience with his knowledge of the subject and the perceptive focus of his intentions should he be elected President. He promised to appoint a peace envoy to Ireland; he was willing to support the issue of visas enabling Gerry Adams and other prominent Sinn Féin figures to enter America; and he endorsed the McBride Principles, which embraced equal opportunity guidelines for US firms operating in Northern Ireland, where there was a legacy of job discrimination against Catholics. As legendary veteran civil rights lawyer Paul O'Dwyer commented at the time, 'I never heard a candidate who knew more about Ireland.'

Such promises did not endear him to the British government. Many in the Conservative Party were incensed that an American presidential candidate was getting involved in Northern Ireland, and in the run-up to the election they did their best to discredit Clinton personally. They even, at the request of the Bush administration, went so far as to investigate his passport files, in an attempt to detect whether or not he had tried to change his nationality in order to avoid the Vietnam draft. This was to cause deep resentment in the future.

This, then, was the man elected as President of the United States of America on 3 November 1992 and inaugurated on 20 January 1993.

I was interested to learn more. Election promises are one thing, fulfilling them, another.

During that ten-week hiatus, the President-elect was visited by a delegation from 'Irish Americans for Clinton', now renamed 'Americans for a New Irish Agenda', eager to pursue the promise of a 'peace envoy' to Northern Ireland. It was not a success. It was unprecedented for a group of Irish lobbyists to engage with an incoming administration, and for various reasons the approach was not well received. However, Chris Hyland told them the White House would welcome their ideas in written form for future consideration. As soon as the inauguration was over, Mayor Flynn returned with a five-point plan which he took to the White House. Signed by himself and the chairman, Bruce Morrison, on behalf of the other activists, it demanded action on the appointment of a peace envoy.

In London, John Major and the British government viewed this 'promise' with dismay and were determined to get the initiative dropped. In an attempt to alleviate the tension between the two countries, they suggested a 'fact-finding' mission instead of a 'peace envoy'. I watched from afar as the diplomatic manœuvring went on. Speaker Thomas Foley was at one time recommended to lead such a mission. He was a confirmed Anglophile and would have been a most suitable candidate for the British, but not for the Irish Americans who reacted angrily to the suggestion. The President, though convinced America had a role to play, postponed his decision to another day and finally the whole controversy was dropped, but not forgotten.

In Northern Ireland, too, the newly developing Irish American influence was being monitored with interest by the Republicans.

Martin McGuinness:

'From the very beginning of the process we had a small circle of people who were basically our negotiating team, which involved no more than seven or eight people around Gerry Adams, and we were discussing the importance of Irish America and how to mobilize Irish America in support of the work that we were engaged in.

'We were conscious of the fact that there were people in the States like Niall O'Dowd and Ciaran Staunton, Bill Flynn in particular and Chuck Feeney, who were coming together as a group against the backdrop of what was happening here. Also, the fact that a new American President was coming into the White House, in the form of Bill Clinton. It was obvious to some of us who had done a bit of research on Bill Clinton that, when he was educated in England at university, it was the time of the civil rights protests in Derry and other parts of the North, so he would have had considerable knowledge of the political situation in the North of Ireland. Very few people in England were interested in what was happening in the North, but he was and he went on to become President of the US, and even before being elected he showed himself willing to engage with Irish American support groups. At the same time, the fact that people like Bill Flynn and Niall O'Dowd and Chuck Feeney and others came together (we named them the "Connolly House group"), we realized that they would have the ability to mobilize the vast bulk of Irish America behind the need to build a peace process in the North of Ireland. Bill Flynn is extremely well connected in New York, probably more well connected on the Republican side than on the Democratic side, but certainly all of them delivered big time in terms of the influence they brought to bear on the Clinton administration, and on Bill Clinton's willingness to be part of the project which would see a political breakthrough.'

The Irish ambassador in Washington at that time, Dermot Gallagher, was a very good friend of mine who, like me, had been born in a town on the banks of the Shannon, Carrick on Shannon in County Leitrim. I remember him talking to me one day about the special arrangement that the Irish had with the President of America and that we should use it to our advantage.

Dermot Gallagher:

'We have a date each year in the presidential diary for a meeting – 17 March – and it carries on from year to year. It's unique and every other country would give their right hand for it, but although we've sent different ministers and politicians, we've never exploited it.

'Albert had a strategy that made perfect sense, in that he suggested that it should be the Prime Minister, the Taoiseach, who should take the opportunity of meeting with the President.

'It had always seemed to me when I first went to Washington that there was no point in having such access if you didn't use it. The social contacts were enjoyable and good fun, but you've also got to convey a political message when it's required. It was obvious that Albert clearly saw that the US was going to be core, was going to be central to breaking down the Northern logjam, and he had this date every St Patrick's Day in the President's diary and he was going to use it at prime ministerial level. That way, too, knowing that they were going to meet on an ongoing basis, he could establish a relationship and that was critical.

'I had been in Washington for a year and was there to set it up and to plan the day together with the White House. We developed it into a much broader event where we not only had the formal meeting and the presentation of the shamrock but the President then gave a glorious party in honour of the visiting Taoiseach, Albert, and his wife, Kathleen.'

This was not my first visit to America – I had been there on official visits before in my different ministerial roles – but it was my first visit as Taoiseach. In Ireland, security for the Prime Minister is limited to two outriders and two security officers including your driver. In America it is more evident, and as soon as we entered US airspace we were joined by a posse of military planes who accompanied us to our destination.

Our first stop was New York, and here we were astonished at the cavalcade of about a dozen official long limousines and outriders, full of FBI security agents who drove our party to our hotel.

Here at Fitzpatrick's Hotel in Manhattan we were escorted to our penthouse suite and advised by the head FBI man that the floor below was completely occupied by his men, as was usual.

Our son Abbie, who had already moved to New York where he was working as a stockbroker, was anxious for Kathleen and me to see his new apartment. We readily agreed and were about to leave our suite when the FBI man stepped forward, very concerned that such an impromptu visit was not on the agenda! It is now, I told him. I think Kathleen must have recognized the glint in my eye, because she quickly took control and asked what was expected. He explained that before any visit the destination premises had to be secured and an advance detail had to totally check the apartment and the team effect a complete sweep for bugs! But it's our son's apartment, we argued. Sorry, Sir, was the reply.

Abbie handed over the keys, security swept in and out, and we followed on an hour later in our cavalcade of limos. Apparently, Abbie was regarded with suspicion by his neighbours from then on, as the sight of all those heavyweight FBI men invading his apartment led them to believe the worst!

That first meeting with President Clinton was very exciting. We'd met socially on the eve of St Patrick's Day at the dinner organized by the American Ireland Fund, a charity funded by Dr Tony O'Reilly to benefit 'peace, culture and charity in Northern Ireland'. It was attended by many of the big names in Congress as well as visiting Irish politicians, and we were entertained by Irish musician Sharon Shannon and singer Phil Coulter, who had written a song especially for the occasion.

Clinton lived up to every expectation. Everyone mentioned his charisma and with good reason. He engaged with you directly, was totally charming and was very knowledgeable on world affairs, in fact on every subject under discussion; his interest and depth of awareness of what was going on in Ireland were extraordinary.

Kathleen and I, together with Bill Clinton and his wife Hillary, a very bright and welcoming woman, stood together to receive the line of distinguished guests. Everyone was very relaxed, although security was so tight that the traditional Irish piper had to surrender his ceremonial dagger before being allowed to escort the President and myself into the reception!

The Kennedy clan were well represented and we were delighted to meet up with our good friends Edward Kennedy and his wife, Vicky, as well as with his sister, Jean Kennedy Smith. I had already been told that Jean had been offered the position of ambassador in Dublin and I thought it was an excellent choice. The name Kennedy was well received in Ireland, and although she had no former experience as a career diplomat, her whole life had been imbued with politics and I knew she appreciated and understood what we were trying to achieve. I also guessed that her brother had been instrumental in getting her the appointment and that meant we would have his support for all we hoped to achieve with the peace process. I realized, too, that to be able to call on his backing in the White House would prove to be an invaluable asset.

There were others I met that night who were to play key parts in the peace process: Nancy Soderberg and Tony Lake, Clinton's foreign policy advisers; former US judge and senator Chris Dodd; and, of course, all those Irish American power players who had helped to get Clinton into the White House.

It was a great night in every way. There was an air of real optimism – we all felt it. Not just because Clinton and his wife Hillary represented a bright new future for America, but because Ireland too would share in it. I remember lining up with Tom Foley, John Hume, Dermot Gallagher and Tony O'Reilly, and even Clinton joined us as we all sang 'When Irish Eyes are Smiling'.

President Bill Clinton:

'When Albert visited the White House in 1993 for our first meeting, I liked his easy manner, quick wit, and his clear conviction that we needed to work together to end the violence in

Northern Ireland. He knows I agreed with him and he was determined not to let me off the hook. I liked that.'

Bill Clinton and I met the following day for our first formal meeting in the Oval Office to talk through Irish American affairs. Ted Kennedy and Jean Kennedy Smith joined us for the official announcement of her appointment as the new American ambassador to Dublin. I warmed to her immediately: she was a very bright, strong, responsible woman and determined to focus on and succeed with the task in hand.

I shook her hand. 'Welcome home!' I said.

Then it was down to business. I felt an immediate rapport with President Clinton: he was a man after my own heart, a man to get things done.

We had a long talk. He told me about his distant Irish ancestors from Fermanagh, now in Northern Ireland on the border with the Republic, and that he had a strong sense of 'Irishness' and Ireland. He'd visited Ireland back in the late sixties when, as a Rhodes Scholar at Oxford, he was caught up by the whole civil rights movement in the North. He'd come over to Dublin with a friend and joined up with others, two boys and two girls. The media had recently tracked down one of the girls to the Southern US, where she was working as a teacher, and she'd given a glowing report of him as a good friend and said that she thought he'd be a great President.

He told me just how big a part the Irish American vote had played in helping him to the White House a couple of months earlier and that he couldn't have done it without their support. Presidents Reagan and Bush had stolen votes from the Democrats and he was grateful to have got them back; now he wanted to keep them with him to go forward to the next election.

He also had a firm commitment to the Irish American leaders who had led his campaign and would work for peace in Ireland. As he put it to me: 'Now it's over to you. Tell me, what I can do to work for peace?'

His first decision, he said, and top of his agenda was to appoint a peace envoy as soon as possible, and the man he would like for the position was Senator George Mitchell. George Mitchell was the Democratic Senate Majority Leader at the time, a very highly respected and astute man, under whose leadership the Senate had approved the formation of the North American Free Trade Agreement and the World Trade Organization. He was a politician of the highest standing and a very honourable man – in fact, when Clinton offered him the prestigious appointment to the United States Supreme Court, he turned it down in order to continue helping the Senate to pass significant healthcare legislation. I knew of his impeccable career and I believed that when the time was right he would be a fine choice.

So when President Clinton asked me what did I think of Senator George Mitchell for the post of special envoy, I replied, 'Fine, I like the man very much and in the future he would be very welcome – but not now.'

I knew he was looking for my approval, but I also knew it would be a foolish move and I said so. I warned him that to send anyone over as an envoy at that particular time would end in failure. The politicians in Ireland would react badly to such an appointment, I explained; they were about to go into local elections and were operating under duress, striving to find positions for their own parties. It was difficult enough to get them to talk or mix between themselves. And the Unionists definitely wouldn't even meet him. Under the present circumstances such a venture would end in failure and that would only reflect badly on the President. I asked him to be guided on this by me. I knew there were people pushing him to move quickly on this appointment, but the timing was just not right. When it was, I promised, I'd be the first to tell him.

I could see he was a bit taken aback but he agreed to accept my judgement. I was convinced that he was very serious in his intention of helping, not just to satisfy the lobbyists, but for himself; he wanted to make a contribution. That was his primary motivation, and he felt he could make a difference.

President Bill Clinton:

'I thought the timing might be right because Ireland's growing prosperity increased the appeal of peace as a precondition for Northern Ireland's participating in it, because the leaders of Ireland and the UK believed progress was possible, and because leaders of the Irish American community told me the time was right and they were committed to it.'

We started from there. I briefed him on the strategy I had in place, what was going to happen, what I intended to do about bringing peace to Northern Ireland and what I was going to demand from the IRA and the Loyalist paramilitaries before I would accept any of their conditions. Before any talks around the negotiating table, before any constitutional changes, I wanted the guns silenced, the violence to stop: from both sides I intended to get a permanent ceasefire. Then and only then could the talks start and inclusion begin.

He was intrigued to learn I was working alongside John Major. I remember him commenting that he understood there was a tradition of hostility between the British and Irish prime ministers! 'Well, that may be the case in some instances,' I assured him, 'but in this one it's not!'

I told him that John Major and I shared a special relationship going back some years, that we were both determined to work together and that peace in Northern Ireland was at the top of both our agendas. I impressed on him that John and I were working for a common purpose and that although from time to time there would be nuances that would differ, we were very close and the two governments were working hand in glove to achieve a political understanding. I assured Clinton that in his meetings with Major he would get the same message.

'And that is another reason why a peace envoy at this time would be wrong,' I said. 'At this time, it would hold up the process we have put in motion, its benefits would be short-lived and our strategy is too important to risk that.'

He accepted it immediately. 'I'll take your judgement on that,' he said.

I went through the whole situation, explaining that though the IRA's violence was continuing, they were also fearful that the Loyalist paramilitaries were becoming equally if not more powerful, and that neither side wanted to slide out of control into civil war or to condemn their children to a life of similar violence. The British army could not defeat them, and it was evident that more and more people would die unless an alternative solution could be found – which was why now, and only now, Sinn Féin were prepared to try to find a way to a political solution.

I finished by saying that I would come back to him and that when I did it would be with a very firm plan that I would need his assistance in implementing. An envoy would be smoke and mirrors at this time and wouldn't fit into my strategy, which I believed would be successful in delivering peace.

President Bill Clinton:

'That first meeting at the White House on St Patrick's Day 1993 set the pace and tone for the work we did together while Albert remained Taoiseach. During that first meeting, we discussed the Troubles in great detail. Mostly I sought Albert's advice. Among other things, we agreed that I should encourage the resumption of dialogue between the Irish and British governments.'

Dermot Gallagher:

'There are politicians who instinctively understand one another and Clinton understood. I think he clearly got the message that there was a definitive strategy which was going to lead forward.

'I think this relationship with Clinton was something new in that he was prepared to be engaged in a significant way. It showed the depth and quality of the engagement that he wanted to make a difference, but he was a good politician in that he was only going to get involved if there was clear guidance.'

It was evidence of just how serious his intentions were that Clinton gave me his personal private telephone number, so that when I needed to contact him urgently about something important, I got straight through without having to go through anybody else.

It was a good meeting. We were both direct in our dealings and talked openly to one another. He announced his decision in his speech at the shamrock presentation ceremony later in the Roosevelt Room, when he said that, although the envoy idea had been shelved, 'We decided, after our consultations, that it is certainly an option that I should leave open.' He was, he added, 'going to stay in touch closely with Prime Minister Reynolds. We're going to talk frequently, and I expect to have an ambassador in Ireland pretty soon.' More importantly, he added: 'The most significant thing I should be doing now is to encourage the resumption of dialogue between the British and Irish governments which I think is a critical precondition to any establishment of a lasting peace. I'm going to continue to stay on top of the situation, involved in it.'

I left America confident that we had strong support from a

President who was prepared not only to act but also to listen. The group of high-powered Irish Americans led by Bill Flynn were equally eager to help with the push for peace; but, even though they had been eager for an envoy to be appointed, they too were now willing to listen and take their lead from John Major and me.

Dermot Gallagher:

'There were people who initially wanted to move very quickly, and they wanted an envoy appointed, but I think they also realized that Albert Reynolds had a clear strategy and they bought into that once they realized there was a definite track and we had access to information. In a sense Albert controlled the strategy and moved it forward, and they linked into that and realized that it would have been counterproductive, it would have been wrong, to set up a separate track when the people in charge, the Prime Minister in Downing Street and the Prime Minister in Dublin, had set out a strategy and were working closely together in a way that was unique and that had not happened previously. They linked into that and strongly supported it.'

Back in Ireland I received a call from John Major, delighted and relieved at the outcome of the envoy situation. For my part I was very satisfied that my strategy for the peace process had been strengthened by this third vital element – Irish America – and that I had the unqualified support of the most powerful president in the world, President Clinton. I had moved outside the box.

12

DESPERATE TIMES,
LONELY TIMES

That spring of 1993 saw a surge in the level of IRA violence when two bombs planted in a wastebin in a shopping centre in Warrington, England, exploded killing two small boys, Jonathan Ball, aged three, and Timothy Parry, aged twelve. Fifty six others were injured. The attack sickened the world and it did not help the Republican cause. In the Republic itself the killings led to a wave of revulsion and tens of thousands attended a peace rally in Dublin.

Undeterred, the IRA set off a bomb in the Baltic Exchange in the heart of London's financial district, causing billions of pounds' worth of damage, and in Belfast the murders and atrocities between Loyalist and Nationalist paramilitaries continued to escalate.

It was a desperate time and a lonely time. The cynics were all too ready to criticize and undermine any hopes of bringing peace to Northern Ireland – why should I succeed where others had failed? Sometimes it was hard to keep one's courage in the face of such pessimism and such depressing devastation. I could not confide to anyone, certainly not within my own government, my knowledge that, despite the violence, we were slowly progressing with the negotiations that were going on behind the scenes.

Although at the time John Major and I certainly didn't divulge to one another the secret negotiations taking place, I learned later that a few days before the Warrington bombing the British government had received a message from Sinn Féin that had given him hope that things were moving. As John Major recalled, sometimes it was very difficult to keep faith with yourself and believe that what you were trying to achieve was possible:

'Psychologically, I tried to put myself from the outset into the minds of the IRA. I don't think you can negotiate unless you put yourself into the position of those you are negotiating with and think to yourself – how are they thinking and why are they doing what they are doing?

'It's very perverse but when I put myself into their position, it seemed to me that they had a lot of volunteers that they had to carry with them in their policy. They couldn't negotiate from what they saw was a position of weakness. So, ironically, whenever they were making progress they needed something to show the volunteers that they weren't being rolled over by the British and they weren't weak. So it is entirely perverse and difficult to understand, but often those bombs were an indication that they were trying to show their own people that they hadn't just given way to the British . . .

'Warrington was the one that I really despaired about because we'd just received a message a few days before imply-ing we were moving closer towards a settlement and then the bomb went off murdering two little boys. It was Easter Saturday I remember, and I was in Huntingdon in my garden, a sunny Easter Saturday and I'd left my boxes, which to anyone in politics are a perpetual burden, when I heard the phone ring, and it rang and rang. I think Norma was at the wrong end of the house, and I thought, someone's ringing a long time, I bet that's a problem. And we heard about the bomb. We didn't at that time know one little boy had been killed and another was so badly injured that he would die, but we did later on that afternoon.

'That was the one occasion when I nearly despaired and wondered if it was worthwhile, whether we should give up.

'The reason I didn't really was quite simple. Firstly I understood this malign psychology about showing the volunteers that they weren't surrendering, and secondly if we had given up there would have been more Warrington bombs and more little boys. But that was a bad day. No doubt about it. And very difficult to persuade people in the media and in politics that it was still right to continue. You just looked like a naïve fool, so that was tough.'

And it was tough. People were very pessimistic, and so were the officials from both governments who were striving to advance talks between the different political parties, but we had to keep trying and we had to believe that things were moving forward.

I kept in close contact with John Major; Martin Mansergh was continuing his talks with Martin McGuinness and Aidan McAteer and sometimes Gerry Adams; Gerry Adams was in discussions with John Hume; and Adams and I were in regular contact by letter, with Father Reid as the go-between. What I didn't realize at the time was that the Republicans, through back channels, were also talking to the British. So many strands of negotiations were going on to find the path to peace – but they were all vital, as Gerry Adams recounts:

'What we were looking for was an alternative way to achieve democratic and Republican objectives. I suppose in the first instance, the talks were to persuade the IRA there was another way to go forward. More importantly, in terms of Irish Nationalism and the national interest, there needed to be a strategy to bring about the basis for peace and to bring about an end to partition and to bring about peace between the Unionists and the rest of the people of the island. There hadn't been such a strategy there since the partition of Ireland. There may have been at different times in the preceding years, different efforts, but there was really no joined-up approach. There had been efforts by Irish governments, along with the British, to bring forward various agreements or treaties but they all had one thing in common and that was that they excluded the Republicans and indeed, from the British point of view, they were part of their effort to defeat the Republicans.

'What we were looking for was something which was more strategic and tactical that OK, did have to have the ability to persuade the IRA, but also had the ability to allow all of us, who may have been divided by party political allegiances, to actually unite, and to try to move the whole very ancient conflict into a resolution process. So when we were talking to the Irish government, however we talked to the Irish government, we were very much of a view that this was their constitutional responsibility anyway. There may have been, since the partition of the island, huge gulfs politically between Northern people involved in struggle, and maybe Southern governments involved in governance, but if you scratch any of us about anything in politics, it's about improving the life for people and in that regard, nothing is more important than peace.

'From the British government's point of view, we were dealing with the enemy. Now we were never dealing with the enemy when we were dealing with Dublin, the most we were dealing with were maybe opponents, but when dealing with the British government, this is the government which had partitioned the island in the first instance, which claimed sovereignty, which claimed jurisdiction and whose armed wing was, particularly in those days, in military occupation of Republican communities. We also had John Major – I've never met John Major – Albert Reynolds had the opportunity of meeting with John Major and doing business with him. I would have a much more critical view because through the back channel (not just what John Hume and I came up with) he was given the potential to bring about a peace process. I know he was in a weakened position, his was a minority government that would have depended upon Unionist votes. It's hard to know through the "messengers" exactly how accurate the situation was, we certainly were led to believe that the government in London was going to sign on for this process and then were very disappointed when it decided at a meeting not to do so. That created huge problems for us. Remember there were conflicts still going on, and people still being killed and you have to at least be able to, I suppose, convince others that even though you may have not made the progress that you'd hoped to make, that at least you were dealing with people who were dealing with you in good faith.'

At one point the priest's visits were so frequent I felt some explanation was due to Seán Duignan and Bart Cronin. I explained to them that I was trying to get something going with various intermediaries acting on my behalf with a few important people in the North. As Seán recorded in his diary:

'Albert gives Bart and me a sneak preview of a draft document on Northern Ireland, plus run-down on what he's up to, which scares the bejasus out of both of us. He is convinced he can sell it to Major, and he insists Sinn Féin and the army council of the IRA will also buy it. He says: "This is about the IRA being persuaded to lay down their arms . . ." He says it will involve the Republican movement accepting Irish unity coming only by consent (That doesn't sound like the IRA to me!) but what's really scary is that he seems to be fixing to contact these guys. Bart and I are so worried we go back to warn him he could be destroyed if he goes down that road. He says maybe so, but he's going to go all the way . . .'

I pointed out that such contacts would only be through intermediaries and the priest was one of them, but they were increasingly aware of the comings and goings of Martin Mansergh, who would often disappear for a few days without any explanation.

It was very difficult for my family too. There were comings and goings to the house at all times of the day and night. It was becoming too suspicious for Father Reid to keep appearing in Government Buildings, so he took to calling at the apartment, sometimes in the very early hours of the morning. Noel Gallagher, my main contact in the North, was also a regular visitor, keeping me informed of the situation.

Kathleen was especially worried for me. I hated to see the stress it was causing and the strain it was putting on her and the rest of the family, but she understood that it was something I had to do. I just had that gut feeling that we would succeed. In so many ways the stage was set; we just had to pull everything together, and talking and negotiating was the only way, no matter what the dangers.

Then something happened which brought a hint of all this subterfuge going on into the public eye. Gerry Adams was spotted by a neighbour emerging from John Hume's house in Derry and the story hit the national press.

Gerry Adams:

'John and I were talking and maybe we'd become careless because there was no intention to publicize it. I was spotted coming out of his home by a neighbour who just casually mentioned it to somebody else, who mentioned it to Eamon McCann who then broke the story. So that caused a bit of difficulty. It was then clear that we were meeting and against a background of the different statements, made by the different sides, for any journalist, it was clear something was happening.

'My recollection is that I said to John we should put our position out, because my concern was that the Irish government was going to negotiate as a government, which it's perfectly entitled to do on the basis of its own judgement on all these matters. We still had to have a very clear eye on the one hand of what we thought was necessary . . . this was the basis on which we were engaging with the IRA, so if we were hopeful of getting success on either of those fronts, we had to be clear.'

The Unionists and others were outraged. They immediately issued strong statements of condemnation that a leader of the SDLP, a constitutional party, should be seen consorting with the leader of Sinn Féin. It did not go down well with Hume's party either, and led to serious estrangement between him and his deputy party leader, Seamus Mallon.

There was even greater criticism a few days later when Adams and Hume issued a joint statement revealing their joint involvement in a search for agreement. This intensified even more when the press announced that the statement they had faxed to newspaper offices was on Sinn Féin headed paper.

On 16 April 1993, I received a letter from Gerry Adams.

'A Chara,

'By now you will have been informed of the agreement between myself and John Hume. I trust that you will be able to endorse this position.

'I consider this agreement to be a considerable and positive breakthrough which moves our project to a crucial stage.

'It is of the utmost importance, if we are to advance expeditiously beyond this phase and realise the full potential of our project that you personally intervene to move it forward.'

Their joint statement, released on 23 April 1993, accepted that the most pressing issue facing the people of Ireland and Britain was the question of lasting peace and how it could best be achieved. It agreed that a process of national reconciliation was needed, ruled out an internal settlement confined to the six counties of the North, and asserted that the Irish people as a whole had a right to self-determination. It saw the task of reaching an agreement on a peaceful and democratic accord for all on this island as the primary challenge.

It did not refer to other negotiations in progress, with the Irish government or among any other parties. It did, however, put our ongoing work on the joint declaration under great strain.

Hume justified publication of the statement by saying, 'If I fail to achieve the objective of bringing violence to an end, the only damage will be that I have failed, but not a single person will be supporting violence as a result. However, if the talks succeed, then the entire atmosphere will be transformed.'

I warned: 'If we in this part of the island appear to walk away from constitutional Nationalism, by unilaterally abandoning our long-standing position with regard to Northern Ireland, the only Nationalism left in entire possession of the field is a violent form of Nationalism which we all repudiate.'

I would have preferred all secret negotiations to remain secret, but this one had burst into the open and we had no control over it. It certainly put back the peace process and served only to exacerbate Unionist distrust.

Meanwhile, on my behalf Martin Mansergh had been working behind the scenes with Martin McGuinness to moderate and make changes in the June 1992 document that would be acceptable to the Republicans and go some way to appeasing the Unionists. The outstanding major questions that continued to cause difficulties concerned setting a time limit for political agreement, the British government accepting the role of 'persuaders' to Irish unity, and the principle of consent. It was essential that the document we arrived at could also be acceptable to London and could form the basis for negotiations between the two governments.

Huge effort was being put into clarifying various ambiguities when suddenly we received a message from the IRA Army Council rejecting any of our alternative drafts, and declaring that, having examined all the steps and timetable set out in the draft joint declaration, and having discussed them at length, they were falling back on the June 1992 document.

Their message was as follows:

'1 Thank you for your latest draft and other documentation. We have examined all of this, the draft joint declaration/steps/timetable and discussed them at length, hence the relatively lengthy period in coming back with a response.

'2 We are serious about this project. We recognise that what it requires is a package that creates what is a political dynamic for irreversible change, and whose objective is the exercise of the right to national self-determination. We see this as the basis for democracy and the beginning of the process of national reconciliation and a lasting peace. This is the standpoint from which we approach your latest submission.

'3 While accepting the integrity of BAC's [Baile Átha Cliath, the city of Dublin – the Army Council's term for the Irish government] seriousness about the project, we are nevertheless unable to convince ourselves that the outline package proffered or joint declaration/steps/ timetable and BAC's understanding of a 15–40 year timescale would produce the necessary dynamic.

'4   We earnestly believe that the position put by us in the June draft is the surest way of providing what is required. We remind you that in coming to the June position, we've accepted the concepts which form no great part of our traditional political vocabulary. We offer this as proof of our willingness to be flexible.

'5   In this context we remain open-minded about our realisable alternative. We ask only that this seeks to fulfil the criteria outlined in paragraph 2, and we believe this requires an agreement with London to do this in the shortest possible time, consistent with obtaining maximum consent to the process involved. Our preference is for a joint declaration which embodies a clear and specified time for achieving this, but we are prepared to consider various options for dealing with this, and these could involve public and/or private elements to this joint declaration.

'This could include a private agreement on a specified timescale underwritten by independent, international guarantors or a delayed public statement to be released some-time – 6/12/18 months? – after the joint declaration, and as part of an agreed implementation of the joint declaration.

'6   We await with interest your response. We wish to express concern at the protracted nature of this process and the degree of looseness about it which is most unhelpful to the search for a peace settlement. We believe that this demands that we approach our task with increased urgency.

'7   Finally, as we conclude our consideration of this section of our project we have been informed that Gerry Adams and John Hume have reached agreement on most of the June draft and have isolated the one part of disagreement so that this can be given separate consideration. They have agreed in principle to all parts of this document except the "within a period (to be specified in advance by both governments)" section. John

Hume has made some suggestions on this about structures, measures and time which have to be further developed by him and Gerry Adams. We believe that this agreement between Gerry Adams and John Hume is an important breakthrough at this time and propose that we endorse the Gerry Adams/John Hume agreement on the June draft.'

Of course there was no way that the John Hume–Gerry Adams agreement could ever be endorsed by either the Irish or the British government. For an agreement to be considered it had to be at constitutional level only and negotiated between the two governments, besides which the Unionists would be incensed if they thought their future and that of their country was being decided by John Hume and Gerry Adams.

After all of the careful intricate steps forwards, backwards and sideways on our draft declaration, this took us all by surprise. In my opinion the document was far too 'green', too biased towards the Republican point of view. I could see no way that the British would accept it.

Moreover, there were other conditions. They wanted assurances on how an Irish government would react to an IRA cessation. Adams sought assurances on the release of prisoners with IRA associations now held in prison in the South. He also wanted to know how the proposed convention which had been mentioned in various drafts of the declaration would function.

Disappointed though I was at this step backwards, I knew I had to keep the lines of communication open. I tried to answer every point. My response, delivered in May by Father Reid, was, first, that there should be a discussion on the statement by the two prime ministers. I continued:

'2 Finalise statement and consultation on all sides and agree a date for it to be announced and become operational for all sides.

'3 Engage in procedural discussions with a view to establishing a convention within three months along the parameters set out in the statement.

'4 Since the convention, unlike the New Ireland Forum, will be a standing body, it would meet in plenary one or two days a month except August on the model of the European Parliament, but committees could meet in the interim between sessions. It would be complementary to any other institutions either already in existence or to be established.

'5 Section 31 [the order banning the broadcasting of voices of all members of Sinn Féin–IRA from Irish TV and radio] would be lifted simultaneously with the announcement at 3, coming into operation for all sides.

'6 Once public confidence in peace had been established every effort would be made to deal expeditiously with issues such as long-standing prisoners, excepting in cases of serious violence, particularly against the person: and arms and equipment, so that the legacy of the past twenty years and the cost could be put behind us as quickly as possible.'

I knew the document as it stood could not, would not, run with the British but I had to keep the lines open, the contact in place and the conversation going or the whole thing would fall apart. Even though the Army Council stipulated the June 1992 draft as the definitive document, we had to keep trying to redefine it in order to have a chance of London accepting it.

A timeframe was just not possible to predict, and to ask London to be willing to 'persuade' the Northern Unionists that a united Ireland was the way forward was out of the question. Peter Brooke may have raised a ghost of hope with his statement of 'no selfish, strategic, or economic interest in Northern Ireland', but that did not mean selling out the Unionists.

At that time John Major was very dependent on the Unionist

vote to maintain his slender majority in government, but that never affected his decisions: he actually felt a sincere responsibility to make sure that their opinions and wishes were upheld – they had to be if ever we were going to get a permanent peace; but also the Nationalists in Northern Ireland were equally under British jurisdiction and he was responsible for those too, and one has to remember that not all Nationalists wanted to leave Britain and unite with the South.

In our private conversations I confessed that although I refused to give in, for many the prospect of peace was fading, and he confided to me that the increased violence was also making the situation within his own party very difficult for him and that people around him were very pessimistic:

'In the face of all that was going on – and after thirty years it wasn't surprising that people were pessimistic – all the people who said, well, you're being suckered into this, it doesn't mean anything, they were all out dancing on the mantelpiece, that's exactly what they thought. There were many people who thought: close it down, there's too much political risk here, don't bother with it. But I was lucky in that some of the opposition parties . . . were quite supportive. John Smith [then leader of the British Labour Party] was happily cynical about the whole thing. I had a whiskey with him when we started a great deal of all this and talked to him about it and he said, "Look, there are no domestic votes in the UK over Northern Ireland, I'll be supportive." And he cheerily swallowed another whiskey while he talked.'

John Hume and Gerry Adams were trying to run too fast. The exposure of their talks had really upset what could only ever be a slow process, drawing in all the different sides; after all, we were trying to rewrite years of history. This sudden attempt at acceleration served only to impede our fragile progress.

The question of a timeframe for an attainment of unity presented the most difficulty. It was a real chicken-and-egg situation. You couldn't say how many years it would take – it could take a generation or a few months – it was of no consequence. You cannot say 'We will attain unity in a generation'. and at the same time say 'Unity will be obtained only with the consent of the majority in the North.' The two things were contradictory. Consent is the cornerstone of the declaration. The issue of time had to go. There was just no way I could sell it to the Unionists or the British.

I continued pressing this argument while Father Reid and Martin Mansergh tried to turn phrases around into something that would be more acceptable to both sides. To use Martin's expression, he'd 'stretched our position like a bit of elastic – way out to the very point that if it went any further it would break'.

Father Reid:

'Then one day Albert said to me, "Look, I've given enough time to this, my officials have given enough time to this, we're not going to have any more to-ing and fro-ing. This is the declaration as far as we're concerned that's going to go – that's what we're going to present to the British government."

'I went to Gerry Adams and I said – "This whole debate is over, this whole discussion is over." He then had to go to the IRA and say, "We have to go with this or we're not going anywhere." He put on a kind of guillotine, which brought the whole thing to a head, otherwise ten years later they could still be arguing because the IRA would be trying to get every ounce they could get.

'It was a day in May and to some extent I took it on myself. I did write to Gerry Adams and I knew from a discussion we'd had that the wording that was there was OK. I knew that. But he didn't say that to me. I took it on myself to go to Martin Mansergh, to tell him, this is OK. Go with it.

'Martin told Albert, it was OK for him to go to the British government with this version of the proposed Downing Street Declaration.

'Then, I began to say to myself, Gerry Adams didn't say that to me and this was a very big decision for me to say to the Taoiseach – "Go to London, tell the British government the statement's OK and the IRA will stop!"

'I went out to Killiney and walked around . . . I went back to Martin at his office that night and said, "Look, Martin, you'll understand I'm getting very worried here that I told the Taoiseach to take this over to John Major . . . I did have a meeting with Gerry Adams before I did that, I had an express meeting with him – I remember we used to say in peace-making, a rose by any other name would smell as sweet, and if you kind of got the wording right, which wasn't exactly what the IRA wanted, but if it was substantially the same, and he was saying the same thing – 'a rose by any other name would smell as sweet'."

'I remember I was really in stress, and Martin said to me, "The Taoiseach is the kind of man . . . that once he's made up his mind to do something, he's going to do it, so there's no point in you or me going to him and saying, 'We're getting second thoughts'. Forget about it, leave it. Let him go. You're dealing with a Taoiseach who is a man who makes up his mind and that's it."

'I left; I'd tried at least. The point was we were dealing with a business and Albert is a businessman and when he's doing a business deal he'll put up with a certain amount of discussion and then there's a point when he says, "OK, this is it, there's no more . . . We can forget about the whole thing or we go with whatever agreement we have . . . no more discussion, I'm going over to John Major with this statement and say this is the statement we're going to make and I understand that if we make it the IRA will stop!"'

Finally we had a document that the IRA would accept. It was a more modified version of the June 1992 declaration but still left a long way to go before it would satisfy the demands of the Unionists and the British government. Nevertheless, after a great deal of soul-searching I decided to hand it over to John Major. I knew it went to the outer limits of what they would find acceptable but I reasoned I either abandoned it or used it, and to my mind it was better to keep the lines of communication open. If we didn't, I feared we would lose the interest of the IRA Army Council and to my way of thinking we had to keep them on side and talking.

I phoned John Major and tried to inject a positive attitude into our discussion, to make him realize that although the document still fell short of satisfying the Unionists, at least we had a form of response that could be the basis for a break-through. I wanted to take it to London personally, so that the two of us, in confidence, could talk through what we had in order to find some way of building on the document's pro-posals, but Major was worried that news of our meeting would leak out. Instead he dispatched Sir Robin Butler, the British Cabinet Secretary, to meet me at the military air base in Baldonnell. Over coffee I briefed Sir Robin on what I saw as the possibilities arising out of the document for talks and the potential for an end to violence, and I handed over the sealed envelope in the hope that the British would view it with the same open-minded tolerance.

At the same time John Hume sent over a rival document which further complicated the British decision. As John Major wrote in his autobiography:

'Two days later, an irritated John Hume gave us a rival version of a declaration. He was annoyed with Reynolds, complaining that although he was Prime Minister of Ireland he did not understand the complexities of the text, and had given us an unsatisfactory draft.

'We studied the texts carefully. Far from being a break-through, they showed little comprehension of what might be acceptable to the British government, let alone to the Unionist majority – to whom they offered virtually nothing. The word "consent" appeared, which was an advance, but inadequately.'

John Hume had no idea that we were in ongoing discussions with Sinn Féin and his version at this time served only to unsettle the British. As we anticipated, the British were very uneasy about the document and took particular exception to the idea that they should be the 'persuaders' for Irish unity and adopt a timetable for withdrawal from Northern Ireland.

I made further phone calls to Major personally and tried to persuade him that although the changes were minor, they were significant in that they showed a marked progress in where the Nationalist side were coming from and it was up to us to move them on from there. I understood just how heavily weighted it was towards the Nationalist position, but I also understood that unless it accommodated the Unionist point of view, the prospects for peace would be as distant as ever. It was my intention, I said, to redress the balance with input from the Unionists.

There was even more unease and dismay when news emerged of the forthcoming visit of the Irish President, Mary Robinson, to Belfast where, it was reported, she would meet and shake hands with Gerry Adams.

Dick Spring, who was continuing the long-running inter-governmental dialogue initiated by Peter Brooke and Patrick Mayhew, was incensed at the announcement, especially at such a sensitive time in the negotiations, and did his best to dissuade her, but the President was undeterred by any of the criticism.

The upcoming visit dominated the meeting in mid-June with John Major, who insisted that the whole thing should be stopped. Personally I saw no reason to be so concerned. Mary Robinson was a hugely popular figure at that time and I did not see that 'ordering' her not to go would serve any purpose whatsoever.

Before becoming President, Mary had been one of those in Dublin who believed the Unionists deserved more sympathy. In fact, she had resigned from Labour in 1985 over the Anglo-Irish Agreement, regarding it as being unfair to the Unionist cause. In her term of office one of her principal aims had been to reach out to the dispossessed and the underprivileged on the fringes of society in the poorer areas. This included areas of west Belfast, and the purpose of her visit was not specifically to shake the hand of Gerry Adams but to meet with represent-atives from various Belfast organizations dealing with problems of poverty and dispossession. The fact that Gerry Adams was one of many such people was incidental and certainly, as far as I was concerned, did not merit government intervention.

The Unionists, outraged, bitterly condemned her visit, and the press built it into a major political debacle. The Dublin *Sunday Independent* roundly accused her: 'She should know that she has disgraced her office and tarnished her Presidency beyond redemption. Mrs Robinson has shamed the people of this country gratuitously, unforgivably, indecently. She should now resign.'

The general public, when asked their opinion, returned a vote of 77 per cent in approval of her action, indicating a far more tolerant attitude than that exhibited by the political intelligentsia.

Aside from the prospective visit of President Robinson, my

main objective in meeting with John Major that June was to explore how we could build on what I believed was the potential of the declaration we had in hand. Major was cautious. He agreed that the Mayhew talks between government ministers and officials had stalled again and therefore we should at least take the opportunity to examine the text further, but – he was careful to distinguish – although his government would discuss it, they would not negotiate on it. Fair enough!

Several meetings then took place with John Chilcot and Sir Robin Butler representing London, and Seán O hUiginn and Dermot Nally representing Dublin, with both sides working to address the points raised. Mansergh now joined his colleagues on the Irish side to try to help the two governments in redrafting a joint Anglo-Irish Declaration on which both sides could agree. Discussions were now confined to London and Dublin, and had moved on from the dialogue with Adams and the other Northern Nationalist contacts.

There were other complications holding up progress. In London a number of right-wing backbenchers rebelled against Major in several key votes on Europe, and it was only when Jim Molyneaux and the Ulster Unionists came to his rescue that his government escaped defeat. There were immediate suspicions within the Republican movement that a deal had been done between the Unionists and Major.

It was a frustratingly slow process. In September I felt compelled to write a personal letter to John Major exhorting him not to let go of this fragile chance of peace. We had all worked long and hard to get this far, and as the document had the backing of those who were capable of calling an end to violence, it was an achievement worth striving for. I went on to say that the principle of consent was not an issue, that the Nationalists accepted the idea subject to the sort of framework set out in the paper, and that what we were all hoping to achieve was not necessarily Irish unity or anything like it within any limited timescale. What was needed was a period of stability, without violence, in which both sides could put bitterness behind them and come together to work out an agreement on their future rationally and equitably. Time, I said, is not on our side.

At the same time John Hume, still totally unaware of Mansergh's contacts with Sinn Féin and the delicate stage of the intergovernmental negotiations in progress, went to see the Prime Minister to press home the same message.

It got him nowhere. Eventually, irritated at the lack of progress and to increase pressure on both Major and myself, Hume decided to act on his own initiative. He phoned me with the idea that, to break the stalemate and get things moving, he and Adams should issue a joint statement saying that they had made considerable progress in joint discussions and would be passing the results on to the British and Irish governments. I did everything in my power to dissuade him. His timing could not have been worse. The Conservative Party conference was imminent and for Hume to go public at such a time, not only revealing his continuing relationship with Sinn Féin but also claiming their major input into such a controversial document, would cause immeasurable damage both to Major and to the negotiations overall. I strongly advised him not to do it, but he was adamant. At least, I urged him, say you are sending the report to Dublin only; that at least, I said, would limit some of the fallout.

The announcement of this 'Hume–Adams' initiative raised the stakes dramatically. Tensions in the North were stretched to breaking point as the Unionists gauged the extent to which the Nationalists were laying down conditions for peace which the Irish government appeared to be endorsing. Rumours abounded, the press went wild, the British were in uproar –

and the chance of the Unionists agreeing to anything emanating from Hume and Adams was nil!

Hume had timed the announcement to hit the press just as he was about to leave on a trade mission to America. In Dublin we waited for the highly publicized document to appear.

The media in both Ireland and Britain were at fever pitch with speculations as to how the 'man of violence' and the 'man of peace' could be on the verge of agreement. News came back to us from America of the incredible news coverage there, a lot of it critical of Hume's judgement in joining with Sinn Féin.

I found it hard to believe that Gerry Adams would have condoned a statement like this at such a sensitive time. Then, on 24 September, I received a message from him:

'A Chara,

'I understood how the public statement may be causing difficulties for you. I myself only came to support the idea after great deliberation and considering all the issues involved. The bearer of this note can outline those for you, and indeed many may already be obvious to you given the pressures in the North at present and the slowness of the "Sasanaigh" to respond and the matters I told you of.

'I believe that you should respond positively to the statement and take the public initiative. For example by welcoming this development and saying that you are seeking to take up the matter – have taken up the matter with Mr Major etc etc. I will do and say nothing which does not help you in this regard and I am open to suggestions on how this can be done??

'It is of vital importance that we maintain our consensus no matter what the pressures. It is also vital that we seek through this development to advance our project and ensure that the onus is on the British – not you, John or me!

'Le gach dea mhéin,

'Gerry A.'

* * *

And still we had no word from John Hume. Martin Mansergh and I waited, while Seán Duignan did his best to issue evasive statements to the press. As he wrote in his diary:

'27 September 1993

'What's John Hume up to? I have rarely seen the Taoiseach or Mansergh so upset. And not a peep from John. Haven't a clue where he is. I keep issuing – "we look forward to hearing what progress may have been made" rubbish. Either he's lost the head or he is crafty as a fox – or both – because we're getting conflicting reports from US quoting him as already having given Dublin the report, then that he'll give Dublin the report when he gets back. Mansergh says we've got nothing from Hume or Adams. Still, nobody wants a public row with John. So I go on as if everything is perfect.'

As Gerry Adams admitted in hindsight:

'In fairness, it was to keep the pressure on the Irish government. It was to keep that going. The big difficulty for Albert, I think, was that Dick Spring was the other part of the government and clearly ... these matters had to be dealt with in a very confidential way so there was a management difficulty for all the players in this.

'John was coming back and he was going to go and meet the Irish government about this whole business and I picked him up at the airport, I met him before he met Albert. And I said to him – look, we need to keep everybody steady here ... I had difficulties, the most difficult negotiation I found was with your own side. The Taoiseach had difficulties, the most difficult negotiations being with his own side, and John Hume had difficulties, the most difficult negotiation he's ever done I think. None of us had difficulty with broad popular opinion in Ireland, but we all had difficulties with people within our own constituencies.

'This was actually a seismic shift in Republican thinking. Our position was that the Irish government had to do the negotiation. Now we obviously used every device that we could think of to make sure that the Irish government was as true as possible to what we wanted.'

For all of us involved in the process, treading a careful line with your own side was often even more difficult than negotiating with the others. Knowing what to say, and when, could be a real problem. Dealing with the opposition was a political game; dealing with your own constituencies was far more problematical, much more debilitating and exhausting.

This announcement of a 'Hume–Adams' report raised all sorts of questions in the Dáil, questions we often could not answer. The revelation of this mysterious Hume–Adams statement also made the public aware that there were secret contacts – but they still had no knowledge of the years of negotiating that had been going on, or the fact that work was in progress on the declaration between the two governments. Nor did they realize the full significance of the announcement – which I regarded as irresponsible – for that fragile peace process.

Finally Hume came to see us on his return from America. It was a tense meeting with Dick Spring, Martin Mansergh and myself. We asked to see the document. He handed over a paper to Dick Spring, who took one look and said, 'What's this about? There's nothing in it.' I took a look myself. There were a few paragraphs that reiterated all the old aspirations that had formed the substance of a statement Hume and Adams had already published – nothing new whatsoever of any value or worth, no kind of a 'breakthrough' as had been intimated to the press. The so-called 'agreement' was not worth the paper on which it was written. The breakthrough Hume–Adams document that threatened to put back all our efforts did not even exist. In disgust, the Tánaiste instructed Martin Mansergh to tear the paper up. It was scrapped, torn up and thrown away. However, as we left the room, unbeknown to me at the time, Martin Mansergh rescued the torn halves, taped them back together and kept the document for the file.

The Hume–Adams document read as follows:

'The initiative in which we are involved has come a considerable distance since we embarked upon it some time ago. The progress we have made has not been easy or without difficulty. On the contrary the entire initiative has, for everyone concerned, been fraught with danger and risks. However the ultimate objective, the ending of conflict and the securing of a lasting peace, has ensured our continued commitment. We have expended considerable time and energy in exploring the possibility of creating a process which could achieve these objectives.

'The aim of our dialogue has been to establish an overall political strategy to establish justice and peace in Ireland. We have developed this over a series of meetings, building on the progress made in our previous dialogue.

'As a result of these detailed discussions we reached a consensus that the strategy agreed with you in June of this year could provide a basis for peace. The agreement and the public assertion of this consensus is, in itself, significant and gives added weight to the June agreement. We believe, therefore, that a heavy responsibility lies with both Governments, and in particular the British Government, to seize the opportunity and to put together the necessary elements which we are convinced will establish a lasting peace.

'Any lasting settlement will have to be the result of detailed discussions and agreement between the Irish people and their democratically elected representatives north and south.

'The bedrock of our position was set out in our initial statement where we pointed out:

' "Everyone has a solemn duty to change the political climate away from conflict and towards a process of national reconciliation which sees the peaceful accommodation of the differences between the people of Britain and Ireland and the Irish people themselves.

' "In striving for that end we accept that an internal settlement is not a solution because it obviously does not deal with all the relationships at the heart of the problem.

' "We accept that the Irish people as a whole have a right to national self-determination. This is a view shared by a majority of the people of the island, though not by all of its people.

' "The exercise of self-determination is a matter of agreement between the people of Ireland."

'The principle of national self-determination is universally recognized and unassailable. But we equally recognize that the exercise of this right is a matter of democratic agreement between the Irish people and must respect the diversity of our different traditions, as any new settlement to be viable, must earn their allegiance and agreement.

'We hope that the Irish Government would publicly welcome our consensus and agree to incorporate it into their approach with the British Government. We believe that this would considerably strengthen their hand in dealing with the British Government. We have no doubt of the broad public support for this initiative.'

'25th September 1993'

One of my connections in the North, Noel Gallagher, who knew Hume well, told me that, following his visit to Dublin, Hume had returned to Derry that night agitated and stressed:

'Hume had clearly made up his mind he could do it on his own with Adams and without Fianna Fáil or the Irish government. He believed he could do his own deal with the British government.'

In Dublin we tried to cover up the non-existent 'agreement'. I sympathized with Gerry Adams' request that I give it public support, but it was all smoke and mirrors, there was nothing to substantiate it. I instructed Seán Duignan to tell the political correspondents that the report had 'significant potential', that it was 'part of the process', etc., but nothing could have been further from the truth: rather than progressing the situation it served only to thwart it.

For my part, and for the sake of progressing the peace process with the British government, I had to distance myself from John Hume. The media were quick to comment.

In an interview with John Humphrys I said that, although John Hume had spent most of his life working for peace and had advanced some principles on which peace could be built, 'he knows, and he has said, that it is now a matter for the two governments to take up the initiative and to put a formula for peace together.'

At this John Humphrys asked, 'And you are quite clear that any initiative has to be undertaken only by the two governments – by yourself and Mr Major?'

I answered: 'That's the position. And, I think, the logic of the position dictates that's the way it has to be. If you were to come forward with the initiative we would listen to you, we would hear what you have to say. As, indeed, we have heard from many others and I have been taking soundings from way back for quite some time. This is not a new development as far as John Major and myself are concerned . . . we've been talking about it, we have been tossing ideas back and forth between ourselves. And, indeed, the upsurge of violence now demands that both of us must try and bring it to finality. And that's what we intend to do.'

John Humphrys then quoted John Hume as saying that if John Major and I acted on his initiative there could be peace within a week! And he asked, had I been briefed on the contents of his talks with Gerry Adams? I answered:

'I have spoken to him. He has given the Tánaiste and myself a report of his talks. We evaluated that, we see it as pointing the finger at principles that can form part of a peace formula. There are other parts that have to be input as well. And that's why he [Hume] says that quite clearly, it is a matter for the two governments to take up the initiative and run with it ... We have to make our own evaluation, we have to make our own assessment of the situation and we have to come forward with what we believe would command support across both communities.'

I had to emphasize that John Hume's aspiration of 'peace within a week' was a bit simplistic. It was also essential that I sent a clear message to the Unionists that the future for peace was in the hands of the governments and not in the hands of John Hume.

A few days later I received another letter from Gerry Adams:

'6th October 1993

'A Chara,

'The following is our perspective of an elaboration on the joint report forwarded to you by John Hume and myself. Both documents are strictly confidential and will, at our end, be treated with the same sensitivity as all other documents which have passed between us in the course of this project. Our commitment to the confidentiality of this process remains absolute.

'The project in which we are involved has come a considerable distance since we embarked upon it some time ago. The progress we have made has not been easy or without difficulty.

On the contrary, the entire project has, for everyone concerned, been fraught with danger and risks. However the ultimate objective, the ending of conflict and the securing of a real and lasting peace has ensured our continuing involvement and commitment. We have all expended considerable time and energy in exploring the possibility of creating a process which could achieve these objectives.

'The Dublin proposals which we are agreed could provide a basis for peace, are the core of the consensus we have reached. They are also in the private domain while unfortunately the Hume Adams strand of our initiative is in the public domain. The greatest difficulty has been caused by the failure of the British Government to respond to the proposals put to it by Dublin and by the delaying tactics deployed by the British. Their dilatory approach is primarily aimed at undermining the Irish consensus through the growing public pressure on this consensus and primarily directed at the Hume Adams talks.

'Dublin were fully briefed on our concern about these matters and of the pressure involved. The absence of any alternative suggestion which would have relieved these pressures led directly to the issuing of our joint statement of 25th September and the resulting publicity. It is important to make a number of points in this regard.

'The project, or at the very least, aspects of it, was about to become public. The joint statement should have at least ensured that it came out in a controlled manner. This was part of the rationale behind it. It was also an effort to put the pressure, the onus, where it belonged; with the British Government. In all of this we sought to maintain our consensus.

'This statement was agreed with Dublin. You drafted it. We made major concessions in this regard in deference to your concerns. The subsequent "arm's length" approach by Dublin officials and the confusing distraction about the "report" has not helped.

'Furthermore, the defensive approach being adopted by the Dublin Government would appear to be both unnecessary (responding to predictable Unionist pressure when it is the British who should be under pressure to respond) and potentially damaging to the consensus reached, to the project itself and consequently to the objective of the project, the establishment of a real peace process. This approach has already caused some questioning of the project within the Republican community.

'A more supportive public stance from Dublin in regard to this initiative is required. The proposals put by you privately to the British place the initiative clearly with you.

'It is crucial therefore that Dublin adopts an attitude that advances the project. The broad public support for this initiative should not be underestimated. The public declaration of an agreement between Hume and Adams on a possible peace proposal has been warmly received, particularly within the nationalist community North and South and internationally. The opportunity which the present political climate presents cannot be lost. I am convinced that it is now time to move this project forward.'

'Is Mise le Meas

'Gerry Adams'

If Hume or Adams had hoped their 'agreement' would move things forward, they were wrong: it did the opposite. The delicate shoots of progress had been well and truly trampled underfoot by Hume, for although there had been no Hume–Adams agreement, it had been so well broadcast by Hume that the Unionists could not ignore talk of its existence or tolerate what it was supposed to imply. Following on from that, there was no way that the British government could be seen to be dealing with Sinn Féin.

That same month Sir Robin Butler flew over to meet with Dick Spring and myself, to inform us not only that the British government were totally dismissive of the Hume–Adams agreement but that Downing Street was simply not interested in pursuing this document. A letter then followed from John Major effectively ruling out a joint Anglo-Irish Declaration for the foreseeable future.

I was devastated, and for a while there seemed no way forward.

John Major:

'They [Hume–Adams] tied his hands for a long time. They made great political difficulties for him in Ireland and restrained what he could do. That undoubtedly was the case.

'What was Albert's concern? Albert's concern was a deal that could stop the killings. That was Albert's concern. Albert was a trader and Albert was a dealer, he was a bottom line man. At the end of the day Albert will do a deal and he'll get the best deal he possibly can unless it's impossible to sell and providing it meets his objective.

'Now he was restrained in the deal he could do by much of the Hume–Adams dialogue and often by others like McGuinness in exactly the same way people attempted to restrain me with Unionist concerns in London.

'You picture two people held in harness by the people behind them, struggling to meet. That broadly was what it was like for a time. Fortunately the harnesses were elastic and we could meet.'

Sir Roderic Lyne – John Major's private secretary for foreign affairs in 1993 – commented recently, when asked about the difficulties John Hume's statement caused to both governments at this time and how it held up the peace process for three months:

'Yes, he held it up because he went and published – and this was all because Hume's enormous ego had been bruised by the fact that Albert was getting the limelight and not Hume. One has to remember this about Hume, that he had a valiant record over the years . . . I think he'd shown huge courage standing up to the men of violence, but by this period, he sort of felt he walked on water . . . and he thought this was his baby and that he'd taken the risk in going into talks with Adams and he'd come up with this Declaration [presented at the same time as the Irish government version of June 1993] and then Albert had taken it over and was presenting it as Albert's not Hume's.

'Of course Hume's version, which we were refusing to negotiate on, had in a lot of stuff that was completely unacceptable, that we weren't prepared to touch. By then Albert was starting to take out some of this unacceptable stuff . . .

'Then the thought that there was a Hume–Adams document and that this was the pup that was being sold to the British government made it very difficult for us to continue with talks with Albert for quite a while and made it all the more important that anything that came out of our talks with Albert could be seen to be very different from what was presumed to be the Hume–Adams document. So it actually slightly weakened Albert's negotiating position. He probably had to give more ground to us after that than he wanted.'

The fact that the document was now believed to bear Hume's and Adams' 'fingerprints' had effectively ruled out the current Anglo-Irish document. To counterbalance that I had to draw in the Unionists. I had to find a way of earning their trust and making them believe that the Irish government understood their fears and that I would make every endeavour to ensure that in the next round of Anglo-Irish talks – and I was not yet prepared to give up hope of them being resurrected – their interests would be well served. The Loyalist paramilitaries were growing in strength and they were retaliating to IRA atrocities with escalating violence. It was essential that we found a way to convince them too that there was a chance for peace – but how?

The answer proved to be the Reverend Dr Roy Magee. He had started out in the 1960s as a young cleric in east Belfast, working in areas that were strongholds of the Ulster Defence Association and Ulster Volunteer Force. He'd become associated with them when the Troubles started.

Reverend Roy Magee:

'Generally speaking [the Loyalists] were happy enough as long as they were left alone. They were Brits who wanted to see themselves as British and didn't want any disruption to that, and if there was a threat that developed, that caused their hackles to rise and tension to mount within the area. Broadly speaking that was the general picture with the constitutional claim over the six counties that the Republic of Ireland had in their constitution.

'When civil rights marches started they began to get concerned because they felt they were being infiltrated by the Provisional IRA. When the Troubles started in Londonderry, it confirmed their thinking that it was a move on the part of Republicans to get their way within Northern Ireland.

'I was in the dock area of Belfast when the Troubles broke there. I was walking the streets with them trying to keep them out of mischief. The problem began to develop more and more as the tension mounted and the killing started. I think they saw the statement by the Irish government [Jack Lynch's broadcast statement of August 1969, 'We will not stand idly by'] as a real threat, that raised hackles in the Loyalist community.

'I was working independently as an individual within the

church. I couldn't say I had the blessing of my denominational body to do what I was doing, I didn't even think at times I had the blessing of my own congregation to do what I was doing, but I kept doing it.

'Then at the stage when the Loyalist paramilitaries were beginning to show they could do as much mischief and damage as the Provisional IRA and Republican groups, I received a call from Martin Mansergh who phoned me to ask if he could meet with me. I met him in Belfast and we had a chat together.

'After a couple of meetings he asked me would I meet with Albert Reynolds, the Taoiseach. Would I come down to Dublin and meet him. And I said I would because I think, and the Loyalist paramilitaries felt, that it was important to get their views made known.

'My effort was an attempt to explain their thinking but at no time to excuse their behaviour. It was always a matter of trying to interpret where they were at in their thinking, and to try to say to people – you need to be aware of this – and then to . . . nudge the paramilitaries in one direction, and my briefing with the Irish government in the same direction, so that they would meet at a point and understand each other more perfectly.

'When I had the approach from the Irish government, I told the Loyalist paramilitaries, the CLMC, the Combined Loyalist Military Command. I always informed them of what was happening, so that it could never be misinterpreted and they would think a deal was being done secretly behind their backs. They agreed it would be good to get their point of view across to the Irish government and that I should meet with the new Taoiseach, which I did.

'I went totally with an open mind believing that the man was totally genuine and was interested in seeing peace established in the whole of Ireland and I must say that proved to be the case. I think from the first time I met him I was convinced he was a man who could be trusted, he was a man who was a politician, I would say of the people, a man who was not an academic politician, if you understand what I mean, but a man who was interested in practical issues that could be moved and he would do all he could to move them. I found that we could talk together quite openly, a conduit that could be used, not only to the Irish government but with negotiations to John Major who was also prepared to take risks. And that from my point of view was how the situation developed.'

The bombing of the fish-and-chip shop on the Shankill Road on 23 October 1993 was devastating and brought everyone, North and South, to the brink of despair. It was around midday on a busy Saturday when the street was crowded with families shopping. It was a strongly Loyalist area, the heartland of the paramilitaries. The UDA, in fact, maintained an office above the shop and this was the target. Two IRA bombers, in the mistaken belief that a high-powered UDA meeting was in progress, entered the shop intending to plant the bomb when, without any warning, it exploded. The old building collapsed immediately in a huge pile of rubble. One of the two bombers, Thomas Begley, aged twenty-two, was killed instantly. The death toll was tragic: nine bodies were dug out of the devastation, two of them young children, Leanne Baird, aged seven, and Leanne Murray, aged thirteen. Another died a day later. People dug with their bare hands to help rescue the victims. Fifty-seven others were seriously injured.

The chilling UDA response was a public warning: 'John Hume, Gerry Adams and the Nationalist electorate will pay a heavy price for today's atrocity.'

Loyalist gunmen then went on a bloody vendetta rampage

that saw the death toll raised to twenty-three within a week. On the night of Hallowe'en alone, seven men were gunned down when Loyalist paramilitaries burst into a crowded bar in Greysteel, County Derry.

It was the highest death toll of any month since October 1976. The outcry of horror was worldwide. In the House of Commons, in Dáil Éireann, the peace process was pronounced beyond hope, finished. The Hume–Adams initiative was rounded on with derisive condemnation. Michael Ancram, political affairs minister in the Northern Ireland Office, said the Shankill bombing made 'a total mockery of any talk of peace on behalf of the Provisional IRA'; John Hume spoke of it as an 'appalling act of mass slaughter'; and John Major named it 'sheer bloody-minded evil'. Dick Spring called on Gerry Adams to denounce the bombing, saying the peace process had been dealt a 'grievous blow'.

Gerry Adams responded that the bombing could not be excused and added that he was absolutely confident he could secure an end to IRA violence if the British government responded positively to the Hume–Adams initiative. John Hume described this as 'significant'; the Prime Minister said it was 'tantamount to blackmail'. The SDLP called for a unilateral IRA ceasefire, while Martin McGuinness announced that the Prime Minister, John Major, was 'blocking the Irish peace initiative'.

I was in complete despair: both Martin Mansergh and I were at a total loss as to what to do next. I sent a message to Sinn Féin telling them that if I was to continue they had to stop the violence, that I could not go on promising peace with one hand while with all this going on they tied the other behind my back. There's no credibility attached to it, I told them, no point in trying to persuade the British government to come with you. I'd always promised Major I wouldn't let him down, that I'd carry the can and that he wouldn't be responsible if things went wrong. Here was a guy with goodwill keeping peace at the top of his agenda, a man who was giving the Irish problem more time than any other prime minister since Gladstone, and all this was blowing up in his face. They had put him in an impossible place. He was accountable to the British public for this, and it had put him in a precarious and difficult position.

I was so appalled at what had happened that I honestly thought the whole thing would probably blow sky-high.

In an effort to get things moving Dick Spring presented to the Dáil a short speech that drew together the different strands of the peace process. In it the Tánaiste outlined six 'democratic principles' for a sustainable peace. These were that the people of Ireland, North and South, should freely determine their future; that this could be expressed in new Northern, North–South and East–West structures; that there could be no change in the North's status without freely given majority consent; that such consent could be withheld; that the consent principle could be inserted into the Republic's constitution; and that the Republican movement could come to the table if violence were abandoned. This implied a promise to re-examine Ireland's constitutional claim to the North and a strong affirmation of the consent principle. This was well received by the Unionists and was looked upon favourably by the British, but the Nationalists and Republicans took great exception to the fact that it gave the Unionists the right to withhold their consent to any agreement, thus reinforcing the Unionist veto over political or constitutional change. A storm of protest ensued. The speech also made no mention of the role of the two governments, and especially of the British government: it threw the onus completely on the Nationalists and Unionists living in the North.

Then, just when I was beginning to think things could not get worse, newspapers around the world printed pictures and reports of Gerry Adams carrying the coffin of Thomas Begley, one of the IRA bombers responsible for the Shankill Road atrocity. The young man had been given a hero's send-off and the cortège had been followed by thousands of people as it wound its way through the Catholic areas of north and west Belfast. It is hard for anyone not bound up with the complicated reasoning of the militant Nationalists to understand the ritual of such a funeral or the hero's send-off, yet the young man was himself a victim of the Troubles: he had grown up knowing nothing but hatred and had fought for what he believed was right. This was the unbearable tragedy of the North, and it only served to make me more and more determined, at whatever cost, to see it end.

Gerry Adams had, I believe sincerely, expressed his sorrow at the deaths of so many people; but he was also the Republican leader of Sinn Féin, the political arm of the IRA. He had to join in the cortège, he had to take his turn carrying the coffin, as did Martin McGuinness: both had to show respect for someone who had died for the cause. It was expected. If they had not, the community would have ostracized them, they would have lost their support and any influence or power they had within the Army Council. They had no choice, even if it meant the collapse of the Hume–Adams initiative.

I tried to explain all this to John Major when we met that month for a European Council meeting in Brussels. The meeting took place in the British ambassador's residence, a magnificent building in the heart of the city. It was one of our private meetings, where we spoke freely with no officials present. John was absolutely furious.

'How do you expect me to continue with any process,' he

said, 'when I take up the papers and in every paper on the front page is Gerry Adams carrying a coffin?'

'You have to understand,' I said, 'if the guy didn't carry the coffin he wouldn't be able to maintain his credibility with that organization and bring the people with him. If he shunned the funeral he could even end up in a coffin himself.'

It was very difficult for John Major: he had to contend with the British people who had no concept of Republicanism, they simply didn't understand. All they saw were the bald facts, and it was almost impossible for him to continue to try to do something under those circumstances. To the public Gerry Adams was synonymous with the IRA, and if the bomb was going off he must have known the bomb was going off.

Gerry Adams:

'I actually remember Albert articulating that position and doing it well, but what he would not have known was that it wasn't even a conscious decision. It wasn't even a calculation. This was a kid, his parents, whatever he did, deserve our solidarity and our sympathy and the rest of it is culture. If you go to a funeral, you'll be asked to lift and you wouldn't even think. It would be insulting to say no, I won't do that!'

I think John appreciated what I was saying but it took a while to convince him and it was very difficult. Those private meetings helped us both: we were just two men, going over what was going wrong or right, we just used to talk things through. I remember he said over the funeral incident, 'I'm going to have to condemn Adams.' We agreed that we had to distance ourselves from the Hume–Adams initiative, that it was now so tainted as to be unusable; the only way forward was for the two governments to take matters into their own hands, and we had to make a public statement to that effect. Strictly between ourselves, we agreed that I should try to keep the Irish initiative going to see where it would lead. Major was adamant he could not be seen publicly to wear this. But, as we reasoned it out between us, the Hume–Adams initiative was being declared dead in order to keep it alive, in the same way as Adams carried the bomber's coffin, because otherwise he couldn't deliver the IRA.

In our private relationship we could say things to one another that would not get out. We were prepared to take the raps in public: strictly true or otherwise, we let things be said and we said nothing in response, because to prove anything was to expose where you were at – you had to accept the criticism, justified or not.

John and I were fortunate in that we met as friends and even when we had disagreements we managed to thrash things out.

John Major:

'We did and we usually went away with something to be done that could help us thrash it out. We didn't ever say, "Well that's it, tough, we've got to leave it there, we can't do anything. Goodnight and goodbye."

'We never left it that way. We always left it with something we could look at with which we could bridge a gap. That was true in terms of phone calls and innumerable meetings. European meetings were very helpful. We had innumerable meetings in the middle of those without the usual panoply of the press waiting for statements. And those were very useful.

'I'm not quite sure why it was; sometimes two personalities gel. We never grated on one another, nothing Albert did grated. I may have been fed up with some of the things he's done but it didn't grate.

'We had one piece of good fortune that we were able to speak harshly to one another without the bruising lasting. That was very useful.'

Indeed, it was very useful on this particular day. I left the summit with a very heavy heart. In the official meetings I had emphasized that although the term 'Hume–Adams' was in the public focus, the document I had given the British government was one drafted by Martin Mansergh and backed by the Irish government; it was an Irish position paper, developed over the previous two years. I assured them that it had nothing to do with the mythical document from Hume and Adams; it was our own document. However, the meeting was dominated by the feeling that Adams' 'fingerprints' were all over the document and we somehow had to get rid of that notion.

John Humphrys from the BBC was there again to question me just before I left Brussels. I had to inject a feeling of optimism into my answers even though my spirits were low. I had to make sure the message got across to everyone that a solution, a key would be found to unlock the doors to peace. The least I would accept, I told him, was a joint statement that would command the support of both communities in Northern Ireland, one that would draw the attention of all those engaged in paramilitary violence enough that hopefully they might see their way to cease the violence and turn back to a political process.

Such a statement, I continued, would not predetermine the future of either community, but would signal the direction that the two governments would like to see the affairs of Northern Ireland taking in the future. There would be a new beginning, and the starting point for that new beginning would be a permanent cessation of violence.

I stressed: 'It's a question of how far the two governments can come down the line to create a situation, to which we hope the paramilitaries can respond, and which the two communities can strongly support, because at the end of the day we're dealing with people.

'It's not just what John Major would like to have in the statement, or what I would like to have in the statement. It's more how we can direct a message up there that will be listened to and that will point a new direction for the two communities of Northern Ireland, while at the same time not threaten their futures or indeed predetermine their futures . . . one that can allay the fears and suspicions which have been expressed, that we might be engaged in some underhand deal, or under-the-counter arrangement – no – what we want to do is bring it out into the open . . . and provide the environment in which they can sit and discuss and agree their future with both governments, who in turn will support that new arrangement, whatever they may agree . . . A future by agreement, not by coercion and not by violence.'

Seán Duignan, who accompanied me to Brussels, wrote in his diary:

'Hume and Adams told to get off the pitch! Albert and Major met (no officials present) for more than an hour. Joint statement afterwards sent out a clear message to John Hume to butt out and leave it to the two Governments . . . When Brendan McMahon (Dept of Foreign Affairs) and I read it together, we just looked at one another. Brendan said: "Doesn't look great to me." That's for sure. It says only the two Governments can take the initiative; no question of adopting the report (Hume Adams) given to Albert, which it is emphasised, he (Albert) did not give to the British Government. Brits happy at having dumped Hume. Albert says to me it had to be done, that only the two Governments can do the job, but I can see he's not happy . . .'

The statement said that the British and Irish governments welcomed the 'courageous and imaginative efforts' of the SDLP leader, Mr Hume, but agreed that there was no question of 'adopting or endorsing' the Hume–Adams proposals and that any initiative could only be taken by the two governments. If violence was demonstrably renounced, they would 'respond imaginatively', but there could be no secret deals with organizations supporting violence as a price for its cessation.

After all the effort that had gone into the initiative it was hard to be seen to cast it aside. John Hume's health was in a fragile state and I feared what this decision might do to him, but sometimes there is no choice. Some people never forgave me over that Brussels joint statement, but I had to distance myself from Hume in order to keep the British government in negotiations. I had to look as if I was changing position to keep everything going forward.

John Major too was on a knife-edge at the time. Following all the violence there were many in his government who wanted him to give up not only the negotiations, but anything to do with me and the Irish government as well. Our only way to keep things moving forward was to be seen to be taking the political route.

It was a very awkward situation to be dealing with, but politics being what it is, sometimes you have to do things you don't want to do; if it's going to get results, it's a call you have to make.

The reaction following the statement was vociferous. After Sir Patrick Mayhew said the six Spring principles were 'reassuring', Gerry Adams claimed: 'The British have seized upon Mr Spring's remarks in a cynical effort to divert attention from Major's reluctance to be involved in a genuine peace process.'

John Hume called for a meeting with John Major. Fifty figures from the business and public sector of Northern Ireland warned that rejection of the Hume–Adams initiative would assist IRA hard-liners. In Dublin, the Sinn Féin chair,

Tom Hartley, said he would be 'disappointed if the British rejected the Irish peace initiative and the Dublin Government acquiesced'. He said that 'consent was a bogus concept, a euphemism for a Unionist veto'.

From America, Bill Clinton responded that he shared the two governments' condemnation of violence and strongly supported their efforts to renew talks with the four constitutional parties. Meanwhile seven hundred people joined a 'Peace Train' from Dublin to Belfast.

The Prime Minister indicated he would meet the leaders of the four constitutional parties to clear the way for renewed inter-party talks; the DUP and the UUP said they would not negotiate with Mr Hume until his talks with Mr Adams were over.

On Ulster Radio, the UUP leader Jim Molyneaux described the six Spring principles 'as a great improvement' – and the Hume–Adams initiative as 'a recipe for bloodshed'.

Gerry Adams:

'It was a challenged process. The Shankill Road bombing – apart from being overwhelmed by the horror of it, my instinct was – we had to make this work!

'At different times you'd be driven to distraction by an inability to get agreement over a word or a phrase, but I was living in the middle of it, so the imperative was to sort it out.

'In many ways we saw Albert Reynolds coming into Government Buildings as Taoiseach as a positive, as a friend for the process who was also prepared to take risks and chances. Father Reid was also tenacious in doing the circle.'

Suddenly, things were moving. There was an electrifying energy injected into the urge for peace. Thousands attended lunchtime peace rallies in Belfast and Derry. The intergovernmental conference met in Belfast and the two governments agreed to work together 'in their own terms on a framework for peace and stability and reconciliation'.

The Northern Ireland Secretary, Sir Patrick Mayhew, said the six principles would be 'central'. Dick Spring promised the basis for the framework would be developed 'with haste'. John Major told the Commons he wanted to see inter-party talks 'as speedily as possible' but did not want an 'artificially staged event' with no probability of progress.

In the Dáil I tried to assuage the fears of the Nationalists by indicating that the fourth Spring principle which had caused them so much consternation, on the right of Unionists to withhold consent, was not intended to change the majority consent principle of Article 1 of the Anglo-Irish Agreement. I also said it should be clear within four or five weeks whether a breakthrough on the North was possible.

Senator Gordon Wilson, whose own daughter had been killed at Enniskillen, met with Loyalist paramilitaries in his own never-ceasing efforts for peace.

The IRA said it would stop targeting Loyalist paramilitaries if they ended their campaign against Catholics. Loyalist sources responded that a complete IRA cessation was required. At that year's Árd Fheis in Dublin, I told Fianna Fáil that peace could begin by the year's end. 'Peace first' was my message: before we advance any progress on talks, we must have peace.

The people were saying it clearly. People from both communities were yearning and clamouring for peace – now.

John Hume was feeling betrayed and angry at being sidelined. He threw himself into a series of television and radio interviews, still claiming that if his initiative were followed we would have peace within a week. I was being heavily criticized by Patrick Mayhew for pushing the idea of peace before Christmas. He also insisted that talks and the peace process must run in parallel, but the move to seize the opportunity for peace was growing and I firmly believed it should be grasped by both governments and that we should do everything within our power to bring an end to violence.

Unfortunately, an off-the-record comment I made to two journalists was reported in the press. I'd been chatting to them informally at a Whitney Houston concert and had said that, rather than let this opportunity for peace pass, I would walk away from John Major. They decided that the 'confidence' was too important to ignore and printed it. It caused a rift in Anglo-Irish relations; but emotions were running high, the prospects for peace had never been stronger and I was determined to keep up the pressure on the British government.

Dick Spring, who was very supportive, pursued implementation of the six principles while I picked up the threads of the abandoned initiative and worked behind the scenes on my 'peace before Christmas' agenda.

In London, speaking at the Lord Mayor's Banquet, John Major seized the initiative in saying that 'there may now be a better opportunity for peace in Northern Ireland than for many years'. He then added that he eschewed deadlines, but if the IRA gave up violence for good, Sinn Féin could join political talks; however, his government would never talk to organizations which did not renounce violence.

In a statement relegated to the inside pages of the papers, Gerry Adams admitted that Sinn Féin representatives had engaged in 'protracted contact and dialogue' with the British government. The claim was emphatically denied by No. 10, but as I remarked at the time, 'If that's the IRA saying they were involved in talks with the Brits, I believe them. They kill people. They do not tell lies.' I was to be proved right.

In my efforts to get a balanced agreement I had been trying to understand the apprehensions of the Northern Protestants. Archbishop Eames had been particularly forthcoming. I wanted to sound him out on what the Unionists would find acceptable, I wanted to get into their minds. I knew John Major was trying equally hard to ensure that both the Northern Nationalist and the Unionist voices were heard and that the aspirations of both were taken into account.

The Reverend Roy Magee continued to visit me in Dublin to put the Loyalist point of view:

'I always met Albert in Dublin in his office, there was greater security there. This was one thing that always struck me about him, it was always man to man you were talking, it wasn't secretaries taking notes, he was relating to you, you were relating to him, you were asking questions, developing thoughts, you were explaining things. It was in the peace and quiet of two men talking to each other and that ensured security; just the two of us.

'I was also a conduit for another man, a man who was dealing with John Major, and that was Archbishop Eames. I would have transmitted stuff to him and he would have brought it to the British government. My direct link to Albert Reynolds was also the direct link to the Irish government.

'There were other avenues that were open. I think the Loyalists tried to open as many channels as possible to get the message through. I would relay messages from the Loyalist paramilitaries to the Taoiseach and he would talk to John Major, and you would find the things you had been talking about would come out in a public announcement from Downing Street which was a great sign that things were moving in the right direction.

'The one thing the Loyalists were concerned about was the constitutional claim over the six counties as part of the whole island of Ireland, and once we'd got that clarified, that there would be no major change in the position of Northern Ireland within the United Kingdom, unless the majority of the people wished it, the pattern of movement was set towards resolution.'

Archbishop Lord Eames:

'I went to all the lengths I could to get Dublin to accept that they would never get any sort of understanding unless there was recognition of the consent principle in Northern Ireland. Haughey had never got to grips with that, Albert did.

'I began to sense that things were moving despite the horrific death toll and the injuries, and to me there had to be political dialogue and understanding.

'Albert said to me one day, "We're going to get a Declaration together which will embrace what you and others have been saying to me about the nature of consent," and I said, "Well, if you feel that now is the time for this, I believe it will be a major step forward."

'I'd already talked about this with John Major at length and he saw consent as the key to this, that something in the future, whatever the arrangement might be, had to contain outward visible signs of the consent principle; agreement that the future of Northern Ireland would not be swept in without their consent.'

I asked Robin Eames to write a paper for me expressing his concerns and those of the Northern Protestants. He underlined that their fears had to be not only recognized but seen to be recognized; he indicated how far his contacts thought the Ulster Loyalists would move; he analysed why they were suspicious of Southern intentions; and he set out his personal theory of what would follow in the wake of a complete Republican–Loyalist ceasefire.

I shared these ideas with John Major, as did Eames with Jim Molyneaux. We all knew we were talking to each other, but we also understood that, far from being a game, these separate, 'secret' strands of communication were imperative if we were to find an acceptable formula for peace on which all sides could agree. The man we all trusted implicitly in this was Robin Eames. He never betrayed to me conversations or confidences shared with him by either Major or Molyneaux, and in the same way I knew he would never pass on anything I confided to him in our conversations.

Archbishop Lord Eames:

'Then one evening, in Dublin, Albert put a piece of paper in front of me. He showed it to me and I said, "Look, you're going to have to give me a couple of hours to read this." As soon as I read it, it seemed to me there was totally insufficient reference to the principle of consent. By then John Major had come completely on board with this whole idea of consent.

'"Albert," I said, "it's not worth the paper it's written on. There's not enough reference to consent." So Albert said, "You write it, you draft the section which refers to the consent of the Northern Ireland people to their own future. I want to know what they would accept." Now I made my attempt at that and I gave it to him and, of course, I gave it to John Major.'

I was aware that that early draft of the declaration would be unsatisfactory, that we still hadn't really grasped the right wording to assuage the Protestant sensitivities. I thought, if I believe it's unbalanced – what will Eames think?

He was not impressed. I asked him to propose a form of words for me, to think about what he considered would win the approval of the Northern Protestants, and would also be possible for me to include in the document. We considered several drafts until finally he was satisfied.

Archbishop Eames:

'When we got to that stage, I phoned James Molyneaux and

told him I was coming over to London and that I had something I wanted him to see.

'I flew over to London only to find it was the day of the State Opening of Parliament. I got as far as Birdcage Walk before my taxi had to stop and I was forced to finish my journey on foot. However, because the Queen was attending the State Opening, the Metropolitan Police had sealed off the route. A little policewoman stepped forward and said, "I'm sorry, Father, but the road is closed and I can't allow you to pass."

'I said, "Look, it's awfully important I get there, I have an appointment over in Parliament."

'"Well, I suppose I could let you through," she said. "Is there anything of importance in your briefcase?"

'"Only some trivial papers," I answered. She let me through and on I walked from there to Westminster with what was to become an important section of the Downing Street Declaration in my briefcase.

'I handed it to Molyneaux who took it, pondered on it for some time, then returned it with one or two suggestions; but what was important was that he agreed to the substance of it.'

A few drafts later it was included in the Joint Declaration on Peace which was to become the Downing Street Declaration. In my speech on that momentous day I spoke of my concern for Unionist feelings as follows:

'Paragraphs 6–8 reflect my desire to respond to the Unionist fears. They include a willingness to accept and examine representations by them across the negotiating table with regard to the aspects of life in the South which they believe to be discriminatory or which threaten their way of life.

'In the Declaration I also ask them to look on the people of the Republic as friends, who share their grief and shame over all the suffering in the last quarter of a century, and who want to develop the best possible relationship with them, in which trust and understanding can flourish and grow.

'In it I also pledge to consider how the hopes and identities of all in relation to constitutional matters can be expressed in more balanced ways, which no longer cause division. I have stated that the Irish Government will, as part of a balanced constitutional accommodation, put forward and support proposals for change in the Irish Constitution, which would fully reflect the principle of consent in Northern Ireland.'

In parallel with Archbishop Eames presenting the case for the Protestants and Unionists, Roy Magee was discussing the Loyalists' aspirations and the conditions that they hoped to see in a joint declaration.

Reverend Roy Magee:

'We had had a meeting of the combined Loyalist leadership discussing the way that they would be happy with things if certain points were drawn up. I met Mr Reynolds the following day and he asked me, "What was the situation?" I explained about the meeting, which I had the right to do and the permission to do. "Could I see those points?" he said. I gave them to him, and those were the six points that were written into the Downing Street Declaration.'

I included them unchanged in paragraph 5:

the right of free political thought;
the right of freedom and expression of religion;
the right to pursue democratically national and political aspirations;
the right to seek constitutional change by peaceful and legitimate means;
the right to live wherever one chooses without hindrance;
the right to equal opportunity in all social and economic activity, regardless of class, creed, sex or colour.

Reverend Roy Magee:

'It was a tremendous step when the two of them came out of Downing St and John Major spoke and the first thing he said was the part of the meeting we'd held in the Shankill Road. It was mind-blowing almost but it gave the impression that here was a man, Albert Reynolds, who was serious about seeing peace in the island of Ireland and was concerned that the Loyalist paramilitary group and the Loyalist people would not be trampled over by those who wanted a united Ireland.'

But we weren't there yet. Suddenly another leak burst on to the front pages of the Irish press, with an exclusive report by Emily O'Reilly on the contents of an Irish position paper drafted by the Department of Foreign Affairs. It called upon the British to acknowledge the 'full legitimacy and value of the goal of Irish unity by agreement' in return for changes to Articles 2 and 3 of the Irish Constitution. The report continued that the document proposed a greater role for the Republic in policy on the North through joint North–South administrative bodies with executive powers.

I was appalled. It was a highly damaging leak and undid all the trust that we were trying so hard to build with the Unionists. Jim Molyneaux, Ian Paisley and John Taylor straight away pronounced it proof of a planned sell-out of the Unionists.

Paisley immediately sought an interview with John Major, who sympathized with him, saying he would have 'kicked the leaked Irish Government document over the rooftops'. After this, Paisley commented that he believed Major would not now do a deal with me.

The new proposal for a draft joint declaration, including the sections written by Eames and Magee, had been further refined and sent to the British government for discussion at a special cabinet meeting. I waited anxiously for the result. An Anglo-Irish summit was scheduled to take place at the beginning of December and I was hoping that this communiqué would be at the centre of the discussion. A phone call from Major's press secretary, Gus O'Donnell, indicated this was not the case. Instead, they announced in a press briefing that work could not continue on the joint document because they had not received the Irish position paper. This, in my view, was deliberately misleading. We were talking about the peace process; they were referring to a separate paper on the 'talks process'. Relations were further undermined when O'Donnell warned of questions being asked about contacts with the IRA. I had an interview the following day and was not surprised, but angered, when I was asked if Mansergh, my adviser, had indeed had direct talks with IRA representatives. I denied it emphatically, but I resented the way British intelligence seemed determined to undermine the peace process.

The following day, 26 November, Robin Butler arrived from London and to my great consternation and anger presented a new British peace document for the summit peace proposal, as an alternative to the Irish peace document, only this time their paper included proposals for unilateral changes to Articles 2 and 3. I was furious. It was completely altered from the balanced document we had presented to them and showed no understanding whatsoever of what we were trying to achieve.

Roderic Lyne, foreign affairs private secretary to the Prime Minister, recalls:

'As we got nearer to the Dublin summit, we got so concerned about the fact that Albert was still sticking to too much of this "green" language that we drafted a document of our own. We did this as a tactical move. We did not expect Albert to buy that document, but in a negotiation it is fair enough to put down different texts from both sides. Albert was furious and he and Martin Mansergh claimed that it was a deliberate attempt by us to destroy the whole process. It wasn't, it was a legitimate attempt by the British government to show the Irish, as a guideline if you like, what represented our point of view and what we could accept. We were trying, as it were, to bang a peg into the ground and say this is our position, because they had theirs, which was roughly their text of the declaration, and we had to get them to shift to ours. It was a deliberate move to get them to think about the effect on the Unionists; they only thought about the effect of anything on the Nationalists. It was one of the weaknesses.'

I sent a message back to John Major telling him that, as an alternative to the summit peace proposal, it wouldn't wash, and why bother to have a summit at all if this was their attitude? I was disappointed; it was not what I had expected from Major. It seemed to me he was being very badly advised by someone who had no understanding whatsoever of what we were trying to achieve. Since the Halloween Massacre in Greysteel we had had three weeks without paramilitary violence: this was surely as a result of our approaches to the paramilitaries seeking a way forward. Now was the time to build on this; there was no point in proceeding with this British document. To my mind the two documents were irreconcilable.

To make matters worse, Butler had also informed me that the story was about to break that since 1990 the British had been in secret contact with the IRA.

13

BACK CHANNELS

Before the story broke we had no clear evidence that the British were conducting a dialogue with Sinn Féin although, knowing of their contacts in the past, we suspected something could be going on. John Major himself had emphatically rejected such an idea only a few weeks earlier at the beginning of November, following the Shankill Road bombing, when he announced to the House of Commons: 'It would turn my stomach to sit down and talk to the Provisional IRA.' He said it at a time of high emotion, and it was true both he and I had, of necessity, to publicly proclaim our refusal to conduct face-to-face contacts with members of Sinn Féin until all violence had ceased; but, like me, John understood that nothing could or would ever be achieved without communication, and therefore secret links had to be sanctioned.

There had been links in place between them since the early eighties, that much I knew.

Gerry Adams recalls:

'It started away back in 1972 or maybe even as early as late 1971, but certainly in 1972 because I was released from prison to be involved. I was interned to be involved. I didn't know this of course, but I was released to be involved in talks with the British. We talked to Whitehall, we talked to Whitelaw in Whitehall, and that had been set up by a number of people who became the line of communication and unknown to us, that line continued as governments changed. They were probably dormant most of the time, but resurrected during the hunger strikes, during the first hunger strike in 1980, and there were quite a lot of exchanges, particularly during the second hunger strike when, as each of the hunger strikers neared death, or as their condition worsened, then the line became very, very active, so we were very suspicious. It was actually a big thing for us to agree to use such a line of communication and I think it does show a seriousness about our intent, the moral obligation to exhaust all possibilities. You could have stood on your honour and said – look, I'm an MP, I demand it. There's absolutely no reason why you can't come and talk directly, as opposed to sending messages through other people who would then deliver the messages and the whole thing would be wrapped up in such a way as to make it deniable, so that a British minister could stand up and technically use a formulation of words which allowed him to say – "We have had no talks with (what were then depicted as) terrorists." And the thing broke down, maybe the guy regrets it nowadays, but John Major used really offensive phrases like – there would have to be a period of "decontamination".'

Martin McGuinness too, had encountered different British contacts:

'There had been ongoing contact with the British Government over the course of many years and there was contact with the British Government during the course of the hunger strike of 1981 and all of that is on the public record. Effectively the British government, under John Major's tutelage, were involved in some sort of an exploration with us and effectively what they were proposing at the time was that if people like myself and Gerry Adams could deliver what they called "a period of quiet" . . . they refused to use the word "ceasefire" because they believed that because of the bad experiences that Republicans had been through in 1974 through to '75/'76, when talks collapsed, that there wouldn't be much point demanding that . . .

'Republicans had learnt a lot of lessons if you like, that the British government weren't really interested in the causes of conflict or bringing about a real negotiation to resolve the causes of conflict, they were only really interested in stringing out the ceasefire for as long as they possibly could, in the belief that if they did that the IRA would effectively become a defunct organization and war weary and of course history will show that they made a big mistake . . . In the dying days of the Thatcher administration, a representative of the British government who is known as the Mountain Climber came and spoke with me and told me very frankly that the purpose of the meeting was to give me some insight into the thinking of Margaret Thatcher, vis-à-vis her determination to marginalize Irish Republicans, and to build a wall as high as she possibly could so that people would realize that there was no prospect whatsoever of anything being achieved vis-à-vis Republican objectives while she was British Prime Minister. But of course what they failed to see, in agreeing to that meeting, was that rather than seeing that as a hard-line approach, even by Thatcher, I actually saw it as a weakness on the part of the British government that they actually felt, under what was an iron-fist approach Prime Minister, that in the dying days of her administration she recognized that there was no prospect whatsoever of any resolution of the situation unless they spoke to Irish Republicans. She was hoping, I think, that

I and others would be discouraged by the message that we received; in fact the opposite was the case. I was encouraged that she felt that she had to do that.

'That happened in the winter of 1990. In fact the first meeting took place one month before Margaret Thatcher left Downing Street and the person, the Mountain Climber, also announced at that meeting that he was about to retire. We obviously knew who we were dealing with, that we weren't dealing with just someone who was a civil servant or representative of the British government, that this was actually a person who was part of MI6. I didn't go to such meetings unless I had clearance from Sinn Féin and I had spoken to the IRA about it because I wasn't going to stick my neck out; however, following the offer of the meeting it was decided at leadership level within Republicanism that I should go along with a listening brief and hear what they had to say.'

The full exposé of the British negotiations was revealed in the press and so we learned that in February of that year, 1993, a message had been delivered to John Major which was believed to have been sent by Martin McGuinness – although McGuinness denies this – via an intelligence link to the British government. It read:

'The conflict is over but we need your advice on how to bring it to a close. We wish to have an unannounced ceasefire in order to hold a dialogue leading to peace. We cannot announce such a move as it will lead to confusion to the volunteers, because the press will misinterpret it as surrender. We cannot meet the Secretary of State's public renunciation of violence, but it would be given privately as long as we were sure that we were not being tricked.'

It was a most unlikely and dramatic communication, and the obvious suspicion was that it was a ploy or a trick by the IRA to seduce the British government into a trap; the political risk of even entering into preliminary dialogue was high. However, Major's office was assured by the Northern Ireland Office that it had come through a reliable secret source.

John Major:

'We were always convinced that it came from McGuinness and when we responded and a regular response continued we had no reason to believe it didn't come from the high command of the IRA. Whether McGuinness originated it, or approved it, or McGuinness said, "This is what we should say," and someone else wrote it, only McGuinness and those other people will know, but if it hadn't come from the upper echelons of the IRA there wouldn't have been any follow through and there was.

'Our security people were always confident that it came at the instigation of McGuinness.

'. . . There was a lot of debate as to whether it was a trick and whether we were being extremely foolish and whether we should ignore it but at the end of the day the equation was quite simple: we responded and it was possible we were on an escalator to a settlement, and if it went wrong we had got political egg on our face. So the equation was – on the one hand a settlement and the end of killing and on the other hand, embarrassment and egg on your face. I didn't think it was a very difficult position. It was obvious what you had to do and if it went wrong, it went wrong. How could you not have taken that risk? How could you not have done so? I didn't think there was any doubt about it.

'We looked at it very carefully.

'. . . I had a very small number of senior colleagues I shared that message with, just a handful, and we discussed it in great depth and decided how to respond and we did not publicize it, we kept it quiet.

'We didn't publicize it, not because we wanted to keep it

away from my colleagues but because we did not know what was going on at the other end of the tunnel. We did not want to publicize it and unsettle the IRA if they were making gestures to us ... which was also embarrassing and difficult because there we were not telling people what was going on. Easy in a democratic system to make a fuss over that, and of course some years later people did.'

The British government sent back a cautious reply agreeing to 'exploratory dialogue' if there was a 'genuine and established end to violence'. In their response they acknowleged that the result of such a process could be a united Ireland – but only with the consent of the people of Northern Ireland. This became known as the 'nine-paragraph' message, which went on to emphasize that 'the British Government does not have, and will not adopt, any prior objective of "ending of partition"' and that 'unless the people of Northern Ireland come to express such a view (i.e. a desire for a united Ireland), the British Government will continue to uphold the Union'.

The talks were to take place during a 'period of quiet'. Martin McGuinness writes in the Sinn Féin document 'Setting the Record Straight' that early in the year a representative of the British government had been in frequent contact, sometimes on a daily basis, suggesting that there was the possiblity of meetings taking place between British government representatives and Sinn Féin. The request for talks and a 'period of quiet' was passed on to the IRA:

'By this time, the British government had appointed two representatives. By the end of March we had reached agreement in principle about the meetings. The Sinn Féin side applied itself to terms of reference and an outline of policy position. It was during this period that we received the British 'nine-paragraph' document. We prepared an eleven-paragraph response to it. We also appointed a small secretariat under my tutelage.

'At this time we, Sinn Féin, were given a commitment by the IRA that it would create the conditions necessary to facilitate the round of talks and to enable us to explore the potential of the British government's assertion. This would have involved a fourteen-day suspension of operations.'

In the end the escalation of violence by the IRA forced the British government to abandon the text of a second substantive message and to withdraw from such talks until Sinn Féin had 'sufficiently shown it genuinely did not espouse violence'. Sinn Féin viewed this rejection as treachery. Persuading the Army Council to suspend violence for fourteen days had been a hard-won achievement; now they felt let down.

This was the tortuous path to peace that we trod every day.

There are many rumours as to the origin of the message allegedly sent by McGuinness. He adamantly denies that it came from him.

Denis Bradley, who acted as a conduit between the British and Sinn Féin, claims he wrote part of it in an effort to kick-start the peace process. Noel Gallagher, my contact and friend in the North, maintains he saw it completed by the secret back channel who took over from Michael Oatley, the Mountain Climber. Noel claims that he was at the Excelsior Hotel outside Heathrow when he saw 'Fred', the new man, complete the letter in preparation for passing it on to the British government. Whatever the truth, many people were putting in a great effort to get peace, many people were taking risks, and if it led to both sides talking, it was worth it.

However, later that year when the story of British secret back channels to the Provisionals broke in the London *Observer*, the peace process was in serious jeopardy again.

Patrick Mayhew and John Major were then put in the position
of having to explain to the House of Commons that while they
had not actually held talks, or struck any secret deals with the
IRA, messages had passed between them and the Republicans.
The revelation that Martin McGuinness could have sent the
original message, including the word 'surrender', placed him
in a dangerous situation too, within the IRA. As Martin
explained to me:

'Sir Patrick Mayhew was the Secretary of State in the North
and during the course of that he went into the British House
of Commons and attributed a statement to me which I had
never made, which I did view as an attempt by that administration to set me up and that was a very dangerous period for
me. At that time the leadership of Republicanism through
both the IRA and the executive of Sinn Féin were aware that
I had been authorized to do that first meeting, so effectively
people knew that my bona fides were OK, that this wasn't me
going along, a loner, that this was me effectively trying to
ascertain where the British government was coming from. We
then had the ludicrous situation where Sir Paddy Mayhew had
to go back into the House of Commons and I think make
dozens of corrections to the initial statement that he made.

'At that time we could easily have given up on the process,
but we didn't. We were very determined, even in the face of
what we considered to be a mischievous approach, and that
could vary from mischievous right through to Machiavellian
and a very dangerous approach, that we wouldn't give up our
objective, to try and establish whether or not there were
enough people of goodwill around who could effectively bring
about a situation where the British government and the
political leadership of Unionism would be compelled by the
coming together of these important political forces to come to
the negotiating table.'

* * *

I phoned John Major personally to express my anger not just at his government's hypocrisy in talking with the Provos but more significantly at my receipt of the disastrously amended document which I refused to even discuss. I finished by reiterating that there was no point in having a summit, no prospect of success and no way I would collude in such an anodyne joint statement.

That same day I wrote a very strongly worded letter to John, in which I told him that I did not see any prospect of the new proposal working and that we should not be trying to start again from scratch, bringing to nought eighteen months' patient work. I pointed out that the first document we had sent over in June had been a proposal from the Irish government and that we had since improved and refined it to take on board the many legitimate points made by his side. I stressed that we had further incorporated a lot of material given to me by Archbishop Eames which would make the document more acceptable to the Protestants and Unionists, and that we had gone as far as it was possible to go.

I emphasized that I did not accept their reasons for not proceeding with the joint declaration as originally envisaged. I confided that the recent leaks relating to the position paper had been explained to a close confidant of the Loyalist paramilitaries and that in his judgement, if the situation was explained in full to the Loyalists, the feared backlash would not happen.

I argued that we should not allow ourselves to be blown off course by the various attempts to thwart our progress, and I finished by saying, 'The prize is big enough to overcome present difficulties.'

The recent leaks were yet another frustrating setback to overcome. There were always those on every side who did not want to see the peace process succeed, and a leak of information to the media at the wrong time was an effective spoke to stick in the wheel. It was not just Unionist aspirations fighting Nationalist desires, British against Irish; there were politicians in high places, hungry for power, who thought they could foil the ambitions of others by knocking back signs of success in the peace process, and there were those who simply did not want to see peace with the men of violence at any price. There were so many possible ways the leaks could have happened – careless talk or malicious whispers – but whatever they were, it was practically impossible to discover who or what was the source; we just had to trust that what we were doing was right and determine that we would not allow such mischievous actions to derail the process.

The British were clearly very embarrassed at revelations that they had been in secret contact with the IRA, as Martin Mansergh recalled:

'It was clearly a matter of deep embarrassment to them. The embarrassment was that they had told us nothing about it. I was told afterwards by a senior British official that the reason for the contacts was that the British government wanted to check out for themselves what John Hume was saying to them. John Hume is the type of person who likes to take a fairly optimistic assessment, and I think each government wanted their own direct contact with Sinn Féin so that they could form their own independent judgement.'

14

FROM DUBLIN TO
DOWNING STREET

All the revelations and recriminations cast doubt on plans for the summit. John Major was insistent that it should go ahead as scheduled on 3 December 1993. Dermot Nally, secretary to the government and an experienced diplomat, strongly advised that we should not entertain their document at all. He called it 'typical British game playing' and said that if we wanted their respect we should 'get it off the table'!

The arguing, the dealing, went back and forth across the Irish Sea. Roderic Lyne was desperate to fix the summit date for Friday 3 December, but also insisted that the British document presented at the meeting the previous Friday, 26 November, cementing the union and raising Articles 2 and 3, should be on the table. Mansergh phoned back with my answer: 'No way.' There was also the post-Brussels meeting scheduled for Downing Street later in the month. Finally, just as it seemed the two projected meetings were back on, Lyne added that the Downing Street meeting would only take place 'subject to progress'.

I was furious. 'Tell them it's all off,' I instructed Martin

Mansergh. 'I'm not playing any more games. Tell them not to bother to come!'

Martin returned a few minutes later with the news that the two meetings were now on schedule and definitely on!

Then Seán Duignan relayed a message from his opposite number in London that 'negative vibes' from Dublin are being reported in the British press! Seán told me it was his work, that he'd put out a press release expressing Dublin's hurt and anger at British duplicity . . .

Politics!

With tempers frayed and emotions high we prepared for the Dublin summit. The evening before the summit Martin McGuinness revealed that the previous year the British had briefed Sinn Féin–IRA on discussions at Stormont throughout the period of the inter-party talks. This only fuelled my anger. I had always confided discreetly to Major that we had secret contacts as sources of information, and although I always suspected such contacts were going on on his side as well, I was upset that he had not placed the same trust in me.

Major, Mayhew and Douglas Hurd (the British Foreign Secretary) looked tense and strained when we gathered on 3 December in what was known as the King's Bedroom in Dublin Castle. Dick Spring and I sat across from them as they tried to put forward their document for discussion and we refused it. The meeting was becoming more contentious and bad-tempered when John suggested he and I should start off with a private meeting to thrash a few things out together. Certainly the air needed to be cleared before we could get anywhere.

John Major described this meeting in an interview for the BBC programme *Between Ourselves*:

'Albert and I, despite being friends, had some furious arguments in private over the drafting of the Declaration.

'It was in fact at Dublin Castle when I notably snapped my pencil in half, but it was more in irritation than temper. It was a pivotal meeting in which one or other of us was going to walk out or we were going to get an agreement; as it happened we got an agreement, but it was very tense that day.

'We withdrew that morning for a private meeting in a very ornate drawing room and Albert and I spent half an hour telling one another about our respective deficiencies.'

I remember saying to him, 'You're supposed to be my pal, John Major, and there you are talking to the Provos. I don't mind your talking to them, but you're not telling us the truth about it, and worst of all you're not telling me.' I felt betrayed, I told him. I'd put my cards on the table and I'd expected him to do the same.

I raged on: 'Why spend so long on an agreement and then come in with this? That's not you, John Major,' I said, 'that's somebody in the system and as far as I'm concerned I won't even read it and that's the end of it because the principle is all wrong. We agreed it and yet you try to change it at the last minute and that's not John Major. I don't know who gave you that to get in at the last minute, but it's a totally different document!' I raged and he raged – I chewed his bollocks off and he took lumps out of me.

John Major:

'It was the frankest and fiercest exchange I had with any fellow leader in my six and a half years as Prime Minister. Afterwards we re-assembled. All the officials were waiting, they weren't sure if we were going to continue or pack up and go home. We then had a very tense morning but eventually we made sufficient progress to realize that we would get there – but it could have fallen apart that day.'

Roderic Lyne:

'The chemistry between Major and Reynolds was very

important and never more important than in the famous
Dublin Castle meeting . . . that bloodletting sort of opened up
the way to the final negotiations on the Declaration.

'Before the meeting the pressure had built up on both sides.
Albert had been briefing the press and John Major was cross
about that. Albert was very cross that the British back channel
had been published in the press and that we'd been talking to
the IRA and all the rest of it, and because there was all this
fury when we arrived there, two big delegations, foreign
ministers and officials, the meeting started just with Albert
and John in the room together, not even Martin Mansergh and
I were in the room at the beginning. Normally when the heads
meet, you've always got at least one person there, but we
decided they should have a completely private chat.

'Martin and I sat outside the door and you could hear voices
being raised and they were having a real go at each other and
after about half an hour we were summoned in and then the
meeting went on, just with the four of us in there, and they
were still shouting at each other and hurling dossiers – I'd
armed John Major with a dossier of press cuttings that had
Albert's fingerprints all over them – unattributable briefings
that he hurled at Albert while Albert was hurling the back
channel back at John. They were still being pretty rough with
each other and glowering when we went in there. It was like
a couple of guys having a fight, but they gradually got through
this and the temperature got down to a point where we could
then join the delegations who were hanging around and
actually start negotiations.

'There wasn't a great deal for Mansergh and I to do until
then. We were acting more as witnesses and may have been
referred to for certain points but basically this was the two
principals having a go at each other . . . There wasn't much
negotiating, it was really getting the angst out of the system

and deciding do we go ahead with this or do we give up?

'The conclusion of that sort of double session was – "All right we're prepared to continue talking and give this a go, see if we can make it work," and it was only when they'd achieved that that we could sit down . . . [to reach a decision]. Albert sat down with two of his trusted delegation and John Major went with his trusted officials, Hurd and Mayhew, two of his most loyal and rocksolid people.

'We then got into what was still a very difficult negotiation, not least because Spring's people were attacking and we got to some crucial point – there was a point when they asked for a break in the proceedings and went off down the corridor to have an argument among themselves, between the different factions on the Irish side, and it went on for half an hour. There was a long pause while we waited for them to come back and we didn't know if they were going to come back and say "Yes, it's all right, we'll continue negotiating" or "No, we can't accept this, we're out of here."'

From our point of view, I remember a note being passed by John Chilcot to John Major at about the time we left the room that had us worrying that maybe they would pull out and go home. I always believed that Major wanted the declaration to work, that he wanted to be the Prime Minister who would crack the stalemate and end the violence, but that like me he had those around him only too eager to hold him back.

The only good thing was that by now the two sides were working off the one agenda and negotiations were now confined to the most recent Irish position paper which incorporated the paragraphs put together by Archbishop Eames and the Reverend Roy Magee, as well as amendments proposed by the British over the last five months. However, there was no agreement on Articles 2 and 3, although they were still very much 'on the table'.

I wasn't looking for a totally green agreement and Major was not looking for a totally Unionist one. The first might get me in favour with the Republicans, as the second would Major with the Unionists, but how long would it last? We were two well-balanced men, but we were under a lot of pressure from some of our officials – and, just as he had to be firm with his people, I had to be tough with my side too.

The break in the meeting seemed to make us all relax and the atmosphere lightened. We all came back into the King's Bedroom. There was no instant breakthrough in negotiations but there was a distinct feeling that something constructive had been achieved and that we had definitely launched a process that would lead to the joint Downing Street Declaration.

We left the officials to work through the details of the text while John and I conferred with our respective colleagues via numerous phone calls. After months of sparring we were finally into real negotiations.

At one point the British came back insisting on the inclusion of Articles 2 and 3; I parried that I would accept their being changed only if there was reciprocal movement on the Government of Ireland Act!

I agreed that I would talk to the Republicans to draw them in, if Major would talk to the Unionists. We needed them both on side.

The stakes were now so high, an agreement so close, that failure would hit very hard, and yet success was far from certain. There was still tough bargaining to go to draw the two sides together.

The EU summit in Brussels a week later was the scene of another battle, with Major and I both refusing to give ground. The Irish government wanted to retain the 'Irish Convention' introduced in the Anglo-Irish Agreement and so hated –

indeed, vetoed – by the Unionists; however, once we had renamed it and reinvented it as the 'Forum for Peace and Reconciliation' it was finally accepted by Jim Molyneaux as a useful but harmless talking shop and so deadlock was avoided by compromise.

Roderic Lyne:

'We had another round in Brussels which wasn't easy, but we finally got on with a lot of stuff on the phone and I think that the role Albert played in this was critical, because he was prepared to go horse trading, he had to fight his way through his own side in a coalition government where there were people who were urging him not to settle, including very green elements in the Irish Department of Foreign Affairs. There was a sort of middle-ranking, very deep green official called Seán O hUiginn ...

'Now curiously Albert and Spring didn't chuck him out. A middle-ranking official on our side would not have intervened in the way he did – quite aggressively and even rudely towards the Prime Minister of another country. But you could see what pressure Albert was under from his own people. So I give him credit for that.'

O hUiginn was good, a tough negotiator, obviously not acceptable to the British because he was so tough and good – a real Republican!

On 14 December, the day of final reckoning, tensions were high as we battled with revising, refining, balancing and counterbalancing the text of the joint declaration. It was imperative it was acceptable to both Republicans and Unionists or all our aspirations for peace would be lost, our hopes for an end to the violence would be dashed – all our efforts wasted. John Major and I resolved the final issue in the course of two phone calls, when we agreed that the declaration should include a commitment, for the first time in history, that the British government 'will uphold the democratic wish of a greater number of the people of Northern Ireland on the issue of whether they prefer to support the Union or a sovereign united Ireland'.

Although we hardly dared admit it to one another, by early evening the deal was done and the declaration was on!

On the morning of 15 December we flew to London. Dick Spring, Máire Geoghegan-Quinn and various officials who had been involved in the talks accompanied me. Exhaustion had turned to elation. We were very aware of the historic significance of the declaration we were about to sign. It went further than any other British prime minister or British government, or indeed any Irish prime minister or Irish government, had ever gone before. It was the ultimate achievement of a lot of work by a lot of people behind the scenes, a lot of input to strike the right balance that made it acceptable to the two governments and, we profoundly hoped, throughout the communities and indeed among the para-militaries as well.

I'm sure there were still doubts on the British side but, as Martin Mansergh commented later, they 'finally became con-vinced that they had to take hold of the peace initiative if the moral ground were not to be lost, regardless of whether it in fact brought peace, of which they were highly sceptical. Although credit was due to Margaret Thatcher for her part in upholding the Anglo-Irish Agreement, I was always fairly clear that there was little hope of an end to belligerence in Ireland while she remained the British Prime Minister. John Major deserved credit for his political courage in adopting the Declaration and indeed a short time later the Framework Document, which was to be at the expense of the Unionist alliance.'

We arrived at Downing Street, where a welcoming John

Major met us and conducted us to the Cabinet Room. I have to admit I still felt slightly apprehensive that the British might attempt a last minute renegotiation, but it was not to be.

There was a momentary hesitation when we came to sign the draft document. It had gone through so many versions, we realized that we were not sure that we were both signing the same document! In fact, after all the changes and rewording, the drafting and redrafting and dotting 'i's and crossing 't's, we had to appoint people to carefully compare our clean copy with their clean copy, going through them word by word to make sure they were identical in every way. There was a sigh of relief: no problem!

There was a lot of banter around the table, a lot of hand-shaking and back-slapping; champagne was served – orange juice for me, I was still teetotal. As Robin Butler remarked to me, we'd 'come a long way from Baldonnell!'

For John Major and me it was a momentous occasion. We'd fought many battles along the way, against each other and our own governments, but we'd done it, and we both recognized the significance of our achievement. We weren't there just yet, but we were on our way to peace in Northern Ireland.

There was one instant that almost marred the occasion when Roderic Lyne took me to one side and said that the Prime Minister would appreciate it if I would agree to him referring to himself as a Unionist. I did not think it would be a good idea and said so, which I think annoyed Major, but he'd asked and I'd answered – besides, my judgement was that such a statement was provocative. Our agreement had been negotiated from a neutral position and we had gone the distance with that; suddenly to weight it with personal descriptions veering towards one side or another would have negated all our efforts, and to my mind it could easily have been used as an excuse by the Republicans to go against the declaration. Reflecting on this moment, Seán Duignan made an interesting comment:

'In the event, the Prime Minister refrained from such observations but afterwards, as I shook his hand, the thought struck me that he had taken as many risks as Reynolds, Hume and Adams on the way to the accord. It was not that long ago since IRA mortars exploded in the garden we could see from inside No. 10. As Tory leader he was also taking a considerable risk, not just in terms of his reliance on the Unionists in the Commons, but also in terms of the large pro-Unionist element on the Conservative backbenches. However, a British source later told me Major resented Reynolds' rejection of his "I am a Unionist" affirmation.'

Then it was out to the press conference. We stood in front of the brightly decorated Downing Street Christmas tree, John Major and me, side by side, accompanied by Patrick Mayhew, Dick Spring and Máire Geoghegan-Quinn. The declaration was received with an almost euphoric cheer from the assembled crowds and media waiting beyond the barriers outside No. 10 – a welcome that was echoed around the world.

Then, from the press call and celebrations in Downing Street, it was across to the Irish Embassy in Grosvenor Place, where more champagne and another photo-call awaited.

We returned to Dublin that same day. It was hard to believe even then that we'd actually done it, that the Downing Street Declaration was declared and we were on our way to peace. As Dick Spring and I entered the Dáil, there was a standing ovation from all sides of the chamber.

In my report to the Dáil, I commented:

'This is an unusual Declaration between Governments. It does not just reflect the views and interests of the two Governments or provide some compromise between them. Instead it seeks to comprehend the deeply held positions of all who find themselves caught up in the narrow ground of a conflict with ancient roots within a part of this island. It makes clear that the British Government is in no sense an enemy to the rights of the Nationalist tradition, and the Irish Government is in no sense an enemy to the rights of the Unionist tradition.

'The overriding objective, the overriding criterion for the language of this Declaration is whether each statement in it makes a contribution to peace, and whether it adequately reflects deeply held fears and essential interests.

'I am convinced that nobody should be afraid of peace. The purpose of this joint Declaration is to help remove conflicts of interest, and fundamental differences in the sense of identity, out of the arena of violence, and to place them purely in the political and democratic arena.'

We did not promise 'peace within a week' or 'peace by Christmas': the declaration was a set of principles, not a deal negotiated with the paramilitaries from both sides, though it did open the way for that. Nevertheless it was greeted with great warmth and enthusiasm by the media. The *Irish Times* said that it was 'a measured and subtle challenge to parties and paramilitaries of all shades'. The *Irish Press*, the *Irish Independent*, and the London *Independent* called it 'historic', and the *Guardian* spoke of an opportunity 'unparalleled in a quarter of a century'; but *The Times* warned that 'its success depends on factors outside its signatories' control'. In that they were right.

There was cross-party support from both British and Irish governments and from John Hume and the SDLP, although there was a wariness among some of the Nationalists that, in the attempt to reach the middle ground, some of their concerns had been overlooked in favour of supporting the aspirations of the Unionists.

The Unionists' reception was cautious. Even moderate Unionists looked hard at anything emanating from Dublin, especially with the Taoiseach's signature on it, and even more particularly with the names of Hume and Adams hovering in the background. However, encouraged by Jim Molyneaux – who said he did not want to be responsible for delaying peace by a single day – they gradually came on board. As expected, Ian Paisley and his hard-line Democratic Unionists rejected it out of hand, more ready to destroy it than support it. And from the people whose support we really sought, the IRA, there was only doubt and suspicion and a call for clarification!

15

STALEMATE TO CEASEFIRE

From the moment it was announced, the Downing Street Declaration received unprecedented support from around the world. President Clinton was one of the first to convey his congratulations, as was President Jacques Delors, followed by all the European leaders and other political friends. A welcome visitor to Ireland at that time was Yasser Arafat, who also expressed his support in an interview he gave to the *Evening Herald*:

'Peace can solve all issues; we have to remember that. All wars solve nothing. It is in the interest of the people that there should be peace. For every revolution there must be an end.

'Only yesterday, the military wing of the African National Congress decided to dissolve. In South Africa, in the Middle East, and two or three years ago in Central and Eastern Europe, there has been a recognition by leaders of stature that the old ideological conflicts must be brought to an end everywhere and that a new spirit of peace and reconciliation must be brought to bear on the deep differences, which have caused immense human suffering.'

Following the announcement there was praise and re-
joicing, even from the cynics who'd never believed an
agreement could be made or that peace was possible; but I
knew that if things didn't move forward, they would be back
clamouring at the door. Peace was never an easy option. First
we had to see if the declaration would run!

It wasn't even out of the starting box when it faltered.

The IRA did not reject the declaration but they did demand
'clarification'. I was more than happy to comprehensively
clarify any point of confusion, but both Major and I were
adamant that we would not renegotiate the signed document.

The sticking point for Sinn Féin was the twin principles of
self-determination and consent, the very issues that had consumed so much time in my covert communications with
Gerry Adams and Martin Mansergh's meetings with Martin
McGuinness.

The Downing Street Declaration stated: 'It is for the people
of the island of Ireland alone, by agreement with the two parts
respectively, to exercise their right of self-determination on the
basis of consent, freely and concurrently given, North and
South, to bring about a united Ireland, if that is their wish.'

All parties had come a long way in agreeing to this wording. Still, many Nationalists were disappointed it did not go
further in setting out the path to a unified Ireland, while the
Unionists, though accepting it, still felt betrayed, and the fact
that the words 'a united Ireland' were included at all struck
fear into their hearts.

I answered such fears in the Dáil, the day after the declaration was announced:

'As for the notion of betrayal, my Government too feels a
sense of responsibility towards the Unionist population.
Nothing that John Major or I proclaimed on Wednesday
represents a betrayal of the democratic rights of the people of

Northern Ireland. I have stated, and I now repeat, that neither the Government nor the people of this State have any desire to impose either by force, or by some form of political coercion, a united Ireland on an unwilling population and against the wishes of the majority of the people of Northern Ireland. Only a united Ireland based on a clear agreement and consent is worth having.

'I believe there is hardly anyone in Ireland today who believes that unity is or should be on the immediate political agenda. There is no way round the task of first building better relationships, new trust, and developing the practice of co-operation between the two parts of the two communities in Ireland. Any attempt, whether political or otherwise, to move quickly in the direction of a united Ireland in the absence of consent would be totally counterproductive. But that does not mean that the ideal should be abandoned as a long-term aim. Indeed, Irish unity in the right conditions would still be the almost universal wish of the people of this State.

'The most pressing item on the political agenda, after peace, is to create an accommodation between Unionists and Nationalists in Northern Ireland and between North and South, within a broad framework of British–Irish co-operation. An atmosphere of peace will make that task much easier. If overall agreement at first proves difficult, then let us proceed by smaller steps in a balanced way.'

'Smaller steps' it proved to be. I knew that the call for 'clarification' was a delaying tactic by Sinn Féin. They needed time to study the complex document, as well as time to relay its meaning and content not just to the IRA's Army Council but to its many supporters around the world. After all, this was not just another intergovernmental document, a clever piece of rhetoric; this was a life-and-death situation that affected everybody on the island of Ireland.

I understood why they wouldn't accept the declaration immediately – it was too soon for them, they did not want to show their hand – so I let them take their time. I was determined to get a permanent ceasefire, and if it meant playing them like a trout before reeling them in, then I was up for it. There were compromises they were going to have to make, and a huge leap of faith. It would not be easy for Gerry Adams and Martin McGuinness to persuade the IRA or their grassroots supporters that the declaration would live up to its promises.

Martin Mansergh, who on my behalf was now in constant contact with Adams and McGuinness, understood that:

'In a sense Sinn Féin leaders were riding two horses at the same time in trying to reassure the wider leadership that this was still consistent with core demands. But they probably realized that, in practice, it was heading in the direction of a negotiated political settlement that would, certainly for the time being, fall considerably short of Irish unity.'

John Major:

'The IRA were really on the back foot. Their desire for "clarification" was just to give them time to think and we were perfectly aware of that. They could not go against world opinion and particularly American opinion. We knew that. They were caught, and all they were doing was buying time with their "clarification", and I was perfectly happy for them to have as much time as they liked, particularly if they weren't killing people at the time. But when they actually asked for clarification, the points they raised were frankly pathetic. It was clear it was just a tactic while they sorted out their own internal problems and we always appreciated that. We always realized that Adams and McGuinness had their own problems with the IRA and it wasn't in our interest to make their problems more difficult.

'If they had sent the message and we thought they had, then they were interested in making progress, which we thought they were; then we needed to help, not make life more difficult.'

Positive signs were emerging. An *Irish Independent* poll found that 97 per cent of respondents in the Republic wanted the IRA to end its campaign. The London *Independent* reported that ministers were considering contingency plans for scaling down the army presence if the IRA agreed to end violence. In an article published in *Sunday Life*, John Major sought to reassure the Unionists that the declaration was not about undermining the Union or joint authority. Martin McGuinness announced 'nationwide consultations' by his party. Jim Molyneaux denied the declaration was a 'sell-out', while at an EU briefing in Brussels, Dick Spring described it as 'the basis for a lasting political settlement' and urged paramilitaries to 'respond positively'.

But there were also stumbling blocks. The declaration had promised that all those who permanently relinquished support for paramilitary violence would be invited to join in the political process in 'due course'. The British had tried to interpret this as a three-month 'quarantine' or, as John Major unfortunately termed it, a 'decontamination' period. Once we had our permanent ceasefire in place I wanted them included as soon as possible; I knew anything short of that would be seen by Sinn Féin as totally unacceptable – a deal-breaker.

Sinn Féin's president, Gerry Adams, continued to call for clarification through 'unconditional' talks between the two governments and his own party, and he went on to question the interpretation of 'self-determination', seeking an all-Ireland referendum for the 'island' as a whole rather than separate plebiscites North and South; and still he demanded that the British should act as 'persuaders' for a united Ireland. The DUP leader, Ian Paisley, said his party would not join in any talks based on the 'poisoned dream of the declaration'.

All sides caught in the conflict were determined to make their positions clear.

The British produced even more provocative language when, on a pre-Christmas visit to Belfast, John Major answered Sinn Féin's expectations of clarification by declaring: 'There is a gauntlet down on the table. It is marked peace. It is there for Sinn Féin to pick it up. The onus is on them. There is no need for fresh negotiation. There is no need for indecisiveness. There is no further clarification needed – we are not being drawn into negotiations. I am not playing that game.'

The people of the island of Ireland were impatient to move ahead. In America the arguments were also building for an IRA ceasefire and a speedy return to the political process. President Clinton called on all those who justified or embraced violence 'to cast off the works of darkness and put on the armour of light' and accept this 'historic opportunity to end the tragic cycle of bloodshed'.

President Bill Clinton:

'I was initially delighted. I remember thinking that it was a wonderful Christmas present, and one that I hoped would give us an opportunity to help resolve the problem. I hailed the joint declaration and both John Major and Albert Reynolds for the significant steps they both took. The key breakthrough in the declaration was that it both took away the justification for violence – the Republicans now had a peaceful avenue towards their goal – and it reassured the Unionists that their rights would be respected and that no change would occur without a democratic process. The declaration paved the way to the negotiating table.'

On Thursday, 23 December 1993, the IRA announced a

three-day ceasefire to start at midnight. But whatever spark of hope may have been raised that peace might be in the offing was quickly doused when Martin McGuinness reported that 'the political situation hasn't developed to a position where Sinn Féin can use its influence to end attacks on the British Crown forces'.

As if to emphasize the point, just after midnight on 27 December the IRA ended their ceasefire with a bomb attack on a police station in Fintona, County Tyrone, causing huge damage. They followed that, and their New Year statement that 'the struggle' remained 'solid and instant', with a missile attack on a patrol in Upper Library Street in Belfast; and as if that wasn't enough of an indicator, a young British soldier was shot dead by a sniper in Crossmaglen, County Armagh.

Despite this surge in violence, and the defiant words that Sinn Féin and the IRA were feeding to the press, I held firm to my belief that behind the scenes the momentum towards a ceasefire was growing.

I was determined to prove that an end to violence could have its own rewards. If they wanted questions answered on clarification, I answered them, and when they asked for the ban on broadcasting rights to be lifted, I arranged it. It was a nonsense anyway. Established twenty-two years previously, section 31 of the Broadcasting Act was a ministerial order banning members of Sinn Féin, the IRA and other named organizations from speaking on the national airwaves. Broadcasting companies had got around the problem simply by using actors to dub the voices of the offending protagonists. There was outrage at my lifting the ban from John Bruton, Dick Spring and Des O'Malley, but Michael D. Higgins, the minister in charge of broadcasting, was undeterred.

Assurances were also given that an end to violence and an IRA ceasefire could lead to an early release of prisoners and that Sinn Féin would be invited to a meeting at Government Buildings within seven days of a ceasefire announcement. Releasing prisoners once a conflict was over was key, as Martin McGuinness explains:

'It had to be put on the radar screen that in the context of the agreement, prisoners would have to be released. For time immemorial on the island of Ireland, where there has been conflict and where conflict has ended, prisoners have always been released, because not to release them is to allow the situation to fester. Indeed, many times, even though they were released, it still festered because issues that lay at the heart of the conflict were not being directly faced up to. So in our situation what we were trying to do was bring about a process which would see the issues at the heart of the conflict dealt with, and alongside that, prisoners being released. It was crucial, and of course from our perspective we went to great pains to be sure that our people, who were supportive of what we were doing, were visiting the prisoners in the prison to out-line for them what we were doing and the general direction the process was going, so that they in their turn could relay the briefing to all the other prisoners. In that way we could bring the vast bulk of the prisoners with us.'

Increasingly, I was being attacked from all sides, politically and in the media, for 'pro-Sinn Féin tendencies' and for using 'Provo language'. But I knew from my own enquiries what the big issues were for Republicans and the demands that had to be met in order to get a ceasefire. I was satisfied that if I could deliver them it would make a difference, no question about it. I'd made up my mind, too, that no matter what, I was going to do it. I'd come this far; criticisms from the opposition or the media were not going to stop me.

In the same way as the Republicans in Ireland sought to draw in the prisoners, I knew that it was imperative that the

Republicans in America were also informed of the implications of the Downing Street Declaration and that they too were engaged in the cessation of violence and the path to a ceasefire.

Following Clinton's inauguration back at the beginning of 1993, Niall O'Dowd, who together with his colleagues had worked so successfully to get Clinton into the White House, had assembled another ad hoc group of wealthy Irish American businessmen interested in forming a path-finding mission to Belfast. I had already foiled O'Dowd's previous demands for an American peace envoy to Northern Ireland; now he was keen to pursue the idea again with another group of entrepreneurial Irish Americans. At that time, one in four chairmen and chief executives of American companies claimed Irish heritage, so he had a lot of choice.

O'Dowd first asked high-profile New York insurance executive Bill Flynn, boss of Mutual of America, to get involved. Flynn, whose mother came from County Mayo and whose father was from County Down, was a member of numerous charitable and educational boards and in 1992 he had helped organize a conference in Derry on conflict resolution. He had spent time in Northern Ireland with the Peace People, and had already met Gerry Adams and had talks with him and Father Reid at Clonard Monastery.

Charles 'Chuck' Feeney was next to come on board. He was one of those at the very top of the *Forbes* 'rich list' and had made his fortune from, among other ventures, selling duty-free goods to tourists all over the world. A reclusive family man, he had quietly been involved in philanthropic works north and south of the border for many years. He had also contributed generously to the campaign for Irish visas and was interested in promoting peace in the North.

Raymond Flynn and Bruce Morrison added political gravitas, and the whole group was backed by Brendan Scannell, who at the time was serving as a diplomat with the Irish Embassy in Washington.

The plan was to open up a link between Sinn Féin and Irish America to explore the possibility of acting 'outside the box' in an international dimension, as a way of seeking an end to the conflict, and even to begin the process of brokering a ceasefire. Through a Sinn Féin contact a meeting had been set up with Gerry Adams, who had agreed to ask the IRA for an informal seven-day ceasefire to accommodate the visit of the American group. The Americans also planned on holding meetings with the two governments and the political parties; however, to avoid any leaks getting out about their visit, they agreed to put those in place on their arrival.

Confirmation went through that the informal ceasefire would be in place, and the date was set for 4 May 1993.

I was not at all happy when news of this reached me. In his official capacity as Mayor of Boston, Raymond Flynn had relayed the intentions of the group to the Dublin authorities. Again, the timing was wrong; the initiative had to remain with those of us already involved and as always negotiations were at a delicate stage, where any outside influence could tip the balance and upset all we had achieved. I believed they would serve a better purpose at another time. I asked for my official view to be passed on to Flynn, informing him that the government did not believe there should be official contact with Sinn Féin until a permanent cessation of violence had been declared. He followed our advice and pulled out of leading the mission, and the group's visit was cancelled: without Flynn as the political leader, the visitors would have been just another bunch of businessmen. I learned later that Flynn could have had another motive for pulling out: he had been nominated as American ambassador to the Vatican by President Clinton on St Patrick's Day, and as the appointment hadn't been confirmed at that stage he wouldn't have wanted to do anything to jeopardize his chances by becoming personally involved in a potentially controversial action.

As it was, the ceasefire lasted for a few days before orders could go down the line to the various units that it had been called off. Again, it was only when the story broke of the British secret dealings with the Republicans that we realized the ceasefire had also been timed to coincide with secret talks with the British, which had also failed to happen.

At the time Gerry Adams was not at all sure of the credibility of the Irish Americans. It had not been easy getting the IRA to agree to a ceasefire, and then to call it off ... but a personal visit to Belfast by O'Dowd to explain the circumstances of what had happened, and that they had been beyond his control, convinced him they were genuine and a new meeting was set up.

The fact-finding mission, this time led by former Connecticut congressman Bruce Morrison, arrived in Dublin at the beginning of September to start a round of talks with politicians on both sides of the border. This time they had had written confirmation of an ad hoc temporary ceasefire – and had subsequently destroyed the missive for fear news of their mission might break out. Only two days before their arrival, the IRA had heralded the start of the ceasefire by setting off a massive bomb, ravaging the centre of Armagh.

They came to see me in Dublin. I knew them all, we'd met over in America and on their individual visits to Ireland. Chuck Feeney owned a hotel in Limerick, Castletroy Park, and during all the problems with Aer Lingus and talk of changing the routing to fly over instead of into Shannon, he came to see me to discuss the effect such a change would have on local businesses. He had a good head on him and was always a man of great courage.

I asked all my staff to leave the office when the group arrived and we spent a good two hours talking. I told them where we were with the peace process, about my talks with John Major and what we hoped to achieve with the joint declaration. Irish America was important for our success; I knew how powerful these men and others like them were in the States and I wanted to ensure that when the time came I could count on their support. They wanted to get Adams over to America and were eager to push for a visa. I told them that now was not the time; there would be too much opposition, not just from the British, but from the Unionists and Loyalists who would see it as a severe betrayal. I also said that at that time, I would be against it too. It was not the policy of the Irish government to support the granting of visas to members of Sinn Féin or the IRA to travel abroad, but, I told them, when it was right I'd be ready and I'd let them know.

They left me and headed North. They met up with the different constitutional politicians, both Nationalists and Unionists, under the pretext that they were Irish Americans looking at the prospects for developing and investing in business. Ian Paisley called Morrison a 'troublemaker' and refused to see him, but they were well received by leaders of the other parties. They even met with representatives of the Loyalist groups, Gusty Spence and David Ervine, who, they reported back, seemed very earnest in their desire for peace. With Gerry Adams and Martin McGuinness they came to the real point of their visit, which, they said, was to build a bridge between Sinn Féin and Irish America and to ensure that any moves towards peace and a ceasefire would be met by reciprocal political benefits in the States. They also promised to lobby the US administration into helping the parties move forward in a democratic way. Their visit to Sinn Féin head-quarters earned them the name 'the Connolly House group'.

They returned to America, but we were kept informed of what they were planning through our Embassy contact, Brendan Scannell. The White House was also on track. All information on the group's activities was passed through a channel to the White House. Niall O'Dowd then briefed the office of Senator Edward Kennedy. Kennedy, although he was not a friend of Sinn Féin, had a sincere sense of responsibility towards Ireland and he knew that it was essential that the White House was kept aware of any of the group's activities pertaining to the peace process. His sister, Ambassador Jean Kennedy Smith, would have made sure he was up to speed on how things were going in Ireland. At that time she had only recently moved into the American Embassy in Phoenix Park, but she was a good friend and became a frequent visitor to my home and my office, and we kept closely in touch on the way things were progressing. I made it clear that though I welcomed the enthusiasm of the Connolly House group, they had to follow our lead and should not try to go it alone. If they were to have any credibility with the White House, or indeed with us or any of those involved, it was essential they followed our strategy.

In America, Nancy Soderberg, staff director of the National Security Council, a key official in the White House whose brief included Northern Ireland, worked closely to monitor what was going on in Ireland, with a colleague of hers, another expert on Irish affairs, Trina Vargo, who had in fact taken over Nancy's position in Edward Kennedy's office. Trina's expertise on Ireland was highly regarded on Capitol Hill. She was also extremely discreet and highly valued by Kennedy, who relied on her to keep him fully informed. In addition, she was a close associate of O'Dowd and Scannell.

In the lead-up to the election Clinton had promised that he would give an entry visa to Adams or any other elected politician. Since then Clinton had become President, and Adams had lost his political status when he was defeated in his West Belfast constituency. Nevertheless, in April 1993 Adams had applied for a visa and been turned down as ineligible under the US Immigration and Nationality Act, which prohibited the issue of a visa to any alien who had engaged in terrorist activity.

In October that year the New York Mayor, David Dinkins, perhaps in an attempt to win over the Irish American vote and revive his chances of re-election, wrote to President Clinton requesting him to reconsider granting a visa for Adams in the light of the ongoing dialogue between Hume and Adams and the search for peace.

His appeal was thwarted when news of the Shankill Road bombing hit America. Nancy Soderberg and her immediate boss, Tony Lake, said later that they had looked at the letter but then immediately dismissed it. At that particular time all hope of an imminent ceasefire vanished. However, there was an outcry over the snub to an important Democratic mayor, and a great deal of publicity was created by Irish Americans over the refusal letter, which referred to the PIRA, the Provisional Irish Republican Army, instead of the IRA. The importance of the distinction was easy to overlook: however, as only the British or the State Department use the initials PIRA, the Irish Republicans took great exception to it. The effect was to soften the attitude towards giving a visa to Adams. Revelations in the press about the British secret negotiations with the Republicans further enhanced his chances.

Inspired by this, the Connolly House group decided to try again. They believed it was imperative that Adams should have the chance to come to America to explain the position of his party and what he and his colleagues were doing to engage the IRA in agreeing to a ceasefire.

In one of his many roles, Bill Flynn was chairman of the National Committee on American Foreign Policy, a non-profit organization which sought to stimulate debate on foreign policy in the United States. For some time that particular body had been considering setting up a conference to discuss peace in Northern Ireland, to which they intended to invite Northern Ireland party leaders. Bill had a track record of organizing such events on conflict and was a credible and effective operator with a known reputation; so, he argued, if he invited Gerry Adams to participate in the debate, it would be hard for the White House to turn down yet another application for a visa.

Meanwhile the joint Downing Street Declaration was signed and I started looking for effective ways to draw the IRA not just into accepting its terms but into constitutional politics.

I was well aware that Adams wanted and needed to get into America. If we were to have any chance of peace, it was vital that he went over there and briefed his grassroots supporters on the intentions of the joint declaration; and I wanted him there to use his influence to build their support for a ceasefire.

As Martin McGuinness explains:

'Right through the course of the conflict in the North of Ireland, there was a substantial section of Irish Americans who were hugely supportive of Sinn Féin and Republicanism and indeed were supporters of the IRA, and over the years many of these people had made contributions to the Nationalist community in the North. It was much easier to get a decision from the constituency here, to understand if all those that you represented were behind the process. Here we could send our representatives around the country to gather information about their decisions. It was different when your constituents were three thousand miles away. You have to remember that for most people that was pre-internet.'

Gerry Adams:

'The Irish American factor was just totally critical and in our own way, as we came to terms with reorganizing Sinn Féin and trying to develop and find effective ways of delivering the objectives of our struggle, an idiot could have realized that the international dimension was part of any successful liberation struggle. Again, we had ongoing connections into Irish America, into Irish Republican Irish America which, as time had gone on, over thirty years, had become smaller, just by the sheer war of attrition, but then there were a number of people like Ciaran Staunton, who did a huge amount of work on immigration legislation and was a member of Noraid at the time, and Niall O'Dowd, who were watching what was happening and who were saying we can bring other people in here, there's corporate America   '

I knew that the British and John Major in particular would be strongly opposed to my supporting the call for a visa for Adams, but I also knew it was the right way to go. I knew too that I could not be seen to call for it myself or there would be an outcry from the Unionists and the Loyalists. It had to be seen to come from the Irish American lobby, my allies in the Connolly House group.

It was going to be difficult. Both Jean and Edward Kennedy, following the murders of two of their brothers, had a deep hatred of terrorism and terrorists that would be hard to overcome. However, they were both passionate about Ireland and about bringing peace. The senator was well informed about the talks John Hume had been having with Adams, and Jean herself was convinced that Adams was sincere in his desire to find a peaceful and political solution to end the Troubles. We had to convince Ted that the time was right to allow Adams back into the States and that we needed him to sell the idea to Clinton.

That New Year, Senator Kennedy, his wife Vicky and their son, Patrick, came over to stay with Jean at Phoenix Park, and we invited them over to the apartment in Ballsbridge for dinner with the family: Kathleen and me, Cathy, Abbie, Leonie and Andrea. Patrick was flying into Dublin that same evening, after a meeting with the Pope in Rome that day, and was driven directly to the apartment in time for dinner.

I seem to remember we spent a lot of time thrashing out the problem of the visa. I think Jean was up for it by then but Ted needed a lot of persuading. It seemed they'd been going over and over it, because Ted was beginning to come round to the idea and was starting to understand the necessity of getting Adams into America. Jean had a lot of influence with her brother and he relied on her good sense to advise him. Also, where Jean and I were restricted in what we could do, Ted was free to lobby openly when Adams reapplied to visit America.

The Connolly House group had set a date for their conference that February, 1994, and to make sure Adams was there they had already begun their push for a visa. Jean told me that she was concerned that it was too soon, that as Sinn Féin still had not signed up for the declaration, there would be resistance in America to the visa application. Both she and Kennedy looked to John Hume for advice, but at that time he was shying away. Hume was in a difficult position. As leader of the Nationalist SDLP he was held in high regard by members of the Irish American community, and I'm sure he realized that once the charismatic leader of Sinn Féin, the rival Nationalist party, with his enormous media appeal, was allowed into America, some of the limelight would switch from him to Adams and the special esteem he enjoyed could be diminished.

When Jean asked my opinion on the visa situation, I offered my complete support. Go for it, was my advice.

I phoned Dermot Gallagher in Washington and warned him that I was about to change government policy. I believe we need a visa for Adams, I told him, and no reflection on you or the Embassy, but I'm going to inform the President, myself, of my decision.

When Adams sent in his application for a visa, he did so at the American Embassy in Dublin rather than Belfast, which he was entitled to do as leader of a party in both parts of the island and as an Irish citizen. Here again Brendan Scannell had been instrumental in advising Adams that his best chance of success was via Dublin.

The British were totally against a visa being granted, and had he put in his application in Belfast, because of the British–American special relationship, the American ambassador Raymond Seitz would most likely have rejected it out of hand.

As Dermot Gallagher recalled: 'The advice had come from a colleague of mine, Brendan Scannell, to put the application through Dublin rather than the consulate in Belfast or London, because ... the application would come with a recommendation. Ultimately it is the President's decision but it would be helpful if it came with a recommendation.'

On its receipt, Jean Kennedy Smith immediately forwarded a cable to the State Department recommending that, in the interests of pushing the peace process forward, they should waive the visa ban on Gerry Adams.

There was opposition from all sides, not least from some members of my own government. The British government was forceful in its opinion that a visa should not be granted until there was a permanent end to violence. Its position was supported in America by Secretary of State Warren Christopher, the Attorney General Janet Reno, House Speaker Tom Foley and the head of the FBI, Louis Freeh. On the other hand, encouraged by a now supportive John Hume, Edward Kennedy had agreed to lend the weight of his name in backing the visa, and together with three other Democrat heavyweights, Chris Dodd, John Kerry and Daniel Moynihan, had written to the President to register support for the application.

John Major was extremely angry, but I had to do what I thought was right and I didn't believe it would threaten our future relationship or cause conflict between us.

All I wanted was to get Adams into America to prove to Sinn Féin and the IRA just how highly regarded we were there, that we could get him a visa. My mindset was such that I thought, if I can show the IRA that we can win the argument over the British and over American policy, it will make the IRA sit up and take notice. I wanted to prove to them that there could be an alternative to violence.

Roderic Lyne, on behalf of John Major, certainly presented his opinion very forcefully to the White House:

'Obviously we wanted to use the Americans for leverage and particularly for leverage on the IRA, after the Downing Street Declaration had been achieved, to get them to give up violence, and so working pretty closely as we were at the time with Albert, we were trying to put maximum pressure through every possible means on the leadership of the Provisionals to buy into the Downing Street Declaration and say "All right, now we've got a basis for giving up violence." Part of that pressure was to try to persuade the United States to maintain its view that they should not be welcomed in the United States while they were committing violence. Keep the carriage in front of the donkey and say if you give it up, then you can come over here, we'll give you a visa. And the American ambassador in London, Ray Seitz, was completely firm on this; the American consul general in Belfast was completely firm on this; the State Department were completely firm on this; and the White House was sort of wobbly, and one had to shore them up all the time, so I had to keep reminding Tony Lake, the National Security Adviser, that this was the deal. And John Major would remind Clinton in phone calls and he said, "Fine, fine, fine, I completely agree!"

'Adams then applied for a visa and the American consul, who was over in Belfast, interviewed him and it was made clear to Adams that he would only get the visa if he would sign up clearly to giving up violence, which of course he couldn't do, so he was told no visa. Adams then got the Irish lobby in the States to lobby the White House . . . [Clinton] suddenly flipped because he'd come under pressure from Ted Kennedy or whoever to give Adams a visa.

'We were extremely angry at this because he'd taken the pressure off Adams and he was basically saying, "Well, we didn't mean it when we asked you to give up violence."

'So we then had to get the Americans back on side and the way to do that was first of all to have a big row with them so that they realized – so that Clinton personally realized – that he'd done something very stupid.'

On Capitol Hill the Connolly House group used all their muscle to lobby the President, while Irish America rallied to the cause with full-page advertisements in the *New York Times* calling for the US to support the efforts to find peace. It was signed by the chairs of over eighty-five leading American corporations and over one hundred high-profile Irish Americans.

I phoned the President directly on the private number he'd given to me on St Patrick's Day specifically for such an occasion.

He was still not absolutely resolute in his decision but I told him that the Downing Street Declaration was a big leap forward and that Sinn Féin and the IRA would only sign up for it once the grass roots were fully versed in what it meant for their future. If Adams was allowed into America it would prove that he and Sinn Féin were being accepted politically and internationally on a completely new level and it would make everyone realize that the years of violence could be over.

I talked him through the significance of such a visit, not least that it would also be seen that the Irish had not bowed to the demands of the British. I also pointed out that to grant the visa put an obligation on Adams to deliver the peace. He would be out on the world stage, his actions and words up for judgement by a very big audience, and if he failed to deliver, the price would be very high indeed.

Allow him in for a short period, I suggested, two days, just enough to attend the conference. No fundraising, I agreed, a short-term visa, just enough time to sell the message to Irish America that they're moving forward to peace.

I made the same phone call to Tony Lake and Nancy Soderberg while Jean Kennedy Smith continued to push through her own connections. More and more people were joining in the crusade. Suddenly even those who professed themselves repulsed by the violence were beginning to realize that there was a sudden shift, a mood of progress, that peace was looking possible.

President Bill Clinton:

'Very few people in my government supported the granting of the visa – my Secretary of State, the FBI and CIA directors, and the Attorney General all strongly opposed it, on the grounds that it would undermine the fight against terror and cause the UK to cease important cooperation with us. Neither, of course, happened but the feelings against it were strong.

The British government also weighed in strongly against the move. I took their concerns very seriously. Ambassador Smith was the only administration official outside the White House in favour of the visa, as were several Irish American members of Congress. I knew there were risks in the decision, but in the end I felt there was a key shift in the Irish Nationalist movement. I thought we should test it. If Adams was in fact serious about peace, then it was worth supporting him. If he was not, granting him a visa and having him fail to deliver a ceasefire would backfire on him and hurt his standing in America. This was the argument made by Tony Lake, my National Security Adviser, and Nancy Soderberg. And it was also made forcefully by Albert Reynolds. My conversation with him was very important to the decision-making. The decision did impact on our relations with the British for a time – but eventually we got back on track and today there is peace in Northern Ireland.

'There was a great deal at stake in making this decision. It risked our relationship with the British, our greatest transatlantic ally. It also would inflame our relationship with the Unionists and with their supporters in the United States. The opponents argued there was no difference between Gerry Adams and the hard-line IRA and that we had no business meddling in the affairs of the UK. I didn't believe peace could be made without the involvement of the US, and I believed that if the efforts succeeded it would have a profound impact on the trouble spots torn by violence.'

The decision was made: a visa would be granted – but not before Gerry Adams had made a personal declaration that he had renounced violence.

On 28 January 1994 Adams travelled to the American Consulate in Belfast where, under instructions from the White House, the consul general, Val Martinez, asked him to answer two questions about his attitude to violence and the political process. The wording of the questions made it difficult for Adams to answer the questions in all honesty and he had to refuse. It looked as if the visa would also be refused – but then Niall O'Dowd suggested that if Adams wrote out his own statements that would satisfy the White House, the situation could be saved.

Adams wrote: 'My sole purpose in coming to the United States is to advance the cause of peace and move the process forward. I want to see an end to all violence and an end to this conflict. I don't advocate violence. It is my personal and political priority to see an end to the IRA and an end to all other organisations involved in armed actions. I am willing to seek to persuade the IRA to make definitive decisions on the conduct of its campaign.'

He also added that he was anxious to be persuaded that the joint declaration could be a basis for peace.

While pressure was brought to bear from various quarters to make the statement public, in one of those twists of fate that had bedevilled the whole peace process a news bulletin reported in San Diego that the 'Southern California IRA' had placed hoax bombs in British stores in the city! Immediately there were calls from O'Dowd and Soderberg for Adams to denounce the threat. It was a nonsense; as Adams retorted to O'Dowd, 'Does this mean I have to apologize every time an Irishman gets into a fight with an Englishman in a pub?' But he did it, the visa was issued and Gerry Adams flew to New York.

Gerry Adams:

'There's no doubt that the American access did become critical and there's no doubt that Albert's ability to talk to the President, cutting through all the bullshit, worked. And of course Jean Kennedy Smith was a big player in this.

'It was actually in the scheme of things quite a small thing, but it assumed such symbolic importance. The visa was limited to New York for just forty-eight hours but it marked a complete change in US foreign policy in relation to Ireland. If you trace US foreign policy in relation to Ireland, it simply did not get involved. It was always regarded as an internal matter for the government of the United Kingdom, under Reagan and Thatcher and Bush Sr. So it wasn't the visa per se that was so important, it was that Ireland became an international matter.

'It marked the beginning of a new relationship. It was a huge coup for the Irish, and Irish America responded. Also by this point, again under Albert's tutelage, the Minister for Arts and Culture had got rid of section 31 [the broadcasting ban]. The British still had censorship and I remember when I was being interviewed in the States remarking on the stupidity that that just wasn't possible back home.'

As expected, Gerry Adams was fêted in New York; now we had to see just how far that would take us on the road to peace. In the end I believe even John Major understood that it would benefit the process. Dermot Gallagher, the Irish Ambassador in Washington, makes this assessment:

'I think with hindsight, John Major thought it was the right decision. Gerry Adams was trying to lead a very complex movement into the political dialogue, out of the political cold and into the political centre, and I think the visa gave him an enhanced status in his own community that was very important. If I remember right, Clinton said to Albert – and certainly Tony Lake, the head of National Security, passed on Clinton's message to me – that, if we let Adams in for just forty-eight hours, and restrict him to no fundraising and just New York, and it's successful and makes a difference, then we'll all be delighted. If it isn't – there's nothing lost. I'm only allowing him in for forty-eight hours, so if there's no delivery, if it doesn't move things forward, then I don't have to do it again. So, as far as Clinton was concerned, it was a pragmatic decision, it was very sensible and he over-ruled a lot of his own administration in doing that.'

For the Americans, the visa was a very significant move and they expected it to deliver peace within a couple of weeks. I'm sure they thought the visa gave them the right to call the shots, but it doesn't work like that. Sinn Féin and the IRA are a law unto themselves: they deliberate, they discuss and they confer. Before they could even think about declaring peace, there were years of history and historical decisions and agreements to unravel, and the process was slow and intricate. Word of what they were planning had to be assessed by the Army Council, who in turn would send that information across the country to be filtered down through the various cells of the organization. They in turn discussed and argued and took views on the different decisions before returning their responses for further investigation by the leaders of the IRA.

At the peace conference in New York, in the glare of all that publicity, Gerry Adams made all the right noises to win over his Irish American audience. He said that if the joint declaration was the 'first step' on the road to peace then he wanted to know what was the 'second' so that he could sell it on to every Irish Republican. He talked of national self-determination, the British being persuaders for Irish unity, guarantees for Unionists and demilitarization of the conflict, ending with the statement: 'It is our intention to see the gun removed permanently from Irish politics.'

The British, of course, were outraged; they saw only that it shook the hard-won confidence of the Unionists and served to relieve the Republicans from pressure to accept the joint declaration.

Again I went to Downing Street and again I pressed John Major to relent on his refusal to bow to the request for 'clarification'. I urged him that it was time to concentrate on the Nationalists; the Unionists were already signed up to the declaration, now we had to reel in the others. It was all taking too long and I was anxious to see that part of the process concluded so that we could move on. The British government met with the SDLP, the UUP, the DUP and the Alliance Party, but Sinn Féin was excluded.

As for the intention of seeing the gun removed, well, that would be anyone's guess. Martin Mansergh and Martin McGuinness were still in close contact, but no one as yet knew when a ceasefire would be called. We only knew there would be other demands before that was a reality, and meanwhile the violence and the killings continued.

I was in New York when news reached me that the Provos had fired mortar bombs on Heathrow Airport for the third night running. Though none of them had gone off – they were all duds or not primed – once more the IRA were demonstrating their power and their determination not to surrender easily. It did not bode well for the peace initiative. The news was very black from Downing Street and very pessimistic on the streets of New York.

I was on my way to Washington to celebrate St Patrick's Day. My entire family, all the children and their spouses, had been invited and it was to be a memorable night; but the Heathrow mortars had cast a very dark shadow. Many in Clinton's administration who had supported the visa for Adams were now angry and perplexed, while many others were only too ready to say 'I told you so!'

Tony Lake, Nancy Soderberg and Trina Vargo remained depressed but silent in the face of bitter criticism. I had no explanation to give. Even John Hume was lost for words. It was what they did – 'The Armalite and the ballot box' – and the Armalite was still there. We just had to believe it would change. As Martin McGuinness observed in a recent conversation, not specifically about the Heathrow mortars, but in a general reference to the retaliatory action that attempted to foil the progress towards peace:

'Never at any stage of the process would I allow a situation to stop the decision-making process that I and others had to make, in the interests of peace and justice and indeed freedom on this island. So we always knew that there would be people who would be opposed to what we were doing, the question was the percentage of people who would oppose us. I think, and many people believe, that we'd done what many people thought was not do-able and that was to bring the vast bulk of Republicans and the vast bulk of the IRA in behind the process. Now that said, your family and others and your friends consider the possibility that there might be people out there who would be prepared to resort to the violent way, and to attack us, but at no stage of the process did I say – well, we can't go down this road because somebody might shoot me dead. That was an occupational hazard. I would have been doing a grave disservice to the role I was playing within the struggle. I had made up my mind that the peace process was the way to go, the course of negotiations was the way to go, tackling the issues like establishing a power-sharing government, and all-Ireland institutions. If I was to allow myself to be intimidated, and threatened, and to not embark on a course which effectively changed Irish history for the better, then I'd have felt I was a cheat, to be quite honest, that I was doing a disservice to the people that we represented. Of course – and a lot of people choose to forget this – since the early 1980s we had consistently put ourselves before the electorate and the electorate gave us a mandate, so we had a mandate to negotiate on behalf of the Republican constituency, who voted us into office. I think that we were always very conscious that at the end of the day there would have to be a negotiation to resolve the conflict.

'You had successive British governments or British military generals doing theses for different universities in which they were conceding that the British army had not the capability to defeat the IRA. And Republicans were challenged by that, I think, because Republicans had to consider whether the IRA had the military capability to defeat the British army. And if you answered the questions honestly, either on the British side, as some British generals did, or on the Republican side, as some Republicans do, and you conclude that neither could defeat the other, then you were in a stalemate; a stalemate that could go on for a very long time with an awful lot of people losing their lives. So that stalemate had to be broken, and our view was that we should do the unthinkable, that the people should break the stalemate and a vicious circle of injustice and discrimination and violence should end, and then equality should be ours.'

That was what we all had to believe: that we had to go on despite the background of violence. We could not be intimidated by the few when the gains would be so great. I tried to persuade our American hosts that the peace process was not a fraud and we would succeed.

To celebrate the beginning of what we all hoped was a brighter, peaceful future for Ireland, the White House had opened its doors as the setting for a magnificent party. Before the evening began, Kathleen and I and the President and First Lady were led into one of the ornate drawing rooms for a photo-call. Our children were also invited to attend to meet the President. As my daughter Cathy reminds me, Hillary

Clinton almost fell over when she saw all seven children standing attentively. 'My God, Kathleen!' she gasped. 'Are those all yours?'

They were charming hosts and posed for individual photos with each of my children.

Then it was on with the evening.

As President Clinton recalls of that St Patrick's Night:

'We were there to celebrate hope and leaving the hard un-answered questions behind, drowned out for a moment by the music.'

Evidence of this hope was apparent when on that particular evening, 17 March 1994, as President Clinton stood to say a few words, the hundreds of guests gathered to celebrate St Patrick's Day rose with calls of 'Bravo!' and a thunderous standing ovation. As guest of honour I headed the Irish contingent, but there were people from all walks of life, from corporate America and the trade unions, impresarios and some of the biggest names in show business, all eager to hear about the future of Ireland. It was good to meet socially with those who had worked to get the visa for Adams, not just Tony Lake and Nancy Soderberg, but Senator Kennedy too. Senator George Mitchell, who was to be so instrumental in delivering the final surge for a permanent peace, spent a long time chatting with me. Niall O'Dowd, Bill Flynn, Chuck Feeney and Bruce Morrison – so many people!

The White House had opened up a whole floor for the party and everyone was free to wander the beautiful rooms. I remember talking to Richard Harris, Michael Keaton, Conan O'Brien, Paul Newman and Joanne Woodward and many more. The Belfast flautist James Galway entertained us, as did Sharon Shannon and Phil Coulter, who was becoming a 'regular'. I remember Phil joking that if the President and I had followed our other careers, Clinton with his saxophone and his band, I as a promoter, then on a night like tonight the posters might have read – 'Albert Reynolds presents Bill Clinton and his Arkansas Blues Band!' The evening finished as it had done on the previous St Pat's night with John Hume and I joining with the President to sing, 'When Irish Eyes Are Smiling'.

As he said goodnight the President shook my hand and said, 'Whenever you've finished, remember to pull the door to when you're going out!'

There was a pub somewhere in downtown Washington, called The Four Provinces, named after the four provinces of Ireland. It was owned by a fellow from Longford and I'd already promised that I'd try and stop by. My son-in-law Kevin loves this story, as he tells it:

'So, we pulled the door on the White House and, much to the consternation of the hovering security, we all piled into the waiting entourage of limousines. Albert's directions to take us to The Four Provinces were met with astounded concern from the head FBI man. "You can't do that, Sir, the place hasn't been swept!"

'"Then get a f— brush!" he said. "We're going!"

'We set off in the usual cavalcade, with outriders and lights flashing, and arrived at the pub. Again the security men tried to hover protectively around Albert, but he'd have none of it and strode straight into the pub where he stayed until the early hours, in his element, talking to everyone, working the room! The story of Albert's visit lived on for years!'

The party was over but we left our American hosts in no doubt whatsoever but that we had to push forward; that whatever the violence, it would be overcome.

Dermot Gallagher:

'I think that it may have encouraged them because what we were saying to them was – look, here is the strategy. We believe it's going to deliver a permanent ceasefire but there are going to be ups and downs on the way because clearly it's a very complex situation, but we shouldn't let the last atrocity discourage us, if anything it should motivate us to try even harder. They saw the reality and the sense of that. They understood that you don't give up if you have a clear strategy, which you're convinced will lead to a ceasefire and a broader political dialogue with everybody around the table, and, hopefully, with everybody getting up from the table with something to sell to their own constituency. That is the essence, the core of good negotiations.'

Now it was back to John Major and another attempt to get the British to agree to 'clarification'. This was in the face of news coming from the Sinn Féin Árd Fheis that Gerry Adams was demanding a wider agenda for peace. However, he acknowledged in his speech that 'For the Downing Street Declaration to address the issue of Irish national self-determination was a significant departure for the British Government.'

Adams wrote to Major asking for meetings. His office replied: 'Not until there was a cessation of violence.'

Meanwhile Martin Mansergh urged his contacts to re-consider the benefits of the Downing Street Declaration and to take on board that it was a mistake to reject what it offered as a potential first framework for peace. That Easter we were informed that, as a demonstration of goodwill and to prove that the IRA was sincere about the peace process, there would be a ceasefire for what, we heard, would be a month. It was three days. Politicians and the public reacted to this with cynical disbelief. If the IRA had hoped to win favour or acceptance by this brief respite from violence, they were wrong. Personally I was bitterly disappointed.

It was another stultifying stalemate. In an effort to kick-start something I offered Northern politicians 30 per cent of places in an enlarged government, in the event of an all-Ireland settlement. The Unionists rejected it with contempt but the seed was sown.

There were more waves of sectarian killings and a message from London. It came through Patrick Mayhew and requested that I advise Sinn Féin that the British might be forthcoming on clarification as long as it was clearly understood there would be no renegotiating whatsoever. I told Sinn Féin to put down their queries on paper and I would forward them on to Major.

This was a significant moment in the peace process: it was imperative that nothing went wrong. I went through their questions myself, vetting each issue raised. Those that I knew were answerable and acceptable to the British I passed on, but there were some I refused to transmit. I insisted my stamp was on all the questions that were sent, because only in that way could I ensure there would be no excuses for the British to react negatively.

When I was satisfied there was no room for error, I forwarded the list to the British government with the advice that not only should they answer the questions, they should also make sure that the 'tone' of their response was correct; in other words, whateverthe content of their verdict, as in all their dealings with Sinn Féin they should express themselves with respect and parity of esteem.

Then I was off to Chicago. A message came through from Dermot Gallagher that the President had agreed to meet with me the following day in Indianapolis. I wanted to convey to him what was happening in Ireland at the time and to keep him informed of how things were progressing. It was a sign of his support and keen interest that he agreed to see me at such short notice.

I met the President in Indianapolis on the wettest morning. I just remember the rain came down in bucketloads. Clinton had no umbrella, I had no umbrella. Flash rain, they called it: one moment sun, the next down it came. The meeting took place in the tiny robing room of Mount Helm Baptist Church. The church was not far from the site where Senator Robert Kennedy had spoken in 1968 just moments after learning that the Reverend Martin Luther King had been assassinated. Earlier that morning the President had broadcast his radio address, in which he said: 'On that awful night twenty-six years ago, Robert Kennedy beckoned Americans of all races to show compassion and wisdom in the face of violence and lawlessness.'

We then went on to the nearby Martin Luther King Memorial Park for the ground-breaking ceremony for the Landmark for Peace Memorial. It was an appropriate occasion on which to discuss our progress. The chairs in the presbytery were not the most comfortable, but that didn't matter: Clinton wanted to hear directly from me how Sinn Féin and the IRA were reacting to the declaration and what progress was being made. I explained that Major had finally agreed to answer their questions on 'clarification' and that I had made sure they were on track to be acceptable. It was their way of buying time, I told him. Sinn Féin might accept certain things, whereas the Army Council might not. They were waiting for things to progress further, but they didn't want the world to see them turning anything down because Molyneaux had already accepted the declaration on behalf of the Unionists. It was a waiting game and we had to play along.

It was a big decision for them. They had to decide whether the declaration would advance Republican and democratic goals, or whether it was a trap. This was not just a temporary ceasefire: this was for ever and a day, and it was a huge decision, so they had to be sure. Clinton and I talked man to man; this was what I called 'real politics'.

President Clinton agrees: 'It was a metaphor for our inter-dependent world: meeting with Irish leaders in an African American church to promote peace half a world away.'

Then it was out to the platform and into the rain for the ground-breaking ceremony. Clinton opened his speech with the words: 'Ladies and gentlemen, now we're all being tested by a little rain. Those of us who grew up in farming areas know that rain is a gift from God. It's going to help us all grow a little!' There was no shelter up there on the platform, although Nancy Soderberg, who was accompanying Clinton, managed to borrow some umbrellas. Even so, I don't think I've ever been so wet.

Dermot Gallagher laughs about it still:

'In the hotel in Indianapolis, which isn't the most exciting town, Albert had to take off his suit and Clinton was in a dressing gown. They both had to send down their suits to be sponged, dried and pressed. I'd never seen such rain in my life. I managed to get a little shelter but the others couldn't leave the platform. We were only in Indianapolis for two hours so Albert was wandering around the hotel in just his dressing gown.'

We left there for South Bend, Indiana, and Notre Dame University, where I had been invited to give the commencement address. It was a great moment for me to stand there in mortar-board and gown before 12,500 young Catholic students. I talked about the principles and realities on which the peace process was built. 'It will take real courage', I said, 'to begin a new and different journey by accepting that only through dialogue and peaceful negotiations can we build a new Ireland.'

The cheers of those hopeful young people made the hard path that still lay ahead more endurable.

Better news awaited my return. The British had responded to the Sinn Féin questions with 'clarifying' answers. The British response was welcomed by Sinn Féin; now we had the agonizing wait for their decision, and that of the IRA Army Council, on the declaration. At the news of the British response the Unionists again grew nervous that they were about to lose out in some underhand deal and the Loyalists took to the streets with a furious escalation of violence.

In the following weeks Martin Mansergh and Martin McGuinness continued meeting up in all sorts of places, trying to work out the future position for Sinn Féin – its acceptance as a political party and its inclusion in talks – as well as other areas of confrontation that still headed their concerns, such as the amnesty for prisoners and demilitarization.

Martin McGuinness:

'My meetings with Martin Mansergh were wide-ranging discussions. From our perspective, they were very much part of our attempt to address the concerns of the broad Nationalist and Republican community on the island of Ireland, coupled with engaging with the United States – Irish Americans – and to put in place a very convincing argument for the IRA to take their decision to call a ceasefire.

'What we wanted . . . was to assure people that, as a result of in-depth discussions with Albert's administration and Irish America and John Hume, we believed that a credible alternative was in place and that in the aftermath of a ceasefire, all sides would become engaged and try to bring about inclusive negotiations. There were quite a number of discussions and the meetings with Mansergh were secret meetings in a number of different places. Without identifying specific places, they were in a number of religious establishments, mostly south of the border, which were made available to us.'

Dick Spring was conducting talks with the American

administration while at the same time continuing his inter-party negotiations on a framework document with the British government. I was still in contact with Gerry Adams through Father Reid, still pushing for the ceasefire.

At the same time I threw myself into a series of countless interviews and speeches both at home and abroad, encouraging and promoting the case for peace. I had to be meticulous in the language I used because I knew the different factions would be monitoring everything I said and that one slip, one insinuation of bias weighted in whichever way, would be pounced on and used to undermine the peace process.

Everything had to be studied and exact. There was huge input into every speech, every line was analysed as to what it could convey and how it could be construed, because the IRA, and the Loyalists, and the Unionists, were always listening and ready to react, either for or against. Martin Mansergh would go through everything, saying you can't say this or that or it will be misinterpreted.

During that particular period, when we were trying to draw in the IRA, every communication carried a message – and that went for everyone, not just for me. Whenever John Major said something a bit ambiguous, there'd be an immediate reaction, 'Why did he say that?', and sometimes I would have to phone John Major and say, 'What are you trying to do?' And sometimes he would do the same thing to me. He was in an equally sensitive position; we both had to be so aware of hidden meanings.

One of the perks of the job was that occasionally you got invited to a special sports event. I was in New York in June when the Republic of Ireland was playing Italy in the soccer World Cup. We'd had a great time, a great view of the game from a first-class private box, and what's more we'd won – Ireland 1, Italy 0. I, Kathleen, Diggy, Tom Savage and the rest of the party had all crowded into the dressing rooms to congratulate Jackie Charlton and the boys when news came through that a Loyalist death squad had marched into a pub in Loughinisland in County Down and opened fire, slaughtering six men aged between thirty-four and eighty-seven, who had been watching the game on television, cheering on their team; five more were injured.

It was a bleak time. The continuing atrocities in the North perpetrated by both sides made it very hard to keep the faith. Many did not, and pessimism began to weigh heavily even on those most willing to believe that the process was still alive. My critics were all too ready and eager to jump up with accusations that I was wasting my time on a failed initiative at the expense of the talks process, crying that it was about time I realized that the peace process was dead. It was a very lonely time, a desperate time, when I had to dig deep and summon up all my courage and belief that despite the continuing wicked killings and senseless loss of life, there was still hope of peace and that what I was doing would show results. I had chosen a path that I knew would be unacceptable to my own government: only Martin Mansergh and I knew of the ongoing negotiations and contacts still being conducted between Gerry Adams, Martin McGuinness and ourselves. We could confide in nobody, but I refused to bow down and give in.

Word had still not been received of Sinn Féin's reaction to the British government's clarification paper. However, we were aware that the Sinn Féin Árd Chomhairle had decided to call a special delegate conference in July to examine the Downing Street Declaration in detail and to agree its formal attitude to it and its relationship to the peace process. It was to be held in Letterkenny, County Donegal, and I knew the outcome was going to be critical. Father Reid had already given me a copy of Adams's speech, which I thought was fair and acceptable if somewhat ambiguous. Martin Mansergh had also conveyed to me that there was a positive feeling in his talks with Martin McGuinness that a lasting ceasefire had effectively been decided upon. I felt encouraged by his words that he had found them 'in a very, very, practical-orientated mood, and essentially that the decision had been made. I'm not saying in formal terms, but just mentally the decision had been made, and it was a question of choreographing the next few weeks.'

And there were hopes that Letterkenny might be the occasion for a ceasefire announcement.

Martin McGuinness:

'It was "hoped for" but it was never a realistic proposition that the Letterkenny conference, which was a meeting of Republicans from all over the island of Ireland, would be the meeting to take the decision on a ceasefire. That decision was only ever going to be taken by the seven members of the IRA Army Council. They were the people who had to decide. Gerry Adams and I met with them on a number of occasions to update them on our approach and our progress and to make hopefully a convincing case that they should consider calling a cessation, to break what I've described as the vicious circle of inequality and domination and violence that was happening at the time.'

Nevertheless, I had received word that it was going to happen at Letterkenny. However, the night before the meeting Father Reid arrived with the news that the announcement was off. The reason for the cancellation was that news of the ceasefire had been leaked to the British press and until the source of the leak was found the Army Council was suspending the announcement.

Apart from the disappointment that there was to be no ceasefire announcement, I felt even more despondent that as yet there was no news of the declaration being accepted. Even I began to wonder if maybe Adams and McGuinness had lost their influence with the Army Council.

Martin McGuinness:

'Persuading them was very difficult because of the bad experiences that the IRA had been through in the 1970s and because of the bad faith effected by the British government. What we had to do was construct a credible case that the British government and the Unionists could be compelled to come to the negotiating table against the backdrop of an IRA ceasefire. And an essential component of it all was the involvement of Irish America, the White House, the Irish government, John Hume and of course Gerry Adams on behalf of Sinn Féin.

'There was also the backdrop of quite a number of submissions by very senior generals within the British army, who had produced different theses that effectively admitted they could not militarily defeat the IRA. By the same token, Republicans listening to that, and I was one of them, had to also contemplate whether the IRA had the ability to beat the British army.

'At the time the Loyalists were killing as many Catholics as they could get their hands on, so we had this vicious cycle of discrimination, injustice and inequality, conflict, violence and death, and in my opinion if we had waited for the British government to break that cycle of conflict, we would have waited a very long time. So my view was – let's be audacious, let's do what nobody's expecting, let's get the IRA to break the cycle.'

Father Reid continued to reassure me that all was not lost and things were moving forward. He worked tirelessly, shuttling back and forth between Adams and me, feeding information, encouraging and urging and nudging us on. I think at that stage my wife Kathleen almost gave up on me. We'd no sooner be in bed than Father Reid would arrive, and he and I would be engrossed in conversation for most of the night. Kathleen was definitely relegated to the distant back row at that time, and if a planned holiday on a friend's yacht hadn't been on the cards, the strain on us both would have been unbearable. Certainly the strength of our relationship was tested to the full.

I was still getting positive messages that things were on target and although it took courage to hold on to that belief I kept driving it forward. John Hume was facing rebellion inside the SDLP, with his deputy leader Seamus Mallon and others challenging his judgement in continuing to believe that the peace process was alive. He was under enormous pressure, not just from his party but also because of his association with Adams: even the homes of his party members were sometimes under threat or actually attacked by the Loyalist para-militaries. It was a time of extreme tension and emotion for all of us.

I had given my word to both Major and Clinton and I had promised a ceasefire. On the eve of my holiday in mid-July 1994, I sent an ultimatum to Adams and McGuinness. I could not live with the uncertainty any more. I demanded a ceasefire by the end of August or I was closing everything down. I'd put my life and career on the line to support them: now they had to call it, or I was walking away and the chance for peace would be lost for another twenty-five years.

It was a risk worth taking.

Martin McGuinness:

'I think the judgement that had to be made by Republicans at the time was – what do you believe the effect of calling a cease-fire would have on the Loyalists, on the British army, on the Conservative government, on the Republicans? All had to be assessed and judged. My assessment at the time was that if a ceasefire was called, that would place huge pressure on the British government, on Unionist politicians and on Loyalist paramilitaries to recognize that something fundamentally had changed.'

Pressure was being put on the Republicans from the American side too. Bill Flynn, on a private visit to Adams that summer, had warned him that if the killings continued corporate America would pull out. In Washington, Nancy Soderberg, growing impatient at the lack of news, phoned Niall O'Dowd, demanding to know whether his promise that a ceasefire was imminent was real or not. Despite everything, O'Dowd said, he was still being reassured that things were on course.

In response to a request passed through Republican contacts, he listed certain goals that could be delivered by Irish Americans if an unarmed strategy was pursued. These included promises of unrestricted access to the States for the likes of Adams and McGuinness and other Sinn Féin members; parity of treatment with other Northern Ireland leaders in Washington; release or transfer to Ireland of IRA prisoners held in America; funding for a Sinn Féin office in Washington; and American business investment into Northern Ireland. All this carried great weight with the IRA. A message was delivered to the Connolly House group asking for confirmation of the list in writing and, more significantly, requesting that they made sure they were in Belfast for the end of August for what was about to happen.

The British, too, were playing their part with an offer to amend section 75 of the Government of Ireland Act, which asserted its claim to sovereignty over Northern Ireland, in exchange for changes to Articles 2 and 3 of the Irish constitution.

As the end of August approached there was a feeling of anticipation that things were coming to a climax. Mansergh seemed confident, Father Reid was confident and I prayed that the positive messages we were receiving would soon be reflected in reality. John Major remained doubtful, no matter how much I assured him, 'You'll get peace, and soon.'

On 25 August the Connolly House group led by Bruce Morrison arrived in Dublin and crowded into my office. Along with Morrison were Niall O'Dowd, Bill Flynn and Chuck Feeney, plus two trade union fellows, Joe Jamison and Bill Lenihan, representing the American labour movement. Dick Spring was with me as we listened to what they had to say. They were on their way north to meet with Gerry Adams, where they hoped to hear exciting news. They explained that they had this idea that a ceasefire was about to be declared, but that it would be one of limited duration; they hoped, they said, to get Adams to agree to a period of at least six months.

Dick Spring and I looked at each other. I was furious. 'Who gave you permission to go negotiating for me with your six months?' I said. 'There's no way. If you come back from Belfast with your six months I'll not be taking it. You can tell Gerry Adams that if six months is on the table, he can take it off again. It's permanent or nothing! You may accept it from them but I won't.'

They were taken aback. They genuinely thought six months was a good deal, but I was adamant it was all or nothing, permanent or nothing. They didn't see it as I saw it. People were being killed every day, there was no way I was going to wait around. I had worked hard to clear every obstacle in the way of a permanent ceasefire, and the IRA knew that. I had agreed to the release of prisoners, I'd lifted the broadcasting ban, and I had got Adams a visa for America. I had also promised I would allow them into inter-party talks, the chance to develop and be accepted as a constitutional political party and that I would take up opening the border roads with the British government. Now I expected them to deliver a permanent ceasefire.

The Connolly House group were all keyed up, they thought they were doing well if they could achieve a six-month ceasefire. It would be a waste of time; I told them, I did not waste my time and I would not waste their time by even talking about it. We either get a complete cessation or we don't, but I'll accept no compromise!

I knew Bill Flynn and the others were surprised that I just discarded the prospect of a six-month period of peace, but I knew the Republicans were tough negotiators and we had to be tougher. My view of the Republican movement was that they were honourable people, and if I made an agreement with them it did not have to be written down on paper, it would be kept. They never broke their word to me. They may have done to others, but not to me. Not Gerry Adams or Martin McGuinness; they never did. They had promised a permanent ceasefire and that was what I intended to get.

I told the Americans bluntly, 'Anyone who goes up there to that meeting with Gerry Adams and says a short-term ceasefire is on the cards is wrong! It's not, not as far as I'm concerned. They can forget it!' I told them straight out: 'Tell Gerry Adams and Sinn Féin, from me, Dublin wants a permanent cessation of violence and on that basis only will Sinn Féin be allowed into the political process. I'll take no limits of six months or a year. No temporary, indefinite or conditional stuff. It has to be an all-out IRA ceasefire or nothing!'

I had made my point. The group left for the North and a media frenzy. Word of their arrival had preceded them, and although their publicity stated that they were on a personal visit to investigate openings for American investment, no one believed it. Rumours were rampant that they were there for the announcement of peace and a ceasefire.

Just about the time that the American party were preparing to leave the States for Dublin, Gerry Adams and Martin McGuinness had met with the IRA Army Council for a final assessment of the situation before the call to cease fire. The various justifications for an end to violence were all in place: the strands of Nationalism in Ireland had come together, supported by the US administration and President Clinton; the Irish American support was there, plus corporate America was offering various guarantees; the Irish government was on board connecting in a comprehensive way with the North not seen since 1920; and through John Hume they had the support of the Northern Nationalists.

The IRA had one final demand, one last assurance before they sealed the peace. They wanted a US entry visa for Joe Cahill. This was a tough call. Joe Cahill had a notorious record where the US was concerned. As a leading member of the Provisional IRA as far back as 1940, he had been convicted of murder and sentenced to hang, only to have his sentence commuted; in 1974 he had been caught smuggling several tonnes of arms into Ireland from Libya. He had been deported from the States and spent many years in prison. Since then he had become a senior figure in Sinn Féin and a key proponent of the peace process, but as a former 'terrorist' he was still banned from America.

When Father Reid turned up with that request, I was staggered. It was a week before the end of August, a week to go before we expected to hear the call for a ceasefire. It was the last throw of the dice – I had to do it. I also understood it. The Republican power base in America could not be under-estimated and it was of vital importance that the announcement of a ceasefire was handled properly. They could not risk a schism in the movement. It was imperative therefore that an emissary be despatched to the US to brief the support base when news of the ceasefire broke. As McGuinness later told me, 'it was important that Joe Cahill, who had a record second to none in terms of Republican credibility, was able to go to the States and meet with all of those people who had supported the struggle over many years'.

Joe Cahill was, in fact, the only man who could talk to the die-hard IRA and sell them the fact that the peace process was for real. It was important he got their support because they were the fundraisers and if they didn't back the cessation there would be no money to help rebuild the organization, in its new political form, back at home in Ireland.

It was the height of summer and everyone was on holiday, including all my usual contacts in America. Ambassador Jean Kennedy Smith was in the South of France when I finally reached her. She understood at once the urgency of the request and, willing to help as ever, she flew back to Dublin. Her first move was to contact Nancy Soderberg who, as Clinton's leading foreign policy adviser on Northern Ireland, had been so instrumental in the Adams visa waiver. She was on holiday in Madrid when Jean finally tracked her down, but this time she was reluctant to get involved. The Adams visit had been successful, but his visa had been granted on the promise that a ceasefire would be delivered; she refused to offer any more concessions until that promise was put into effect. 'And the administration agrees with me,' she said. 'No more visas until we have a ceasefire!'

I got on to the American State Department and got the same answer: no more visas. The line was endorsed by the Justice Department, the Attorney General's Office and the State Department. Only the President himself, I was informed, could over-rule that decision.

After all the rows over a visa for Adams, I guessed the British too would be against it – but they let it pass.

Roderic Lyne:

'I had to make a middle of the night decision on Cahill. I mean, having fought against Adams, rightly I believe, I had a phone call from Tony Lake at about two o'clock in the morning, when we were starting to get these positive indications, saying they'd had an application from Cahill to come in and they believed that Cahill was being sent to deliver a message to the hard-liners in the community in America, that they were going for a ceasefire. They had to make a quick decision on it and would we basically agree to them doing it, because they'd learned from the previous row that they needed to consult us. It was in the early hours of the morning and I thought – I'm not going to wake John Major or Paddy Mayhew on this one. I have a notion I said "All right" in the course of the phone call without consulting anyone. I may have called John Chilcot but I did not wake Major . . . It was one of a number of things that happened preparatory to the ceasefire . . . but we didn't oppose and we didn't complain afterwards. We basically said, "Fair enough!"'

Father Reid was ceaseless in his calls and visits, urging me on to keep trying, saying the ceasefire depended on it. Just this one last thing, he insisted, and we'd be there. By the time I reached Soderberg, she was in Los Angeles. 'You've always told me you were one quarter Irish,' I said. 'Use it now, we need every bit of it. In fact, make it 75 per cent for this issue. If we don't win that visa, peace will be lost!'

We had two days to go, it was the evening of 29 August, when Soderberg finally gave in and agreed to contact President Clinton.

'You've no chance with this,' she warned.

'Please, Nancy,' I begged, 'take the file to him yourself,

drive up or fly up. Don't trust it to anyone else. We'll win this one,' I told her, 'if I can get it into his head he has a ceasefire waiting.'

'Sure,' she said. 'Fire it up!'

'One other thing. Before Clinton signs the file one way or another,' I said, 'tell him to phone me first.'

The President was on holiday in Martha's Vineyard in Massachusetts, but he called me back. It was around three in the morning and as usual he was well informed.

'Have you seen this guy's CV?' he asked.

'I didn't need to,' I told him. 'If he was in the IRA, he'd hardly be a saint!'

Clinton was very dubious about the benefit of letting Cahill into the country. 'You're looking for the impossible!' he said.

'I'd hoped to convince you,' I told him. 'I don't think I'm looking for the impossible. What's a ceasefire worth?'

He argued that they'd granted Adams a visa and no peace had followed – why should this be any different? I explained it was the last piece in the jigsaw, that the whole Republican organization had to be on side and they wouldn't be able to carry it without Cahill. The IRA was adamant that only this man could deliver that, and the Army Council had put out the word: nothing happens unless Cahill gets in.

'You have to understand,' I explained, 'there was a split in the IRA in 1970. Cahill went with Adams and McGuinness and those guys. The other half broke away with Ruairí Ó Brádaigh as leader, a fellow from my own town, Longford. Now, the only one capable of holding both sides together once news breaks of the ceasefire is Cahill. He has to be in the States to contact them and warn them that it's coming.'

President Clinton then told me that Pat Traynor, another Sinn Féin ex-prisoner, had tried to enter the country a few days earlier and had been sent back to Ireland. I knew nothing about that. I did know, however, that Cahill was in poor health, so obviously – and stupidly – Traynor had been sent ahead to care for him on the tour. The President was un-convinced. He was clearly annoyed that he was now being asked to waive visas for not one but two ex-prisoners.

'If you don't do it,' I warned him, 'there will be no peace. I'm talking a permanent ceasefire here. What's that worth to you, for a start, politically now? Let's talk politics. Politically, if it makes a difference between electing you and not electing you, is it worth it or not? All the criticism over Adams's visa will disappear if you pull it off. It's up to you!'

'All my experience tells me', he said slowly, 'that if there's going to be a ceasefire soon, the statement has already been put together by those guys. Do you know if it's been put together?'

I knew I had one last card to play. 'I do,' I said.

'How do you know?'

'Because', I answered, 'I have a copy of it here in my pocket.'

'Then read out the paragraph that matters.'

'I'm afraid I can't do that, Mr President. All I can tell you is it's there. I gave them my word. There has been trust between us all the way on this and I can't break it now. But what I will do is, I'll send the priest up to Belfast to talk to them. He'll be back with an answer within six or seven hours. Call me then.'

I worked through the night, speaking with Father Reid and with Jean Kennedy Smith, getting her to convince her brother Ted Kennedy who was also holidaying not far from Clinton on Martha's Vineyard.

Some hours later the message came back. 'Yes, you're free to do what you would with the statement, in relation to the President.'

Clinton called back, I read out the statement – and waited. It was his call.

'OK,' he said. 'We'll go for it. But this is the last chance.

And if this one doesn't run, I never want to hear from you again! Goodbye.'

As President Clinton recalls:

'Adams's visit encouraged important Irish Americans to push for peace. The role of Irish Americans was crucial to ending violence. Much of the funding and weaponry for the violence had come from America. Albert understood the need to make sure Irish America was on board, and that's probably why he asked me to give a visa to one of the hardest-liners of the IRA, Joe Cahill. It was August, and I hadn't seen a cease-fire since I gave Adams a visa in January – so I was hesitant to give out any more visas. But Albert Reynolds and Jean Kennedy Smith told me I had to do it to get a ceasefire. They persisted and convinced me to grant the Cahill visa. Had Irish America not been on board, there would have been no ceasefire.

'I thought at first it was a mistake; they were asking for two hard things before delivering anything. But Albert, Tony Lake and Nancy were convinced Gerry Adams was acting in good faith so I went forward. Adams and Cahill came through. I'm glad I finally got the chance to meet Cahill and thank him shortly before I left office.'

Joe Cahill arrived in America only hours before the cease-fire. There is a wonderful moment he mentions in his biography:

'The day we arrived in America, I attended a function in Hartford, Connecticut. This was accepted as an ordinary Northern Aid function with nothing special to it. But I have a very vivid memory of talking to people that night and know-ing that around six o'clock American time, the ceasefire was to be announced. It was sort of a wee bit strange. I was talking to them about support and continuing their work for the prisoners, and the political work that they were doing, and all the time knowing that within a few hours the whole thing would be changed. I had to be very careful.'

It was 31 August and I was on tenterhooks. I was attending a meeting of the Fianna Fáil parliamentary party in Leinster House when the news came through that the IRA had issued its statement:

'Recognising the potential of the current situation and in order to enhance the democratic peace process and underline our definitive commitment to its success the leadership of Óglaigh na hÉireann have decided that as of midnight, Wednesday, 31st August, there will be a complete cessation of military operations.

'All units have been instructed accordingly.'

The whole of the island of Ireland heaved a sigh of relief – and then the cheers began.

My speech in the Dáil that day began with the words I'd been waiting to say since first I had been appointed Taoiseach:

'Every Irish person at home and abroad will welcome with relief and thanksgiving the decision announced today of an end to the 25-year-old IRA campaign. It is a day that many had begun to fear they might never see. We all hope that it will be followed by an end to paramilitary violence on all sides and consolidated by a gradual and general process of demilitarisation, and that it will facilitate the achievement of a comprehensive negotiated political settlement.

'A long nightmare is coming to an end, where the legacy of history went so tragically wrong. While the IRA, like others, must take responsibility for their actions, and those that have had terrible human consequences, it would be simplistic to make them solely responsible for the national disaster that has struck this island over the last twenty-five years, holding the whole country back and poisoning relations even further in the North of Ireland.'

Euphoria swept the land. In Belfast a platform was rigged up outside the Sinn Féin headquarters, loudspeakers blared out Republican anthems, and Gerry Adams and Martin McGuinness were fêted with flowers and champagne. In Dublin there were scenes of joyous celebration. Dick Spring and I forgot the strained relations that were building between us, and congratulated one another on the historic achievement. Even the non-believers whooped and hollered in amazed relief.

John Major phoned, still cautious and slightly sceptical, pointing out that the word 'permanent' had not been included in the text. It's their way, John, I assured him, they couldn't in all honesty have said it, they could not answer for future generations. He still didn't believe it was for real, but I reassured him. 'We did it together, John. You've achieved something that no other British prime minister could.'

President Clinton phoned, overjoyed at the news. 'We couldn't have done it without you, Mr President,' I said.

'Listen for the Angelus bell, o'er the Liffey swell, ring out on the foggy dew.' That was the IRA message to all the units for a call to cease fire. As soon as the Angelus ceased and the noon-time announcement hit the airwaves, IRA supporters took to the streets in triumph. To the victors, the prize! But the celebrations struck dread in the hearts of the Unionists, who swore that a deal had been done. They were completely demoralized as they saw their enemy exulting at their success. The air was thick with rumours of secret deals, of being sold out, and of covert pacts.

Martin McGuinness:

'We had the situation where it was quite clear that Irish America were very interested in what was happening here, we had key people like Bill Clinton and Niall O'Dowd and people like Chuck Feeney and others, who were very anxious to help, and it became clear after much considerable work that there were enough people around in the shape of Albert in Dublin, John Hume and Gerry Adams, with Clinton coming to power in the USA, to be able to make a convincing argument to the leadership of the IRA that the most important, the most powerful thing that could actually happen after much of this work had been done behind the scenes, was for the IRA to call their ceasefire. Of course the decision by Bill Clinton, against advice from the State Department, to give a visa to Gerry Adams, and later to Joe Cahill, so that we could engage with our supporters in the USA was of tremendous importance. And Gerry Adams and I, as is recorded in history, engaged with the Army Council of the IRA and made an argument, made a case, that we believed that the British government and the Unionists could be compelled to come to the negotiating table.

'A key element of all that would be, obviously, a recognition that all of the major issues would have to be dealt with, and a key element of all of that would be that these powerful political forces would stay together as a cohesive group within the process to effectively present both the Unionist political leadership and the British government with a fait accompli, that the only really sensible thing that they could do was to come to the negotiating table.

'I regard it as probably the most significant and most important quote of the last fifteen years that on the day that the IRA called their cessation, David Trimble's predecessor, who was then leader of the Ulster Unionist Party, the largest Unionist party in the North, Lord Molyneaux, described the IRA decision to call a ceasefire as "the most destabilising event since partition"! And that gave us, I think, a tremendous insight into his thinking.

'Let me put it like this, we recognized that if there was to be progress made, then a key element to our strategy was to begin an engagement with people within civic Unionism, people within the churches, in the hope that ultimately we would begin engagement with the political leaderships of Unionism. Now, remember, James Molyneaux's approach to any of these developments was to hunker down and pull the bedsheets over him, in the hope that things would just remain the same.'

I did not agree with Martin McGuinness on this. I believe Molyneaux was as keen to see peace as anyone, and from my talks with him I was sure he was eager for the situation to progress.

16

'ABJECT AND SINCERE REMORSE'

I had already been working on the premise that an IRA ceasefire would not necessarily mean a ceasefire by the Loyalists, and that there would be difficulties in persuading them too to join the peace process. As it was, none of the Loyalist paramilitary groups had signed up for the Downing Street Declaration; I had to draw them into the political world, but first I needed them to agree to a cessation of violence.

The general conception of the Loyalists was that they were the paramilitary side of the Unionists. This was not quite the case. As Archbishop Lord Eames explains in Alf McCreary's biography: 'Loyalism is a term that has emerged during my years in church leadership. In my early days the vast majority of the Church of Ireland membership in Northern Ireland would have been classified as Unionists, whereas Loyalism emerged with the birth of Protestant paramilitarism. I always felt it was a flag of convenience for the Protestant working-class areas which wanted their own sense of identity

411

in the face of the growing strength of Republicanism.'

The trouble was, the Loyalists were somewhat out on their own. Traditional Unionism did not really appeal to them; most of them were poor, working-class Protestants outcast by discrimination, poor housing, poor education and no jobs.

For the sake of peace, I needed their assurances that if the IRA called a ceasefire, they would too. I had to draw them into the process, only this time I had to do it myself – I could not confide in anyone, not even Mansergh. If any word had leaked out, not only would it have endangered the peace process but I'd have been thrown out of government.

As the likelihood of an imminent IRA cessation had grown, unbeknown to anyone I had got in touch through a contact with leading figures of the Combined Loyalist Military Command, the Loyalist version of the Army Council that represented the different factions of Loyalism, and I had sent a message with my private secure telephone number asking them to call me.

One of the most influential figures in the Loyalist movement at that time was Gusty Spence, and it was he who returned my call. I told him I wanted a meeting but that it had to be in complete confidence. No one could know about it or we'd all be in real trouble. I knew it would be equally extremely dangerous for him if word got out that he had been talking to me, the Taoiseach. However, as far as I was concerned I had no option: if peace was to become permanent in Northern Ireland, I had to trust in him and his integrity.

I hinted that I was working towards a ceasefire from both sides and I needed to discuss what they would want in return for delivering a Loyalist cessation of violence. We needed to meet and talk.

He agreed immediately and suggested a meeting south of the border. 'Fair enough,' I said. 'If you're prepared to come south that'll suit me, or we could go to some neutral place abroad, doesn't matter to me.'

He suggested we met just south of the border in Dundalk. I thought that would be foolish, I told him, as I had no intention of risking us being seen talking together or even meeting.

'What about all your security?' he asked.

'I won't be bringing them,' I told him. 'They won't be told. This is just between you and me, and I hope you'll do the same or we're wasting our time. If we meet in Dundalk, believe me the security guys will know, the Gardaí will know.'

I had another suggestion, I told him, a hotel in Dublin. 'It's called the Berkeley Court Hotel,' I explained. 'You can drive straight in, down into the underground car park. You'll see a private lift down there. Park beside it, get in the lift, press floor seven and keep pressing. Don't take your finger off the button until it stops. It's a totally private situation and I'll be there to meet you.' Our first meeting was agreed.

Floor seven went to only one place, the penthouse suite. I had it reserved for the appointed day. It was close by where we lived and I knew the hotel and the management, as well as the Doyle family who owned it.

The penthouse had served me well on previous occasions. It was the place I'd chosen for some very significant events. It was where I'd taken Kathleen to celebrate my becoming Taoiseach, at a time when she was too ill to go out to a restaurant; we'd enjoyed a quiet family dinner together with our daughters Cathy and Andrea. I had spent time there on my own, selecting my first cabinet, accompanied only by Cathy, who was there to assist me in making phone calls, typing, and ordering tea and biscuits to keep me going! I'd had a very important first meeting there with Dick Spring, the day I'd returned from that very successful Edinburgh EU summit with IR£8 billion for

Ireland, a sum of over €10 billion in today's market, and Dick and I had agreed to take our parties into coalition together.

And now it was to serve as the venue for a vitally important meeting that I hoped would lead us on another step towards peace.

On the appointed day Cathy was home from college and I warned her that I might need her to drop me off somewhere that morning, no questions asked. She remembers it well:

'It was a Saturday morning, otherwise Dad would have gone to the office early on. I was in the kitchen having my breakfast around ten o'clock when Dad came in and asked if I would drive him to the Berkeley Court for a meeting. I agreed, but I also asked where his car was with the driver, and he said he'd told them not to come in until lunchtime as he didn't want anyone to know about the meeting. We'd all learned by this time that when Dad said that, you didn't ask. I drove him to the hotel which was only about five minutes from the Hazeldene apartment. He instructed me to drive around to the back to the underground car park where the management had arranged for him to use the private and direct lift to the penthouse and we arranged that he would call me when he was ready to be collected.'

I waited alone up in the penthouse. I wasn't even sure if they'd actually come, but I had to put it to the test. Sure enough they arrived, Gusty Spence accompanied by David Ervine. I opened the door and they walked in, looking around. They were a bit nervous, not quite sure what to expect and quite shocked, I think, to find me alone.

'You fellows make yourselves at home,' I said.

Gusty Spence:

'We met in secrecy, in Dublin at the Berkeley Court Hotel. Albert passed a few remarks that a couple of Irish governments had been made up there. That he'd thrust them out! – politicians in the South, thrust them out! – and that he'd put together an Irish government on two occasions up on the seventh floor of the Berkeley Court. I was in hysterics at the grandeur of the place.'

Gusty Spence still had the upright bearing of an old soldier, while the younger fellow, David Ervine, had an open and honest face. They were obviously apprehensive, a feeling I shared, and clearly were intrigued as to what I had to say.

I suddenly realized that in my nervous haste that morning I had picked up the wrong briefcase – I always had two which I used – and so I phoned Cathy to bring me the other one and to come directly to the seventh floor. As she recalls:

'The lift was waiting when I arrived, and as instructed I kept my finger on the number seven until I arrived at the penthouse where Dad was waiting. He asked me in to the lounge where he was having tea with two gentlemen. I recognized David Ervine but not the other man, but they were both warm and welcoming. Only some time later when I was watching the Loyalist ceasefire announced did I realize that it was Gusty Spence.

'On the way home I asked Dad if his meeting had gone well. He said it did and that he hoped it would lead to the out-come he had in mind. He left it at that and I didn't ask anything further.

'I've no doubt that Mum knew all of this as she was Dad's counsel throughout all that process and still is in all aspects of his career and life.'

Gusty Spence and David Ervine had met in Long Kesh where they both were serving long prison sentences. Gusty was a former UVF commander of the old school, who had got twenty years for killing a Catholic barman in 1966. David, also a former member of the UVF, had received an eleven-year sentence for being in possession of explosives with the intention of endangering life. While in prison they had become firm friends and, under Gusty's guidance, had both turned away from violence in favour of a political route.

Gusty Spence:

'It was a matter of common sense. It had to be done because there was no other way. If you wrote out mass extermination of one side or another, or mass evacuation of one side or another, you're left with accommodation, and why shouldn't there be accommodation? I haven't suddenly become a liberal Republican or they liberal Unionists, you keep your own identity, but most important your integrity, that was the way. After the UVF ceasefire in 1974 broke down, I thought there has to be another way, a manifestation of another goal here. The obvious thing was that people should meet and accommodate one another. I was speaking with Republicans not directly but indirectly through Father Green and the Cardinal himself, Cardinal Ó Fiaich.

'He would meet anyone. He actually gave me my sense of direction, and whenever he came to Long Kesh we were pleased to see him. What the authorities did at the time was reprehensible – they backed the van that brought him up to the wire that divided us from the IRA and he could barely see me, they wouldn't let him see me. But he spread his hands flat on the wire, I did the same and we pressed our hands together. Finally they allowed him in to see us. He was brilliant. Matter of fact, I put him on the pipe – mellow mixture Benson and Hedges.

'They used to ration out the poitín to the men for Christmas and I used to mix mine in a tin with tobacco, which I then dried, so that the taste would last longer. I got the Cardinal to try it. "Take a couple of ounces and try it," I said. He didn't want to take it away from a prisoner but in the end he took a

Left: 'Tell me what I can do to work for peace' (Bill Clinton). St Patrick's Day at the White House, 17 March 1993. President Clinton, a supportive friend, took a keen interest in the peace process from the very start.

Right: 'Welcome home, Madam Ambassador!' With Jean Kennedy Smith and her brother, Senator Edward Kennedy, at the White House on the day of her appointment, 17 March 1993.

Below: With Kathleen, attending a special St Patrick's Day dinner at the White House, as guests of Bill and Hillary Clinton, in 1994.

Above: British and Irish delegations meet at Dublin Castle, 3 December 1993. This was a pivotal meeting and a very tense day. *With me, from left to right*: Patrick Mayhew, Douglas Hurd, John Major, Dick Spring and Máire Geoghegan Quinn.

Above: Entering Downing Street with John Major and Dick Spring. Great relief! The Downing Street Declaration had finally been agreed, 15 December 1993.

Below: An historic day. Formally announcing the agreement of the Joint Declaration on Peace, Downing Street, 15 December 1993.

Left: The leaders of the three strands of Irish Nationalism make an historic handshake at Government Buildings, 6 September 1994. *With me, from left to right*: Gerry Adams, leader of Sinn Féin; John Hume, leader of the SDLP.

Above: 'Abject and sincere remorse.' As was agreed, Gusty Spence (*third right*) declared the Loyalist ceasefire on 13 October 1994, six weeks after the IRA announcement of 'a complete cessation of military operations'.

Below: Chequers, 24 October 1994: making progress on the Joint Framework Document. *With me, from left to right*: Dick Spring, John Major and Patrick Mayhew.

Right: With my friends: (*above*) Martin McGuinness, now Deputy First Minister, Northern Ireland; (*below*) Martin Mansergh, my 'highly valued adviser'.

Left: Kathleen and me with Pierce Brosnan and his wife, Keeley Shaye-Smith.

Below: At Barretstown Castle with Paul Newman, to whose Hole in the Wall Camps charity for sick children my government offered a 99-year lease on the estate for just IR£1 per year.

Above: With my namesake, Prince Albert of Monaco.

Right: Sharing a joke with Prince Charles.

Right and centre:
A man of peace and a woman of mercy. It was an honour to meet both Nelson Mandela and Mother Teresa.

Right: Meeting Yasser Arafat, who expressed his support: 'A new spirit of peace and reconciliation must be brought to bear on the deep differences which have caused immense human suffering.'

Left: Working to secure inward investment. Meeting with Don Keough, former President of Coca-Cola, and Bill Gates, Chief Executive of Microsoft.

Right: Talking with Brian Crowley, Fianna Fáil MEP.

Left: A touching moment during a visit to the Saddam Central Hospital in Baghdad, 8 November 1998.

Above: Receiving an Honorary Doctorate at Law from the University of Notre Dame, Indiana, 15 May 1994. I was also the Commencement Speaker that day.

Above: With my brother Jim after receiving an Honorary Doctorate of Law from the National University of Ireland at UCD.

Left: The four of us, *from the left*, Jim, myself, Teresa and Joe (R.I.P).

Below: Outside the High Court in London, on 8 July 1998. With my daughters Miriam and Leonie, supportive as ever.

Right: Finally at 'number one': sharing a joke with the Reverend Dr Ian Paisley, the former First Minister, Northern Ireland.

'One of the proudest days of my life.' Leading the St Patrick's Day Parade as Grand Marshal, New York, 1998.

little to try. Later I heard through the lines of communication, he'd offered a priest "a bit of the hard stuff"! Next time he came, we sat with our pipes and gungered business together.'

Gusty Spence, David Ervine and I spent about three and a half hours talking. I told them I wasn't talking a political settlement here: that could only come after a ceasefire, a permanent ceasefire. When I hinted that there was a possible IRA ceasefire in the offing, they didn't believe it – they couldn't see it happening. They didn't believe the IRA would listen to anybody. Their reasoning was simple: the British army couldn't defeat them, the RUC couldn't put them down, so why should they stop, why now would there be an end to it?

'Fair enough,' I said, 'we'll see. Just tell me, what could I do for you, to get you all to stop?'

Their answer was straightforward: 'Get the IRA to announce a permanent ceasefire and we'll stop. We'll stop twelve weeks after they do. Just to make sure it's for real.'

That was their offer. We agreed at six – six weeks after an IRA ceasefire, they would call a cessation of Loyalist violence. That was their only demand.

'Right,' I said. 'I suppose next time we'd be meeting in Belfast?'

'How can we have a private meeting in Belfast?' they asked.

'Just leave that to me.'

I instructed them to check on a certain hotel and to make sure there was a back entrance easily accessible from the men's toilets, and to have a car waiting there to take me to wherever they chose where we could have a meeting undiscovered and undisturbed – same rules.

Suddenly I knew: there would be problems, but we'd get there. They wanted peace just as much as me. It was all going to be fine.

The day of our next meeting dawned. I told my security guard and driver that I was going up to Belfast. I had a meeting inside the hotel, I told them, and instructed them to wait until I called to let them know when I was ready to leave. I left them at the entrance, walked through in the direction of the toilets and out of the back entrance where Gusty himself was waiting with his car.

Gusty Spence:

'I drove him to a place on University Avenue, not far from the Shankill Road, just off it. A place we kept under wraps. I remember telling him it was a Quaker house and did he know anything about Quakers. He said he had a family of Quakers in Granard in County Longford who always voted for him, welcomed him in and gave him a cup of tea.'

We suddenly realized the risk we were both taking: me, the Taoiseach, in a car with Gusty Spence, former commander of the UVF and a leading Loyalist. If we'd been caught he could have been arrested for kidnapping me!

The meeting took place in a small room upstairs. The owners were a lovely couple; the woman had baked the most wonderful apple tart, I remember, and kept our cups filled with tea. Again David Ervine was there, along with a third man, Billy Hutchinson, another close associate of Gusty Spence, who had been sentenced to life in Long Kesh for the murder of two Catholics on the Falls Road in 1974. Like the others, Billy was a hard man who had decided to follow the political path. They were very concerned to be reassured that in the event of an IRA ceasefire I would ensure that no deal would be done with the British, that they would not be sold out and that their wishes for the future of Northern Ireland would be taken into consideration. I assured them they had my word and promised that once a Loyalist ceasefire was in place I would include them in the political process in the same way I intended to include Sinn Féin.

No one knew of these meetings and all those present had given their word that the trust would not be broken. With the announcement of the IRA cessation of violence, I had to hope that their promise of a reciprocal peace would be delivered. First, however, following the IRA's victorious triumphalism, Loyalist paramilitaries flexed their muscles in a flurry of activity. On the very first day of the cessation, they shot dead a young Catholic man.

Reverend Roy Magee:

'I never got into why they were doing things. It may have been a backlash to test the Provisional IRA. One of the things was that the Provo IRA were on the streets proclaiming a victory. We had a meeting on the Shankill Road that night, and I said, "Why don't you accept it as 'the IRA have surrendered'? There is no changing this, just look on it in a different way." That night the graffiti went up on the walls – "We accept the unconditional surrender of the Provisional IRA" – and they were as happy as anything with that. Nothing had changed – only their mindset had changed.'

Gusty Spence:

'Things progressed being put into place and we knew what was being put in place. The IRA were going to call a ceasefire and when they did, they made a whole hullabaloo as if we had been put into an "all Ireland" overnight.'

It was important that I was seen to fulfil my promise of drawing Sinn Féin into the democratic process as quickly as possible. I also hoped that it would serve to demonstrate to the Loyalists that I was a man of my word. Within a week of the ceasefire a meeting was set up at which I would come face to face with Gerry Adams for the first time, and I wanted John Hume, after all his heroic efforts in working for peace, to share the historic moment with me, so that all three strands of

Nationalism from North and South would come together to celebrate a new way forward.

Hume was in yet another turmoil of disagreement with his deputy, Seamus Mallon, when they came down to Dublin. He was also still smarting from my former rebuff, when for the sake of my relationship with John Major I had distanced myself from him. It was an awkward meeting, filled with tension, and I found it difficult to persuade Hume that his presence was needed at that first, much heralded meeting of the three leaders of Nationalism. His excuse was that he was going to Vienna and would not be back in time. Dick Spring had already told me he would not be present. Like many sceptics, he still could not believe that the IRA would be as good as their word and that the ceasefire would last; all too soon, he thought, it would be broken. He did not want to be seen supporting what he believed was only a temporary pledge, and had made a visit to Germany his excuse.

Hume held out until the night before the meeting, then phoned to say he'd be there.

That momentous day, Gerry Adams arrived at Government Buildings in Dublin accompanied by Jim Gibney and Rita O'Hare, Sinn Féin's director of publicity. It was a dramatic moment. Gerry Adams insisted on walking in through the gates: the excited world media crowded round, and I reached out to shake his hand and to welcome him in. We walked through to my office where tea and buns were waiting. He seemed rather nervous, but he came in and sat down. I was impressed by his manner: he was not at all what I'd expected. I thought he would be more assertive and aggressive, but he was softly spoken and I found myself liking the man. Then John Hume turned up and joined us. The main topic of conversation was the proposed Forum for Peace and Reconciliation which had been part of the Downing

Street Declaration. We set the first meeting for the end of October, and I secretly hoped that the Loyalists would be there too.

Then it was out on to the steps for the photo-call and speeches to the world media.

It was a great day for Ireland. In a gesture that was symbolic and significant, Adams, Hume and I shook hands, and in so doing the three leaders of Nationalism declared themselves 'totally and absolutely committed to democratic and peaceful methods of resolving our political problems'.

This was the coming together of three people who had driven the peace process, a historic occasion that ended over seventy years of conflict and war.

Some people who had lost their loved ones in the Troubles expressed their revulsion that I should be there on the steps, shaking hands with Gerry Adams. My only thought that day was that it marked the end of violence, and that if it ensured not one more life would be lost in sectarian killings, then I was honoured to do it.

In the spirit of the day we held a quiet celebration in the foyer of Government Buildings, toasting all those who had been a part of the process – people like Martin Mansergh, Dermot Gallagher, Seán O hUiginn, our friends in America, the priest Father Reid, and so many more who had worked behind the scenes to get us to this point.

Loyalist violence continued after the ceasefire – it was as if they wanted to test the sincerity of the IRA's commitment to a lasting peace. Gusty Spence and I remained in touch as I continued to urge them to push for a cessation of violence, but they and the Unionists were still highly suspicious that a deal had been done.

On 6 September the CLMC publicly announced its six pre-requisites for a Loyalist ceasefire, reflecting the concerns we had discussed in our meetings: they included assurances that the IRA ceasefire was permanent, that no deal had been done with the IRA and that Northern Ireland's constitutional position was secure.

Reverend Roy Magee:

'There was quite a bit of work to be done in getting the Loyalists to see they weren't being duped in any way and that this was for real as far as the paramilitary groups were concerned.

'I arranged a conference for the leadership and for others from the various Loyalist paramilitary organizations where they were addressed by academics and other politicians in order to convince them that this ceasefire was genuine and that there was nothing in it that was a threat to the Loyalist position. That established a basis from which to work. In the talks I made it absolutely clear that my ambition was to get the guns put away, that the violence should stop because their violence would just reactivate one set of violence with another. It wouldn't solve anything, it would only create greater mayhem and more deaths. It was up to us to take control, we had to make negotiations to get a ceasefire.'

It was the absence of the word 'permanent' in the IRA state-ment that continued to bother the Loyalists, along with the suspicion that a deal had been done by the British with the IRA. There was even more intense contact now between myself, Roy Magee and Archbishop Eames as we sought a way to bring the Loyalists in from the cold, while Gusty Spence and David Ervine were working hard to convince their colleagues that the political path was the only way forward.

Following the IRA ceasefire, the border communities in the North, who for so long had been bound by border controls, took matters into their own hands. The border stretched across the country for some three hundred miles and cut across hundreds of main and secondary roads as well as lanes and even cow tracks. People were cut off from local neighbours, farmers from their land. Road blocks, razor-wire fencing, craters filled with explosives forced communities to take long detours to travel just a few metres. Now local communities started initiatives whereby razor wire was cut, bollards were lifted, even craters were filled in, and in some instances where the concrete blocks were particularly substantial, new roads were built bypassing them. Demonstrations of this magnitude led to the British opening several cross-border roads, a welcome sign that times were very slowly changing.

On 8 September a Loyalist bomb exploded on a train from Belfast as it drew into Connolly Station in Dublin, sparking fears of a renewed onslaught of Loyalist violence. A few days later, at a highly secret meeting south of the border in the Ballymascanlon Hotel, Gusty Spence met with two Republicans from the South, one of whom was a trusted 'messenger' with the power to negotiate on behalf of the Army Council. Spence was there to ask yet again whether or not a deal had been struck between the British and the IRA. The messenger was adamant: there was no deal, and they would get no deal. Everything they did had to be up front.

Gusty Spence:

'I wanted them first to see me. That I wasn't the ogre I was painted to be. And, someone, probably for the first time . . . No, I think the first time that a Unionist spoke openly, truth-fully and faithfully, was whenever James Craig met Michael Collins. He put himself totally in the hands of the IRA to meet Collins.'

The Reverend Magee had already conveyed the same answer as the messenger to the CLMC, but Gusty wanted to check for himself – and even then he still needed further reassurances at another meeting with me.

The British were still sceptical about whether the IRA peace would hold, and all calls from Gerry Adams for a meeting were rebuffed with the excuse that they wanted more evidence before exploratory dialogue could take place. However, they had taken a few modest steps. They had lifted the ban on broadcasting the voices of Sinn Féin, and in response to the hopes for a Loyalist ceasefire they had approved visits by Loyalist paramilitary leaders to the Maze to inform the Loyalist prisoners on the way things were moving.

Others, too, were being drawn into the Loyalist search for peace. Archbishop Eames was once more to play a vital role:

'They asked to see me. It was our friend Roy Magee who opened the door for that. He said, look, these characters are absolutely at a loss, they need some sort of guidance, would you be prepared to see them? . . . The day was appointed and in they came and there were something like a dozen of them in their best Sunday suits and my memory of that was when they left the aftershave was still wafting in the room.

'They came in and I said to them, if these are the terms that you want then really you are asking me – has Major done a deal with the Provos? They said, if you can get a categorical answer, we will accept your answer, but you must guarantee it's the truth from John Major. And I agreed and I went over to London and said to John Major, "John, look me straight in the eye. You are the Prime Minister of Great Britain and Northern Ireland, I'm the Archbishop of Armagh, Primate of all Ireland, have you done a deal with the IRA?"

'He said, "I can look you in the eye and I'll go on looking you in the eye. I have not."

'I went back and told them, and that was the foundation for them making a ceasefire. You see they were afraid, they had nobody to turn to politically, there was this vacuum. I suppose I was there, I knew them, they knew me, I had been in and out of their areas so often, and for some reason they felt that I could get an honest answer from John Major.

'I often wondered afterwards if he had said to me, "Privately? Yes, I've done a deal! But publicly – no!" what on earth would I have done? But he didn't, he said, "No, I didn't do a deal, there was no deal done with the IRA." And he said, "You can tell them that."

'So I told them and that was my run-up to the ceasefire. The other angle to the ceasefire was I asked Gusty to express regret. I said to Gusty, you've got to express regret because the IRA at that stage hadn't and as you know it was included [in the Loyalist ceasefire statement].'

Gusty Spence:

'Abject and sincere remorse. It's important. And I say it now, about fifty years after the most devastating war the world has ever seen, the Second World War – I'm sorry. People should say it. I think everybody in Northern Ireland should turn to everybody else in Northern Ireland and say "I'm sorry!" Abject and true remorse was very, very important. In fact, big Bill Flynn turned to me and said, "I wish the IRA had said that!" You have to be remorseful.'

On the day – 13 October 1994 – the day that he had promised me, when Gusty Spence announced the Loyalist ceasefire, big Bill Flynn was there. He'd done as much for the Protestant cause as the Catholic. He was a man who abhorred violence, and although he was a convinced Nationalist and believed fervently in a united Ireland, he was just as vehement about getting to it by peaceful means and politics and not by bloodshed. He had guaranteed the Loyalists equal treatment in the States, and his presence there that day was a sign of the good faith they had in him. In a coded message they had informed him of the date of the Loyalist call to cease fire and had invited him over from America for the announcement. He was hidden away in a back room, away from the press and media frenzy, but he had been a powerful ally and, like myself, came to trust Gusty Spence as much as Adams.

Just before that memorable day, I had received the call I had been waiting for when Gusty Spence rang and asked if he, David Ervine and one other could come for a meeting under the same conditions as Sinn Féin. I told them, 'If a ceasefire is on the cards, I'll see you there.'

The following day the Loyalist ceasefire was announced. Now the work could begin to make the country whole again. Back to the Berkeley Court, seventh floor, Gusty Spence, David Ervine and Billy Hutchinson. This time they walked in proudly and we all shook hands on a deal well done. Then it was down to business, discussing aspects of the future: Articles 2 and 3, and the big question that was to govern and beset the next few years in the ongoing peace process – decommissioning and the giving up of arms. I had hoped they would join in the forthcoming talks at the newly established Forum for Peace and Reconciliation, but although they said on radio that they might make a submission, as yet they were not quite ready to put in an appearance.

At that meeting I remember, as they were leaving, Gusty suddenly turned to me and, with a glint in his eye, looked around the luxurious penthouse suite.

'There's one last thing I'd like to ask,' he said. My heart sank. 'We only have half the fare home. Could you give us the other half?'

Gerry Adams and Martin McGuinness came down to see me in Dublin, and this time Dick Spring joined us. The Sinn Féin representatives were anxious that talks with the British government should begin as soon as possible so that they could engage in the gradual disentanglement from British rule and move forward into the promised process of self-determination.

I could only promise to do my best to urge John Major on, just as I had reassured the Loyalists at my meeting with them that I would make sure that the principle of consent remained intact.

17

DOWN AT THE SMALL
HURDLE

Although Dick Spring and I had set our minds to bring peace to the North, our political journey in government together had not been a smooth one.

In the last days of July 1994, the final results of the Beef Tribunal were published.

Dick Spring had already let it be known that should the verdict report censure me in any way he was ready to leave the coalition. The end had been on the cards for some time; Labour were just looking for the right excuse. It came with yet another leak by Labour to the press: this time it was the *Sunday Business Post* that carried the story, with the added confirmation that it came 'straight from the horse's mouth'!

They were publicly prejudging the verdict and, what was worse, casting me in the role of the guilty party while painting themselves as the righteous moral guardians of government, who would walk away rather than be tainted by association.

It was that time in the summer when hopes for peace were low. The rumours of a ceasefire announcement at Letterkenny had been heralded in the press and media, and when it wasn't delivered the jeering and derision from the sceptics clamoured loud and clear. Many in the Labour Party were eager to scramble away and distance themselves from what they now predicted would be the 'failure' of the peace process.

Charlie McCreevy:

'I always felt from the day Dick Spring came into government with us, he was being pulled in two directions. People who had voted for Labour in that election had voted on the assumption of keeping Fianna Fáil out; suddenly they found themselves in coalition, in government with Fianna Fáil, and there were many key people very close to Dick who didn't want that. They saw Fianna Fáil as the enemy and coalition was the last thing they would have expected to happen. So there was tension the whole time and Dick was in that middle position trying to do the right thing by the party and the country, whereas some of the others, judging by the way things evolved, did not play off the top of the deck.

'The last government week was in July and I believe Dick Spring put out an understanding that as there would be no meeting of the Dáil in August, when the Beef Tribunal report came out it should be handled in a certain way.'

'In a certain way' meant: no briefings to the press before consultations with Spring on the results of the verdict.

Before the Dáil broke for the summer adjournment, Spring threatened publicly that under no circumstances would Labour 'hide or walk away' from the implications of the verdict.

I was annoyed that they were judging me culpable, and in public, before Justice Liam Hamilton's report was even published. There were many in the Labour Party who were most definitely looking for a fight and a pretext for a final knockout blow to Fianna Fáil. I had a definite premonition that the end was nigh.

Spring and Fergus Finlay were on holiday when the 900-page document setting out the Beef Tribunal's verdict was delivered, according to established practice, to the Minister for Agriculture, Joe Walsh, in Government Buildings one Friday night in late July. At the same time copies of it were sent to various departments for analysis by a team of barristers, advisers and civil servants.

I waited anxiously in my office. It was a long and complicated document. My Beef Tribunal team, senior counsel Henry Hickey and Conor Maguire, had split it up between them and Paddy Teahon, Frank Murray, Tom Savage and Donal Cronin were also reading it. They examined and scrutinized every sentence, paragraph and page while I looked on and awaited their verdict.

The time passed slowly, but finally they all looked up, conferred and agreed. The consensus was that though there were a few minor criticisms of some of my decisions, the findings did not question my motives or impugn my integrity. I was in the clear.

I could take the criticism; now I wanted the world to know that my integrity, my honesty, was vindicated. This tribunal had hung over my head ever since the beginning of my premiership. Originally the accusations had been aimed at Haughey, then when he left office they'd tried to nail them on me; they'd failed, and now it was over. After all the spurious assertions fed to the press by Labour, it was my turn to tell my side. I wanted the verdict known, that I was exonerated from all culpability.

'Tell the pol corrs [political correspondents] I'm vindicated, Diggy,' I told Seán Duignan. I remember he looked at me in shock, and started reminding me of all the warnings he'd received from Dick Spring before he left that no such briefings to the press should take place before consultations with him on the results of the verdict.

Wrongly or rightly, I was not in the mood to wait. I'd been tested to the brink by all Labour's public protestations; I wanted the verdict out there for everyone to see. Others joined in advising me to wait. I'd won, why risk a row with Labour?

I didn't want to hear. I'd suffered too much adverse publicity and now I wanted the record put straight and the truth released.

'Do it, Diggy,' I insisted. 'Tell them I'm vindicated or I'll do it myself!'

Of course there were repercussions. Before Diggy had even finished his briefing to the political correspondents, accusations of treachery, locked doors, broken promises and the end of government were echoing through the building.

The sinister story of the locked doors was bizarre. Maybe the door in the corridor had been closed, but certainly no one had ordered it to be locked. Seán Duignan was there and he had no problem: 'I don't remember it being locked, although I do recall it being closed, which was unusual. However, I went back and forth through the door to the Taoiseach's office on a number of occasions that night and have no memory of encountering any hindrance or delay. I later queried senior and other officials who were in the Taoiseach's office on that occasion, and they maintained they knew nothing of locked doors.'

Dick Spring called in the early hours of the morning to express his anger that I had pre-empted the government's perusal of the verdict. Not a word of congratulations, you're in the clear, only more dire warnings and threats. 'Would you deny me my hour in the sun, Dick?' I asked him.

'There may be no sun,' he answered. 'This is bad.'

It didn't happen on that occasion, but the end of the government was on the horizon, as it had been from some time earlier.

Looking back, was I wrong to publicize the verdict immediately? I only know I'd had enough of all the Labour back-stabbing and adverse rumours which continued to haunt me. Despite my vindication, the press, encouraged by Labour, viewed the result with suspicion; but I was in the clear and that was all that mattered. As for Labour, some of them were furious I was exonerated: the verdict had thwarted the potential collapse of the coalition, which would now have to wait for another day.

I had emerged from the report with my political and personal integrity intact. Dick Spring maintained that the way the report had been handled damaged trust between the government partners, but that he was prepared to work to restore it. For both of us the peace process, now at a highly delicate stage, was of paramount importance; petty squabbling could wait. However, in the shadows there were others trying to take advantage of the crumbling coalition. John Bruton, still aspiring to advance his prospects of a rainbow coalition, reminded Spring that he could collapse the administration and become part of a new government without calling a general election. Spring declined, knowing the option was there.

August and the Angelus bell rings in the IRA peace; September and the storms start again.

Only this time it's over Attorney General Harry Whelehan, my nemesis.

It started when the position of Chief Justice of the Supreme Court became vacant. It should have been a normal appointment, processed in the usual way. As a partnership government, we shared out official appointments. I would have the choice of one, Spring the choice of another. Justice Liam Hamilton, then president of the High Court, looked a likely candidate for the position of Chief Justice, but Spring's first choice was Mr Justice Donal Barrington, who at the time was with the European Court. In the meantime Harry Whelehan had advised Dick Spring that in the event of Liam Hamilton becoming Chief Justice, he would be interested in the vacant presidency of the High Court. This was conventional procedure, in that the Attorney General traditionally has first option on any senior judicial position that becomes vacant. However, Spring and his party made it quite clear that they opposed Whelehan. Spring informed me that he didn't think he was the man for the job, and that he was also too conservative for Labour's liberal tastes, as he had clearly demonstrated with the 'X Case'.

I knew that Harry Whelehan had been going round members of Fianna Fáil gathering support and that most of them had agreed to back his appointment. It was another impasse. Then word came through that Spring's favoured candidate, Donal Barrington, because of a constitutional legal difficulty, was not eligible for the position of Chief Justice.

Spring was in the Far East, I was about to leave for Australia. As far as I was concerned, the decision on Justice Hamilton's appointment was therefore a fait accompli and I announced it as such at the final cabinet meeting before I left. The business of the appointments of Chief Justice and other sequential jobs had been left over from the previous week's agenda and it was quite legitimate that I dealt with it and other postponed business before I left. Labour members were loud with accusations that I was trying to 'slip' it in while Spring was out of the country and that Hamilton was not their first nominee. True, but as their man was not qualified, there was no other choice. However, the row was grave enough for

Labour to issue more threats that they would walk out. I phoned Kathleen and warned her things were looking bad and that Australia might have to be postponed, and that this time the boys might mean what they said.

Soon afterwards, Ruairi Quinn and Brendan Howlin returned from their emergency call to alert Dick in Hong Kong. They reported back that he had agreed to the Hamilton appointment without conditions, but had instructed that all other jobs must wait to be decided between the two us when we were both back in the country. Fair enough. I had other things on my mind. We had the IRA ceasefire in place, now I needed the Loyalists to make their announcement. But first it was off to Australia.

We were fêted in Sydney. There is a big Irish population in Australia and many IRA supporters. Peace in the North had been headline news throughout the continent and the crowds were out on the streets to celebrate. After the tensions of the last few days it was a relief to be part of those emotional and joyful demonstrations. It made the quarrels over a judicial appointment seem very insignificant indeed.

All hopes that Labour would be discreet in their dealings with the press were quickly dispelled with leaks and reports of how Labour had stopped me 'ram-rodding' through Whelehan's appointment. All gloves were off, and our dispute was now in the public ring yet again. Even the press were taken aback at the onslaught of vitriol from Labour against us, their coalition partners. An election was looking more and more inevitable.

As an editorial in the *Irish Times* of 26 September 1994 reported, under the heading 'Coalition Pains':

'Is it seriously in the contemplation of either Mr Spring or Mr Reynolds that the dispute over the High Court Presidency could lead on to a break in the coalition and a general election?

'... Correspondents travelling with the Taoiseach have been advised that Mr Spring says he will leave Government if Mr Harry Whelehan is appointed. Labour's minders are making it clear that as far as the Tánaiste is concerned Mr Whelehan will not have the job, although he is willing to accept a compromise candidate. There is a game of brinkmanship in play here. The Taoiseach is on a winning roll. He has a breakthrough in the North, he has survived the worst of the Hamilton report, the passports affair, the tax amnesty and sundry irritations. Mr Spring is seen by many in the rank and file of his own party as out-manoeuvred and humiliated.

'Those who know Mr Spring recognise that he can be at his most dangerous when he feels taken for granted or condescended to. In those circumstances his aggressive side comes out. It is not beyond the bounds of possibility that he could decide to bring the whole house down simply to teach Albert Reynolds manners, as he might be inclined to put it himself ...

'Mr Spring has made a gaffe on the High Court issue. He purported to run a candidate – Mrs Justice Denham – whom he never even consulted and who, it now turns out, is not even interested in the post. And he has blocked the man who, as Attorney General, acts as chief legal adviser to the Government of which Mr Spring is deputy premier. If Mr Whelehan is not fitted for the largely bureaucratic post of President of the High Court, how can Mr Spring have confidence in him as Attorney General? All in all Mr Spring is on shaky ground.'

There was condemnation of Labour's public abuse and their personal attacks on me were without precedent. I was extremely angry, and further irritated at evidence of more Labour briefings when the *Sunday Business Post* of 25 September 1994 printed claims that Spring and his people were describing me, the Taoiseach, as 'power-drunk following the IRA ceasefire' and as 'the High King of Ireland on a roll'!

As Martin Mansergh reported later to the Oireachtas sub-committee:

'It is totally destructive of trust to attack a partner in Government, and especially its head, in that fashion. It is nevertheless indicative of the subterranean tensions created by the breakthrough on the North, despite every effort on the Taoiseach's part to share the credit with the Tánaiste, without whose support it could not have happened. The Taoiseach was politically soaring and had to be pulled down to earth.'

Whether we reached a compromise or not on the appointments, with all this invective being played out in the media relations would be difficult to rebuild. Besides, there was now no other candidate but Harry Whelehan in the offing. But a call to Dick Spring resulted in the same obstinate rejection – no job for Harry.

We were back from Australia in time to greet the arrival of a very high-profile guest who was arriving in Shannon Airport on a short stopover on his return journey from the United States.

I was waiting along with the rest of the reception party when the message came through that our very important visitor, the Russian President, Boris Yeltsin, was 'indisposed' and therefore there would be a delay in his arrival. We looked at each other knowingly and waited and watched as the plane circled, presumably to allow the effects of his 'indisposition' to wear off. An hour later his plane landed and we all walked out on to the tarmac to greet him.

The door opened and out stepped not Yeltsin, but his Deputy Prime Minister, Olev Soskovetz, who descended rapidly, hands outstretched in greeting, his face furrowed with

DOWN AT THE SMALL HURDLE

concern as he expressed the apologies of his leader, who sadly, he announced, was still slightly 'indisposed'!

I duly expressed my deep concern and offered, if it would help alleviate the difficulty under the circumstances, to go on board to greet the President. My kind offer was met with cries of horror!

In Government Buildings the dispute rumbled on. Dick Spring and I had not met for over a month; when we did I confronted him immediately. 'This can be a long or short conversation,' I said. 'Do you, or do you not, want an election?'

He backed off immediately. 'What gave you that idea?'

I told him in no uncertain terms that I did not appreciate the adverse press that had besieged me over the last few weeks and that it could not go on.

The meeting finished with a decision to appoint a sub-committee consisting of two ministers from each party to find a resolution to the problem.

Why Dick was so adamantly against Whelehan I have no idea, other than that he considered him too 'conservative'. He certainly had not objected to his appointment as Attorney General when I first formed my government with Dick Spring as Tánaiste in 1993, and he had the opportunity to do so at that point. Neither did he or his ministers complain of inefficiencies or inadequacies on the part of the Attorney General in the pursuit of his duties during the course of our administration. In fact, Whelehan was admirable in his conduct.

As far as I was concerned, it was traditional that if the chief constitutional officer of the state and legal adviser to the government indicated an interest in a major position, it was normal that that request should be acceded to, if the Taoiseach was so minded. The Attorney General had indicated his strong interest in being appointed president of the High Court, I had agreed and given him my word, and that was that.

This sub-committee was briefed to come up with any proposals that might resolve the impasse reached regarding the appointment to the presidency of the High Court. As Brian Cowen, one of the Fianna Fáil members of the sub-committee, reported:

'The sub-committee met on a few occasions that week and suggestions had been made by the Labour members of the sub-committee to broaden out the context in which this appointment had to be filled, by looking at the whole system of judicial appointments generally. Noel Dempsey and I were prepared to discuss this matter with them, on a without prejudice basis, as I made it clear that there could be no question of Fianna Fáil agreeing to such a new system of judicial appointments without the present vacancy being dealt with and that the new system would not apply in relation to the filling of the vacancy of the President of the High Court.'

There was now a change of direction from the media, with a sudden show of support for me in the press. No one wanted an election, no one wanted an unstable government; one or other of us had to back off. Dick was now getting mauled in the polls, and even members of his own party were calling 'time' as they saw their support evaporating. Labour back-benchers were getting very nervous and publicly began calling on Spring to find a compromise: the Whelehan debacle was certainly not worth the fall of the government.

I was occupied with other things. Two by-elections were in progress and I was out choosing candidates when a meeting was arranged between Dick and myself. I was flying in from Cork at the same time Dick was on his way to somewhere else, so we agreed to meet at Baldonnell airport.

Seán Duignan recalls the episode:

'The extraordinary memory I have of it is that it went on for a long time, until the Labour backbenchers said to Dick, "This can't go on." And Dick, at an extraordinary midnight meeting, at that small airport, arrived and said, "OK, OK, I accept that it's over. Harry gets the job!" And I remember Albert leaving the building and Dick saying I need a little time and Albert saying – not too long, these things have a way of unravelling.'

The meeting seemed to go well. I did not want to see the government fall. There were too many good and positive things happening. We had achieved the impossible in bringing the beginning of peace to Northern Ireland; the economy was building, unemployment was coming down and the European billions were starting to take effect. If we could only hold it together, I said to Spring, and not let this situation deteriorate, we had the makings of a very successful administration. Dick Spring, well aware that his position was weakened, agreed that there would be no call for an election as a result of the row. He accepted Whelehan's appointment, but pointed out that past events had proved the need for a complete overhaul of the judicial appointments system. It was fair comment and I agreed that we should do it. I also agreed that nothing would be announced until the heads of agreement for a new Courts Bill, embracing the major reform package, were approved by the government. As far as I was concerned we had a deal, and implicit in that was that the Whelehan appointment would be implemented – but, as Diggy later commented:

'Albert Reynolds always knew he was going to win this bargaining. We won't go into why Albert wanted Whelehan or why Dick didn't, but Albert knew he would win it and that Labour would accept it. What he didn't know was that the priest was there in the background. So when Albert won it as he'd predicted and Dick accepted, that was it – until, as Labour said, "The priest changes everything!"'

The story of the paedophile priest Father Brendan Smyth had been revealed on *Counterpoint*, a television programme that detailed his sexual offences against young people. Suddenly the full significance of the investigative report erupted into a political crisis when it emerged that there had been a seven-month delay in processing extradition papers for the priest at the time he was wanted in Northern Ireland on sex abuse charges, and that the source of that delay had been traced to the office of the Attorney General. This delay had been severely criticized in the media, although the priest had subsequently given himself up to the Northern Ireland authorities and was now in prison.

I did not realize the full implications of this until some time later, although Spring did. As far as he was concerned it was the excuse to block Whelehan's appointment and the deal was off. I did not agree. I never break my word when I give it. The new Courts Bill had already been processed and had received government approval some two weeks previously. Spring and I had agreed a quid pro quo deal, by which Fianna Fáil agreed to judicial reforms in this new Bill and Labour agreed to the appointment of Mr Whelehan, and earlier that month, on 5 October 1994, agreement on this had been reached between Fianna Fáil and Labour members of government.

Labour was now adamant that there could be no question of Whelehan's being appointed, and totally refused to accept any part of his explanation for the delay in the extradition matter.

The Attorney General explained that he was never personally informed of the extradition request, knew nothing of it until it was reported in the media, and had himself played no part whatsoever in the delay. The actual request for extradition had been dealt with by a senior officer in his department, Matthew Russell, a senior civil servant and barrister of considerable experience in extradition matters, and it was common practice that the Attorney General would only be informed of any such requests once the departmental officer concerned had formed a view on the legality of the request, at which point he would then pass that view on to the Attorney General.

At issue was the fact that the delay was not unusual considering the complexities of the case and the many years that had elapsed since the alleged offences had been committed, a time lapse that was considered a possible obstacle to extradition. The offences were said to have taken place between twenty-five and five years prior to the issue of the warrants. In 1987 legislation was passed to protect people against extradition in respect of offences committed so long ago that it would be impossible to defend them and in other exceptional circumstances such as adverse publicity in the requesting country.

Whelchan also stated that it was the first time this new legislation had been called into play, and that the case therefore had no precedent. Additional factors were the very heavy workload of the departmental officer, whose work on the case was constantly interrupted by more urgent matters, and, more importantly, the fact that the offending priest had voluntarily returned to Northern Ireland before the examination of the extradition request had been completed, which seemed to lessen the urgency of presenting his views on the request to the Attorney General for his decision.

I was extremely annoyed that I had been put into this situation. I did not think the excuses for the delay were adequate and I was very concerned that a paedophile should have been at large in the community for seven months. The

Smyth case had been mishandled by the Attorney General's office. He himself had not been made aware of the case immediately as he should have been, and therefore was not culpable. Archaic practices were to blame, and these were in the process of being reformed. I could see no reason why this affair should prevent his appointment as president of the High Court. However, Dick Spring was still not satisfied and demanded that Whelehan's report be discussed further and a more detailed explanation be offered to the public, either by the Attorney General or through me as Taoiseach in the Dáil.

At the time, I was more concerned with a shooting incident at a post office in Newry. Republican paramilitaries were to blame and I feared the repercussions. The cabinet meeting that day was dominated by this incident, and we agreed that the Minister for Justice, Máire Geoghegan-Quinn, should cancel the planned release of nine Provisional IRA prisoners. The judicial appointments therefore were postponed to the following day's business.

The whole episode had now been on and off so many times, I just wanted it finished. But, yet again, word came through that Spring and the Labour Party were warning that they would not come into the cabinet meeting if the appointment was to go ahead. As it was, they were there. The Attorney General also attended the meeting and was questioned at length by all the ministers. It was again generally agreed that the explanation for the delay was most unsatisfactory, but all accepted that Whelehan himself had acted in good faith and that he had known nothing of the file. He left the meeting, there was further discussion on the Whelehan report, and the business of appointments was raised. The candidates were Eoghan Fitzsimons for Attorney General, and Harry Whelehan for president of the High Court.

Again Spring reiterated he could not accept the Attorney

General's explanation for the delay in the extradition of the priest, and before a decision could be taken he led his Labour ministers out of the room. I was not particularly perturbed. At the time we all thought that the walk-out was a means of having their dissent recorded in the cabinet minutes – in other words, facilitating the recording of a non-vote as a tactical move. As far as I was concerned I had allayed the Labour Party's concerns expressed to me on the previous day by arranging for the Attorney General to speak at the cabinet meeting and by arranging for myself to address the Dáil at the earliest opportunity, namely the following Tuesday, 15 November.

There was unanimous agreement and approval of the appointments by the ministers of Fianna Fáil, without one word of objection.

Dick was with the others in his office, waiting to see what we would do. I called him and told him the result of the vote. 'What will we tell the press?' I asked. 'Is it over or what?' He said he'd consult with his people and call me back.

It was while we were having tea that the call came through from the President's residence, informing us that she was going away for a long weekend but that if we could get over to Áras an Uachtaráin within the hour, the formal judicial appointments could be made immediately.

We left Government Buildings and were driven through the Dublin rush hour to Phoenix Park and the Áras, where Máire Geoghegan-Quinn, Fitzsimons, Whelehan, Seán Duignan and I met with President Mary Robinson for the official appointments ceremony.

Dick Spring called me and was appalled to find that we were at the Áras. I whispered to him that only a short while back he and his people had been quite happy about the promotion and even he had agreed to it, but as far as he was concerned I was presenting him with a fait accompli; and, he warned, once news of this was in the public domain it would soon become clear that the Labour ministers had not participated in Whelehan's appointment.

The crisis was under way. That same Friday evening we arranged for negotiators from Fianna Fáil to hold discussions with political negotiators from Labour to address their concerns. They still did not indicate that they were pulling out of government.

The press had now swung round from flaying Spring to ranting against me. Spring was back as the moral guardian and I was the villain – or rather, Harry was the villain, and by promoting him I had made myself complicit in what had happened. Paedophilia is the most heinous of crimes, and the fact that the Attorney General's office had not dealt with this case for seven months but had allowed a child abuser to remain at large in the community was the subject of outraged debate filling most of the Sunday columns.

I knew a marathon Labour Party meeting was under way and I guessed that this time Dick would have the full weight of his party behind him on whether to stay or resign once I had delivered my account of the Smyth case to the house. Again I spoke with Spring, who simply advised me of a press statement he was going to make; but by now I realized that the continuance of the government was indeed in jeopardy.

The Attorney General cannot go into the Dáil to represent himself; it is the Taoiseach who politically carries that responsibility, although it is up to the Attorney General to make sure he has all the facts. On Monday, 14 November, under the heading 'A Matter of Accountability', an editorial in the *Irish Times* summed up the situation:

'The die is cast. The appointment is made and cannot be unmade. The former Attorney General is now President of the High Court and cannot even if he wanted to, add to or amplify his account of events. He could, of course, if he were so minded resign and thus defuse the immediate crisis.'

The problem was Harry was not so minded. He was convinced that, despite mismanagement by his officials, he had acted correctly.

Charlie McCreevy:

'I thought Labour were unjustified in their criticism of Harry Whelehan. His biggest minus was that he had no political antennae at all, but he definitely was independent minded and honourable, and if you were thinking of appointing people to the bench, that's the kind of people you should make judges, and it's always been the tradition that if the Attorney General wants a position on the High Court he gets it, whatever the government. The Labour Party didn't want Harry and used the excuse of what happened in the 'X Case'. At the end of the day, whatever you say about Harry and the 'X Case', he did exercise independent judgement.

'Now it was agreed, and I was party to this with Albert, that Dick would allow Harry to become president of the High Court, but before the decision could be put to cabinet, a matter of some weeks, the problem about the priest came up and Labour insisted that changed the circumstances.

'Now, we never knew about this case; and I think this is all credit to Albert – although some say it's a weakness, I say it's his strength and we would never have had the peace process if it was not for his type of approach – Albert had made a deal, and Albert had made a deal with Dick to appoint Harry. And in Albert's view Dick walked away. Albert had promised Harry and Albert would not walk away. It's as simple as that.'

Nothing is as simple as that. There was still the question of Whelehan's accountability to be settled. In readiness for that I asked Máire Geoghegan-Quinn, the Justice Minister, to instruct the new Attorney General, Eoghan Fitzsimons, to re-examine Whelehan's handling of the case and prepare a report for me.

Monday, 14 November proved to be a day of confusion and political crisis. Rumours fed rumours and all sorts of irresponsible allegations were tossed about. I held several private meetings with Fitzsimons to discuss a number of topics, one of which was the necessity to reorganize the Attorney General's office. There was another meeting later that morning with me and some of my ministers when we addressed the current instability and, more importantly, the threat this posed to the peace process.

Fitzsimons then told us that following his brief examination in preparation for his report on other extradition cases, he had come to the preliminary view that the Smyth case might not have been the first case in which the 'lapse of time' had been at issue. He did not remember the name of the case but the Minister for Justice, Máire Geoghegan-Quinn, who had asked her own officials to produce a list of extradition cases dealing with child sex offenders, recalled the name Duggan. Fitzsimons thought that could be it. He then tried to explain the possible implications of the new evidence he'd uncovered, but in very vague terms – 'this or that' and 'if and maybe' – until finally I said, 'Sorry, sorry, you can't say this or that or the other. Give me the explanations clearly on a piece of paper so that I can study it and know precisely what it means and I can decide on what action, if any, to take.'

I felt that as Taoiseach I was entitled to require from the Attorney General a definitive legal view in writing and I sent him away to produce it.

I had hardly slept that week for stress about the implications of this sudden disastrous situation that was threatening to pull down one of the most stable administrations for decades; I was exhausted, he was new to the job and I found his explication of the new scenario unclear and confusing. On the one hand he said that a note on the new file stated that the Duggan case was not relevant to the 'time lapse' question dealt with in the Extradition Act, although he said that in his opinion – on a quick initial view – he thought the time lapse question could be 'considered', whereas a senior official in his office – Mr Russell, the expert on extradition – disagreed. I wasn't a lawyer; I wanted a clear statement of the position.

I was also conscious that Fitzsimons had only been in the job for three hours, whereas Harry Whelehan had done it for three years. 'What does Harry say about it?' I asked. He told me that he didn't know, he had not informed Harry as he had only just come across the file. I told him to go and see Harry and to come back to me with his definitive view of the situation.

It seemed that whereas Whelehan had reported to the cabinet that the Father Smyth case was without precedent, Fitzsimons had discovered that actually it was not the first case to come under the new Extradition Act with its principle of 'justice delayed is justice denied'. Fitzsimons, in fact, had unearthed a file in the Attorney General's office, signed by Harry Whelehan, in which this very principle could allegedly have been considered only two years previously, in the case of another paedophile, a monk, John Anthony Duggan. In that instance, far from dragging his heels, Harry had arranged the monk's extradition expeditiously. Exactly what bearing this would have on the Smyth case no one knew.

As Brian Cowen said in his evidence to the inquiry into this affair in 1995:

'Our attitude collectively can best be described by saying that we felt it was obviously an unresolved conflict of opinion on an initial enquiry and that further work would have to be done on it. On reflection, the issue did not appear to me to be very significant at the time because our concern and total focus was on the seven-month delay in the Smyth case.'

I tried to put the whole thing aside. Until we had all the information there was nothing more we could do; besides, I was more concerned about the effects this unstable situation would have on the peace process. For several days, as further news of the disintegrating relationship between the coalition partners penetrated into the general public consciousness, I had been receiving very concerned letters from the North. The arrangements for negotiations following the ceasefires were at a crucial stage of development, and an unstable political situation in the South was becoming a potential danger to that process. I was deeply anxious to resolve the problems between ourselves and Labour, and to right the situation in my Dáil speech the following day.

Fitzsimons then drew my attention to the fact that Whelehan was to be sworn in as president of the High Court the next day – the very day on which I would be presenting Whelehan's account of the Smyth case. Fitzsimons then said that he had been requested by the Minister for Justice to ask Whelehan, in the current circumstances, to consider postponing the ceremony. I asked Fitzsimons to tell Whelehan about the different problems we were facing, to emphasize the current instability of the political situation, and to impress on him the desirability of putting back his swearing-in for a few days.

There were meetings late into the night on how to resolve the situation. No one was clear as to the implications of the Duggan case, although Máire Geoghegan-Quinn was concerned that in her evidence she might have misled the Dáil by saying the Smyth case was the first to fall under the new Extradition Act. Fitzsimons was then dispatched to ask

Whelehan to delay his swearing-in as president. Whelehan refused. In the confusion none of us thought to tell him rather than just to ask; we were all too preoccupied with trying to save the situation.

During all this my team, led by Martin Mansergh – Savage, McCreevy, Cowen and Geoghegan-Quinn – worked late into the night on the speech I was to make the following day, setting out the background to the Smyth case and the handling of the extradition request. However, our main concern was to answer the five points that Spring and the Labour Party had raised in a lengthy press conference the previous day; in doing so, we hoped we would resolve the situation – and save the government.

As was customary, the next morning, Tuesday, drafts of my speech were circulated to government departments for comments. Two drafts were sent to Fitzsimons' office; but he did not comment on any inaccuracies as regards the Duggan case. The Duggan case was not mentioned in the speech as I still did not have a definitive answer from him on that. However, although I had personally received no further advice note from the new Attorney General throughout the whole of Tuesday, I learned later that he had in fact prepared a memorandum commenting on the Duggan case that had not reached me personally. It had four paragraphs. The first repeated Whelehan's explanation that the Smyth case was the first in which the new extradition law had required consideration. The second paragraph begins: 'It is clear that the above advice to Mr Whelehan was incorrect.' This was crossed out and revised as: 'It does not appear that the above advice to Mr Whelehan was accurate.' The penultimate sentence read: 'That being the case it is clear that the question of lapse of time was going to possibly be a real issue in the Smyth case whereas arguably it presented little difficulty in the Duggan case.'

Again this was revised to: 'That being the case it is clear that the question of lapse of time was arguably going to be a live issue in the Smyth case whereas it presented little difficulty in the Duggan case.' He concluded: 'Mr Russell is very strongly of that view.' It is clear to me now, although I did not receive or read this memorandum, that Fitzsimons was not at all sure of the position but that Mr Russell, a man of great experience in extradition cases, considered that Duggan's case was not relevant to Smyth's at all.

The memorandum continued in this vein, providing no definite view on the matter – reflecting very much the confusing explanations given by Fitzsimons to me and my ministers at that first meeting with him.

Of one thing we were sure: until we had clear and definitive advice I was not prepared to take action, nor could I properly do so without that firm guidance from the government's chief legal adviser.

A second memorandum, it transpires, was also written on that day – by an official in the Attorney General's office – and this too I did not see or read at the time. This one read: 'The official who dealt with the Smyth case is of the opinion that the Duggan case would not have provided him or the Attorney General with assistance in the Smyth case by virtue of the disparity between the lapse of time in each case between commission of offences and the proposed extradition.' This also did not reach me in time for my Dáil address, but it confirmed Russell's view.

Work continued on my draft speech all that Tuesday morning and again, as was common practice, the later drafts were circulated for comments. The speech still contained no reference to the Duggan case and no comments were received back from the Attorney General's office on this point.

The swearing-in of Harry Whelehan took place that

morning before I went in to the Dáil to make my speech.

I was administratively accountable for the Attorney General's office in the house, and it was my duty to answer for his conduct. I apologized to the people of Ireland and to Dick Spring for the time lapse in extraditing the priest Brendan Smyth, and went on to cover the five points on which answers had been demanded by Labour. The debate and the questioning went on for five hours, during which time I expressed my revulsion that such a depraved man as Father Smyth, a man trusted as a priest, should have been left free in the community because of archaic systems in the Attorney General's office, and I promised that reforms were already under way to ensure such a thing would never happen again.

Only later did I learn that Fitzsimons had arrived after I had gone into the house and had handed in a document containing his definitive advice on the Duggan case. In fact, I later learned that copies of the document had been handed over that morning to both Geoghegan-Quinn and Bertie Ahern, although I was not aware of this and neither had raised it with me.

Mr Fitzsimons had in fact delivered a copy of the document to my office while I was in the Dáil. He had asked an official in my office to take a copy of it to the Dáil for me to see. That copy never reached me.

My copy of the document had been passed from the official to the secretary of the Department of the Taoiseach, Paddy Teahon, who read it and made notes on it for me to see, then passed it on to the government secretary, who passed it on to the Chief Whip. The live Dáil television coverage of the day shows what I understand was the Fitzsimons document being passed along two rows until it reached Bertie Ahern, who looked at it, read it and appeared to put it in his pocket. Only when I returned later to my office at 9.00 p.m. did I discover a copy lying on my desk.

It began: 'The reply is the best I can do, it does not in fact answer the question.'

Why, I asked myself in frustration, did it seem that I could not get a straight answer? I wanted black and white; all I could get was shades of grey.

More importantly, Fitzsimons had summarized: 'In my view it would be absolutely incorrect to inform the Dáil that this was the first time that this Section was considered. It would also in my view be similarly incorrect to say that this was the first time that the Section was applied.'

In other words, the main explanation for the delay in the Smyth case was flawed in that this was not the first time the legislation had been considered and applied, and the cabinet and the house had, in effect, been misled.

The significance of this advice was clear. I would now have to criticize the account given by Whelehan, now a member of the judiciary, sworn in as president of the High Court that very morning. The advice had reached me too late.

I was furious that I had not received the vital document earlier. I realized the impact it would have on the fragile negotiations with Labour and, more importantly, on the even more delicate state of the peace process. I felt bitterly let down by Whelehan, and I dispatched Fitzsimons to ask him to con-sider stepping aside for the sake of the government.

He refused.

It was another long night. There was a frantic moment of hope that things could be saved when Charlie McCreevy came rushing in to say that behind the scenes he'd been talking to Pat Magnier, a Labour senator and close friend of Dick Spring, and that there was a possible deal to be made. We were all gathered working on my speech for the following day when Brendan Howlin rang. He spoke to Noel Dempsey and outlined the conditions of the new offer on the table. They wanted me to go into the debate the following day and express my regret at making the appointment of Harry Whelehan as president of the High Court against the wishes of the Labour Party; to say that Dick was right, I was wrong!

It was a bitter pill and a pound of flesh rolled into one. Everyone was looking to me – Brian Cowen, Michael Smith, McCreevy, Diggy: it would be a humiliating contradiction of everything I'd said the day before, but I had no choice; I did feel very badly let down by Harry, and if it saved the government from falling – I had to do it.

'Has Spring agreed this?' I asked.

'We're waiting to see,' said Charlie. Ah!

The question of the Duggan case was raised. I was annoyed I had not received the Attorney General's definitive response of the day before, but I consoled myself and the others with the thought that I still had a chance to bring it up the next day. However, despite the document from the Attorney General, none of us were clear as to its exact implications for the Brendan Smyth case: even Geoghegan-Quinn, the Justice Minister, and Brian Cowen, with his legal brain, were still puzzled and uncertain about its significance and what it meant exactly.

'Get Fitzsimons over,' I said. It was about one o'clock in the morning. He was there within half an hour. I discussed his advice with him. This time he said that he considered that as Whelehan had been incorrect in what he told the cabinet and the Smyth case had not been the first case to be considered under the new extradition law, he was of the opinion that if Whelehan were still Attorney General he would have to resign. I asked him to prepare a paragraph for insertion into my speech to that effect, making the point that Whelehan must take personal responsibility for the report to the cabinet. Even as I instructed him I was conscious that it was legally and constitutionally dangerous to cast aspersions on a member of the judiciary in the Dáil, but I had little to no choice. I was also concerned that Fitzsimons himself still seemed uncertain about the precise legal position.

Work on the speech to address and answer all Labour's demands went on until the early hours. McCreevy and Howlin, Dempsey and Quinn kept up a running analysis of what was or was not acceptable to Spring. I went along with it but I had little hope of its achieving anything. I didn't know what game they were playing, I only knew that Spring had made up his mind – or if he hadn't, those around him had. Howlin and Quinn were doing their best, but there were other advisers around Spring, more influential, who had resented joining with Fianna Fáil from the very beginning and now saw this as their opportunity to break away.

In fact I said to Diggy at the time, as he recalls:

'I remember something Albert said at this stage – "I'm being led to my execution, somebody is doing this, somebody is orchestrating it."'

By the early hours of the next morning the draft of the speech – including the paragraph drafted by Fitzsimons – was approved. In it I said that I regretted my decision to proceed with the appointment of Harry Whelehan in the face of the express opposition of the Labour Party and promised that this breach of the trust on which the partnership was founded would not happen again. Howlin said it would be enough to satisfy Labour, but McCreevy and the Fianna Fáil team wanted written confirmation that Spring now approved and was happy. They wrote out a statement which McCreevy and Dempsey took across for Spring to sign. It read: 'On the basis of the statement, prepared by me, being incorporated in the Taoiseach's statement, I will lead my ministerial colleagues back into Government, to complete the programme for

Government. Signed Dick Spring 10.22 a.m. 16-11-94.'

Dick Spring then came over to my office and we confirmed the deal with handshakes and backslaps all round.

Before the hour was up the truce was over. A phone call to Dick Spring that morning, from some mystery informer, revealed that I had known of the Duggan file the previous Monday.

They came to confront me – Dick Spring, Howlin, Quinn and Mervyn Taylor – and accused me of lying, of deliberately withholding information about the Duggan case and of deceiving the house. Of course I denied it vehemently; but all my explanations – that I had not wilfully misled the house but had been waiting for the Attorney General's definitive advice, as was correct procedure – fell on deaf ears. I produced the final advice letter from Fitzsimons and told them that now I had all the facts I intended to make a full disclosure of the Duggan case to the Dáil that day. Spring not only refused to listen, he also refused to read the letter. They wanted me to call for Whelehan's resignation immediately. I told them I had already done so and that he had refused. As far as he was concerned it was a simple matter of human error on the part of one of his officials – and as for the Duggan case, he confessed it had been overlooked. They wanted him impeached. I said it wasn't feasible.

Ruairi Quinn's next remark is now in the annals of Irish political history: 'We have come for a head, Harry's or yours – it doesn't look like we're getting Harry's.'

We walked into the Dáil. The Labour Party deputies, significantly, were no longer sitting on our side, a sure sign that the government was over. I called to suspend the sitting for one hour to allow the whips time to discuss the arrangements for the day's sitting. The opposition, sensing blood, opposed. John Bruton, leader of Fine Gael, had tabled a motion of no confidence in the government and I needed time to consult with my advisers on the consequent crisis situation. There was the usual baying from the usual suspects. Dick Spring silenced them with his words, 'Whereas a week is considered to be a long time in politics a request for a one-hour adjournment is very reasonable.'

He knew he had all the time in the world. I knew it was all over.

It had never been a harmonious relationship – we were not natural partners – but we had made it work and we had achieved much together. In my speech that day I felt honour bound to read out the three sentences requested by Labour, but I also informed the house of the Duggan case, its significance and its consequences as far as Whelehan was concerned, in the passage drafted by Fitzsimons. I knew that the government must fall, but in bowing to Labour's wishes I also felt justified in lauding all that we had accomplished. As an administration we had achieved the most ambitious and impressive programme for government that had ever been implemented and we had initiated the biggest breakthrough towards peace in the North in twenty-five years. We had established the highest level of economic growth and the biggest investment plan in the history of the state. We had strong economic growth, social partnership, European inflows and the peace dividend – the economic outlook was the best in years.

All true. Many wished the administration to continue; surprisingly, that day there had been strong editorials to that effect in the London papers. I knew the work would continue without me and that I was honour bound to resign. There were others who had been waiting in the wings, all too eager to assume the mantle of power. That's politics.

Yes, I was devastated – there was so much more I wanted to

achieve, particularly with regard to the ongoing peace process in the North – but I was also realistic. The Whelehan debacle had weakened my position as Taoiseach beyond redemption and given Spring the reason to walk away. Even if a reprieve had been granted, it would not have lasted. Labour had decided months ago that it was over; all they had wanted was the right excuse foran exit.

There was a sense of bewilderment as we left the house that day and walked up to my dining room for tea. No one could believe what was happening. For all the frantic manœuvring and negotiating over the last few days and hours, the prize had slipped through our fingers and no one quite knew how. Máire Geoghegan-Quinn, Brian Cowen, McCreevy – all of us were struck dumb one minute, bursting with remorse the next. How could it have happened? It just didn't add up, didn't make sense!

As always, Kathleen was there; she was my support and my strength. Kathleen knew of my decision, we'd talked it through together, as we did everything. The family were there, too – as many as could get there – waiting in a show of shared courage and support. Even so, neither the family nor I could comprehend or believe what had happened or why. Everyone was so subdued, it was like a wake, as people lined up to express their sorrow at the turn of events.

Only my little grandson Robert made me smile. 'Don't worry, Poppy,' he said. 'Now you'll have time to come to Disney World with me!' Fair enough!

I resigned as Taoiseach and as leader of Fianna Fáil. Ironically enough, Harry Whelehan resigned twenty-four hours later. Would it have made a difference if he'd done it before? I doubt it. The marriage of Labour and Fianna Fáil had irrevocably broken down. It might have limped on for a few more weeks, months even, but the end was in sight and inevitable. I don't think Harry had any idea of the enormity of the circumstances he'd created. I still maintain he was an honourable man; it just seemed to me he had no political nous whatsoever.

In my resignation speech that November day, I was proud to say:

'When I became leader of Fianna Fáil and Taoiseach I set myself two political objectives – to achieve peace in Northern Ireland and on the whole island, and to turn the economy around. I was fortunate in such a short space of time to achieve those two political objectives. Many political leaders set themselves in life certain priorities and goals but for whatever reason were not around long enough to achieve them. I was fortunate to work with a team and together we were able to achieve our objectives in a very short time.'

I was one of the last to leave the Dáil that day. I'd listened to the tributes, shaken hands, embraced and patted friend and foe alike in the tradition of the retiring Taoiseach. I looked up at the press corps in the gallery where the boys and girls who'd criticized and reported my every word were still hanging on for the last story.

'It's amazing,' I said to them, 'you cross the big hurdles, and when you get to the small ones, you get tripped up.'

18

'IF MISTAKES WERE MADE, THEY WERE MADE ELSEWHERE'

As I left Government Buildings that bleak November day and drove through the streets of Dublin and into Phoenix Park up to Áras an Uachtaráin to tender my resignation to the President, I saw my Gardaí outriders peel away. The significance of this suddenly hit me: I was no longer Taoiseach, no longer worth guarding, and my privileges would slowly be stripped away. I was so utterly exhausted by the long hours of the last few days, the sleepless nights, the mental agonies, the devastating situation, the emotion of the day, that I was now like a zombie on automatic pilot completing the final ritual of my office, my resignation.

I went home to Kathleen and closed the door on the world.

My governing thought in resigning was that I did not want to do anything that would hold up or endanger the peace process. That was paramount. By stepping down I believed I had ensured a smooth takeover by whoever was chosen as the next Fianna Fáil leader and that the partnership with Labour

459

would continue. The trust between Dick Spring and me had been breached and could not be mended. A head had to roll and it was mine. My single-mindedness in the pursuit of what I believed in had brought the achievements I'd desired: the guns were silenced, the economy flourishing. This time that single-mindedness was to my own detriment.

Charlie McCreevy:

'As he said himself, having got over the big things, it's the little things that trip you up; never was anything more true than that. The peace negotiations, the economy, we'd done all those things right: good government, good decisions, running the country very well. Then to fall over something that no one understands to this day.

'Albert didn't have to resign. If that was Charlie [Haughey] he'd have said – "Let the party put me out! Have a vote of no confidence. Whatever!"

'But Albert would have guessed and guessed correctly. You see, when Albert did the "night of the long knives", he really had created a plethora of enemies within the parliamentary party. He made no secret of it, he had put them out and that was it.

'So I reckon he thought, I'm not going to wait for a vote of no confidence. There was enough of that in Haughey's day. If you look back at the records of that night, no one suggests Albert should resign but he must have guessed the whole thing would be in a mess, because if he had stayed on Labour would not have come back into government with us. He reckoned if he stepped down then Bertie [Ahern] would come in dealing with Labour and the whole government and the peace process and everything else would go on.

'You see, Albert's very noble, he'd do it, step down and that was it. Another leader would probably have battled on, but Albert reckoned if he stood down the party could survive.

Charlie Haughey wouldn't have done it, Bertie Ahern wouldn't have done it, but for Albert there were other more important things.'

Martin McGuinness:

'Well, the circumstances [of Albert's resignation] were a big shock obviously and a huge disappointment. I think by that stage Gerry Adams and many of us had met with Albert and the world was looking on with incredible interest at what was a rapidly developing peace process, something that was beyond the wildest dreams of most people, and for a key part of that to be lost as a result of a paedophile priest was just a madness that we couldn't understand.

'So that was a big shock to people here in the North and within the broad Nationalist community. But it was not just in the Nationalist community; I think by that stage many within the Unionist community were looking on with considerable interest at what was developing and what was happening and how life was changing.

'It was in everybody's interests that the key players in all of this remained together, because remember – the big challenge was to bring about negotiations.'

The press yet again were in a feeding frenzy. However, when I closed the door on the world on Thursday, 17 November 1994, I also closed the newspaper coverage out of my world. Yes, the papers were delivered as usual, but nobody, least of all me, had the stomach to read them. The entire family were completely exhausted, traumatized and shattered, both emotionally and physically.

Yet, on the Sunday evening of that weekend, Miriam telephoned from Edinburgh to ask me if I had seen that day's *Sunday Times* (Miriam lives in Edinburgh and had not been physically present throughout that week). She was incensed about a one-page article entitled 'Goodbye Gombeen Man'. This article presented 'the facts' of my resignation by stating, in effect, that I had deliberately and dishonestly misled both the Dáil and my colleagues, and that I had deliberately suppressed information and then lied about when I got the information.

Miriam told me much later that she had agonized for hours on that Sunday as to whether or not to make the call. She was feeling the pain of the week as much as the rest of us. On the one hand, she knew her call would add further fuel to the already enormous fire, but on the other hand she was livid about the article. Although having no idea at the time what the consequences of her call on that Sunday evening would be, Miriam later explained why she decided to make the call. She knew that she had been reared in a home where lies were not tolerated under any circumstances. The truth, the truth, the truth; she recalls that in our home, the truth was all that mattered.

Imagine how we both felt when I phoned her back within the hour to say that the Irish version of the *Sunday Times*, which had until then been lying unread in a pile with the rest of the newspapers, contained a completely different article by a different journalist. In total contrast to the article in the British edition, the report in the Irish edition of the *Sunday Times* was more or less a true explanation of the events of the week and it had covered my detailed speech in the Dáil.

Freedom of the press and freedom of expression are precious rights that I firmly believe should be protected. However, I have always and for ever held the very strong belief that reputation, which goes to the very core of a person, deserves equal protection.

On that Sunday evening, despite my completely exhausted state, I resolved to take things further. Little did I or anyone else know that my issue with the *Sunday Times* on that day would play a major part of my life and my family's life for the next six years.

Just as my resignation had been clouded in complexity and confusion, so too was the battle for my reputation. This battle had to be pursued in England because the paper containing the damning article had been published there. At the time, many viewed my actions as utter madness. But it was all down to my integrity and my reputation. As I saw it, there was only one way to go.

This book is not the place to cover the legal complexities of my case against the *Sunday Times*. The detail of it has been covered in numerous books and articles ranging from legal textbooks to works on journalism, the media, and privacy and the press. There is also a full record of the judgement in the records of the UK parliament!

My battle against the *Sunday Times* was conducted in London. The case was initially heard in the High Court, then in the Court of Appeal and eventually in the highest legal forum in the land, the House of Lords.

Round one took place during a five-week trial before judge and jury from 14 October to 19 November 1996. It was a mixed victory for me. Although the jury decided in my favour, namely that 'the facts' as reported were not true and that the article was not a fair and accurate report of events, they made a 'nil' award of damages (later changed to 1p by the judge). This would leave me with massive legal bills despite the jury's vote in my favour.

As this stage of the proceedings came to an end, my son-in-law Kevin recalls: 'Albert made a very dignified speech to the press before meeting with his legal advisers, Lord Williams, Andrew Caldecott and Pamela Cassidy. It seemed to me that there was a feeling of general embarrassment around the table about the way the English justice system had dealt with the case. At the end of the meeting, Albert buttoned up his jacket and with that glint in his eye said, "Why apologize – I will take it all the way to Europe if I have to." He would not suffer any injustice, as he saw it.'

Later, at a legal consultation to analyse the outcome and the options, Miriam specifically recalls my asking the lawyers: 'Where's the justice in all this?'

Round two: I appealed the decision to the Court of Appeal on the grounds that the judge in the case had misdirected the jury. I won a retrial in the Court of Appeal, the Lords of the Court noting 'with regret . . . that the misdirections were such as to deny Mr Reynolds a fair trial of his claim'.

The significance of this statement was not lost on me, an Irish man pursuing justice in the English courts. I was entitled to a new trial. The *Sunday Times* sought permission from the Court of Appeal to rely on a defence of 'qualified privilege' in the new trial. The Court of Appeal refused.

Round three (October 1999): The House of Lords. The thrust of this hearing was all about the legal complexities of the defence of 'qualified privilege'. Bear in mind that I was still entitled to my new trial, but the paper was arguing for an expanded version of this defence which, if it succeeded, would not only represent new law in this area but, from a personal point of view, would both strip me of my right to a new trial and have enormous implications for the costs in the case, which were nothing short of massive at this stage. It was a tense day to say the least. Many of the family were there to support me, as they had been from the beginning, including Miriam, who had, at various stages, expressed the thought that perhaps she should never have made that Sunday night call from Edinburgh.

The result? The House of Lords agreed with the *Sunday*

Times that the law should be extended to allow journalists (and, it turns out, authors) to rely on the defence of 'qualified privilege' where the subject matter is in the 'public interest'.

Various guidelines were laid down in the judgment as to what circumstances need to exist before this 'public interest' defence is available. I am told that in legal circles, this is now known as 'the Reynolds defence' or 'the Reynolds privilege defence', and that it has been cited in many major libel cases since 2001 involving parties such as the BBC, the *Daily Telegraph*, Lance Armstrong, journalist Graeme McLagan (in respect of his book *Bent Coppers*) and the *Wall Street Journal Europe*.

However, for me and my family, it was enough for us on that day of judgment in the House of Lords to hear the Lords say that by a majority of three to two they had concluded that although the law should be extended to include this 'public interest' defence for the media, the *Sunday Times* was not entitled to rely on it in my case because (very simply), it had represented its commentary as 'fact' and had not reported the details of my explanations in my Dáil speech.

On Sunday, 10 September 2000, almost six years after publication of the offending article, the paper announced the settlement. More importantly, the *Sunday Times*, in that report, accepted my position, which I had fought so long and hard to defend, that I had not lied to either the Dáil or my government colleagues. The battle was finally over.

As regards the Irish media, I suppose I was my own worst enemy. I'd started off as Taoiseach with a policy of regular and frequent press conferences. Perhaps it was a case of 'familiarity breeds contempt', or maybe it is just the way things are with the media. Fair criticism I can take; abuse of my integrity and defamation of my character I will fight all the way. I had several run-ins over the years with various journalists from a number of newspapers. If I felt the articles they printed about me were damaging in a serious way, I would demand a retraction and an apology. Most editors were fair, they would assess the situation and for the most part an apology would be forthcoming; but where it wasn't I felt completely justified in suing, although I never made any personal financial gain from so doing.

I justify my actions simply with this quote from Iago in Shakespeare's *Othello*:

> Good name in man and woman, dear my lord,
> Is the immediate jewel of their souls:
> Who steals my purse, steals trash; 'tis something, nothing;
> 'Twas mine, 'tis his, and has been slave to thousands;
> But he that filches from me my good name
> Robs me of that which not enriches him
> And makes me poor indeed.

Years later, on his retirement from the editorship of the *Irish Times*, Conor Brady was asked if he had any regrets over the past sixteen years. He said:

'I suppose there are a lot of things really. A newspaper is a very imperfect thing. I think maybe we were a bit hard on Albert Reynolds. We got into an adversarial position with Albert for a number of reasons that I don't really want to get into. But he's a man who made a significant impact and probably, at the time, the paper didn't give him enough credit for it.'

I've reflected long and hard over the intervening years as to what was the true reason for the fall of my government. Was it simply disagreement over a judicial appointment? In his testimony recorded at the Oireachtas Committee inquiry and shown during the *Sunday Times* trial, former Attorney General and High Court president Harry Whelehan stated that 'Mr Reynolds did not seriously mislead the Dáil in relation to the Duggan affair'. In fact, he went on to relate how Fitzsimons had delivered the message to his home from the Fianna Fáil ministers asking him to step aside. During that conversation they had also discussed the Duggan case, its relation to the Smyth affair, and their interpretations of its relevance. He continued:

'Mr Fitzsimons listened to me, he appeared to understand and I took the impression that he was sympathetic to the interpretation which I put on the Duggan case.

'When the Taoiseach made his speech to the Dáil on the Tuesday, it did not altogether surprise me that he did not refer to the Duggan case because while in the Duggan case there was an inaccuracy, perhaps, which would require clarification, I do not believe that the Dáil had been seriously misled because my view was that the Duggan case had required not a consideration of the section but, as Mr Fitzsimons put it, a perfunctory reference to the section.'

The Smyth case and the Duggan case were no more than convenient pretexts, not sufficient reason for bringing a government down. There have been many worse scandals.

In fact, journalist Vincent Browne set the record straight when almost a year later he wrote:

'Dick Spring sought to explain in the Dáil on Wednesday why the Michael Lowry affair was of little consequence as compared with the crisis that brought down the Government of Albert Reynolds 11 months ago.

'He said that the Lowry affair involved – at most – the minister overstating his case, whereas the crisis of last November involved the concealment of vital information from the Dáil. Isn't it wonderful how accommodating memory can be?

'The proximate issue that brought down Reynolds last November was his failure to tell the Dáil on Tuesday, November 15th, about the discovery of the Duggan case. This allegedly had an important bearing on the excuse given for the eight-month [*sic*] delay in dealing with the Father Brendan Smyth extradition order. In fact it had no bearing on the issue. The Duggan case was irrelevant.

'There was no concealment of relevant information from the Dáil on November 15th last. The government fell only because the pretext on which Reynolds said that Spring was right and he was wrong over the appointment of Harry Whelehan to the Presidency of the High Court was found to be false. That is all. It was a storm in a teacup in which Reynolds, Whelehan and Matt Russell were drowned.'

It was a time clouded by confusion, mismanagement, mis-interpretation, missing ministers at times when they were needed, missing documents, misinformation, mischievous dealings and sinister forces working behind the scenes. Rumours have reached me over the years of documents being deliberately lost and miraculously found, but when a crisis remains as baffling as this one, conspiracy theories will always abound.

There was also a theory about at the time that the government had worked in collusion with the Catholic Church and buried the report while the Church authorities had conspired to transfer the priest from one diocese to another rather than deal with his sordid activities. Anger grew at the arrogance of the Church and its failure to understand the outrage of and on behalf of the abused. This was fed by more stories as scandals erupted across the front pages of the press. There were reports that a priest had died of a heart attack in a gay sauna in Dublin and was given last rites by two other priests who just happened to be there; another priest was convicted of a sexual attack on an eighteen-year-old hitch-hiker. The hypocrisy of the Catholic Church, and its tolerance of the abuses perpetrated by its clergy, deeply offended every community and reflected badly on the government, who were held responsible for the erosion of our core values and bore the brunt of the public outcry. We were not only responsible, we were held culpable.

On top of all of this, Fianna Fáil had suffered defeat in two recent by-elections.

Charlie McCreevy:

'The Government fell on top of its head over the appointment of Harry Whelehan – even those involved in it are still confused and to this day it doesn't make sense. But there was a small thing that nobody paid enough attention to in this and I didn't either, I suppose. There was a by-election in Dublin South Central, and Eric Byrne won the seat back for the Democratic Left. Without us realizing, if Fine Gael, Labour and the Democratic Left came together, they would have had eighty-three seats. This, together with the loss of the Cork seat, allowed an alternative government to be contemplated. No one thought about it like that but it may have changed the dynamic in the Labour Party.'

I expected Bertie Ahern to move smoothly into the role of party leader, but then at the last moment Máire Geoghegan-Quinn threw her hat into the ring before realizing she had little support and bowing out fairly quickly. The public were overwhelmingly opposed to an election or a change of government; in their view the Fianna Fáil–Labour government was working well and they favoured it continuing under Ahern and Spring. John Bruton again raised the issue of a 'rainbow' coalition with himself and Spring rotating the position of

Taoiseach; Dick Spring informed the media that such an option was no longer relevant.

Bertie Ahern was in the process of opening formal negotiations for a new Fianna Fáil–Labour deal and I was acting as caretaker Taoiseach when an article by Geraldine Kennedy in the *Irish Times* turned everything upside down. In it she alleged that Fianna Fáil ministers, including Bertie Ahern, had been informed of the Duggan case on Monday, 14 November, and that I was not alone in being privileged with the information. That itself was not sensational new information; it was already in the public domain. Dick Spring was already well aware of it at the time, and indeed I had referred to it in my speeches in the Dáil on the two following days, as had the Minister for Justice, Máire Geoghegan-Quinn, when she apologized for inadvertently misinforming the house. What is more, I had referred to the Duggan case in the text of my speech that Spring himself had been given to approve before he signed the statement of intent to stay in government. However, for whatever reason, Dick Spring now treated it as a new and shocking revelation, and his advisers, Fergus Finlay in particular, pounced on it as telegraphing the final knockout blow to Bertie's aspirations of leading another Fianna Fáil–Labour coalition, and used it as an excuse to strongly advise Spring to consider the alternative.

Vincent Browne made a bid to save the Fianna Fáil–Labour government when, after the suspension of the talks, he spent an hour on the phone with Fergus Finlay trying to convince him that he was completely wrong and that there was nothing new in Geraldine Kennedy's story. In fact he reminded him of what we all knew, that Máire Geoghegan-Quinn had related the same fact in the Dáil debate on the crisis only two weeks earlier.

Fergus Finlay actually reread that self-same speech by the

Minister for Justice, but said that as far as he was concerned the evidence that she had had prior knowledge of the Duggan case was only alluded to in 'heavily coded hints' and that he couldn't possibly have made any sense of it without being in possession of the true position.

I reread Máire Geoghegan-Quinn's speech to the Dáil on 16 November. In it she stated:

'On Monday, the Attorney General contacted me by phone and advised me that an important piece of background information which had previously been given to me about this case was incorrect. There had, as the Taoiseach has stated, been a previous case, in 1992, when the Attorney General considered the provisions of Section 50(2)(bbb) of the 1965 Extradition Act. I asked the Attorney General to come immediately to join myself and other Fianna Fáil members of the Cabinet who were meeting together at the time . . .

'. . . Although the information provided was, as the Taoiseach has stated, of a technical nature, and was made known to other Fianna Fáil Cabinet colleagues at the same meeting, I believe it was my particular responsibility as Minister for Justice to insist that a reference to the previous case should have been included in the Taoiseach's speech.'

Later in the same speech she refers directly to the monk Duggan, identifying him as the aforementioned man in the previous case.

All this completely refutes Finlay's assertion of 'heavily coded hints'. Nothing could have been more clearly stated or understood. It also makes a nonsense of Spring's shock, horror and consequent actions following Geraldine Kennedy's 'sensational new evidence'.

Looking back, although Finlay was in court most of the time, it is interesting that he was not called to give evidence by the

Sunday Times, even though he apparently was a source for the offending article. This time he had got his way, however, and Spring pulled the plug on the coalition. In my opinion it was a shameful excuse to end a government and served only to prove that for all the posturing about trying to save the partnership, Labour were only intent on seeking any excuse to pull it down. They'd come for my head; next for the guillotine was Bertie!

Eyebrows were raised at Labour's hypocritical change of allegiance, but change they did. Suddenly Bertie and Fianna Fáil were cast aside and John Bruton, who had been in a vulnerable position and about to be put out by his own disillusioned party, was given a new lease of life and suddenly installed as Taoiseach – without the rotation!

The circumstances surrounding the fall of the Fianna Fáil–Labour partnership government, one of the most successful governments of recent years, were considered so ludicrous, complex and baffling as to merit the setting up of an investigation by the Select Committee on Legislation and Security. This was not a judicial tribunal but a self-investigation by the Dáil. On 6 December, the government through its Chief Whip proposed a motion to the Dáil: 'To request a person of judicial or senior legal status to inquire on behalf of the House into all the circumstances surrounding the Father Brendan Smyth case and to give that person the necessary powers to summons all persons relevant to the inquiry and to report back to the House as a matter of urgency.' The past few weeks had been so traumatic that I welcomed such a device in the belief that it would cut through all the controversies that had arisen and arrive at the truth.

The first people called to give evidence to the investigating sub-committee were all those associated with the office of the Attorney General, that is, the non-politicians. I attended closely to all the evidence and especially to that given by Eoghan Fitzsimons, much of which, I have to say, seriously differed from my recollections and any notes I had of the same events.

The investigation was the subject of huge interest and the televised parts were keenly followed by the general public, sparking off discussions in pubs and bars across the country. Inevitably, too, there were Dáil reports and acres of newsprint, much of it expressing opinions coloured by subjective political point-scoring, self-serving partisanship, ventilation of personal spleen or self-righteous posturing. It seemed almost impossible that an inquiry could succeed in arriving at a fair and impartial conclusion. However, the sub-committee, under the chairmanship of Mr Dan Wallace, then bent to its task and called the politicians to give their version of events.

As a key witness, I was one of the first to give evidence. In welcoming me to the meeting, the chairman reminded us all of the matters which were to be investigated by reiterating that the task of the sub-committee was to question all persons deemed appropriate on the circumstances surrounding:

1 the appointment of the president of the High Court on Friday, 11 November 1994;
2 the request on Sunday, 13 November 1994 from the Taoiseach and the Minister for Justice to the Attorney General to re-examine all the details of the Brendan Smyth case;
3 the alleged request from the Taoiseach to the then president of the High Court to resign on Monday, 14 November 1994;
4 the draft reply and covering letter provided to the Taoiseach by the Attorney General in advance of the Dáil debate on Tuesday 15 November 1994 on the issue of the

prior application of section 50 of the Extradition (Amendment) Act 1987, and the identification of all persons involved in or approving the draft reply and covering letter; and

5 the identification of all those involved in the preparation of the Taoiseach's Dáil speech for Tuesday 15 November 1994.

I began my evidence by stating that my fundamental position was best summarized in that part of my speech to the Dáil on 6 December 1994 in which I said:

'It seems ironic that the Government should be able to survive a badly bungled extradition case about which there was huge public concern, and rightly so, but that it was also brought down by the omission to refer to an expeditiously conducted extradition case which raised few serious legal issues. The issue is that neither I nor any of my colleagues tried to mislead the Dáil, nor was there any conspiracy. The facts are that Fr Smyth is serving a sentence and that the Duggan gentleman has served his sentence.'

Rigorous questioning by my fellow politicians ensued and I answered them all in good faith. Others involved followed suit, members of my cabinet who had been with me and advised me and remembered those long days and nights in November when Labour had held us hostage over events which were, for the most part, beyond our control. Máire Geoghegan-Quinn, Brian Cowen, Charlie McCreevy, Martin Mansergh and others were all called to account, as were Dick Spring and various Labour deputies concerned in the debacle. It was a long process.

Máire Geoghegan-Quinn related all that had gone before concerning the Father Smyth case and the extent of the information revealed by the Attorney General's office which led to her erroneous statement to the Dáil. The Chief Whip, Noel Dempsey, had also made statements to the Dáil to broadly similar effect based on the information provided by the Attorney General's office.

In its summing-up report the sub-committee stated:

'This misleading on his [Dempsey's] part as well as on Minister Geoghegan-Quinn's part was inadvertent. The blame for the giving of the incorrect answers lay with this [the Attorney General's] office.

'Official A, who dealt with the Smyth case, provided the material to answer the above questions. At the time of preparation of this material he states that he was not conscious of the existence of the Duggan case and that he had apparently forgotten or overlooked the other cases. He agrees that the information provided by him was not correct. In this context also it should be stated that Official B who had actually possessed the Duggan file states that he did not recall it when the investigation commenced. The file was actually turned up by Official C who was assisting in the investigation.'

During his evidence Official A, Matthew Russell, in my opinion an excellent and experienced man in matters of extradition law, also gave a number of reasons why the Smyth case had taken seven months to come to the attention of the Attorney General and why it had not been expedited with the urgency that the case necessitated. He claimed that he erroneously believed 'that Fr Smyth was residing at Kilnacrott Abbey and that in consequence he was not a danger to the community at large'. He added that had he known that Fr Smyth was at large within the community, he would have given the case priority over other cases. He also stated that the fact that the UK authorities and/or the RUC did not press the extradition request and made no contact with the Irish Attorney General's office until 29 September 1993 indicated a lack of urgency as far as they were concerned. The combined effect of these factors, together with other inordinately heavy demands on his time and the need also to consider the legal issue, was that the file was simply not processed and – the legal issue apart – was left to lie dormant.

Official A's letter of apology was also included in the report. In it he stated: 'I also very much regret the embarrassment which this whole affair has caused to the Government and to Mr Harry Whelehan, S.C.'

The conclusions eventually reached by the sub-committee were as follows:

1   The seven months delay was totally unacceptable notwith-standing the explanations given;
2   The only person who knew of the Fr Smyth extradition request and Warrants was Official A in whose custody the file remained at all times from the date of commencement of the extradition process until the time the controversy arose;
3   There is no evidence that any outside influence was involved in the delay in the processing of the Warrants;
4   Neither the former Attorney General, nor the Government were made aware of the existence of the Fr Smyth extradition request until the controversy arose in the Autumn of 1994;
5   The Smyth case was not the first case in which section 50(2)(bbb) of the Extradition Act 1965 as amended was considered;
6   Inaccurate information was given to the Taoiseach, the Minister of Justice and the Chief Whip;
7   The procedures in place in the Attorney General's office at the relevant time for the processing of extradition cases were seriously defective;

8   Had the new procedures been in place it is clear that no delay would have occurred.

The conclusions of the investigation were a huge relief to me. I had suffered so many personal attacks on my conduct during the days and weeks following the fall of the government that it was good to see my own and my cabinet's actions fully vindicated.

In his statement to the Dáil on 4 April 1995 the chairman of the investigating sub-committee, Mr Wallace, expanded on the unusual background to the fall of the government when 'what was widely considered to be an excellent Government fell in mid-term because of disagreement over a relatively small matter, namely the appointment of a new President of the High Court. The fact that the crisis emerged within a few months of the Northern Ireland ceasefire, undoubtedly the greatest political breakthrough on this island over the last 25 years, added to the general sense of disbelief and shock.'

The chairman then assessed the various issues which the inquiry had addressed in its task of understanding why the crisis arose. The first was the appointment of Harry Whelehan. On this point, he said, the evidence was clear that most people, including myself, considered the matter settled when the cabinet sub-committee arrived at an agreement. 'When the Courts and Court Officers bill was drafted in retrospect, it seems clear, that Deputy Reynolds should have appointed Mr Whelehan immediately as President of the High Court. While his sensitivity to Deputy Spring's pre- dicament was admirable, it was not politically wise. Similarly, his agreement to various requests for postponement of the appointment ultimately paid a poor dividend. By the time the Cabinet met on the fateful Friday events had been complicated further by the Fr Brendan Smyth case.'

The chairman then continued with the observation that although the government partnership was most successful, there existed a serious difference of opinion within the Labour Party on the desirability of being in that partnership. Many members were committed to the administration, but there were other very influential figures who viewed the partnership as a liability, especially as they watched their party's initial popularity diminish in its performance in the European elections, various by-elections and a range of opinion polls, and came to realize that there was a definite possibility of Labour losing seats at the next general election. Dick Spring, consequently, was being pulled in two different directions, thus rendering the government extremely vulnerable in a crisis.

The opposition parties, too, realized that they were in an extremely poor position to pressurize the then exceptionally strong government and that they could face another seven or eight years on the opposition benches unless they found some means of undermining the Fianna Fáil–Labour partnership. The government was performing so well on the economy and Northern Ireland that the only realistic prospect of bringing it down was on smaller issues. The emergence of the Brendan Smyth case offered such an opportunity.

It was clear that Harry Whelehan had no knowledge of the Father Smyth case. The core issue, therefore, was whether or not his failure to deal with the administrative problem in his office was sufficiently serious to affect his suitability as president of the High Court. As the sub-committee agreed, 'the presence of the Taoiseach, Deputy Reynolds, the Tánaiste Deputy Spring and Mr Whelehan at the Friday Cabinet meeting should have made it possible to deal with the dilemma immediately ... However, the request to the Attorney

General, Mr Fitzsimons, to undertake a full examination of the Fr Smyth file, can be interpreted only as indicating a determination on the part of the Taoiseach, Deputy Reynolds, to obtain as much information as possible on the issue for the forthcoming Dáil sitting.'

The chairman then addressed the problem of the confusion over the relevance of the Duggan case by saying:

'In my opinion Deputy Reynolds was absolutely correct not to have mentioned the Duggan case in his Tuesday speech in the House because the implications were too great for its introduction without absolute written confirmation by the new Attorney General. In fact Deputy Reynolds could rightly have been criticised had he detailed the Duggan case on the Tuesday.

'On Wednesday 16 November 1994, Deputy Reynolds strongly criticised Mr Whelehan because of the omission of a reference to the Duggan case in his report to the Cabinet, based largely on a text supplied by Mr Fitzsimons and the Labour party. With the benefit of hindsight, since those specific criticisms were advanced in an attempt to bestow a grossly exaggerated importance on the relevance of the Duggan case, they were extremely unfair to Mr Whelehan. Deputy Reynolds honourably expressed regret in that regard when giving evidence to the subcommittee. The fact that Deputy Reynolds left those comments in his speech, even when the agreement with Deputy Spring had broken down, is a clear indication of the integrity of his behaviour throughout those events.'

The part played by the new Attorney General, Mr Fitzsimons, was summarized as follows: 'Mr Fitzsimons was the central figure in the events of 14–16 November. Before assessing his role, it is important to fully accept the difficulty of his position. A highly respected member of the Bar, he had what can only be described as a baptism of fire on his first full day as Attorney General. His performance proved to be critical in the overall matter. In particular his insistence on the importance of the Duggan case provided the defining issue on which the fate of the Government was eventually sealed. There is no evidence to suggest that Mr Fitzsimons acted in anything other than an honourable manner throughout. However, his inexperience of the political environment, combined with his failure to keep working notes, probably contributed to the large number of instances in which his evidence seems to be a source of disagreement.'

The chairman then listed the various inconsistencies of the evidence in the 980-page report, and concluded by saying, 'no matter how one assesses the evidence it seems clear that the crisis originated and developed because of political mistakes and misunderstandings rather than any act of wrong doing. Hopefully those who made extremely critical and hurtful comments in the immediate aftermath of the crisis will now generously set the record straight.'

Martin Mansergh, in his evidence, had also vindicated me when he said:

'Albert Reynolds is no longer Taoiseach. The suggestion that he misled or sought to mislead the Dáil or practised deceit is in my opinion a grossly unfair and unjust slur on his reputation and integrity. Mr Reynolds did this country great – and I hope lasting – service, by the courage he showed in helping to bring about peace over his three-year tenure. As one of his closest advisers, I appeal to this committee, whatever other conclusions it may come to about these unhappy events, to exonerate Mr Reynolds and his colleagues from the charge of misleading or deliberately withholding important information from the Dáil. If mistakes were made, they were made elsewhere. Is it not enough for the Labour Party, whose work in partnership with Fianna Fáil will be remembered with honour, that the relationship is now terminated, that they continue in Government with others? I would hope, but I am not so naïve as to expect, that the dishonourable charges made against Mr Reynolds will be dropped as unjustified and unsustainable, so that he will have his good name and reputation restored to him in the highest assembly of the nation.'

19

A WIDER WORLD

In December 1994 I returned from an EU meeting in Essen at which John Major and I had received a standing ovation and Helmut Kohl had delivered a speech in which he paid tribute to what we had achieved in bringing peace to Northern Ireland. It was, he said, unprecedented not just in the history of the two islands, but also in terms of the European experience. A few days later, on 15 December, we celebrated the first anniversary of the Downing Street Declaration.

The new Framework Document setting out the political, legal and constitutional way forward for the people of Northern Ireland was ready to go to press – the very document that would become, in essence, the 'Good Friday Agreement'. Both British and Irish government officials had engaged in developing the document. I must say I agreed with John Major's opinion when he said: 'Much of what was the Good Friday Agreement was in fact the Downing Street Declaration and the Framework Document with knobs on. I don't wish to undersell what was achieved but that's what it was and it wouldn't have been obtained so quickly had they not been in place.'

I still hoped that, despite everything, I would remain involved and that I would be able to play a part in forging and implementing future developments in the peace process. Indeed, Bertie Ahern had already told me that he wanted me to stay on with special responsibilities for the North – but he then appointed Ray Burke as shadow Minister for Foreign Affairs. One of the snakes had come out of the grass, as I had been warned by Seán Duignan they would. Ray Burke had been one of the fellows I had dropped when I was appointed Taoiseach: so no love lost there, and not a hope of any future official involvement. My time in government was over.

John Major:

'I was very sorry to lose Albert. Extremely sorry, because we had a good relationship and we were making progress and I knew we'd continue to make progress. So yes it was a blow and I also felt extremely sorry for him. I wondered whether malign fate was snatching away a chance for peace – but we were lucky with John Bruton.'

I was not so sure about John Bruton. He was seen to favour the Unionist side more than the Nationalists, and I feared that progress in the peace process would now slow down. I was desperately concerned that this should not happen. We could not just sit back and wait for it to evolve; it was at a fragile stage of its development. Unless promises were kept and things were seen to move forward it would be all too easy for some of the more extremist paramilitary groups, who were still out there, to use any sign of stalling in the process as an excuse to return to violence.

Martin McGuinness:

'The difference between Albert and John Bruton was that

Albert had, for want of a better word, a way with him. He had a certain way of dealing with people that clearly suggested inclusivity. Albert also comes from Longford and it's almost a border constituency. He travelled extensively in the North, knew Northern Nationalists, Republicans, Unionists, Loyalists of all descriptions, so he had an easy-going way with him. John Bruton wouldn't have been as grounded in the North as Albert was, and in my view, his inclination to be grounded wouldn't have been as grounded as Albert's was anyway. So we had a situation where, I suppose – when I met Albert or Gerry met Albert, we felt at ease with him, he felt at ease with us. When we met John Bruton he didn't feel at ease with us, and we treated him with considerable suspicion because he came from the Fine Gael party.'

Gusty Spence:

'Albert had played a pivotal role and vital beyond a question of doubt . . . I'm trying to think of another person that would have carried it, definitely Bruton wouldn't have done it nor Haughey, there was too much suspicion of him with the arms trial.

'Cometh the day, cometh the man.'

Reverend Roy Magee:

'I think the Loyalists were convinced that he [Albert] had delivered a very good end, that it was a real decision that would be carried on between governments rather than individuals. I know in my own mind there was a concern, would there be anyone that would be able to take his place, who would get the support and the trust of the Unionist and Loyalist people of Northern Ireland.'

I remained a member of the Forum for Peace and Reconciliation which we had established at the time of the Downing Street Declaration. It provided a bridge for all parties to join in the democratic process and we met regularly.

I realized that, following the ceasefires, people would want a place where they could go to discuss the way forward. The 'Friday Forum' was that place where all sides could join in the process of reconciliation, and certainly it brought Sinn Féin to the table, together with other political groups and parties.

The DUP, led by Paisley, were still resistant to joining in any talks. They were growing in numbers as a party but, as their leader had forewarned me some years back, he would not join in any talks until he was number one. And he would be.

I had so much experience to offer, I could not sit back and do nothing. I contacted people on all sides and told them that I was available if I could be of any help. Sinn Féin responded immediately. Gerry Adams was travelling extensively by this time, so it was agreed that Martin McGuinness and I should stay in touch. Both Sinn Féin leaders were very concerned about the new government in Dublin, its attitude towards the Republicans and the effect the change would have on the prospects for developing the peace process. If we wanted to keep the thing alive, it was important that I kept myself available.

Martin McGuinness:

'I had never met Albert in my life before those initial meetings, and in the aftermath of those original meetings, it was obvious that he and I were friends and that we both recognized that we, along with many others, were a part of something that was very important for the island of Ireland in terms of the development of the peace process. I think also I was struck that Albert had a particular soft spot for Northerners and passionately wanted to use whatever influence he had to encourage the process along. I think I was convinced of his bona fides and he was convinced of my bona fides, so we were effectively working to achieve the same objective.

'We still maintain contact – even to this day Albert will ring me every now and again. Back then he would come up and speak with me on a regular basis. Honestly, I think that his contribution to the process has been very important.

'We would have useful discussions and there were many opportunities down the years, even after he left government, when he and I got together to discuss how the situation was progressing, for me to get his view of where things were at, and for him to get my view. And every now and again Albert would offer to talk to people – and to talk to people on the Unionist side, particularly focusing on people who were fairly negative about the process in an attempt to get them to be more positive.

'I wouldn't say he was acting on my behalf but he was acting in the best interests of the process.

'For example, the conversation I had with Albert in the aftermath of the Paddy Mayhew statement was around our concern that the issue of arms was being used by the Conservative government to prevent discussions taking place, and we were concerned that if that was the case it would be very damaging to the process.'

I had always been of the opinion that the question of de-commissioning should be put aside until all parties came together for inclusive and democratic talks around the negotiating table, and we had deliberately excluded all reference to the subject in the Downing Street Declaration. Sinn Féin had been eager to join such talks as soon as possible, but John Major was insistent that peace should be seen to hold and that a period of non-violence should elapse before this could happen. This became one of the conditions of the cease-fire: that Sinn Féin would be included in such talks once there had been a cessation of violence for six months.

I had always argued with John Major that asking the IRA

to hand over their weapons before Sinn Féin could be included in multi-party talks simply would not work. Throughout the history of Republican uprisings, the IRA, by tradition, had never surrendered to the demand for decommissioning and I knew failure to recognize that would be a serious stumbling block. The strategy, the priority in all our talks had been peace first, followed by detailed negotiations which would then lead to a political settlement. This had been the understanding throughout Martin Mansergh's discussions with the Republicans and my contacts with Gerry Adams, and one of the subjects in my talks with John Major and the British government. To make decommissioning a precondition to talks was to take a path to certain failure. I believed John Major had understood this, but after I left government the British, now supported by John Bruton, had other ideas which delayed progress.

They were still concerned that the IRA ceasefire statement did not include the word 'permanent', and to compensate for this they now determined that before Sinn Féin could be included in multi-party talks the handover of weapons had to be initiated. Before I stepped down there was a meeting between Sinn Féin and British civil servants; but there was no trust, despite the ceasefire, and the situation remained at stalemate.

Decommissioning had been a point of contention waiting to break through since the first attempts to negotiate a ceasefire. This issue was now being used by the British to hold up the talks. I had always asserted that once peace was truly negotiated and a political settlement agreed, then the disposal of arms should be dealt with expeditiously. As far back as the 1980s, in earlier ministerial roles I had held meetings with Qadhafi in Libya, on state business, and from our personal talks I had gained a very good idea of the extent of arms and weapons, supplied by Libya, that were still being held by the IRA. McGuinness rebuffed Martin Mansergh when he tried to raise with him the subject of arms from Libya. I had expected as much, but he let them know that I knew the details.

Unfortunately John Bruton was quite hostile in his attitude to Sinn Féin, although as the outgoing Taoiseach I had briefed him on the state of the peace process. To his credit he had asked Martin Mansergh, with his intricate knowledge and invaluable contacts in the Republican movement, to stay on as an adviser, but Martin's loyalty was deeply rooted in Fianna Fáil, and he refused: he simply could not see his way to working for Fine Gael.

John Bruton took over at a very delicate stage of the negotiations when, as McGuinness has already pointed out, the people involved respected and understood one another and were engaged in working for the same objective. Bruton was not part of that continuity, as was evident when he joined with the British in making decommissioning a precondition for talks, in breach of my agreement with Sinn Féin.

The British were also seeking to prevent Gerry Adams going back to America. They lobbied to prevent him getting a visa, they lobbied to stop him from being invited to the President's St Patrick's Day event, and most of all they lobbied to stop him fundraising for Sinn Féin. It led to very angry confrontations between Britain and America, and most of all between the President and John Major. By then I was not Taoiseach, but in the past I had warned Major during our private talks that if Sinn Féin were to pursue a political route, they would need funding. The Connolly House group had promised Sinn Féin financial help in setting up a headquarters in Washington, but like any political party it could only be maintained by serious fundraising, and in talks with them and with Ted Kennedy I had emphasized that it was important

Gerry Adams should be allowed into America to do just that.

With my help, Ted Kennedy, along with other high-profile Irish Americans, was very persuasive in getting the President's support on this issue, but Major was livid:

'There was one occasion when Clinton and I had a furious row that went on for days over whether Adams should be let in to fundraise for the IRA after the Americans had promised us he wouldn't be. That was the worst single argument I had with Bill Clinton. Our personal relations were very good. He's a difficult person not to like and he's very charming, but on this issue I felt let down and we had a furious row about it – but I can't recall that it caused any difficulty between Albert and me. I mean, Albert was bound to wheel America in to help on his side, of course he was, but I was quite pragmatic about that and it wasn't going to make much difference to me. As far as I was concerned the issue was between London and Dublin and I considered New York, Washington to be a subsidiary player, to be frank. They could be helpful or they could be a hindrance, generally they sought to be helpful, generally they were helpful . . . and I was grateful for that, but at the end of the day the agreement was going to be between Dublin and London.'

It seemed to be a deliberate attempt by both governments to stall the peace process. The situation was further exacerbated when, on a visit to Washington in March 1995, the British Secretary of State for Northern Ireland Patrick Mayhew set out his three preconditions for talks which became known as the Washington principles. The key demand was that the IRA disarmed progressively, and it spelled out that this would entail 'the actual decommissioning of some arms as a tangible confidence building measure'. Only by agreeing to these conditions, he told journalists, could Republicans remove what he described as 'their self-imposed disqualification'.

As Martin Mansergh comments:

'The Mayhew principles were laid down partly to spoil the effects of Adams being received in the White House. It was also to help the British Tories keep the Unionists on board in Westminster.'

Martin McGuinness:

'The position we were in at the time with Sinn Féin, the British and the Irish governments was that decommissioning was a stupid precondition put forward by Paddy Mayhew. It was not mentioned in the Downing Street Declaration ... in fact Mayhew's statement was made when Gerry Adams was there in Washington and we in the Sinn Féin leadership were very angry that it should be used as an excuse by John Major ... which we effectively saw as an attempt by the British government to block the prospect of negotiations. The negotiations did begin but we in Sinn Féin did not join in until 1997.'

The stance on decommissioning was indeed proving to be a big stumbling block in the progress to peace. Even within the new Irish government under Dick Spring and John Bruton there were radically different views about whether or not it was included in the ceasefire deal. Dick Spring understood that it was, Sinn Féin was adamant it wasn't. I just knew I had a gentleman's agreement with John Major that Sinn Féin would be included in talks after six months of non-violence.

John Major:

'If we'd let them in without decommissioning we'd have lost everybody else in the talks. This was like a multi-faceted Rubik's cube, trying to keep everybody on board: for every action there is a reaction, and if they had come in without decommissioning we would have lost other people we needed to talk to elsewhere in the system, that was the point.

'That was a political reality we had to face. I wasn't being obstructive or inflexible: I was just boxed in.

'... There wouldn't have been any Unionists, there might not have been any non-Unionists, there would have been nobody else there: that was the problem.

'Who was it who was the problem? The people with the weapons were the problem, so if you wished to have talks you obviously had to hold out for decommissioning.

'If it hadn't been for the necessity of the "action–reaction" thing, one could have accelerated things, but it was a reality. It wasn't us being difficult, it was stone cold political reality, without commitments on that we couldn't do anything.'

Early in 1995, the long-heralded appointment of an American envoy to Northern Ireland was made. I had met George Mitchell at the St Patrick's Day celebrations the previous year. He was Democrat Majority Leader in the Senate at the time, but had decided not to run for re-election. That month, March 1994, President Clinton had called him into a meeting.

George Mitchell:

'I had decided not to seek re-election that year. I went to the White House where Clinton and I had a long talk for a couple of hours and he tried to talk me out of it. I told him I'd made up my mind. He said to me, "If I call upon you to do a mission, would you be willing to do it or are you sick of politics?"

'I said, "No, I'm not sick of politics, this is a hard decision for me."

'He did not at the time mention Northern Ireland but it's very clear to me in retrospect that that's what he had in mind.'

George Mitchell was the man Clinton had recommended to me that day in March 1993 as a possible envoy for Northern Ireland – the one I had turned down until the timing was right. Now the timing was right; but Clinton was also aware that the British were still sensitive to the word 'envoy'; so they designated him 'special adviser to the President on economic affairs in Northern Ireland'. His specific function was to organize a White House conference on trade and investment in Northern Ireland to take place in May of that year. First, however, he was introduced to Tony Lake, Clinton's National Security Adviser, and my other friends in the White House security office, Nancy Soderberg and Trina Vargo, who filled him in on Northern Ireland. He was also dispatched to Dublin to meet with me in early February 1995.

George Mitchell:

'Albert was deeply involved. In my book I made it clear that the foundation for all this [the Good Friday Agreement] was laid previously in the prior agreement and discussions that Albert was instrumental in organizing between himself, John Hume and Gerry Adams. The key was in all those prior efforts. The decision to get the three strands of Nationalism, the Irish government, Sinn Féin and the SDLP, into a discussion really made the difference.

'When I first came the IRA ceasefire had been in effect for about six months, and the Loyalist [ceasefire] for about three months. At that period I was working solely on economic things. I had no conception, really no idea, I would be staying on. My commitment was simply to do the economic conference which was in May 1995 ... the day before the conference ended, ... Clinton called and said, "I'm going to speak at that conference tomorrow and I'd like to be able to say that you'll stay on for another six months," but as far as I was concerned, it was all in the economic context.

'Later in that year the governments asked me to chair a commission on the subject of paramilitary decommissioning. The way it worked was that the two governments agreed on me as chairman and then each government nominated one other person. The Irish chose Harri Holkeri, a previous prime minister of Finland, and the British chose John de Chastelain, a Canadian general.

'That's when we met with Albert as a group because we were trying to get as much information as possible and we felt that Albert was a key figure in the whole thing, in the entire process of getting the ceasefires and in his previous work with John Major.'

We met at Dublin Castle on a Sunday – Holkeri, de Chastelain, George Mitchell and myself – and we spent hours, far more time than we'd intended, going over every aspect of it, so that they would have a feel for it all. I took them through the years leading up to the peace process and the ceasefires, the secret negotiations and the gentlemen's agreement that had existed between John Major and me that Sinn Féin would be brought into talks with the other constitutional parties within six months of a ceasefire, and Sinn Féin's frustrations that it had never been honoured. I explained the Sinn Féin attitude to decommissioning and that it had never been part of the Downing Street Declaration, and I warned that it was a sensitive subject and that they should tread carefully.

Following my resignation, my colleagues at Fianna Fáil had put my name forward for the Nobel Peace Prize. I was deeply honoured to be nominated and to have my name considered along with that of John Major and John Hume. I was still passionately determined to see the conflict ended on our island and, despite being 'retired', I undertook a gruelling round of lectures and interviews promoting the peace process around Europe, the United States, Australia and Canada. I was determined to play as visible a part as possible in stirring the two governments into action to find a formula for inter-party talks. I was concerned and very disappointed that the promises we had made to include Sinn Féin were still not implemented. In an interview with the London *Observer* I remarked that 'there was supposed to be a generosity from both governments. The Irish government has shown it, but the British have not. The British may have miscalculated that they can sit back and do nothing. But if they [the IRA] went back to the armed conflict people won't blame them because they have shown good faith.'

John Major:

'We were aware it was frustrating. We had done what I thought was a great deal. At some political cost, we had lifted many restrictions on the IRA, and were waiting for progress. And the IRA was marking time. They'd seen the opinion polls, they saw the Conservative Party was in trouble and unlikely to be re-elected. They thought they might get a different and better deal from an incoming Labour government and so they were holding back. If we had been ahead in the opinion polls instead of behind I think we would have made much faster progress because they would have continued to deal with us.'

As far as I was concerned – and Sinn Féin – it was frustrating all round. They were calling on the British to allow them into talks and the British were firmly keeping them out. I tried to warn John Major that things were breaking down. I was very aware of how fragile the situation was, and so was Martin Mansergh from his continuing contact with the Republicans. In every interview I gave I pushed the British to be generous in their approach; I even sent a personal message to Downing Street that unless they accepted Sinn Féin into multi-party talks and moved the peace process forward, there was a possibility that the violence could return.

In the *Irish Independent* I stated:

'Commitments were given in the Downing Street Declaration, and in many, many statements by both governments and by both prime ministers, that if there was a full

A WIDER WORLD

cessation of violence the British government would be
generous in its approach, and that all parties which had left
violence behind as a means of achieving political progress
would have the right to fully participate in the democratic
process.' I added that political leaders were 'lagging behind the
views of the people and that the younger people, especially
those who have never seen such a quality of life, have no desire
to return to the bad old days'.

However, only a few months later, on 9 February 1996, the
bad old days returned with a vengeance. Shortly before, I had
written to John Major to tell him that I had received
indications from Republican sources that peace was heading
for breakdown within a matter of weeks. Tragically it did
when a bomb ripped through Canary Wharf in the City of
London, killing two people and inflicting millions of pounds'
worth of damage. It seemed the ceasefire was broken. Tired of
peacefully waiting for inclusion in talks, the IRA were back to
seeking their objective in the bad old way. The report of
George Mitchell's International Decommissioning Body had
been published just a couple of days before. It recommended
that arms should be decommissioned at the same time as
political talks began, as a compromise between the British
stance of decommissioning in advance and the Sinn Féin
demand that it should come as a result of multi-party talks
began and negotiations. The Canary Wharf bombing
annulled all that. The ceasefire was over and Sinn Féin was
banned from the political process. It was impasse for another
year.

In Dublin, the rainbow coalition was experiencing
difficulties, in-fighting and personality clashes. It had been
hard enough trying to blend two parties in a coalition government; with three there was bound to be trouble.

There were serious disagreements between Dick Spring

and John Bruton, as well as between the Taoiseach and officials in Iveagh House – particularly between Bruton and Seán O hUiginn, who, on the recommendation of Martin Mansergh, was acting as his adviser on Republican affairs. By June 1997 it was all over and another election was called. Fianna Fáil was back in government with the help of three Independents and the PDs, now under the leadership of Mary Harney. Bertie Ahern was appointed Taoiseach, with Harney as Tánaiste.

Sadly, the rainbow coalition had had a negative effect on the peace process. Within little more than a year of their taking power, the ceasefire was over.

Martin Mansergh assesses the situation as follows:

'Sinn Féin were prepared to give John Bruton the benefit of the doubt and they tried to work with him but things got increasingly difficult and it broke down. Now, of course, there would have been difficult problems to face even if Albert had stayed in power, but I don't believe it would have broken down. Bruton did meet with Sinn Féin but he would never meet Hume and Adams together, in fact even in the autumn of '95, before the breakdown, he refused a request from John Hume to meet with himself and Gerry Adams because he thought it might have an adverse effect on the Unionists and that went down very badly.

'With hindsight, looking back on the fall of the Fianna Fáil–Labour government, I think it had a negative effect on the peace process, but I would say also that politically, while Fianna Fáil lost out in the short term and went into opposition, the Labour Party were the people who lost out in the longer term. If they had remained in government with Fianna Fáil, they would have been there almost certainly following the next general election. Instead they lost the '97 election, they lost the 2002 and the 2007 elections. So their strategy proved to be a very expensive one from their point of view.'

During the previous year, Bertie and I had had a couple of lunches at his request, during which he had proposed that my name should go forward as the Fianna Fáil nominee for the coveted post of President. At first I turned the suggestion down. But then I agreed that, in the event that Mary Robinson did not seek a second term, I might consider it. We met again in early 1997 at McGrattan's restaurant near Government Buildings. It was evident at the time that the Bruton government was about to fall and an election was on the cards. Bertie was after as many seats as he could get for Fianna Fáil and wanted me to stand again as deputy for Longford–Roscommon to ensure the seat for the coming general election. He also pointed out that my son Philip could hold the seat in a by-election if I succeeded in winning the presidency, which he was sure I would, or so he said.

I had actually been considering retiring from politics at that election, but the challenge of becoming a presidential candidate was tempting. At that point nothing was decided. My family, Kathleen in particular, were not at all keen on me running for the Phoenix Park; and besides, Mary Robinson had still not announced her intentions. Bertie, however, was very persistent and persuasive, saying he believed that I had the right credentials for the job. He also brought up the prospect of my becoming involved at government level in trying to re-establish peace in Northern Ireland should Fianna Fáil get back in, which I had no doubt they would.

In March that year Robinson made public her decision to stand down as President. In June I was re-elected deputy by my loyal constituency, Fianna Fáil was back in government with the PDs and Bertie, as Taoiseach, endorsed me for the presidency and confirmed that my name would be the only one from Fianna Fáil in the running for the Áras. I began to organize my campaign with the support of Brian Cowen and Charlie McCreevy.

My hopes of being brought into government as a peace envoy for Northern Ireland were quickly dashed. Ray Burke, back as Minister for Foreign Affairs, made sure of that. Also Bertie Ahern, who had retained the services of Martin Mansergh as his adviser on Northern policy, was keen to follow things through and to keep the central role for himself. It was obvious there would be no official appointment for me; but the opinion polls for my nomination for President were looking good.

Mary McAleese, at the time vice-president of Queen's University, had also put her hat into the ring and in mid-July had sought the backing of Ahern. Significantly, her backers had sent him and all other Fianna Fáil deputies, outgoing senators and MEPs her eleven-page CV and academic record. I did not receive a copy. It was evident that she was working hard to win the support of those who were opposed to me, and there were quite a few. Ahern had brought back a number of those I had removed from office, and there was little love lost between us.

There were rumours of others entering the race: John Hume and David Andrews were mentioned, but both declared they would not be running. Bertie continued to proclaim in the press that he was endorsing me as the only Fianna Fáil candidate. I knew that Mary Harney and the PDs had told Bertie they would not support my nomination bid, but I knew many members of Fianna Fáil would. Then, suddenly, the name of a former Minister of Agriculture, Michael O'Kennedy, was put forward – encouraged, it was rumoured, by Bertie. He was a strange choice. I didn't dwell on it at the time because he had little chance of winning, but he would serve to split the vote.

The race was now intensifying and my backers were confident that I was the front-runner. Of the members of the cabinet, only David Andrews, Brian Cowen and Charlie McCreevy – and Bertie; or so he assured me – were supporting my vote. Many of the backbenchers, however, were behind me, and the opinion polls, too, seemed strongly in my favour. I was still feeling confident that I was in with a very good chance; after all, I appeared to have the backing of the Taoiseach, and as a former Taoiseach myself, I had experience in international affairs at state level and I had been a leading figure in the peace process. The other main contender, Mary McAleese, though a worthy academic, was nevertheless an unsuccessful Dáil candidate who had never served any time in government; and Michael O'Kennedy, the wild card, seemed to be gathering very little support at all.

However, behind the scenes, although I did not realize it at the time, forces were gathering behind McAleese. On the eve of the election I had a phone call from the journalist and broadcaster John Cooney, who had received an authoritative 'deep throat' message informing him that the vote was swinging behind McAleese and he should say as much in his hourly radio news bulletins. He didn't mention the source of his information, but both he and I knew that his tipping McAleese to win would definitely sway those who were still undecided as to which way to go. Everybody forecast that O'Kennedy would not be in the frame but I had no idea the competition would be so close. In the event, during his bulletin on the morning of the vote Cooney hedged his bets by moving McAleese up the field, calling it 'a neck and neck race with the former Taoiseach'.

Rumours had filtered through that Bertie wanted McAleese as the Fianna Fáil nominee and that, unbeknown to me, he had held a meeting with Fianna Fáil very late the previous night, at about 1.30 a.m. I was advised by a number of friends that I should pull out as I was being set up. I could not believe this was true.

I felt reassured when, on the very morning of the vote, Bertie phoned me at home to ask if I thought I had the required number of votes to win. I said I believed I had, and we discussed who would be my director for the presidential election campaign itself. We even talked about a fundraising event in America. He also made a point of telling me that there would be no need to give a speech at the meeting before the vote. Imagine my shock, then, when at that very meeting the chairman, Rory O'Hanlon, announced that the candidates would each have five minutes in which to speak!

Neither O'Kennedy nor I was aware that we would have to speak, but Mary McAleese was well prepared; she delivered her speech with confidence from an impressive three-page script whereas O'Kennedy and I were completely thrown and forced to speak off the cuff. I believed we had both been set up.

There was a further surprise when none of the three declared candidates was formally proposed and seconded, which was extremely unusual. I became even more suspicious when I won the first vote with only a very narrow majority, getting only forty-nine votes to McAleese's forty-two and O'Kennedy's twenty-one. Now I knew why O'Kennedy had been rowed in. In the second ballot his vote was split: four of his supporters backed me and the rest went for McAleese, while I also suffered four defections and one of my supporters left the meeting.

I suppose with hindsight the fact that I had nothing to offer the backbenchers as an incentive – no jobs to offer or, more significantly, to take away – might go some way to explaining the result. Cynical, perhaps, but realistic. Whatever the reason,

I lost the vote and McAleese emerged triumphant. I was sure that Bertie's pretence of remaining neutral was just that, a pretence. He even made a big show that he had cast his vote in my favour – the first vote, that is: no one knew how he voted with the second – but I remember Brian Crowley, a Fianna Fáil MEP, sitting next to me and, as Bertie, smiling, held up his first vote card with my name on it, whispering: 'You're f—ed!'

Of one thing I was sure – it was inconceivable that Fianna Fáil would have backed McAleese without their leader's connivance or encouragement, albeit through intermediaries. Bertie had 'shafted me' again, as John Cooney recently wrote in the *Irish Independent*. It became obvious to me that, in a tactic worthy of Machiavelli, O'Kennedy had been persuaded to join the race at a late date for the sole purpose of getting Mary McAleese elected on transfers when he was, inevitably, eliminated.

I learned later that O'Kennedy had been about to leave the contest at one point because of what he saw as shabby treatment by the Taoiseach, but that others had persuaded him to stay on. I also learned that his supporters had been strongly canvassed, with Ahern's approval, to ensure they transferred their votes to McAleese.

I admit I was bitterly disappointed, but there were other challenges out in the world and I was ready to take them on.

By that stage all my children had received university degrees. Now it was my turn. In 1995 I was very proud to be awarded an honorary degree as a Doctor of Law by the National University of Ireland. All my family came to my graduation ceremony on that occasion; but they were not able to be present at all the other ceremonies that followed, at the many other universities, in America and Australia, Canada and Europe, where I was honoured for my part in the peace process.

Perhaps one of my most treasured memories is of 17 March 1998, when, wearing the traditional silk top hat and tricolour sash, I marched down Fifth Avenue behind the 'fighting 69th', the military escort that led the New York St Patrick's Day parade – a singular honour for an Irish politician. It was one of the most exhilarating and proudest days of my life. Proposed by my friend Bill Flynn, I had become the first ever Irish-born Grand Marshal of the annual St Patrick's Day parade. Two million people gathered to watch. Many of them were dressed in traditional Aran sweaters. The more extrovert among them sported green painted moustaches and bald heads, most were swathed with the tricolour. It was an experience I savoured – to lead one's fellow Irish living abroad, men and women from every county in Ireland, in that great celebration. That year marked the bicentenary of the 1798 rebellion and felt even more special for that, imbued as it was with the spirit of all those who died for the cause of religious freedom for all.

It was time to travel the world. My experiences with the peace process in Ireland led to invitations from around the globe to lecture and advise on conflict resolution in divided countries, where violence continues to inflict misery and human suffering. Of course, the peace in Ireland was only in its first delicate stages of development, and there would be many stumbles before it was firmly established; but at least it was on its way. The peace process was always at the forefront of my consciousness and my constant priority, and if I had experiences that could help others then I was happy to share them.

Such travels also gave me the opportunity to meet up with old acquaintances, people whom I had met during my years in government. One of those was Pervez Musharraf, whom I had met and got on well with when he was Prime Minister and Chief of Staff of the Pakistan Army. In October 1999 he effected a coup d'état, ousting Nawaz Sharif. Dismissing the national and provincial legislative assemblies, he assumed the title of Chief Executive and in so doing became Pakistan's de facto head of government, the fourth army chief of Pakistan to have assumed executive control of the country. It was at this point that he called me. Pakistan at that time was seen as a haven for terrorists, and most Western countries had in place a policy of sanctions against it. One of Musharraf's objectives was to change this, but he had no idea how to get his message across that in future things were going to be different in Pakistan. He asked for my personal advice.

I happened to be over in Pakistan at a time when Clinton's presidency was coming to an end. One of his final engagements was a state visit to India and Bangladesh. Musharraf was not an internationally accepted head of state at the time and so Pakistan was not on Clinton's agenda. Besides which, there were strained relations between India and Pakistan; you were friends with either one or the other – and at that time India was the preferred friend.

However, Musharraf was anxious to restore trading relations between the West and Pakistan, and he insisted that it would be seen as an immense insult if Clinton was in the East and did not pay his respects to him as the new Prime Minister of Pakistan. He asked me if I could arrange for the American President to make a stop in Pakistan.

I consulted with the American ambassador, who informed me that he was aware of the delicacy of the situation. For Washington to ignore Pakistan represented a breach of protocol that could lead to what little relationship there was deteriorating even further. However, officials in Washington were more concerned with competing with Russia for the trade in India, and were not listening to his advice.

I saw that such a situation could easily have serious consequences, and I considered it right and proper that the President himself should be made aware of this and have the opportunity to make his own decision. Our relationship, begun that St Patrick's Day in 1993, had grown in trust. So I called him on his private number and explained in full the political repercussions of his excluding Pakistan from his state visit. I also added that Musharraf had every intention of combating terrorism in his country, but he needed support; I said he would prove a good ally, but that he and his people would be deeply insulted if the US President were to ignore Pakistan on this final visit to the region.

I'm delighted to say that, following my intervention, Clinton changed his arrangements and spent several hours talking with Musharraf.

Given my role in the peace process in Ireland, Musharraf sought my counsel on other problems he faced, particularly in developing relations with India and structuring a way forward for his country's economy, which was suffering badly from the effects of the constant border tensions. The economy was in a very poor state, and it was hard to see it improving because so much of the national budget, a good 40 per cent, was being spent on the military instead of the social infrastructure. Musharraf was concerned that if he did not deliver a strong economy, the Islamic extremists would become more powerful and influential. It was imperative that good relations with India were restored. Following my advice, a mediator was introduced into the situation – a man I knew well: Senator Edward Kennedy – and a meeting between leaders of the two countries was arranged. Talks continued for over three years after that.

Unfortunately, in 2007, just as the two capitals were discussing plans for a historic summit, Musharraf became embroiled in a public feud with his country's highest court. Eventually he left office, and the peace initiative began a downward slide. Today, however, although there are still outbreaks of violence and terrorism from the different militant factions, the conflict is slowly being resolved and the two sides are talking.

Colonel Qadhafi was another such acquaintance. In my various ministerial roles I had made many contacts in the Middle East through my involvement with different business delegations. Ireland had supplied investment and medical staff for hospitals in Libya, as well as developing the export trade in food, beef and chemicals. We had a good relationship with Libya, at a time when America and Britain were highly sceptical of Qadhafi and particularly suspicious of his support of terrorism. Both countries had sanctions in place against Libya, America because of the Lockerbie plane bombing and Britain because of arms supplies to the IRA.

Two hundred and seventy people had lost their lives in the Lockerbie bombing of 1988, and it was alleged that Qadhafi himself had authorized the atrocity by two of his own officials. When the two Libyans responsible were finally handed over and taken into custody, Qadhafi asked me if the trial could be held in Ireland. I told him that was not possible and that the only place where they would get a fair trial was in The Hague. In the end a special court was set up at Camp Zeist in the Netherlands.

During my talks with Qadhafi I had discussed the subject of compensation for the victims, and an idea had emerged. As many of the victims of the bombing were American, Senator Edward Kennedy had become involved; so I called Senator Kennedy and explained Qadhafi's proposal. I believe it was the first time that compensation to the families of terrorist victims had ever been offered by a state designated as a sponsor of terrorists. The principle established was that compensation should be offered in return for the lifting of sanctions. I was not involved with the actual negotiations, only the principle – which was actually more of a business deal than an acceptance of responsibility by Libya; but it resolved an impasse and helped move things forward.

By 1997 the peace process in Ireland was in crisis, bedevilled by the inactivity of both British and Irish governments who, politically paralysed, still refused to take risks for peace. That year saw the twenty-fifth anniversary of Bloody Sunday in Derry, and the second of the regrettable breakdowns of the ceasefire with the bombing of Canary Wharf. We had travelled a tortuous path to peace and I was loath to see us slip back into more years of violence, death and destruction. Negotiations over decommissioning had been undermining the peace process for eighteen months or more, and although it had never been a precondition for Sinn Féin's entry into talks it was still being used as an excuse. I called on both the British and the Irish governments to seize the initiative to get everyone around the table; to demand an immediate restoration of the 1994 ceasefire by both sides; to immediately and unequivocally accept the Mitchell Principles, and Senator Mitchell's interpretation of how they should be implemented; and to announce the entry of Sinn Féin into talks within a matter of weeks after the first three principles had been implemented and accepted.

I finished by saying: 'The saving of human life is the greatest challenge facing all of us and we must take up that challenge now!' I firmly believed that, and also that a lasting solution to that challenge could only be found through dialogue leading to agreement among all the people living on this island, without outside interference.

On 10 April 1998 the Good Friday Agreement (also known as the Belfast Agreement), almost identical in terms to the Downing Street Declaration and the Framework Document put together by John Major and myself several years previously, was finally ratified, and three new interlocking institutions were set up. Relations within Northern Ireland were addressed by a power-sharing Assembly, designed to operate on an inclusive basis in which all main parties would share in government as members of a permanent coalition. Key decisions were to be taken on a cross-community basis. Relations between the North and the Republic were dealt with through the creation of a North–South Ministerial Council, which would allow cooperation on certain functional issues between the Northern Ireland Assembly and the Irish parliament – which, as a safeguard, could not function without one another. And under strand three, a British–Irish Council was established.

The Omagh bombing on 15 August 1998, in which twenty-nine people were killed, was a cold-blooded and cynical return to violence by a splinter group of Republican paramilitaries calling themselves the Real IRA and was part of a concerted campaign in opposition to the Good Friday Agreement. It was a particularly vicious attack in the middle of a shopping area on a busy Saturday afternoon, and the scenes of bloodshed and human distress were unbelievably harrowing and depressing. It was perhaps one of the worst atrocities of the Troubles, and it received universal condemnation. The mainstream IRA warned the 'Real IRA' that it should disband, and at the time it did suspend operations – but there were others, calling themselves the 'Continuity IRA', who resisted the call to cease fire and operate on occasions even today.

Following the Good Friday Agreement, although everything seemed neatly parcelled up, the political issues of
decommissioning, demilitarization and policing remained
unresolved for a long time, and continue as points of
contention even to this day. The guns had been silenced, but
the old tribal suspicions hadn't, and behind the scenes I was
still meeting with both sides.

The Unionist parties were deeply divided over the agreement, many thinking too much had been conceded to the
Republicans when David Trimble, then leader of the Ulster
Unionist Party and the first Unionist leader to negotiate with
the Republicans, cut the historic deal that led to power-
sharing with Sinn Féin. The Reverend Ian Paisley, leader of
the DUP, was incensed and labelled Trimble a traitor. As
ever, the road to peace was a turbulent one and in 1999, with
Republicans still refusing to decommission arms, Trimble
took the decision to lead his party out of the Assembly.

I still made myself available to anyone, regardless of party,
who wanted to come and see me for advice, and it was during
this troubled period that two members of the DUP met with
me and asked me questions, which I was sure were coming
from Paisley. These meetings were set up by my friend Noel
Gallagher.

The DUP representatives wanted me to explain the ramifications of their new situation in relation to Sinn Féin and the
IRA, and what I thought the Republicans might settle for in a
new democratic process. At the same time, I remonstrated
with Sinn Féin that they would have to accept new arrangements for policing and participate in them, not reject them.
Police reform was an area of both real and symbolic conflict
between Unionists and Nationalists and remains so.

The power-sharing did not last long. In 2002 police in
Northern Ireland raided Sinn Féin's Stormont office and their

other offices in Belfast on suspicion that Republicans were seeking to gain access to sensitive political information. The Unionists, the UUP and the DUP, then refused to remain in government unless Sinn Féin were expelled. This was impossible under the terms of the Good Friday Agreement, and so regrettably the Northern Ireland Assembly was suspended and, for the fourth time in its history, the government of Northern Ireland reverted to direct rule from Westminster.

I looked on in dismay. Over the years there have been so many setbacks and breakdowns in the progress towards peace – though despite them all we are getting there. The UUP remained vulnerable to attack from the DUP and it lost support in succeeding elections. Paisley was on the march to number one, I believed. And on the Nationalist side Sinn Féin was making inroads into the SDLP vote.

In September 2004, as a meeting at Leeds Castle was being organized at which it was hoped intensive negotiations would produce a new agreement between Republicans and Unionists and the restoration of devolved government in Belfast, I gave a speech to a group of students and graduates of the Washington– Ireland programme and a number of business people in Belfast. In it I said:

'A unique opportunity is available these three days at Leeds Castle to all party leaders and the British and Irish governments to grab the advantage now offering itself, to bring to completion the outstanding fundamental aspects of the Belfast Agreement, with all the parties and the two governments agreeing to re-establish an Assembly, that with some adjustments, not fundamental ones, to do with say, accountability, but not leading to a return to a veto situation. Power-sharing must be maintained as the only successful and equitable way forward for all parties, especially the two largest ones: Sinn Féin and the DUP. Then Dr Ian Paisley can be installed as

First Minister for Northern Ireland, a singular honour, that I am sure he has worked all his political life to achieve, and can now lead his party into a bright and peaceful future. He is the man to lead change.

'But before this can take place or simultaneously, I believe that a total and full decommissioning must be carried out, leaving no doubt in anyone's mind about its totality and veracity. The IRA must reduce themselves to a commemorative organization only; demilitarization must take place by all involved, including the British army, and thereby return normality to society. Devolved power, bestowing full management control and legal authority to the Belfast Assembly in relation to policing, justice and equality and that Sinn Féin could then join the PSNI [Police Service of Northern Ireland] Board with confidence – no more political interference from any quarter. When all these actions are completed and all other smaller issues that will arise along the way are complete, then everybody can redirect their energies towards the economic and social development of Northern Ireland.'

The future could be wonderful, but the present still rumbled with strife.

In Drumcree the conflicts of the marching season escalated. Again I was called to secret meetings with parties from both sides to try to resolve this annual battle. The Drumcree marches took place every July and August to mark the anniversary of the Battle of the Boyne in 1690, in which the Protestant William III – William of Orange – defeated the deposed Stuart – and Catholic – king, James II. Before 12 July every year the Orange Order marched to the service at Drumcree church, then followed the same route along the Garvaghy Road that they had walked since 1985. Since then Nationalist housing had been built along the road, and that had led to an annual incitement to violence between the marchers and the residents, until finally the parades were banned. The problem was, it was the Chief Constable of the RUC who proclaimed the ban, which he had no authority to do. It was also outside his remit to stop people worshipping at the church. Archbishop Eames had been called upon to close the church; this he refused to do, earning him some severe criticism, but he preferred to take the long view. He realized that if he took a strong moral tone he might lose control of his church and maybe also his influence with the Orangemen.

I had several meetings over the years with the different bodies involved, including an official one with Martin McGuinness, a separate meeting with John Pickering, rector of Drumcree church, and yet another meeting with Daryl Hewitt, the district master of the Orange Order, to try to mediate a solution to a problem that remains unresolved. Again, it is a question of getting people around a table to talk. The Orangemen, whose slogan at one time was 'No walk, no talk', are more amenable than formerly, but now it is some of the residents who are resisting negotiations. For the time being it is relatively peaceful.

The St Andrews Agreement on 13 October 2006 timetabled a series of steps leading back to the restoration of power to the Northern Ireland Assembly.

Finally, in new elections to the Assembly after the St Andrews Agreement, the DUP returned the biggest vote and Sinn Féin overturned the SDLP majority. My prediction that had been received so cynically by those young American students in Belfast in September 2004 had finally proved true: Dr Ian Paisley had become number one and he and Martin McGuinness became joint First Ministers of the North. Fair enough!

As Martin McGuinness related recently:

'I had my first meeting with Ian Paisley on March 26th, 2007 and during my discussions with him it became clear that as a result of the political strength of the DUP and Sinn Féin we would be the largest parties in the Assembly and it was clear to us both that we were going to be joint First Ministers of the North ... It was at one of those first meetings that he said something that corresponded with what Albert had once said to me ...

'We were up in the parliament building at the time and Paisley said that maybe I should write to Peter Hain, the British Secretary of State, and tell him to get out of Stormont Castle because we wanted it for our own purposes. That was a very clear indicator to me, and something I've learned since, that Ian Paisley and many other Unionist leaders totally abhor being told what to do by British ministers and that his attitude was – we can govern ourselves. That was a comfort to me because that was common ground between us and something that I felt we could all build on. And I think that Albert had a sense of, not just Paisley's nature or his approach to life or politics, but Albert had a sense of where most Unionists came from, that they would want to be in government, they'd want to be taking decisions and that ultimately they would want to effectively work in government together with ourselves.

'Privately behind the scenes there were many people out in the public who if you had said, even in 2003 for example, that we would be in government with the DUP by May 2007, they would have had men in white coats take you away!'

Back in 1990 when Ireland had the poorest economic record in Europe, with 15 per cent unemployment, if anyone had predicted then that we would have the highest growth rate in the developed world, I think they too would have been called a lunatic and taken away by men in white coats – but it happened.

There was a time, before the current financial crisis, when everything I'd hoped to see on the island of Ireland was being realized. I was a businessman, a risk-taker, and the core values that had made me a successful businessman were the same values I called upon in my drive to jump-start the economy and to help bring about peace. If business taught me anything, it was the truth of the saying that 'opportunity comes to pass and not to pause', the need to seize the moment. In building C&D back in the seventies, it was the three-day week affecting British industry at that time that gave me the break which allowed us to penetrate the market, and we never looked back. Of course, luck can play a part; but recognizing it and knowing how to use it is an essential business skill. It's being aware that you're in the right place at the right time that enables you to seize the opportunity.

As a businessman I'd suffered the frustrations of trying to build an international business with the primitive and limited telecommunications system that existed in Ireland at that time. When I became a minister I seized the opportunity to put that right. We were a small, poor, agriculture-based economy and we were bleeding people. Look at our intellectual heritage: we had a nation of bright, talented young people, but we had nothing to offer them and they were continuing to leave our shores to seek a better life elsewhere. They were our main resource, our chief asset, and they were draining away. My investigations into new technologies and the emerging power of telecommunications suddenly revealed an opportunity for Ireland that could simultaneously resolve the two major problems besetting our country: a poor economy and excessive emigration.

To develop this new industry we turned to America and

Europe and fostered business recovery by focusing primarily on public initiatives to attract foreign investment and to develop infrastructure. To service this growing industry we needed a workforce; so we made a strategic decision to make a big investment in education, to shift the focus from turning out workers for an agriculture-based economy to producing a technology-based workforce.

My business instincts told me this was a revolutionary way forward for Ireland, and that if we made ourselves competitive and marketed our assets well, we could attract more and more companies to our shores. As Minister for Finance I started reducing our corporate tax rates to the lowest levels in the European Union and inward investment dramatically increased. I called on Irish Americans and persuaded the high-flyers of corporate America to take a risk and invest in our future – and an integral part of that future was peace.

My dealings in the North had already taught me that the Unionists were pragmatic. They wanted to do business, and if we could offer a strong economy to compete with that offered by Britain, they would be willing and eager to trade. For the sake of Ireland's future and that of its people we had to have peace, and I was willing to risk everything to get it. As Taoiseach, I was lucky that at that seminal moment John Major and Bill Clinton came into power; and there were others in the North, too, who realized that the timing was right and were ready to take the risk and seize the moment.

Europe and the single market opened up, and as the billions I'd negotiated started to flow into our economy and our infrastructure grew, investors were drawn to our high-tech environment – companies like Intel, Microsoft, IBM and Cisco – certifying to the world that Ireland was serious about growth.

Our self-esteem grew with our economy; our young people

stopped leaving, and many who had gone earlier came back to their roots. We became the gateway to Europe and a bridge to America. We no longer looked merely to Britain for support. The peace process was tortuous but the North was watching, and as they saw our economic status growing to rival that of Great Britain, many realized there was an opportunity looming and could see an alternative way of life.

So the Celtic Tiger roared and peace finally came to Northern Ireland – but nothing in life is ever permanent. Now we are in a recession, as is the rest of the world; but we've entered it stronger than we have ever been in our history, and it will pass. Peace is holding well; of course, there have been the odd incidents from extremist groups and probably there always will be, but it's the attitude of the people in the North that has changed. Republicans and Unionists now speak as one: they want peace, and nothing and no one is ever going to be allowed to take them back into the dark days of violence. Once they would have sheltered the killers, now they offer no refuge – as was clear when, in the spring of 2009, two British soldiers were murdered at the Massereene Barracks in County Antrim, and PSNI officer Stephen Carroll was killed in Craigavon: the criminals were caught within days.

The island of Ireland now lives in harmony and the border matters less and less. What we began with the Downing Street Declaration, which subsequently became the Good Friday Agreement, and more recently was subsumed into the St Andrews Agreement, has changed the face of politics and with it the parameters of the argument. The constitutional principles adopted in these agreements, although complex, have endorsed equal treatment for all. The Nationalists accept that it is for the majority of people in Northern Ireland to decide when or whether there will be a united Ireland. In return they insist on the right to equal treatment, on respect for their citizenship, and on freedom to conduct their lives according to their culture and tradition, and openly pursue their political objectives, without being regarded as surreptitious or subversive by the Unionist population. In the same way, the Unionists in the North must be regarded as equally Irish and be accorded the same rights and respect by Nationalists. We are one people, on one island, and whatever our individual creeds or beliefs they must be respected so that we may live in harmony.

There is a new awareness on the island of Ireland: you can be Irish, you can be British, and you can be British and Irish. And when a united Ireland comes, it will come by voting, and not by war.

Who knows where the path will lead?

EPILOGUE

In the years following my resignation, Kathleen and I left the apartment in Hazeldene and moved to a larger home in Dublin. Our children had grown up and flown the nest, but there were grandchildren and big family occasions to accommodate. With seven children and their partners, our original family home in Longford, Mount Carmel, was sold.

Several of the children are also living in the city, although Philip and his wife Anne, and their three children, live in Mullingar. Emer married her long-time sweetheart, Kevin, and they settled in Dublin, as did Leonie and her husband Garret, and Cathy, who is married to Niall. The others are scattered – Miriam, with her husband Niall, in Edinburgh, Albert junior (Abbie) in New York with his wife Erika, and our youngest daughter Andrea in London, forging a new life with her new husband Jamie.

Kathleen and I have been blessed with a deeply loving family. We have also welcomed our grandchildren into the world. Philip and Anne were the first with Robert (who, very fortunately for all of us, came into the world in December 1991 during the tense and difficult time following my sacking and Kathleen's diagnosis), Stephanie and Mark. Albert junior and Erika have three children, Katie, Jack and Sarah, all born in Dublin, as was our youngest grandchild, Charlie, who arrived in June 2008, born to Cathy and Niall. Some years before that Miriam and Niall produced two little girls, Phoebe and Heidi, and Kathleen and I both flew to Edinburgh to welcome them into our extensive family. We still get together for family holidays and family occasions, only now Kathleen and I have moved to live in an apartment in our favourite Dublin Hotel, The Four Seasons – more rooms for more children. In 2008 the youngest of our daughters, Andrea, married Jamie, and with him came his children, Milo, Georgia, Edie and Finn – and so our family grows.

Kathleen and I have been blessed in our life together, in our love and in our family. After Kathleen's diagnosis of cancer and her successful treatment, we both decided to dedicate much of the rest of our lives to assisting cancer organizations. Kathleen became honorary president of Children for Children and Adult Care Foundation, which led to the collaboration between Our Lady's Hospital for Sick Children in Dublin and St Jude Children's Research Hospital in Tennessee. The latter is one of the world leaders in the successful treatment of children with cancer. It was the first partnership between St Jude and a west European hospital. To enhance the collaboration, we raised funds to install a telemed unit in Crumlin. This unit enables consultants in the two hospitals to confer, studying X-rays and individual patients in real time as if they were in the same room. We saw such benefits from tele-medicine that the Foundation donated two more telemed units to Crumlin; many such units were donated to hospitals throughout the island of Ireland, North and South.

In 2006, in recognition of this contribution to health care services and particularly of my role in Ireland's Children for Children and Adult Care Foundation, I was awarded the Stearne Medal. I felt a huge sense of pride receiving it, as this medal has been awarded on only three previous occasions: to Princess Magriet of the Netherlands in her capacity as President of the International Red Cross, to Lady Valerie Goulding in recognition of her work in rehabilitation, and to Dr Catherine Molloy in acknowledgement of her singular contribution to Irish medicine. Although the medal was awarded to me it belongs to Kathleen also. As always, when we set about doing something, we do it as a team.

With the perspective of time passed, I look back over my life. I have had the great good fortune to serve my country and my countrymen and women, and I am immensely proud of that, as I am that, along with so many others, I led the quest for peace on our island of Ireland. I pray that it will continue.

I said at the beginning of this book that I was a risk-taker. Sometimes I won and sometimes I lost. But one thing I do know: I entered the arena and, being there, I made a difference.

As Theodore Roosevelt said in a speech he delivered in 1910:

'It is not the critic who counts, not the man who points out how the strong man stumbled, or where the doer of deeds could have done better.

'The credit belongs to the man who is actually in the arena; whose face is marred by the dust and sweat and blood; who strives valiantly; who errs and comes short again and again; who knows the great enthusiasms, the great devotions and spends himself in a worthy cause; who at the best, knows in the end the triumph of high achievement, and who, at worst, if he fails, at least fails while daring greatly; so that his place will never be with those cold and timid souls who know neither victory or defeat.'

APPENDIX

Joint Declaration on Peace:
The Downing Street Declaration,
Wednesday, 15 December 1993

1. The Taoiseach, Mr. Albert Reynolds, TD, and the Prime Minister, the Rt. Hon. John Major, MP, acknowledge that the most urgent and important issue facing the people of Ireland, North and South, and the British and Irish Governments together, is to remove the causes of conflict, to overcome the legacy of history and to heal the divisions which have resulted, recognising that the absence of a lasting and satisfactory settlement of relationships between the peoples of both islands has contributed to continuing tragedy and suffering. They believe that the development of an agreed framework for peace, which has been discussed between them since early last year, and which is based on a number of key principles articulated by the two Governments over the past 20 years, together with the adaptation of other widely accepted principles, provides the starting point of a

peace process designed to culminate in a political settlement.

2. The Taoiseach and the Prime Minister are convinced of the inestimable value to both their peoples, and particularly for the next generation, of healing divisions in Ireland and of ending a conflict which has been so manifestly to the detriment of all. Both recognise that the ending of divisions can come about only through the agreement and co-operation of the people, North and South, representing both traditions in Ireland. They therefore make a solemn commitment to promote co-operation at all levels on the basis of the fundamental principles, undertakings, obligations under international agreements, to which they have jointly committed themselves, and the guarantees which each Government has given and now reaffirms, including Northern Ireland's statutory constitutional guarantee. It is their aim to foster agreement and reconciliation, leading to a new political framework founded on consent and encompassing arrangements within Northern Ireland, for the whole island, and between these islands.

3. They also consider that the development of Europe will, of itself, require new approaches to serve interests common to both parts of the island of Ireland, and to Ireland and the United Kingdom as partners in the European Union.

4. The Prime Minister, on behalf of the British Government, reaffirms that they will uphold the democratic wish of a greater number of the people of Northern Ireland on the issue of whether they prefer to support the Union or a sovereign united Ireland. On this basis, he reiterates, on behalf of the British Government, that they have no selfish strategic or economic interest in Northern Ireland. Their primary interest is to see peace, stability and reconciliation established by

agreement among all the people who inhabit the island, and they will work together with the Irish Government to achieve such an agreement, which will embrace the totality of relationships. The role of the British Government will be to encourage, facilitate and enable the achievement of such agreement over a period through a process of dialogue and co-operation based on full respect for the rights and identities of both traditions in Ireland. They accept that such agreement may, as of right, take the form of agreed structures for the island as a whole, including a united Ireland achieved by peaceful means on the following basis. The British Government agree that it is for the people of the island of Ireland alone, by agreement between the two parts respectively, to exercise their right of self-determination on the basis of consent, freely and concurrently given, North and South, to bring about a united Ireland, if that is their wish. They reaffirm as a binding obligation that they will, for their part, introduce the necessary legislation to give effect to this, or equally to any measure of agreement on future relationships in Ireland which the people living in Ireland may themselves freely so determine without external impediment. They believe that the people of Britain would wish, in friendship to all sides, to enable the people of Ireland to reach agreement on how they may live together in harmony and in partnership, with respect for their diverse traditions, and with full recognition of the special links and the unique relationship which exist between the peoples of Britain and Ireland.

5. The Taoiseach, on behalf of the Irish Government, considers that the lessons of Irish history, and especially of Northern Ireland, show that stability and well-being will not be found under any political system which is refused allegiance or rejected on grounds of identity by a significant

minority of those governed by it. For this reason, it would be wrong to attempt to impose a united Ireland, in the absence of the freely given consent of a majority of the people of Northern Ireland. He accepts, on behalf of the Irish Government, that the democratic right of self-determination by the people of Ireland as a whole must be achieved and exercised with and subject to the agreement and consent of a majority of the people of Northern Ireland and must, consistent with justice and equity, respect the democratic dignity and the civil rights and religious liberties of both communities, including:

- the right of free political thought;
- the right of freedom and expression of religion;
- the right to pursue democratically national and political aspirations;
- the right to seek constitutional change by peaceful and legitimate means;
- the right to live wherever one chooses without hindrance;
- the right to equal opportunity in all social and economic activity, regardless of class, creed, sex or colour.

These would be reflected in any future political and constitutional arrangements emerging from a new and more broadly based agreement.

6. The Taoiseach however recognises the genuine difficulties and barriers to building relationships of trust either within or beyond Northern Ireland, from which both traditions suffer. He will work to create a new era of trust, in which suspicion of the motives or actions of others is removed on the part of either community. He considers that the future of the island depends on the nature of the relationship between the two

main traditions that inhabit it. Every effort must be made to build a new sense of trust between those communities. In recognition of the fears of the Unionist community and as a token of his willingness to make a personal contribution to the building up of that necessary trust, the Taoiseach will examine with his colleagues any elements in the democratic life and organisation of the Irish State that can be represented to the Irish Government in the course of political dialogue as a real and substantial threat to their way of life and ethos, or that can be represented as not being fully consistent with a modern democratic and pluralist society, and undertakes to examine any possible ways of removing such obstacles. Such an examination would of course have due regard to the desire to preserve those inherited values that are largely shared throughout the island or that belong to the cultural and historical roots of the people of this island in all their diversity. The Taoiseach hopes that over time a meeting of hearts and minds will develop, which will bring all the people of Ireland together, and will work towards that objective, but he pledges in the meantime that as a result of the efforts that will be made to build mutual confidence no Northern Unionist should ever have to fear in future that this ideal will be pursued either by threat or coercion.

7. Both Governments accept that Irish unity would he achieved only by those who favour this outcome persuading those who do not, peacefully and without coercion or violence, and that, if in the future a majority of the people of Northern Ireland are so persuaded, both Governments will support and give legislative effect to their wish. But, notwithstanding the solemn affirmation by both Governments in the Anglo-Irish Agreement that any change in the status of Northern Ireland would only come about with the consent of a majority of the

people of Northern Ireland, the Taoiseach also recognises the continuing uncertainties and misgivings which dominate so much of Northern Unionist attitudes towards the rest of Ireland. He believes that we stand at a stage of our history when the genuine feelings of all traditions in the North must be recognised and acknowledged. He appeals to both traditions at this time to grasp the opportunity for a fresh start and a new beginning, which could hold such promise for all our lives and the generations to come. He asks the people of Northern Ireland to look on the people of the Republic as friends, who share their grief and shame over all the suffering of the last quarter of a century, and who want to develop the best possible relationship with them, a relationship in which trust and new understanding can flourish and grow. The Taoiseach also acknowledges the presence in the Constitution of the Republic of elements which are deeply resented by Northern Unionists, but which at the same time reflect hopes and ideals which lie deep in the hearts of many Irish men and women North and South. But as we move towards a new era of understanding in which new relationships of trust may grow and bring peace to the island of Ireland, the Taoiseach believes that the time has come to consider together how best the hopes and identities of all can be expressed in more balanced ways, which no longer engender division and the lack of trust to which he has referred. He confirms that, in the event of an overall settlement, the Irish Government will, as part of a balanced constitutional accommodation, put forward and support proposals for change in the Irish Constitution which would fully reflect the principle of consent in Northern Ireland.

8. The Taoiseach recognises the need to engage in dialogue which would address with honesty and integrity the fears of

all traditions. But that dialogue, both within the North and between the people and their representatives of both parts of Ireland, must be entered into with an acknowledgement that the future security and welfare of the people of the island will depend on an open, frank and balanced approach to all the problems which for too long have caused division.

9. The British and Irish Governments will seek, along with the Northern Ireland constitutional parties through a process of political dialogue, to create institutions and structures which, while respecting the diversity of the people of Ireland, would enable them to work together in all areas of common interest. This will help over a period to build the trust necessary to end past divisions, leading to an agreed and peaceful future. Such structures would, of course, include institutional recognition of the special links that exist between the peoples of Britain and Ireland as part of the totality of relationships, while taking account of newly forged links with the rest of Europe.

10. The British and Irish Governments reiterate that the achievement of peace must involve a permanent end to the use of, or support for, paramilitary violence. They confirm that, in these circumstances, democratically mandated parties which establish a commitment to exclusively peaceful methods and which have shown that they abide by the democratic process, are free to participate fully in democratic politics and to join in dialogue in due course between the Governments and the political parties on the way ahead.

11. The Irish Government would make their own arrangements within their jurisdiction to enable democratic parties to consult together and share in dialogue about the political

future. The Taoiseach's intention is that these arrangements could include the establishment, in consultation with other parties, of a Forum for Peace and Reconciliation to make recommendations on ways in which agreement and trust between both traditions in Ireland can be promoted and established.

12. The Taoiseach and the Prime Minister are determined to build on the fervent wish of both their peoples to see old fears and animosities replaced by a climate of peace. They believe the framework they have set out offers the people of Ireland, North and South, whatever their tradition, the basis to agree that from now on their differences can be negotiated and resolved exclusively by peaceful political means. They appeal to all concerned to grasp the opportunity for a new departure. That step would compromise no position or principle, nor prejudice the future for either community. On the contrary, it would be an incomparable gain for all. It would break decisively the cycle of violence and the intolerable suffering it entails for the people of these islands, particularly for both communities in Northern Ireland. It would allow the process of economic and social co-operation on the island to realise its full potential for prosperity and mutual understanding. It would transform the prospects for building on the progress already made in the Talks process, involving the two Governments and the constitutional parties in Northern Ireland. The Taoiseach and the Prime Minister believe that these arrangements offer an opportunity to lay the foundations for a more peaceful and harmonious future, devoid of the violence and bitter divisions which have scarred the past generation. They commit themselves and their Governments to continue to work together, unremittingly, towards that objective.

GLOSSARY

Anglo-Irish Agreement   An agreement signed on 15 November 1985 at Hillsborough Castle by the British and Irish governments. The agreement gave the Irish government an advisory input into Northern Ireland's governance but also confirmed that the constitutional position of Northern Ireland would change only if a majority of its people agreed to join a united Ireland. It also established the Anglo–Irish Intergovernmental Conference, with a secretariat made up of officials from the British and Irish governments, concerned with political, legal and security matters in Northern Ireland, as well as the promotion of cross-border cooperation.

Áras an Uachtaráin   The official residence of the President of Ireland. It is located in Phoenix Park on the north side of Dublin.

Árd Chomhairle   The Irish term for High Council. The reference in this book is limited to the term's usage as Sinn Féin's National Executive or ruling body.

Árd Fheis   The Irish term for the annual conference of a political party.

Attorney General   The government's chief legal adviser and chief law officer in Ireland.

Cathaoirleach of Seanad Éireann The Chairperson (or Speaker) of
the Senate, the 60-member second chamber of the Irish
parliament.

Ceann Comhairle of Dáil Éireann The Chairperson (or Speaker) of
Dáil Éireann, the 166-member House of Representatives
of the Irish parliament.

Celtic Tiger The term used to describe the period of rapid economic
growth in Ireland between 1994 and 2007.

Combined Loyalist Military Command (CLMC) Umbrella
organization of the main Loyalist paramilitary groups.

Dáil Éireann The Dáil (as it is more commonly referred to) is the
principal chamber of the Irish parliament to which the
government is responsible. Members of the Dáil (TDs) are
directly elected by proportional representation. It meets in
Leinster House in Dublin. The Dáil can be dissolved at any
time at the request of the Taoiseach to the President of
Ireland (Uachtarán na hÉireann), but the President has the
right to refuse a dissolution, where the Taoiseach has lost the
confidence of Dáil Éireann.

Democratic Unionist Party (DUP) One of the two main Unionist
parties in Northern Ireland. Founded by the Reverend Dr
Ian Paisley, it had strong links to the Free Presbyterian
Church.

The Downing Street Declaration A joint declaration issued on 15
December 1993 by the British and Irish Prime Ministers,
John Major and Albert Reynolds. It included, for the first
time in the history of Anglo-Irish relationships, the principle
that the people of the island of Ireland, North and South,
had the exclusive right to solve the issues between North and
South by mutual and concurrent self-determination. The
declaration, after 'clarification', was considered sufficient by
the Provisional IRA to warrant its announcing a ceasefire on
31 August 1994, which was then followed, on 13 October, by
an announcement of a ceasefire by the Combined Loyalist
Military Command.

Drumcree A village located just outside the town of Portadown,
County Armagh. Since 1995, Drumcree has been the scene of

a prolonged dispute between the Orange Order and local Nationalist residents over a parade from a church service on the first Sunday of July.

Fianna Fáil One of the two main political parties in the Republic of Ireland. The party was originally formed in 1926 from those who opposed the Anglo-Irish Treaty in 1921 (in particular Eamon de Valera). There are two separate chief posts in the party, that of Leader of Fianna Fáil (elected by Fianna Fáil TDs in the Parliamentary Party) and President of Fianna Fáil (elected at the Árd Fheis).

Fine Gael One of the two main political parties in the Republic of Ireland. It was originally formed in 1933 from a merger of the parties which supported the Anglo-Irish Treaty.

First Minister of Northern Ireland Leader of the Northern Ireland Executive (the executive arm of the Northern Ireland Assembly).

'Four Horsemen' A leading group of Irish American politicians in the 1980s, consisting of Senator Edward Kennedy of Massachusetts; Senator Daniel P. Moynihan of New York; Speaker of the House of Representatives, Thomas 'Tip' O'Neill; and Governor Hugh Carey of New York.

Garda Síochána The Irish term for 'Guardians of the Peace'. The official name of the police force of the Republic of Ireland, known in everyday language as the Gardaí.

Good Friday Agreement Also known as the Belfast Agreement and, occasionally, as the Stormont Agreement. An agreement concluded in Belfast on 10 April 1998 (Good Friday) by the British and Irish governments and the parties in the talks. The principal provisions of the agreement included the establishment of a Northern Irish Assembly; the establishment of a 'power-sharing' Northern Ireland Executive (both established in December 1999); and the establishment of a British–Irish Intergovernmental Conference (replacing the former Anglo-Irish Intergovernmental Conference, established by the Anglo-Irish Agreement).

Government of Ireland Act An Act passed by the parliament of the

United Kingdom in 1920 which partitioned Ireland and established two different jurisdictions, that of Northern Ireland (comprising the six counties of Antrim, Armagh, Derry, Down, Fermanagh and Tyrone) and Southern Ireland (comprising the remaining twenty-six counties). Southern Ireland never functioned as an operative political entity and was superseded by the Irish Free State in 1922.

'hunger strikes' A tactic of fasting in order to bring attention to an injustice which was first used by Irish Republicans in 1917. In this book, the term refers to the main hunger strike in the Maze prison during 1981, which culminated in the deaths of ten prisoners who had demanded political prisoner status.

Irish Republican Army (IRA) A paramilitary organization, whose name went back to the War of Independence, which in 1969 split into two groups, the Official IRA and the Provisional IRA (PIRA).

Labour Party The Irish Labour Party, the third largest of the political parties in the Republic of Ireland. It was founded by James Connolly in 1912 as the political wing of the Irish Trade Union Congress.

Loyalist The term Loyalist refers to one who is loyal to the British Crown (monarchy). In the context of Northern Ireland, the term is sometimes used interchangeably with 'Unionist', but 'Loyalist' is more often associated with particularly hardline forms of Unionism. It was commonly used to refer to those who gave tacit or actual support to paramilitary groups 'defending the union' with Britain.

Nationalist In the context of Northern Ireland, the term is used politically to describe those who support a united Ireland. Mainstream Nationalist parties such as the SDLP are distinguished from those from the militant strand of Nationalism, who call themselves Republican.

Northern Ireland Assembly The term used to describe the devolved legislature for Northern Ireland, one of the three devolved governments in the United Kingdom.

Northern Ireland Executive The term used to describe the executive arm of the Northern Ireland Assembly. It consists of a First

Minister, a Deputy First Minister and various other ministers with individual portfolios and remits, elected using the d'Hondt system. It was established under the Northern Ireland Act 1998.

Oireachtas The official Irish term for the national parliament or legislature of Ireland. The Oireachtas comprises the President of Ireland (Uachtarán na hÉireann) and the two houses of the Oireachtas, Dáil Éireann and Seanad Éireann.

Progressive Democrats (PDs) The Progressive Democrats were a right-of-centre liberal party in the Republic of Ireland, formed in 1985 by Des O'Malley and Mary Harney (former members of Fianna Fáil) and Michael McDowell. They disbanded in 2009.

Progressive Unionist Party (PUP) A Loyalist political party linked to the Ulster Volunteer Force (UVF). The PUP was formed in 1979, and its main support base is the Loyalist working-class communities of Belfast.

Provisional IRA (PIRA or IRA) The Provisional Irish Republican Army. Generally referred to as 'the IRA' or 'the Provos'. Established in 1969 at the outset of the Troubles, following a split in the IRA at that time.

Republican The term literally refers to a person who supports the style of government based on a republic rather than a monarchy. In the context of Northern Ireland during the Troubles, the term was often used to describe a person who tacitly or explicitly supported the IRA. However, in the Republic the Fianna Fáil Party describes itself as the Republican Party, and expresses a democratic and constitutional Republican philosophy.

RTÉ Radio Telefís Éireann is Ireland's national television and radio broadcaster.

Seanad Éireann The term used to describe the Irish Senate, the second chamber of the Irish parliament.

Sinn Féin The name of the Irish political party, led by Gerry Adams, has been transferred many times since its original use by Arthur Griffith in 1905. It is an Irish Republican party, whose core aim is to bring about a united Ireland. From

1970, Sinn Féin was associated with the Provisional IRA, the two together forming 'the Republican Movement'.

Social Democratic and Labour Party (SDLP)   A Nationalist political party in Northern Ireland founded in 1971. Born of the civil rights movement, it supports the aim of a united Ireland but only through non-violent means. John Hume was leader of the SDLP from 1979 to 2001.

social partnership   A term used to describe the tripartite, triennial national agreements reached in Ireland, voluntarily, between the government, the main employer groups and the trade unions. The process was initiated in 1987, following a period of high debt and weak economic growth. The first agreement was the Programme for National Recovery (1987–90), followed by the Programme for Economic and Social Progress (1991–4). Positive industrial relations and wage moderation were important outcomes and contributed significantly to the Celtic Tiger.

Tánaiste   The Irish term for 'heir of the chief': Deputy Prime Minister in the Irish Government.

Taoiseach   The Irish term for 'chief': the official term used to describe the Irish Prime Minister.

Teachta Dála (TD)   The Irish term for 'assembly delegate', or 'deputy to the Dáil'. An elected member of Dáil Eireann.

'The Troubles'   A term used to refer to political conflict and violence in Ireland, both from 1919 to 1923 and, in Northern Ireland, from 1969 to 1998.

Uachtarán na hÉireann   The President of Ireland whose official residence is Áras an Uachtaráin. The President is directly elected by the people.

Ulster Defence Association (UDA)   The largest of the Loyalist paramilitary groups, formed in 1970. Its main objective is to resist the unification of Ireland. Its militant cover name was the Ulster Freedom Fighters (UFF). The UDA officially ended its campaign of violence on 11 November 2007, when it ordered the UFF to stand down.

Ulster Freedom Fighters (UFF)   The cover name of the Ulster

Defence Association (UDA), used to claim responsibility for acts of violence.

Ulster Unionist Party (UUP)   Sometimes referred to as the Official Unionist Party or OUP or, simply, the Unionist Party. Founded in 1905, it is one of the two main unionist parties in Northern Ireland. In 2009 the party agreed to an electoral alliance with the (British) Conservative Party of 'Conservatives and Unionists'.

Ulster Volunteer Force (UVF)   The second largest of the Loyalist paramilitary groups in Northern Ireland.

Unionist   In the context of Northern Ireland, the term is used politically to describe those who wish to see the Union with Britain maintained.

ABOUT THE AUTHOR

Born in Roosky, County Roscommon, in November 1932, Albert Reynolds served as Ireland's eighth Taoiseach from 1992 to 1994 and was a pivotal player in the advancement of the Northern Ireland peace process during that time.

Reynolds was first elected to Dáil Éireann as a Fianna Fáil TD for Longford Westmeath in 1977 after an early career as a successful businessman, and continued to be re-elected as a TD until his retirement in 2002. In that time he served as Minister for Finance (1988–91), Minister for Industry & Commerce (1987–88), Minister for Industry & Energy (1982), Minister for Transport (1980–81) and Minister for Post & Telegraphs (1979–81).

He is married with seven children.

Jill Arlon is a broadcaster, lecturer and actress. With her husband Deke she formed a very successful international artist management company. Jill has also written novels, and this is her second biography.

BIBLIOGRAPHY

Gerry Adams, *Hope and History: Making Peace in Ireland*, Brandon Books, 2005

Brendan Anderson, *Joe Cahill: A Life in the IRA,* O'Brien Press, 2002

David Andrews, *The Kingstown Republican*, New Island Books, 2008

Liam Clarke and Kathryn Johnston, *Martin McGuinness: From Guns to Government*, Mainstream Publishing, 2003

Feargal Cochrane, *Unionist Politics and the Politics of Unionism since the Anglo-Irish Agreement*, Cork University Press, 2001

Tim Pat Coogan, *Tim Pat Coogan: A Memoir*, Weidenfeld & Nicolson, 2008

Dáil Éireann: Report of the Sub-committee of the Select Committee on Legislation and Security, 1995

Deaglan de Beadun, *The Far Side of Revenge: Making Peace in Northern Ireland*, Collins Press, 2008

Seán Duignan, *One Spin on the Merry-Go-Round*, Blackwater Press, 1995

Johnny Fallon, *Brian Cowen: In His Own Words*, Mercier Press, 2009

Fergus Finlay, *Snakes and Ladders*, New Island Books, 1999

Roy Garland, *Gusty Spence*, Blackstaff Press, 2001

Alf McCreary, *Nobody's Fool: The Life of Archbishop Robin Eames*, Hodder & Stoughton, 2005

John Major, *John Major: The Autobiography*, HarperCollins, 1999

ALBERT REYNOLDS

Eamonn Mallie and David McKittrick, *The Fight for Peace: The Secret Story behind the Peace Process*, Heinemann, 1996

Martin Mansergh, *The Legacy of History for Making Peace in Ireland*, Mercier Press, 2003

Frank Millar, *David Trimble: The Price of Peace*, Liffey Press, 2008

George Mitchell, *Making Peace,* University of California Press, 2001

Ed Moloney, *A Secret History of the IRA*, W. W. Norton and Co., 2003

Brendan O'Brien, *The Long War: The IRA and Sinn Fein*, O'Brien Press, 1993

Conor O'Cleary, *The Greening of the White House*, Gill & MacMillan, 1996

Oireachtas Archives, debates and speeches, see www.oireachtas.ie

Jason O'Toole, *Brian Cowen: The Path to Power*, Transworld Ireland, 2008

Kevin Rafter, *Martin Mansergh: A Biography*, New Island Books, 2003

Paul Routledge, *John Hume: A Biography*, HarperCollins, 1997

Tim Ryan, *Albert Reynolds: The Longford Leader. The Unauthorized Biography*, Blackwater Press, 1994

Jeffrey A. Sluka, *Hearts and Minds, Water and Fish: Support for the IRA and INLA in a Northern Ireland Ghetto*, JAI Press, 1989

PICTURE
ACKNOWLEDGEMENTS

All photographs not credited below were kindly supplied by the author. The publishers have made every effort to contact copyright holders where known. Copyright holders who have not been credited are invited to get in touch with the publishers.

First section

pp 4/5: AR with Charles Haughey and Bertie Ahern: Maxwell's; John Major, AR and Theo Waigel, 1 April 1990: Maxwell's; AR, Dublin, 31 January 1990: Getty Images; AR after his election as Taoiseach, Longford: photo by Bryan O'Brien

6/7: Mary Robinson gives AR the seal of office, 12 January 1993: Lensmen; AR making a speech as Taoiseach: Maxwell's; AR and Cabinet, 11 February 1992; AR and Cabinet, January 1933: both Lensmen

8: AR in conversation with Chancellor Helmut Kohl on a visit to Bonn in preparation for the European Council meeting in Edinburgh, December 1992: Bundesbundstelle Bonn/ Fassbender

Second section

9: AR and Bill Clinton, 17 March 1993; AR, Jean Kennedy Smith and Edward Kennedy, 17 March 1993: both official White House photos; Bill and Hillary Clinton and AR and Kathleen, 17 March 1994: Greg Gibson/AP/Press Association Images

10/11: British and Irish Minsters at Dublin Castle, 3 December 1993: *left to right*, UK Ulster Secretary, Sir Patrick Mayhew, UK Foreign Secretary, Douglas Hurd, UK Prime Minister, John Major, AR, Irish Foreign Minister, Dick Spring and Máire Goeghegan Quinn: Adam Butler/PA Archive/Press Association Images; AR and John Major entering 10 Downing Street, 15 December 1993; Joint Declaration, Downing Street, 15 December 1993: © Matthew Polak/ Sygma/Corbis; Gerry Adams, AR, John Hume clasp hands, Dublin, 6 September 1994: PA Archive/Press Association Images; announcement of Protestant paramilitary ceasefire, Belfast, 13 October 1994: *left to right,* Davy Adams, David Ervine, Gary McMichael, William Smyth, Gusty Spence, John White and Jim McDonald: McCullough/PA Archive/Press Association Images; AR and John Major (*front*) and Dick Spring and Patrick Mayhew (*back*), Chequers, 24 October 1994: Adam Butler/PA Archive/Press Association Images; AR and Martin Mansergh: Lensmen

12/13: AR and Mother Teresa, 1993: Liam Lyons

14/15: AR with MEP Brian Crowley: Maxwell's; AR in the Saddam Central Hospital, Baghdad, 8 November 1998: Reuters/Faleh Kheiber; AR with daughters Miriam and Leonie outside the Royal Courts of Justice, London, 8 July, 1998: Reuters/Paul Hackett; Ian Paisley and AR, 6 November 2007: Paul Faith/PA Archive/Press Association Images

16 AR leading the St Patrick's Day Parade, New York, 17 March 1998: AFP/Getty Images

INDEX

Andrews, David
  in AR government 177
  in partnership government 212
  on AR's party leadership 171–2
  on George Bush Sr 268–9
Andrews, Todd, and Turf Development
    Board camp 29–30
Anglo-Irish Agreement 142–3, 235–41
  Dublin summit preparations 333–5,
    344–5, 346–7
  proposals 284–302, 322
  Reagan and 269
Anglo-Irish relations, FitzGerald and
    140–3
Arafat, Yasser, on Downing Street
    Declaration 358
Ardmore Film Studios, closure 136
Arnold, Bruce 139
Associated Ballrooms 50
AT&T, AR and 112–15

bacon business, AR and 63–5, 75
Baker, James, and American–Irish
    relations 268
Ball, Kenny 52
ballrooms
  AR's business 40–58, 62–3
  AR's father's 17, 38, 39
  bingo sessions, AR and 58
Ballydermot, Kildare, Turf Development
    Board camp 29–31
Ballymote, AR with CIE at 35–6
Bangemann Report 265
banking, AR rejects as career 28–9
Barr, Sammy
  and Democratic Unionist Party 229
  and Flamingo Ballroom 54–5
Barrett, Sylvester, and Hillery 157
Barrington, Justice Donal, and Chief
    Justiceship 433
Beatles, The, and Royal Showband 43
Beef Tribunal 190–200
  report 428–32
Begley, Thomas 316, 319
Belfast
  American peace envoy mission at
    369–70
  attractions in 60s 51–3
  Quaker house meeting 418

Berkeley Court Hotel meetings with
    Loyalists 413–19, 426–7
Bilk, Acker 52
bingo sessions, in ballrooms, AR and 58
Birmingham Irish Association, and
    Longford News 72–3
Blaney, Neil
  and assistance to violence victims 82–3
  and community swimming pools 60–1
  and weapons for IRA 1969 plot 83–4
  election campaigns 59, 144
border communities, barrier removals
    422–3
Bowyer, Brendan, and Royal Showband
    42, 50
Brady, Conor, on *Irish Times*, and AR
    466
Brennan, Joe, and assistance to violence
    victims 83
Brennan, Seamus
  and O'Malley leadership bid 132
  in AR government 177
Briscoe, Ben, challenge to Haughey 140
British Government
  offer to amend Government of
    Ireland Act 398
  peace counter-proposals 334–5
  secret contact with IRA 335, 336–41
  see also Major, John; Thatcher,
    Margaret
Broadcasting Act, Sinn Féin/IRA ban
    lifted 364
Brookeborough, Basil Stanlake Brooke,
    Viscount, AR and 37
Browne, Vincent, on AR and Duggan
    affair 467–8, 470
Brussels meeting, Forum for Peace and
    Reconciliation agreement 351–3
Bruton, John 12
  and 1992 election 201, 202
  and Framework Document talks
    483–4
  Major on 483
  McGuinness on 483–4
  no confidence in AR motion 455–6
  Taoiseach 469
Burke, Ray
  on Goodman meat plant affair 196–7
  phone-tapping bill 170–1